Rationality and Nature

Rationality and Nature

A Sociological Inquiry into a Changing Relationship

Raymond Murphy

Westview Press

BOULDER • SAN FRANCISCO • OXFORD

Copyright © 1994 by Westview Press, Inc.

Published in 1994 in the United States of America by Westview Press, Inc., 5500 Central Avenue, Boulder, Colorado 80301-2877, and in the United Kingdom by Westview Press, 36 Lonsdale Road, Summertown, Oxford OX2 7EW

A CIP catalog record for this book is available from the Library of Congress.
ISBN 0-8133-2168-9 — ISBN 0-8133-2169-7 (pbk).

Printed and bound in the United States of America

 The paper used in this publication meets the requirements of the American National Standard for Permanence of Paper for Printed Library Materials Z39.48-1984.

10   9   8   7   6   5   4   3   2   1

To Ruth,
Patricia, Lorrie,
Kiernan, and Maya

Contents

PART THREE
Toward a Symbiotic Relationship with Nature

Preface

Sociology has been constructed as if nature didn't matter. It has failed to take the processes of nature into account, perceiving only the *social* construction of reality. Environmental problems are beginning to send shock waves through this myopic sociological structure. Sociology fabricated as if nature didn't matter constitutes pre-ecological sociology. It was the product of a way of thinking in pre-ecological society at large and is increasingly being exposed as shortsighted by the looming environmental crisis. That crisis and the ecology movement have a profound lesson for sociology: the sociological construction of the relationship between the social and the natural must be done in a way that maintains the importance of social constructions without reducing reality to a social construction. Nature does matter, even for sociology. The sociological thesis of the social construction of reality is viable only if tempered by an ecosystemic sociology that takes into consideration the reality of the processes of nature. The relationship between social action and the dynamic processes of nature will have to be incorporated into sociological theory. A restricted focus on only social action just will not do.

Catton and Dunlap (Catton and Dunlap 1978, 1980; Dunlap and Catton 1979, 1993; Dunlap 1980) have been making this point for over a decade, but most sociologists were not listening. As a result, general sociological theory has failed to take into account the embeddedness of social action in the processes of nature (Dickens 1992, Jones 1990). Sociology as a whole has been unable to develop a non-reductionist relationship with the life sciences (Benton 1991). The sociology of development has neglected environmental limits (Redclift 1984). The sociology of science has constructed a representation of science that fails to capture its specificity, namely its peculiar relationship with nature (Murphy forthcoming). The sociology of environmental issues runs the risk of degenerating into a social constructivism that ignores the dynamic processes of nature with which such human constructions interact.

Although criticism of these weaknesses of contemporary sociology is important, it is just a first step toward the elaboration of a less partial sociology. There remains the difficult task of developing an alternative that captures the embeddedness of social action in the processes of nature without reducing social action to those processes, as sociobiology did. This book consists of an attempt to develop such an alternative, placing what is distinctively human (reason, culture, language, science, technology, human institutions) within the context of what is shared with other forms of life. It takes into consideration the exceptional traits of humans while recognizing that these do not render humans exempt from their dependence on nature. What it is to be human involves, in part, relationships with the rest of nature.

The environmental problems besetting the human race suggest a new direction for sociology: the study of how human projects attempting to mold and master nature in fact unleash mysterious uncontrollable forces of nature that affect social action and could even destroy the material basis of human existence. This is the dark side of the manipulation of nature by humans and results in the unknown denouement of social change, which counters facile assumptions of human progress. Social relations are constructed to an important extent by acting upon a dynamic natural environment, and being acted upon by that environment. Although humans are not necessarily transformed by their manipulation of nature, the age-old struggles for power and interest are re-equipped by that manipulation. This re-equipping process changes the relationship between social action and the processes of nature as well as the relations between humans.

The debate over environmental issues is replete with themes of the process of Western rationalization that Max Weber analyzed three-quarters of a century ago. "The reason we attend to Weber today is because he appreciated and responded to the strongest intellectual forces in the making of the modern world. He succeeded in both developing them and identifying their thrust and direction which persist to this day. Above all he understood that rationality had become both the irrational drive and rigid frame of modern life" (Albrow 1990: 12). The work of Max Weber provides a valuable framework for the examination of the relationship between social action and the processes of nature, a relationship Weber himself did not examine in any detail. The present book will draw out the implications of Weber's work for the development of an environmental sociology, or what could be expressed in more Weberian terms as an ecology of social action. Thus it seeks to show that Weber's work constitutes not "an impenetrable barrier" (Benton 1991: 12) but rather a catapult to a comprehensively naturalistic approach to the human sciences.

A focus on the interdependence of human social action, of natural processes of non-human species, and of non-living processes of nature forms the perspective of an ecology of social action. Such an ecology does not reduce explanation to human perceptions and constructions. An ecology of social action does not, however, reduce explanation to biological, geological, chemical, or physical constituents either. It concentrates on the relationship between social action and the processes of nature. Hence it consists of ecology from a sociological perspective, thereby differing from biological forms of human ecology, and it consists of sociology from an ecological perspective.

Part One analyzes the culture of nature, that is, the ways humans view nature and their relationship to it. The social ecologist Bookchin (1987: 72) argues convincingly that "the view we hold of the natural world profoundly shapes the image we develop of the social worlds, even as we assert the 'supremacy' and 'autonomy' of culture over nature." The process of rationalization and its intensification described by Weber will be used to distinguish different world images of the natural-social relationship.

The first view holds that the distinctive characteristic of humans -- rationality -- has enabled humanity to remold plastic nature according to human desires. This view promotes the intensification of such rationality in order to achieve mastery of nature. An opposing view contends that nature is much more implastic than previously thought, resulting in irrational ecological consequences if action is based on an assumed plasticity of nature. Hence development must be rendered sustainable or growth limited in order to attain a more thorough rationalization. A third view, "social ecology," argues that environmental problems result from the hierarchical character of social relations in rationalized institutions, and suggests decentralized institutions and the reorientation of reason toward egalitarian values as the solution to those problems. Yet another view, "deep ecology," claims that ecological problems go deeper still and have their origin in the present anthropocentric culture upon which Occidental rationalization is based. Hence it advocates a world image based on the intrinsic value of nature and a re-enchantment of the world through a return to the rituals and institutions characteristic of primal peoples. Feminists are torn between values based on the equality of men and women and ecofeminist values postulating that women are inherently closer to nature than men.

Part One critically appraises these beliefs about the relationship of humanity to nature, beliefs that motivate and steer social action. It uses Weber's analysis of Western rationalization as the departure point for the examination of its irrational ecological consequences, thereby extending the study begun by Weber of the paradoxical relationship between rationalization and irrationality. The conflicts between instrumental rationality and value rationality, and between different forms of value rationality expressed by these divergent images of the social-natural relationship, are studied in this first section.

Part Two analyzes the material side of the relationship between social action and the processes of nature, and develops a sociology of environmental degradation. Waste has been the forgotten element of political economy. The process of production has created commodities, yet it has created waste too. Private wealth has been amassed by not paying the waste cost of the production, distribution, and use of commodities, that is, by dumping waste upon the commons and causing a public environmental debt to accumulate. A Weberian theory of the accumulation of capital that takes into account the accumulation of waste is proposed as a more inclusive alternative to Marxian theory. The striking contrast between the extensive development of accounting for capital and commodities, which has resulted from economic rationalization, and the undeveloped character of accounting for waste, is related to the lack of accountability for waste. These issues then lead to the construction of a conception of environmental classes. Nature is a medium that carries a social relationship between environmental classes. A way of analyzing the conflict that has erupted over the environment is proposed in terms of the classes that have contributed to environmental degradation or benefitted from it at the expense of classes that have been victimized or will be victimized.

Part Three examines the possibility of throwing off the present parasitic relationship with nature. Although every species eats other species in order to survive and prosper, the intensity and scale of humanity's destruction of species and their habitats constitutes a parasitic relationship with nature that jeopardizes the satisfaction of the long-term needs of humanity itself. Chapter 9 demonstrates that science and applied science, being incomplete and favoring some interests more than others, have been part of the problem of the intensifying parasitic relationship with nature. Yet it also demonstrates that they can be part of the solution, reoriented in favor of a more symbiotic relationship. The final chapter evaluates possible ways of bringing about social change concerning the environment: force and coercion, practical reason, ecological ethics, ecological consciousness and values, and ecological experience and knowledge. To modify slightly Weber's well-known expression, Chapter 10 appraises their potential for transforming parasitism from an ecological iron cage into a cloak that can be thrown off.

This book has benefitted immensely from the insightful comments of Professor Frederick H. Buttel of the University of Wisconsin at Madison and Professor Neil Guppy of the University of British Columbia. I would also like to thank the team of Ginette Rozon, Francine D'Amour, and Manon Leclerc at the University of Ottawa for their very professional work in preparing the typescript.

Raymond Murphy

PART ONE

The Intensification of Rationalization and Its Alternatives

1

Rationalization
Under the Premise of Plasticity

In 1798 Thomas Malthus (1798, 1801) published his theory of the relationship between social action and the processes of nature. He argued that human population grows geometrically but agricultural production, or more generally the means of subsistence, only grows arithmetically. Thus population increases beyond the means to sustain it, the excess population that cannot be sustained by the natural environment is eliminated, and then the population and the means of subsistence grow once again at their respective rates until their interaction produces the next crisis. Boom and bust cycles are, according to this theory, written into the relationship between humans and their natural environment. Malthus concluded that, although population growth could be limited by "preventive" checks (birth control, infanticide) and by "moral restraint" (sexual abstinence), it is usually brought back to equilibrium by "positive" checks (famine, epidemics, and war). He arrived at this conclusion because he believed that sexual abstinence was improbable and, like many Protestant ministers of that age, that birth control was morally repugnant. The famines in Ireland in the 1700s and early and middle 1800s seemed to support his theory.

The Intensification of Rationalization Under Plasticity

The relationship between humans and nature has appeared in the two centuries following Malthus to be a great deal more malleable than he believed. The means of subsistence have grown much faster than the population, to the extent that most industrialized nations now have a continual surplus in their production of food. Population is limited by the "preventive" check of birth control to the point that, if there were no immigration, those nations would decline in population despite a great leap forward in life expectancy. Until environmental problems became increasingly severe, it seemed that both the population side and the means-of-subsistence side of the Malthusian dilemma had been transformed by human rationality: nature had been mastered, the dilemma solved, Malthus refuted. The development of a modern rational society, and in particular the development of science and technology, led many people in the industrialized world to look upon the theory of Malthus as a mere curiosity in the history of ideas: an intellectual museum piece. Furthermore, his theory had other limitations even in his own day. It was class biased. Malthus obscured the fact that the crises he described decimated the poor but hardly touched the rich, severely affected the conquered Catholics of Ireland but less so the conquering Protestants, etc. He failed to perceive the social determination of human vulnerability to his laws (see Moore Lappe and Collins 1970).

At the beginning of the Twentieth century, Weber (1958: 139) characterized the intellectualized culture in the modern, rationalized world as the following belief: "there are no mysterious incalculable forces that come into play, but rather that one can, in principle, master all things by calculation. ... One need no longer have recourse to magical means. ... Technical means and calculations perform the service. This above all is what intellectualization means."[1] Belief in mysterious forces is replaced by belief in the power of knowledge and by instrumental rationality in the form of technology. The world becomes disenchanted as belief in magical and religious spirits is eroded. This dynamic of intellectualization has been strongly associated with the pursuit of mastery, notably, of nature. "What men want to learn from Nature is how to use it in order wholly to dominate it and other men" (Horkheimer and Adorno 1972: 5).

Nature, and the relationship of humans to nature, are seen in this intellectualized, rationalized worldview as plastic: humans can mold and reconstruct the natural environment. They have confidence that they can "master all things," in particular nature and the environment, through their planning by technical means and calculations. A senior population economist with the United Nations, Paul Shaw, argues that since the time of Malthus people have been forecasting disaster. "It has never happened.' Technology is the crucial difference between humans and animals, and in the past, technology has always increased the carrying capacity of the earth, says Shaw. 'Why should it be any different now?'" (Southam 1989: 7). If one resource runs out, a better one will be found in time. If coal becomes scarce, oil will be substituted. If oil resources become depleted, energy will continue to be supplied by nuclear fission reactors. If fission reactors prove too dangerous, then humans will develop a benign process of nuclear fusion.

Hamilton (1973: 41), who was the industrial editor of the *New Scientist*, has given a strong expression of this view that human rationality is no longer subject to the constraints of nature, because rationality has rendered the natural environment plastic. "Technology can achieve practically anything today if we spend enough on it. It gives Man unprecedented powers over his environment and over himself. ... There are few technological barriers left in the way. Virtually everything is possible for those with the money and the will. The barriers are political, economic, social."

Enterprises and states have acted as if the relationship of humans to their natural environment were plastic, treating pollution and depletion of resources as inconsequential. They have justified their actions by developing the corresponding ideology. Humans are assumed to have superpowers, capable of manipulating, domesticating, remolding, reconstructing, and harvesting nature. Editorial pages of newspapers carry articles entitled "Ecologists take heed: The End is not near" and argue that "if Eden exists it lies in our capacity to control our environment, not to retreat from scientific progress and human ingenuity" (Howard 1989: B3). Such assumptions have provided the basis of the legitimating ideology for the exploitation of nature. They have led to the assumption that future discoveries will repair present damage. The plasticity premise is the cultural support for discounting the effect of dumping waste in the environment, for depleting its resources, and degrading it.

In 1967 the futurists Kahn and Wiener (1967: 116) argued that the "capacities for and commitment to economic development and control over our external and internal environment and concomitant systematic, technological innovation, application, and diffusion, of these capacities are increasing, seemingly without foreseeable limit." In 1972 Maddox (1972: 65-6) stated that "sheer physical exhaustion of the resources of space-ship earth is obviously an exceedingly remote possibility." These conclusions were arrived at not so much because of the discovery of enormous resources but much more so on the basis of a faith in the capacity of humans to reshape nature to meet their needs. Beckerman (1974) argued that "man is the measure of all things," that it is not nature itself but man's reason that gives nature the characteristics it possesses, and that nature, far from becoming depleted, expands as human reason grows. Humans, through their rational, enterprising activity transform what was not previously a resource into one. Oil was just a gooey liquid in the ground until humans extracted it and transformed it into a source of energy. Beckerman (1974: 229) gives the example of ore that was discarded in 1880 as uneconomical because it had less than 3 percent copper. Such ore can now be refined economically with copper contents as low as 0.4 percent. Not only have new deposits of resources been found when needed, but also substitutes for previous resources have been developed. If a resource becomes depleted, humans will rationally discover a replacement (Hess 1979: 73).

Shortage has, according to this line of thought, been made obsolete by scientific and technological development (Smith 1979; J. Simon 1981; Simon and Kahn 1984, Wattenberg 1984). Since price is assumed to be a measure of scarcity, the decrease in the price of many natural resources that has occurred over the long term, relative to other goods and services, is taken to indicate that those resources are becoming less scarce (Dryzek 1987: 14-5). J. Simon (1981: 42) answers with a resounding "yes" his question: "Can the supply of natural resources really be infinite?" The Earth can be reshaped to achieve plenitude. "Some proposals have recently been put forward for using nuclear power to heat the deep-sea water in the Caribbean sea, so that the phosphorus-rich water rises to the surface in an area of abundant warmth and sunshine, with consequent expected rapid growth of plankton, and of edible fish" (Clark 1970: 170). This is seen by Clark (1970: 170) as "science fiction come true." Shortage will not be a problem, provided that humans continue to strive to master nature. If shortage there ever is, it will not be of natural resources but rather of rationality and technology when backward, anti-rational ideologies are allowed to gain ascendancy. Even the rapid increase in world population is perceived in terms of its sunny side, resulting in books entitled *Population Growth: The Advantages* (Clark 1975) and *The Ultimate Resource* (Simon 1981), namely the amount of people.

Expectations of growth are deeply ingrained (Cotgrove 1982; Milbrath 1984; Dunlap and Van Liere 1984). The Reagan era in the United States was, among other things, an anti-environmental backlash against new movements premised on the idea of ecological limits (Mitchell 1990; Dunlap and Scarce 1991; Dunlap and Catton 1993b: 3). Its reversal of long-term U.S. support for population control was related to this mastery-of-nature line of thought (Holden 1984; Dunlap and Catton 1993b).

Humans use technology to fashion nature in their image, and, when the need arises, they can solve the problems provoked by the use of technology itself. "When one has wealth and technology without worrying about how to use them, problems are created. But the moment that serious concern arises over their actual and potential uses, the problems can usually be alleviated or prevented" (Kahn 1979: 74-5).

This view is characterized by an unbounded faith in the superior strength of human reason over natural forces. Human reason can be counted on to vanquish and remold nature. Scientific discoveries and technical solutions are found when needed. Rationality enables humans to become the only living species that is "exempt" (see the critique by Dunlap and Catton 1979, 1993a) from dependence on nature, the only species that does not have to adapt to the forces of nature. This assumption of the social reconstruction of nature by humans according to their needs and wants underlies the "cornucopian faith" (Dryzek 1987: 14) that economic growth can continue without foreseeable limit and without exhausting the resources of "space-ship earth." The very titles of the books by proponents of this view, *The Doomsday Syndrome*, and *Doomsday Has Been Canceled*, as well as the interpretation of public reaction to technological risk as pathological phobic thinking (Sjoberg 1987), suggest that concern about the limits fixed by nature to economic growth is not founded on facts rooted in reality, but on a social psychological sickness.

Humans have already constructed factory farms in which the lives of other living species are transformed so as to make them more useful to humans than they would be in their natural habitat.

> In the United States, over 90 per cent of all chickens, 30 per cent of turkeys and nearly 40 per cent of pigs are born and bred under controlled conditions. The animals are regarded as units for converting given amounts of feed into outputs of protein, fat and so on, for human consumption. In order to minimize the space they occupy and make the farmer's job easier, they are often enclosed in small pens which allow them enough room to move but not enough to dissipate their energies in free movement. ... Such methods can bring quicker, fatter returns than free-run open-air farming. (Hamilton 1973: 237)

Humans show off their mastery of wild-animal species and indeed of nature itself through nostalgic references on coats of arms of territories. Thus the American eagle, the Canadian beaver, and the Swiss bear, decimated in their respective territories by humans, are reduced to a remembrance similar to a notch on a cowboy's gun.

In his article "What's Wrong with Plastic Trees?" the resource economist Krieger (1973) reminds us that society conditions the way we experience nature, and therefore concludes that advertising and the rewriting of history can be used to condition humans to find appealing plastic trees, artificial prairies, and other simulated forms of nature. Since society, and not nature, determines what appeals to humans, the natural environment is not only malleable, it is disposable. The artificial is taking over from the natural as humans weed the Earth of undesired pests and bring out its full potential.

In this view, there is no conception of limits and requirements of the human-supporting natural environment. Rather there is a "faith that there will always be another resource to move on to ... [and] a metaphysical commitment to the existence of ever more resources and 'sinks' for pollutants as we use up current ones" (Dryzek 1987: 19-20). Nature as an active force disappears from view, replaced by nature as a passive, mastered material to be shaped and reshaped. "Space-ship Earth" is a telling metaphor. The planet Earth is perceived as having become constructed by humans, much like a space-ship is socially and technically constructed, obeying the commands of its human constructors and operators in mission control. In fact, *An Operating Manual for Spaceship Earth* (Fuller 1971) had already been published by 1971. The obedience of the planet to the dynamics and laws of nature has been replaced by its obedience to the directives of its new human masters. Nature recedes into passivity as humans take control.

Nature's evolution is seen as too slow and inefficient and is being supplanted by rationally planned action to humanize the Earth (Dubos 1980). "Through chemical technology, Man can adapt and improve on naturally occurring materials; he can make them more cheaply from alternative sources, with more consistent quality and higher standards of quality and performance; and he can formulate materials of all kinds with properties quite outside the scope of natural substances" (Hamilton 1973: 69). The belief that nature is being improved upon by human rationality prevails in this way of thinking.[2] "Each of the vast number of other transmutations that he has attempted and achieved is a cause for self-congratulation, a feeling of satisfaction that another corner of Nature's kingdom has fallen to his power" (Hamilton 1973: 78).

History is perceived as having a discontinuity: the point at which human reason expels nature from the dynamic of history. "Progress is seen as the extrication of humanity from the muck of a mindless, unthinking, and brutish domain or what Jean Paul Sartre so contemptuously called the 'slime of history,' into the presumably clear light of reason and civilization" (Bookchin 1987: 50). In this worldview, consciously implemented mechanisms are taking over nature's regulation. "Should we find it desirable, we will be able to turn the Sahara Desert into farms and forests, or remake the landscape of New England, while we create the kind of future we dream. ... We are the legitimate children of Gaia; we need not be ashamed that we are altering the landscapes and ecosystems of Earth" (Vayk 1978: 61). Even new forms of life are being created by human reason as instruments to achieve specific goals. For example, a genetically engineered micro-organism has been produced that can live off oil spills. The United States Supreme Court ruled in 1980 that this bacterium was a human invention rather than a product of nature, and hence patentable. Since then, genes with specific applications (usually medical) and hitherto unseen forms of life have been fabricated, ruled products of human reason rather than of nature, and patented.

Humans are seen as on the threshold of a grand transition: "the transition from being a *passively produced organism* to being the *active controller* of life and destiny" (Christian 1981: 381-2). It is as if scientific knowledge were almost complete, and nature had no more major surprises for humans. In the more extreme philosophical statements of this view, humans are perceived as evolving away from their roots in material nature toward a pure consciousness: "cosmic evolution ... is completed in and as human evolution, which itself reaches ultimate unity consciousness and so completes that absolute gestalt toward which all manifestation moves" (Wilber 1983: 100. See also Wilber 1981).[3]

This vision of progress in terms of human reason rationally dominating both nature and society characterized the thinking not just of right-wing futurists, but much more generally of intellectuals in the period from the Enlightenment until the outbreak of present environmental problems. The French philosopher Ferry (1992: 219-20), marshalling support from Sartre, Kant, and Rousseau, sums up Enlightenment philosophy as arguing that humans are anti-nature beings *par excellence*: they revolt against nature and free themselves from it, thereby becoming authentically human and ascending to the ethical and cultural spheres. Firestone (1970) constructed an antibiological feminism by arguing that reproduction should be removed from women's biology and become a technological procedure.

The sociologist Daniel Bell (1960, 1973, 1977) optimistically claimed that the planning of post-industrial society enables indeterminacies to be progressively reduced and social change to be controlled, and that if limits to growth exist they are social not material. Other well-known sociologists (Dahrendorf 1977, Lipset 1979, Nisbet 1979) also refused to accept the idea of ecological limits. Dunlap and Catton (1993b: 11) documented that in this respect mainstream sociology resonated well with the Reagan administration. They (Dunlap and Catton 1979, 1993a, 1993b) have argued that mainstream sociologists reacted this way precisely because they had constructed a sociology that was written as if humans were exempt from ecological constraints and independent from their ecosystem.

Berger and Luckmann (1967: 1) summarized the core argument of their influential book *The Social Construction of Reality* as follows. "The basic contentions of the argument of this book are implicit in its title and subtitle, namely, that reality is socially constructed. ... [They] define 'reality' as a quality appertaining to phenomena that we recognize as having a being independent of our own volition (we cannot 'wish them away')." In short, phenomena that we recognize as beyond being 'wished away' are none the less socially constructed. Nature is conspicuous by its absence in this argument.

This thesis of the social construction of reality is based on the assumption that the relationship between humans and their natural environment can be characterized by an immense plasticity and that humans, rather than having a nature, construct their own nature: "the human organism manifests an immense plasticity in its response to the environmental forces at work on it. ... While it is possible to say that man has a nature, it is more significant to say that man constructs his own nature, or more simply, that man produces himself" (Berger and Luckmann 1967: 48-49). This in turn is based on the premise of a radical discontinuity between humans and non-human animals. Whereas the latter have a closed and fixed relationship to their natural environment, humans have an open relationship.

> It refers to the biologically fixed character of their [non-human animals] relationship to the environment, even if geographical variation is introduced. In this sense, all non-human animals, as species and as individuals, live in closed worlds whose structures are predetermined by the biological equipment of the several animal species. By contrast, man's relationship to his environment is characterized by world-openness. (Berger and Luckmann 1967: 47)

Recent work from this perspective has dismissed ecological problems as socially constructed "social scares" (Fox 1991, Buttel et al. 1990, Buttel and Taylor 1992, Taylor and Buttel 1992) rather than as a change in the natural environment that could in turn affect social action.

Thus the social ecologist Bookchin (1987: 51) concludes that

> sociology sees itself as the analysis of 'man's' ascent from 'animality.' ... However warped these self-definitions of our major social and humanistic disciplines may be, they are still embedded in nature and humanity's relationships with the natural world, even as they try to bifurcate the two and impart a unique autonomy to cultural development and social evolution.

Sessions (1985: 255) concludes that "the dominant trend of the academic social sciences (especially psychology and sociology) have by-and-large both reinforced anthropocentrism and promoted a view of humans as being malleable and totally conditioned by the social environment."

The assumption of a relationship between humans and nature characterized by plasticity and related goal of mastering nature also underlie the work of Marx and Marxists. "Freedom in this field can only consist in socialized man, the associated producers, rationally regulating their interchange with Nature, bringing it under their common control, instead of being ruled by it as by the blind forces of Nature" (Marx 1966: 820). Marx even praised capitalism's attempt to bring nature under human control. "The *Communist Manifesto* and many passages in the *Grundisse* reveal an extraordinary admiration for the rationalistic side of capitalism -- its aggressive attempt to bring all the 'forces of nature' under human control" (Bookchin 1987: 178). In his critique preceding his reconstruction Gorz (1982: 18) contended that contemporary Marxists perceive history as "the progressive appropriation of nature by human labor. ... Society would be able to mould nature to its needs until, once mastery had been achieved, humanity would recognize itself in nature as its own product." Fidel Castro has been quoted by Marxists as stating that "no one who is conscious of what man can achieve with the help of technology and science will wish to set a limit to the number of human beings who can live on the earth. ... *We shall never be too numerous* however many of us there are, if only we all together place our efforts and our intelligence at the service of mankind" (quoted in Enzensburger 1976: 174). Benton (1991: 6) argues that there has also been "a 'corporatist' commitment to economic growth and indefinitely rising living-standards, and to a reliance on an ideology of 'technological fixes' within the labor movements."

Even New Age/Aquarian proponents, some of whom appear aware of ecological insights, have been caught up in this mind-over-matter ecstasy. "For the first time in history, humankind has come upon the control panel of change -- an understanding of how transformation occurs. ... The paradigm of the Aquarian Conspiracy ... says that we are *not* victims, not pawns, not limited by conditions or conditioning" (Ferguson 1980: 29). Ferguson (1980: 50) discovered that "Teilhard was the individual most often named as a profound influence by the Aquarian Conspirators who responded to a survey." It was Teilhard de Chardin who postulated that mind was in the process of transcending the natural world. According to him, the phenomenon of man is infallibly destined to develop a "noosphere" of expanded collectivized consciousness, an "ecstasy transcending the dimensions and the framework of the visible universe" (Teilhard de Chardin 1965: 318). The evolution of the human mind establishing its transcendence over the matter of nature is predestined and cannot be derailed by human or natural forces. "I feel entitled to say that we have nothing whatever to fear from these manifold disasters [disasters of nature] *in so far as* they imply the idea of premature accident or failure. However possible they may be in theory, we have higher reasons for being sure *that they will not happen*" (Teilhard de Chardin 1965: 302).

This New Age/Aquarian ideology led serious academic articles to propose, half a century ago, that a "noosphere" was in the process of replacing the biosphere. According to this theory, human rationality in the form of ecological engineering was about to succeed finally in subordinating the ecosphere (Vernadsky 1945).

Although New Age Aquarians speak of human embeddedness in nature, they also claim, explicitly in the work of Teilhard de Chardin and Ferguson, that reason enables humans to transcend the conditions imposed by nature and to take over "the control panel of change" (Ferguson 1980:29) from nature's evolution.   For them, human embeddedness in nature is the starting point -- the alpha -- of evolution, but it is in the process of being transcended by reason as humanity moves toward the end point: omega.   Thus the evolution of nature becomes replaced by "the evolution of consciousness," the subtitle of Roszak's (1975) book on the Aquarian movement. This is, in short, another version of the themes of the plasticity of nature and human mastery of nature, in which reason as it develops makes nature more plastic and enables humanity to master it.

In conclusion, the premise of a plastic relationship between humans and their natural environment has been a cornerstone of a world view, whether secular or religiously New Age/Aquarian, according to which human reason progressively remolds plastic nature in the intensification of rationality. Thought since the Enlightenment has been characterized by a radical uncoupling of the cultural and the social from nature, that is, by the assumption that reason has enabled humanity to escape from nature and remake it. This has led to the celebration of the mastery of nature by human reason.

In the intensification of rationality under the premise of a plastic relationship with nature, the anthropocentric manipulation of nature and of its living species has been the means used to monopolize resources and dominate other humans in the market, in political struggle, and in military conflict.   Those means have subsequently become ends in themselves and have evoked quasi-philosophical statements about the progressive mastery of nature by human reason as the goal of human development. This displacement of means to ends is the current outcome of instrumental rationalization on the cultural level and formal rationalization on the institutional level (see Murphy 1988).

Mastery of Nature or Manipulation of Nature?

Counter-evidence

The premise of the plasticity of nature and the assumed feasibility of attempting to master nature have been confronted by devastating counter-evidence over the past decade (see also Dryzek 1987: 15-23). The growing number of high-tech catastrophes (Bhopal, Exxon Valdez, Chernobyl, exploding Space Shuttle, Persian Gulf ecological warfare, and so on ad nauseam), the rapid accumulation of nuclear waste dangerous for long periods of time and for which no safe storage solution has been found, toxic gases emitted into the atmosphere, toxic chemicals excreted into rivers, lakes, and oceans, the destruction of forests by cutting, by hydro-electric projects, and by an accumulation of acid rain, and the depletion of once-abundant natural resources have called into question the possibility of mastering the environment as well as the wisdom of attempting such a feat (Levine 1982; Sills et al. 1982; Couch and Kroll-Smith 1985; Schnaiberg et al. 1986). Technological manipulations have placed the social fabric at risk (Short 1984) and created the "risk society" (Beck 1992). Perrow's (1984) excellent study of what he calls "normal accidents" -- accidents resulting from the complex interactions involved in the most advanced technology (nuclear reactors, chemical plants, dams, etc.) -- has documented the illusory character of the assumption that nature has been mastered even in these small-scale, relatively closed systems. Authors focusing on ecology have come to similar conclusions. "Complexity, uncertainty, and variability in the ecological environment of human choice are sufficient to overwhelm any ecological engineering project. ... Even at the microcosmic level of sustainable, human life-supporting ecosystems of a size that would fit in a spacecraft, technology has as yet to indicate anything remotely promising" (Dryzek 1987: 43-4). Human control of large-scale atmospheric systems and ecosystems remains trifling. Far from mastering nature, the projects of the human reconstructors of nature have unleashed hitherto unknown dynamics of nature. Humans have only managed to manipulate nature to a limited degree. Mastery of nature has eluded the human race.

Rationalization under the premise of a plastic relationship with nature fails to perceive that humans are limited by the conditions of nature, that human understanding of how transformation occurs is very incomplete leading humans to undertake action that victimizes them, and that the "control panel of change" operated by humans is the one at Chernobyl, on board the Exxon Valdez, at NASA Mission Control at the time of the Space Shuttle explosion, etc. Proponents of plasticity and mastery have seen only that the present generation of humans are "heirs to evolutionary riches" (Ferguson 1976: 29) and have failed to perceive that they are also heirs to the accumulated waste, pollution, means of destruction, and degraded environment their rationality has produced, with all their inequitable social impacts (Schnaiberg 1975, Morrison 1976, Unseld et al. 1979). The accumulation of unintended harmful consequences resulting from attempts to master nature based on incomplete understanding then limits future options.

The Decreasing Price of Resources

The hypothesis that the decreasing price of natural resources indicates abundance of their future supply is based on the dubious assumption that breaking points do not exist. Yet they have existed repeatedly in ecological matters. For example, the improved technology of rifles over bows and arrows resulted in buffalo being killed on the North American prairies in greater numbers. The price of buffalo meat and pelts would have diminished as a result of their increased supply, until the breaking point when there were no more buffalo on the prairies to kill. High-technology boats with radar to locate schools of fish made cod fishing on the Grand Banks of Newfoundland more efficient and reduced the price of fish to the consumer, but the resulting overfishing had the consequence of producing an ecological breaking point beyond which there are now no more cod to catch. The technology of logging has improved to the point where prices of pulp and paper are low making demand high, with the result that whole areas of traditional logging operations are logged out. The operation of supply and demand does not prevent resources from being both cheap and depleting. They could even be cheap until they are gone. Of course, beyond the breaking point when a natural resource runs out prices will increase dramatically, but until that point is reached, present price can be a very misleading indicator of future (as opposed to present) supply.

Plastic Tastes

The assumption that society determines what humans find appealing -- and hence that they could be socialized without injury to find plastic trees and an artificial environment more appealing than nature -- constitutes an extreme social determinism. It is akin to a sociology popular among specialists in marketing, which takes the important influences of socialization documented by sociologists, historians, etc., and pushes them to an absurd sociologism: what sociologists themselves have called "the oversocialized conception of man" (Wrong 1961). In the light of the continuing embeddedness of humans in their natural environment, including their biological make-up, it is dubious that humans could be socialized in this way without provoking harmful psychological consequences to themselves as individuals, harmful social consequences in terms of the quality of democratic life in human collectivities, and harmful consequences to the human-supporting natural environment. Thus aesthetic concerns, such as the ugliness of a clear-cut hillside as opposed to the beauty of a forest, continue to provide a firm and important base of support for environmentalism (Schnaiberg 1980: 388).

Are Knowledge and Ignorance Mutually Exclusive?

A central assumption of human rationality as applied to the environment has been succinctly expressed by Hamilton (1973: 167): "The more Man knows about the environment, the better able he is to control it." Even this assumption -- that greater knowledge of nature leads to greater human mastery of nature -- is now beginning to be challenged. "It is only since science has learned to replicate complex physical, chemical, and biological processes in the laboratory that its actions have been so consequential for the eco-system. The frequency of unintended interventions in the eco-system are likely to increase as the keys to more natural processes are discovered" (Perrow 1984: 296).

Rather than having increased the carrying capacity of our planet, the development of a waste-encouraging technology probably has decreased its carrying capacity in the long run by laying waste to the very resources needed to sustain human existence. "The loss of forests and other wild lands extinguishes species of plants and animals and drastically reduces the genetic diversity of the world's ecosystems. This process robs present and future generations of genetic material with which to improve crop varieties, to make them less vulnerable to weather stress, pest attacks, and disease" (World Commission on Environment and Development 1987: 35).

Increased knowledge of nature -- of nuclear and chemical reactions and of recombinant DNA -- has led paradoxically to an unintentional confrontation with new and little understood forces of nature, precisely because that knowledge is partial. Knowledge and technology have been and remain immersed in ignorance (Stehr 1991: 474), especially concerning ecological matters. Human constructions based partly on knowledge and partly on ignorance have provoked the unwitting disruption of the equilibrium constructed by nature and hence the unleashing of hitherto dormant and unsuspected natural forces. It is even possible that the development and application of science and technology will prove to have resulted in less, not more, mastery of nature (see Ehrenfeld 1978: 107-12).

The development of scientific knowledge has led scientists to become more aware of the extent of its still mysterious character. The discovery of previously unsuspected greenhouse effects, ozone layer depletion, harmful effects to the chain of life, etc., which scientists still do not understand, implies the discovery of levels of human ignorance that humans were unaware of. In this sense, awareness of ignorance has increased as knowledge has increased: "while our knowledge continues to increase exponentially, our relevant ignorance does so even more rapidly. And this is ignorance generated by science" (Ravetz 1987: 100). Most scientists have a strong sense of the vastness of what remains undiscovered. This sense of humility in the face of what is still unknown tends to get lost in the euphoria of the technological application of knowledge and in scientistic philosophizing about it.

Only on the assumption that nature consists of a finite, closed system with no emergent properties can the belief be sustained that increased knowledge results in less ignorance. Where nature is concerned, it is probable that humans are dealing with such a vast system that potential knowledge is infinite, and with an open system creating new phenomena. The premise of a finite amount to learn about nature, with humans approaching totality of that knowledge, may well prove inferior to the premise of an infinite amount in which we learn more without approaching 'learning all' upon which mastery could be based. Hence humans will likely have to get used to the counterintuitive idea that increased knowledge does not imply decreased ignorance. Knowledge and ignorance may not be mutually exclusive. Thus Beck's (1992a: 183) assertion -- that "the sources of danger are no longer ignorance but *knowledge*; not a deficient but a perfected mastery over nature; not that which eludes the human grasp but the system of norms and objective constraints established with the industrial epoch" -- is a little too simple. Ignorance and a deficient mastery over nature, which eludes the human grasp, remain characteristic of human interaction with the dynamics of nature even if the sources of danger are knowledge, norms, and constraints stemming from industrialization. The assumption that scientific knowledge is almost complete has been shown by the continual surprises, at times catastrophic ones, presented by nature to be nothing but a speculative illusion (Raynaud 1987: 36). Faith in mastery-of-nature rests upon such illusions.

The Myth of Nature's Plasticity

In his study of technological accidents, Perrow concluded that "by and large no extensive reductions in complexity seem possible in the nuclear power industry. The transformation system simply requires many nonlinear interactions. The same is true of chemical plants such as refineries; there is probably no efficient way to crack crude oil except in a highly interactive system" (Perrow 1984: 89). The complex interactions that result in explosive accidents in nuclear reactors, petrochemical plants, etc., "baffle us because we acted in terms of our own designs of a world that we expected to exist -- but the world was different" (Perrow 1984: 75). Naive assumptions about the plasticity of the relationship of humans to nature, and about social constructions mastering nature, confront a growing realization of the implasticity of the relationship between humans and their environment.

The plasticity myth -- that the relationship between humans and their natural environment can be reconstructed at will by humans -- is based on the denial of nature's complexity, and corresponding faith in the uniquely human capacity of reason to master simple, plastic nature. But nature is much more complex and resistant to human manipulation than previously thought. For example, pesticides have proved less effective than predicted because pests have the unforeseen capacity to adapt to the pesticide, with the result that increasing quantities, or more powerful variants, of the pesticide must be applied to have the same effect (Dryzek 1987: 19), thereby provoking the long-term, cumulative degradation of the environment. Similarly, drug-resistant strains of bacteria have developed that render some human-produced drugs ineffective. Although belief in the social and technical reconstruction of reality still holds sway in many quarters, environmental problems have led to its confrontation with the realization that nature too continues to take part in the construction of reality.

Paradoxically, the more humanity intentionally seeks to control the natural environment, the more unintended consequences it produces. Rather than mastering the constraints of nature, the human race has merely displaced those constraints in time (e.g., by generating radioactive waste) and in space (e.g., by constructing taller smokestacks) and globalized them. This in turn has the potential to produce a negative-sum struggle among humans as waste accumulates and as the environment becomes less capable of meeting human needs and desires.

Nature's Equilibrium Disrupted by Human Rationality

Although humans believe that they are rationalizing nature -- ordering it according to human ends -- they may be destroying more order than they construct. In their attempt to rationalize nature, humans upset the order nature has achieved, thereby creating disorder. There may be a social equivalent to the second law of thermodynamics: the disorder (entropy) of our planet is increasing as a result of human action. Humans have created local pockets of order, but their actions have had global disordering effects. Coal has powered an ordered industrial infrastructure, but the stripmining to acquire it has destroyed vegetation, and the factories using it are disordering nature's atmospheric equilibrium. Rivers were diverted in the Soviet Union to provide irrigation for a rational production of rice, and the consequence was the destruction of the Aral Sea. Humans mine Uranium-235 in order to produce energy, thereby contaminating the planet with intensely radioactive waste, whereas in the natural environment the 99.3 percent Uranium-238 in Uranium ore blocks the fission reaction of the 0.7 percent Uranium-235 from starting (Commoner 1976: 85-6). Ballast water taken on by cargo ships in one ecosystem and released in another has introduced species (e.g. mussels in the Great Lakes) having no predators nor reproductive controls. Economically rational shipping is breaking down nature's bioregional equilibrium of local ecosystems, thereby turning the planet into one big ecosystem, with ecologically (and perhaps long-term economically) irrational results.

The notion of transforming planet earth into "spaceship Earth" implies the replacement of the regulatory mechanisms of nature by those of human planning. Humans have come to believe that progress consists of their socially constructed projects taking over the functions previously undertaken by nature. But it is unclear how this constitutes progress rather than merely an expression of human vanity. Ecologists warn that human planning may well be inferior to nature's regulation. In his discussion of the dangers of nuclear power and the advantages of using solar energy, Commoner (1976: 125) reminds us that "the sun is a huge, essentially eternal nuclear reactor, assembled by the play of cosmic forces rather than by the hand of man." Better, concludes Commoner, to use the reactor perfected by nature than to construct our own. Nature has established over time through photosynthesis and metabolic oxidation a finely-tuned equilibrium of twenty percent oxygen in the atmosphere that sustains oxygen-using organisms (Commoner 1976: 42). Less than this amount and present oxygen-using organisms could not survive. More and the planet would be ravaged by terrible fires. There is as yet no indication that human reason could achieve an atmospheric equilibrium on such a planetary scale.

By destroying the capacity of nature to maintain the human-sustaining natural environment, humans would be forced to do it themselves in place of nature, a laborious, probably impossible, task. As the World Commission on Environment and Development (1987: 32-3) concluded: Nature is "fragile and finely balanced. There are thresholds that cannot be crossed without endangering the basic integrity of the system." Ecologists have demonstrated that nature has its own requirements and, if humans attempt to reshape nature as if it were plastic, they do so at their peril. Man could well be encroaching upon

> Gaia's [the equilibrium of Mother Earth] functional power to such an extent that he disabled her. He would wake up one day to find that he had the permanent lifelong job of planetary maintenance engineer. Gaia would have retreated into the muds, and the ceaseless intricate task of keeping all of the global cycles in balance would be ours. Then at last we should be riding that strange contraption, the 'spaceship Earth,' and whatever tamed and domesticated biosphere remained would indeed be our 'life support system.' ... [Misjudging the limits would lead to] the final choice of permanent enslavement on the prison hulk of the spaceship Earth, or gigadeath to enable the survivors to restore a Gaian world. (Lovelock 1979: 132)

Humans may well be harnessing nature in a way that a domesticated natural environment will no longer be able to meet their most basic needs:

> by replacing a complex organic environment with a simplified inorganic one, market society is literally dissembling a biosphere that has supported humanity for countless millennia. In the course of replacing the complex ecological relationships, on which all complex living things depend, for more elementary ones, capitalism is restoring the biosphere to a stage where it will be able to support only simpler forms of life. ... The earth will become incapable of supporting humanity itself. (Bookchin 1980: 230-1)

The definition of progress in the relationship between humans and nature has consisted of little more than prejudice in favor of the superiority of human projects over the processes of nature. The assumption that human planning can and should replace the regulatory dynamic of nature is being increasingly seen by ecologists as the "arrogance of humanism" (Ehrenfeld 1978). Human mastery of the natural environment appears more uncertain and unwise at the end of the Twentieth century than at its beginning. The superiority of nature over humans as the maintainer of a human-supporting natural environment has been advanced as a fundamental law of ecology and expressed in the aphorism "nature knows best" (Commoner 1972: 37).

Embeddedness in Nature

The conclusion that humans are intentionally taking over, with their projects, the construction of reality from nature is a spurious conclusion. Rather the two are in continual interaction (Burch 1971; Catton and Dunlap 1978, 1980; Dunlap and Catton 1979, 1993; Dunlap 1980). "One factor believed to be a basic cause of changes in global climate is beyond any imaginable human control: the earth's orbit around the sun, which is not completely consistent" (Yearley 1991: 134). Freedom perceived as bringing nature under the control of humans -- as freedom from the blind forces of nature -- is an unattainable, technocratic vision of freedom. Environmentalists have put forward convincing arguments that humanity remains one of the many products of nature and that humans must learn to live in harmony with its other products and with nature itself. Humans, like other forms of life, are creatures of nature dependent on its processes.

The issue is not just how humans construct their projects within the limits imposed by nature, but more profoundly how humans reconstruct the environment on Earth constructed by nature. This reconstruction has been done in ways that unwittingly unleash forces of nature that threaten to destroy the natural foundation necessary to meet human needs. Only now as a result of growing environmental problems are humans beginning to comprehend the illusory character of the alleged transformation from (1) the domination of human social action by nature to (2) the domination of nature by social action based on human rationality. Only now are humans belatedly beginning to recognize the embeddedness of social action in nature and to realize that the relationship between reason and nature is an ongoing dialectical one between two powerful forces.

A social-construction-of-reality sociology rests, like the technological-fix optimism of capitalists and bureaucrats, on a very shaky foundation. It is true that humans shape nature more than other animals and, in doing so, influence their own nature. But it is the other side that sociological constructivists, like capitalists and bureaucrats, have a tendency to ignore. Both have obscured the immense dependency of humans on their natural environment. By focusing on how humans differ from other species, they have lost sight of all that we share with them. Both have failed to take into account the way in which humans, as a species and as individuals, live in a world shaped by its dynamic ecosystem, a world where each technological innovation only reaffirms the dependence of humans on their natural environment. They have failed to realize that a world technologically open is none the less a planet ecologically closed.

Humans participate in the construction of reality through the processes of industrialization, urbanization, and the development of science and of capitalism, but they also run up against real ecological phenomena such as the chain of life and the ozone layer. The social construction of reality takes place within a wider ecological system of reality in the form of nature. Even the most powerful humans build their constructions within a context imposed upon them by the dynamic processes of nature. The power and wealth of those who have most to say in the social construction of reality have been attained at the price of bequeathing a world to their children stripped of ozone layers and rain forests, a world under the threat of the greenhouse effect and the nuclear sword of Damocles.

Thus ecologically aware Marxists are beginning to rethink their assumptions about socialist abundance: ecologists "have one advantage over the Utopian thinking of the left in the West, namely the realisation that any possible future belongs to the realm of necessity not that of freedom and that every political theory and practice -- including that of socialists -- is confronted not with the problem of abundance, but with that of survival" (Enzensburger 1976: 185). Hence Enzensburger (1976: 195) argues that "the productive forces which bourgeois society has unleashed have been caught up with and overtaken by the destructive powers released at the same time."

Treating other living species solely in terms of instrumental rationality, that is, as a means to increase the pleasure of the human species, forces them to live their lives in an environment that is increasingly artificial. Such treatment is based on the premise that living species other than humans have value only as means to satisfy human desires; they have no intrinsic value. That treatment and the premise it is based upon are now being called into question: "the method of 'factory farming' that is now common throughout most of the industrial world has been condemned as inhuman and cruel, even though it makes economic sense" (Hamilton 1973: 238).

The Cultural Period of Plasticity

The belief in the plasticity of the relationship of humans to their natural environment reached its high-point during the period when the production of plastics grew faster than that of any other substance (Commoner 1976: 199-200), surpassing iron as the principal material produced and used. Humans believed they had developed the capacity to shape nature to their will. It was a period when the power of nature seemed to have been tamed and when the partiality of human knowledge of nature, as well as the fragile dependence of humans upon nature, were forgotten. Although wars and a growing awareness of ethnocentrism and the relativity of values had shaken moral notions of human progress, the apparently increasing control over nature remained as the last bastion of faith in progress on an absolute scale.

> Faith in progress leads to the continuous changing of society into the unknown, without a program or a vote. We assume that things will go well, that in the end everything we have brought down upon ourselves can be turned back into progressiveness. ... Consent without knowledge of wherefore is the prerequisite. ... The productive forces, along with those who develop and administer them, science and business, have taken the place of God and the Church (Beck 1992a: 214).

The ideology of the immense plasticity of the relationship between humans and nature, of world-openness rather than a closed planet, of humans constructing their own nature rather than it being constructed by the processes of nature, as well as the emphasis on what distinguishes humans from other species rather than on the common ecosystem they share, all this was the expression of the mastery-of-nature assumption of human progress. It was a product of the age before waste had accumulated and the environment had degraded to a point where harmful effects on human biology became evident. At low points on the waste accumulation and environmental degradation curves, the world could be treated as an open sewer and it appeared that "man's relationship to his environment is characterized by world-openness" (Berger and Luckmann 1967: 47).

The assumption of a relationship with nature characterized by immense plasticity has been that of an affluent society careless of nature, and has predominated in the wealthiest nations during the period when their citizens shared the belief of being capable of reshaping nature with impunity (Catton and Dunlap 1978, Dunlap and Catton 1979, 1993). The premise that rationality can exempt humans from the constraints of nature was the postulate taken for granted before the cumulative reaction of nature to social constructions became clearly evident. Such pre-ecological thinking obscured the embeddedness of social action in the processes of nature. In terms of the history of humanity, belief in the plasticity of the relationship of humans to nature and in the goal of mastering nature arose in human culture in a brief intervening period between two different forms of awareness of the force of the natural environment, namely, after the end of the age when humans could not manipulate nature but before the age when the mysterious, incalculable and uncontrollable ecological reaction of nature to the constructions of humans came in full view.

At these later points on the curve of waste accumulation, the global planetary consequences of the relationship between social constructions and the dynamic processes of nature became increasingly visible. Humans face the painful observation that they too live with a fixed nature in a closed world -- an ecosystem -- to which they must adapt, or perish. Humans have produced themselves by modifying the environment nature has created in such a way that renders problematic its capacity to sustain human life in the long run. It is precisely the limitations humans face in constructing their own nature and producing themselves that demonstrate their continuing dependence on the natural environment. Even in those instances where humans do directly construct their own nature, as in genetic manipulation, they do so by manipulating nature through only a partial knowledge of the processes of nature, with unknown ecological consequences.

There is some evidence that industrial societies are moving from a technological to an ecological social paradigm (Olsen et al. 1992). None the less the plasticity premise and the goal of mastering nature -- both of which underlie modern culture -- are difficult to supplant, despite the increasing evidence of implasticity. This is because they constitute deeply rooted values tied to consumer, employment, and power interests and particular lifestyles. Such values are easy to camouflage on opinion surveys, with respondents replying to interviewers in terms of what ought to be done ecologically, yet acting according to values that demand the least sacrifice.

An Elastic Rather Than a Plastic Relationship

I would suggest that the conception of a plastic relationship of humans to the natural environment needs to be replaced by a conception of it as elastic. 'Elastic' captures the embeddedness of social action in the processes of nature better than the one-dimensional concept of plasticity, providing that all of the constituents of 'elastic' are kept in mind.

First, the development of peculiarly human capacities such as the brain, language, and reason has enabled humans to stretch their relationship with their natural environment more than non-human species. It has empowered humans with a much greater capacity to manipulate nature than any other species. This is why humans came to believe that their relationship with nature was plastic. The assumption of 'plasticity' is, however, misleading because it fails to capture two more characteristics that are at least as important as the first.

The second characteristic involves the existence of breaking points in the relationship. An elastic can be stretched by humans until it snaps. A bridge holds weight until it buckles. A dam holds back water until it bursts. The disappearance of buffalo on the prairies, and cod fish on the Grand Banks of Newfoundland, are examples of breaking points. There are many more. The capacity of the natural environment to support a growing human population can be expanded through the use of inorganic fertilizers, herbicides, and pesticides until their accumulation in the ecosystem reverses food production per unit of fertilizer. Radiation from nuclear waste, nuclear accidents, and war could contaminate food, water, and air, hence breaking the expanded relationship between humans and their natural environment. Assumptions of the 'plasticity' of the relationship of humans to the environment typically ignore the issue of breaking points, that is, they neglect the possibility that the relationship of society with its natural environment can become ecologically overloaded. Recognition of breaking points returns attention to the interaction of human constructions with the requirements of nature.

The third constituent of a relatively elastic relationship between human social action and the processes of nature is that of recoil. Nature reacts to human projects that try to stretch the relationship between the social and the natural. Attempts by humans to reshape the relationship have repercussions, often unforeseen ones, because they interact with the dynamics of nature. This is especially evident in high-technology accidents (Perrow 1984), but it is equally true, albeit less immediately obvious, for the routine pollution of the ecosystem. Contaminants have been forced deep underground under high pressure, and the result was earthquakes (Perrow 1984). Air conditioning was developed to increase human comfort, but the ensuing depletion of the ozone layer led to greater ultraviolet radiation and a higher death rate among humans from skin cancer. The development of the automobile provided rapid private transportation, but it has brought with it pollution that upsets the atmospheric equilibrium established by nature, with consequences that can only be estimated at the present time. Antibiotics have saved human lives and cured illness, but bacteria are now developing resistance to antibiotics. The recoil character of the reaction of nature to human constructions that attempt to stretch the relationship with nature has also been expressed as "nature's revenge." "No historic examples compare in weight and scope with the effects of man's despoliation -- and nature's revenge -- since the days of the Industrial Revolution, and especially since the end of the Second World War" (Bookchin 1971: 59-60).

These three constituents of an elastic relationship -- stretchability, breaking points, and recoil -- capture the embeddedness of social action in the processes of nature. The assumption of a plastic relationship, on the contrary, exaggerates the first constituent and ignores the other two, thereby concentrating on human constructions and neglecting those of nature. Whereas the plasticity premise leads to a dualism between human masters and plastic nature, the three constituents of an elastic relationship refocus thinking on humans as integral parts of nature.

The present overwhelming tendency in society is, however, that consciousness, perceived interests, and organization are structured by the premise of a plastic relationship between human social action and the processes of nature. This has led to indifference and often opposition to environmental requirements, and resulted in human actions that have promoted the degradation of the natural environment and unleashed dangerous dynamics of nature. An inappropriate worldview underlying both popular ideology and social theory is at the source of our ecological problems (Horkheimer and Adorno 1972, White 1967). Technological accidents, the threat to the ozone layer, the possible greenhouse effect, pollution washing up on beaches, the effects of deforestation, etc. do, however, render more visible breaking points and the recoil effect of nature. These problems tend to stimulate awareness of the need to adapt to the ecosystemic forces of nature in order to maintain an environment capable of sustaining human life (Dunlap and Mertig 1992), that is, they have the potential to promote a greater recognition by humans of their long-term ecological interests. The outcome of the intensifying environmental crisis will be determined by the clash of these two countertendencies.

Notes

1. "Calculation" as used by Weber must not be interpreted in the narrow sense as referring only to numbers and quantitative operations, but in the larger sense of figuring things out, as, for example, in the "'calculability' of judicial decisions" (Weber 1978: 1003).

2. See Regis (1990) for a documentation and critique of the proposals resulting from this world view.

3. Wilber has had both a negative and positive relationship with the ecology movement. Transpersonal ecologists like Fox (1990: 199-200) draw on the transpersonal psychology of authors such as Wilber but

discard its anthropocentric side and develop it in a new, ecological direction.

2

Rationalization
and
Ecological Irrationality

The increasing severity of environmental problems attendant upon the development of science, technology, a capitalist market economy, and formal organization strongly suggests that this process of rationalization has been based on the erroneous premise of a plastic natural world and on the unattainable goal of mastering nature. High-technology accidents, waste accumulation, and environmental degradation have been the perverse, unintended effects of rationalization. These ecologically harmful consequences challenge the assumption that rationalization and irrationality are mutually exclusive. They suggest that the two may paradoxically be related, and imply the need for a closer examination of the process of rationalization itself.

What Is Rationalization?

The analysis of the dynamic process of formal rationalization is the master theme in the work of Max Weber. "The key to Weber's sociology is not his epistemological distinctions [but rather] the analysis of the ineluctable processes of rationalization, routinization and secularization" (Turner 1981: 9, see also 101-2). Weberian scholars (Loewith 1970; Tenbruck 1980; Schluchter 1979 and 1981; Turner 1981; Brubaker 1984; Raynaud 1987; Albrow 1990) are now in general agreement that "rationalization" constitutes "a great unifying theme" and "an idée-maîtresse" (Brubaker 1984: 1) in Weber's work. Weber took into account both this dynamic process and the episodic conjunction of other causal factors so as to avoid both extremes of theoretical overdeterminism and historical descriptivism.

Most analyses of the self-propelled process of rationalization in the work of Weber have to do with the inner logic of religious ethics that led to the formation of the spirit of capitalism. Neo-Weberian analysis need not, however, be limited to these exegeses of Weber's work, but can also extend the work of Weber to the study of the contemporary period: to the examination of the inner logic and dynamics of science and technology, capitalism and bureaucracy, modern and postmodern consciousness. "Instead therefore of delving into the archaeology of Weber's rationalization thesis as contained in the Kantian and idealist tradition, it is equally possible for us to act as architects on it, to develop and improve it, to construct a theoretical edifice adequate for the vastly increased scope, power and comprehensiveness of the rationalized society of our own time" (Albrow 1987: 170). Although that ambitious project as a whole is beyond the scope of this book, Weber's analysis of rationalization can and will be used as the departure point for the critical evaluation of important conceptions of the relationship between social action and the processes of nature, with the goal of advancing understanding of that relationship and developing an ecology of social action.

Rationalization consists of several dynamic institutional components. The development of science and technology constitutes the calculated, systematic expansion of the means to understand and manipulate nature, and this has in turn promoted an intellectualized orientation toward the world. The scientific view of the world as a causal mechanism has tended to replace magical and religious beliefs. Belief in mastery of nature and of humans through increased scientific and technical knowledge, even among those who do not have such knowledge, has been an important part of an intellectualized worldview and of rationalization.

The expanding capitalist market economy is another component of rationalization. The capitalist market economy is formally rational in the sense of being freer from traditional and sentimental obstacles to market transactions than other forms of production and exchange, and in the instrumental sense of consisting of the calculated pursuit of self-interested market opportunities. "Those monopolies ... which are based solely upon the power of property, rest ... upon an entirely rationally calculated mastery of market conditions which may, however, remain formally as free as ever" (Weber 1978: 639).

A further important component of rationalization consists of formal, hierarchical organization, which "is the means of transforming social action into rationally organized action. ... [it is] an instrument of rationally organizing authority relations" (Weber 1978: 987). According to Weber (1978: 223), it

> is capable of attaining the highest degree of efficiency and is in this sense formally the most rational known means of exercising authority over human beings. It is superior to any other form in precision, in stability, in the stringency of its discipline, and in its reliability ... and is formally capable of application to all kinds of administrative tasks ... of church and state, of armies, political parties, economic enterprises, interest groups.

Domination in a formal, hierarchical organization is founded not only on the possession of the means of production by capitalists, but also on control over the means of administration by top managers, over the means of destruction by top military and political leaders, and over the means of knowledge by high-ranking technocrats, corporate lawyers, etc. Thus "the hierarchical dependence of the wage worker, the administrative and technical employee, the assistant in the academic institute as well as that of the civil servant and the soldier is due to the fact that in their case the means indispensable for the enterprise and for making a living are in the hands of the entrepreneur or the political ruler" (Weber 1978: 1394). Weber (1978: 978, 224) argued that such a formal, hierarchical organization "was and is a power instrument of the first order for the one who controls the bureaucratic apparatus" and concluded that "the question is always who controls the existing bureaucratic machinery."

The continual elaboration of a formal legal system to manage social conflict and promote the predictability and calculability of the consequences of social action is another component of rationalization. "Juridical formalism enables the legal system to operate like a technically rational machine. Thus it guarantees to individuals and groups within the system a relative maximum of freedom, and greatly increases for them the possibility of predicting the legal consequences of their actions" (Weber 1978: 811).

These components consist of the development of efficient means of social action. They constitute rationality in terms of the rational choice of means to attain goals (that is, efficiency), and Weber referred to this as formal rationality. He argued, however, that this conception of rationality is only one of two possible conceptions. He contrasted this conception of rationality with a conception based on rational choice of goals, which he referred to as substantive (or material) rationality, and argued that substantive rationality varies according to the values underlying it. "Formal rationality refers primarily to the calculability of means and procedures, substantive rationality primarily to the value (from some explicitly defined standpoint) of ends or results" (Brubaker 1984: 36). For example, the Nazis were formally rational -- efficient, chose the best techniques and organization -- when they murdered 6,000,000 Jews. They were not, however, substantively rational according to most values because genocide is not a rational goal regardless of how efficiently it is accomplished. An old-growth forest can be clear cut with great efficiency, but is it substantively rational from an ecological point of view to do so? The distinction between formal and substantive rationality is the conceptual device suggested by Weber for uncovering the tensions between, on the one hand, the efficiency of institutions and, on the other, substantive irrationalities in their functioning in terms of egalitarian, fraternal, caritative, and we might add, ecological, values.

Formal rationality is the kind talked about by people such as economists and administrators, for whom rationality refers to an appropriate choice of means for bringing about an intended, narrowly defined goal. Irrationality in this sense refers only to an inappropriate choice of means that fails to attain such a goal. The concept of substantive rationality brings with it a broader conception of irrationality, which includes not only ends judged worthless but also results or consequences -- whether intended or not -- that are injurious from the particular value standpoint. For example, capitalism has frequently been condemned as an irrational system by proponents of egalitarian, fraternal, and caritative ethics, regardless of whether capitalists intended to violate those ethics.

Parallel to this distinction between formal and substantive rationality on the institutional and societal levels, Weber suggested a distinction between instrumental (or purposive) and value rationality on the cultural and individual levels (Brubaker 1984). For example, instrumental rationality is characterized by conscious reasoning in which action is viewed as a means to achieve particular ends and is oriented to anticipated and calculable consequences. Value rationality is on the contrary characterized by a belief in the intrinsic value of the action, regardless of its consequences, and is oriented to a set of values. This opposition corresponds to a central cleavage in the debate over the environment, namely, whether non-human species, ecosystems, and nature in general should be viewed as means and instruments to carry out conscious projects for the anticipated benefit of humans, or whether they should be viewed as intrinsically valuable in themselves, regardless of the consequences for the standard of living of humans (see Chapter 5). Thus Worster (1977: xi) casts "the history of ecology as a struggle between rival views of the relationship between humans and nature: one view devoted to the discovery of intrinsic value and its preservation, the other to the creation of an instrumentalized world and its exploitation."

The sense that Weber had of the irony of history and his "idée-maîtresse" of the dynamic of formal, instrumental (or purposive) rationalization, in chronic tension with substantive, value rationality (Brubaker 1984; Murphy 1988: Chapters 9 and 10; Albrow 1990), are promising departure points to analyze the construction by humans of the means to manipulate nature and the unintended consequences of such formal rationalization as nature reacts. They constitute a plausible place to begin the analysis of the dialectical relationship between the social construction of reality by humans and the construction (or destruction) of the human constructors by the reality of nature. Weber himself did not go far in this direction of an ecology of social action, but his approach provides a particularly appropriate basis for examining the embeddedness of social action in the processes of nature.

Formal Rationalization as a Self-Propelled Process

Weber argued that capitalism -- and more generally formal rationalization -- became, after being launched by the inner logic of religious asceticism, a force with its own inner logic that no longer needed to be sustained by religious ethics: "victorious capitalism, since it rests on mechanical foundations, needs its support [of religious asceticism] no longer" (Weber 1930: 181-2). He "concluded that rational structures of all kinds were not only stronger in the sense of providing technically better solutions to enduring problems, but that they evoked, and enlisted, the motivation which contributed to their further development. Western rationalism on this account contained an inherent dynamic" (Albrow 1990: 196). The tension between rationality and irrationality itself generates a motivation to overcome remaining irrationality.

The modern economic "order is now bound to the technical and economic conditions of machine production which to-day determine the lives of all the individuals who are born into this mechanism, not only those directly concerned with economic acquisition, with irresistible force. Perhaps it will so determine them until the last ton of fossilized coal is burnt" (Weber 1930: 181). Specialized occupations are required by the logic of machine production, whether we like it or not: "The Puritan wanted to work in a calling; we are forced to do so" (Weber 1930: 181). What is crucial is the way in which "wanting" and being "forced" are related. Humans are "forced" to suffer the consequences because they "want" to pursue material goods. "In Baxter's [an English Puritan pastor] view the care for external goods should only lie on the shoulders of the 'saint like a light cloak, which can be thrown aside at any moment.' But fate decreed that the cloak should become an iron cage" (Weber 1930: 181). Mommsen (1987: 41) has shown that these dire predictions should be interpreted not in terms of an irresistible deterministic force leaving humans no choice or influence on their fate, but rather as a "self-denying prophecy" to foresee and avoid the harmful consequences of proceeding along the present path.

Central to the dynamic of formal rationalization is "intellectualization": the development of an understanding of nature and of how to manipulate it -- which is closely related to what Weber refers to as "machine production" and the "mechanical foundations" of social action -- and knowledge of how to organize and control humans. This rational knowledge is

> fundamentally systemic, binding individuals together, carried through human history, stored in institutions. Mathematics, logic, the natural and social sciences, law, the systems of religion, administration, and the skills and technology of everyday life make up that total accumulation of knowledge which one can call human rationality. ... One facet of bureaucracy was the accumulation of knowledge, not only technical, but also in the form of a store of documentary information gathered in the course of routine administration. (Albrow 1987: 172-3)

Intellectualization results, however, in the loss of the previously dominant spiritual meaning of life; hence it intensifies the search for meaning in the world. "As intellectualism suppresses belief in magic, the world's processes become disenchanted, lose their magical significance, and henceforth simply 'are' and 'happen' but no longer signify anything. As a consequence, there is a growing demand that the world and the total pattern of life be subject to an order that is significant and meaningful" (Weber 1978: 506). The quasi-religious and mystic currents of environmental and ecological thought have explicitly trumpeted themselves as an effort to enchant the world with new (or perhaps very old) meaning (see Chapter 4).[1]

Albrow (1987: 166) has demonstrated that Weber also applied his concept of rationalization to the "formal structuring of symbolic systems: both professional systems of knowledge and the systematization of beliefs about the world ... [and to] value-intensification: the increasing elaboration of knowledge and value-spheres such as art, law and morality." Albrow (1987: 171) argues that value-intensification "is what he [Weber] understood to happen in the modern world as value standpoints became increasingly explicit, their implications developed and made more rational. The rationalization process in general may indeed be seen as the intensification of rationality."

Albrow then investigated the 1984 British Data Protection Act -- prompted by the development of the computer and related information processing techniques -- and documented the relationship between formal and substantive rationality, and between instrumental and value rationality, in this overall process of the intensification of rationalization: the rational monitoring and control of rationalization itself.[2]

> What has happened is that the technical progress represented by the modern computer, when harnessed to considerations of the rights of individuals, generates argument and reflection leading to the elaboration of the idea of rationality. In other words, rationality does not develop in the abstract as some ideal force, but is the ongoing outcome of an interplay between technical progress and reasoned argument. In the institutions of society the outcomes of that interplay are recorded and provide the premises for the next stage of the argument. (Albrow 1987: 175)

Thus substantive value rationality, in terms "of the rights of individuals", monitors and controls the process of formal instrumental rationalization. Although the formal rights of human individuals have been a powerful type of substantive value rationality in the political-legal system of Western societies, they constitute but one set of values and enter into conflict with other values: "the various value spheres of the world stand in irreconcilable conflict with each other" (Weber 1958: 147). Conflict goes beyond the instrumentally rational / value rational opposition and extends to opposition between different types of value rationality. For example, deep ecologists have argued (see Chapter 5) that the focus on the rights of individual humans amounts to an anthropocentric monopoly by the human species, that it has excluded consideration of the rights of non-human living species and ecosystems, and that it should be replaced by biocentric considerations emphasizing the intrinsic value of nature (Devall and Sessions 1985) and ecocentric considerations based upon an enlarged conception of "self" that includes the whole ecosystem (Fox 1990). At the opposite pole, anthropocentric mastery of nature by human reason is celebrated by its proponents as the valued goal of the intensification of rationality, as described in Chapter 1. Proponents of sustainable development and neo-Malthusians have attempted to find a compromise position, which will be critically examined in the next chapter. Social ecologists subordinate ecological considerations to the primary value of human equality, as will be shown in Chapter 4.

The question is: upon which premises, and in terms of which values, will "reasoned argument" and/or the "intensification of rationality" and intellectualization occur? Which premises will be used to monitor, steer, and control the intensification of rationality and to select intrinsic values? Therein lies the basis of cultural conflict over the natural environment. It is these value premises and resulting ways of perceiving the relationship between the natural and the social that are being examined in Part I. The premises underlying the intensification of rationalization do not have to be based upon arbitrary decisions. They can instead be submitted to rational reflection and debate.

The Dialectical Embrace of Rationality and Irrationality

Albrow argues that, three-quarters of a century ago, Weber highlighted processes that have since become distinctive features of our time. Of the eleven Albrow gives, two are of particular importance. The first is the "intensification of rationality."

> At every level of social action from the individual setting goals to policy of the state, from the pursuit of profit to the process of scientific research to the development of new means of communication, there is a growth of rationality which becomes identified as the universal principle for human action and the best criterion for common understanding. It is institutionalised in systems of action of an ever more embracing kind. Because of its twin features of universal intelligibility and capacity to provide technical mastery of the real world it has, as the rationalisation process, become the driving force in human history. (Albrow 1990: 283-4)

The other distinctive feature associated with the intensification of rationality is, paradoxically, the "magnification of irrationality." "The scope and cumulative effects of irrationality grow with the extension of rationality. More and more people are placed under the constraints of rationalised systems which they do not understand, while those systems produce larger, unmanageable, unwanted effects" (Albrow 1990: 284). This has certainly been true in an ecological sense. On the social side as well, the popularity of the derogatory meaning of the word 'bureaucracy' attests to the generation of substantive irrationalities by the process of rational organization.

Thus "as formal rationality grows there is good reason to think that material irrationalities increase equivalently. ... It would be a fatal mistake to imagine that the one is an alternative, much less a conclusive negation, of the other. So long as human culture survives, rationality and irrationality are locked in a dialectical embrace" (Albrow 1987: 182). One reason is because many natural processes, "population trends, resource limitations, health factors, ... are outside the presciptive rules of rationality. ... it is not possible for system-rationality to provide a closed and eternally predictable environment" (Albrow 1987: 182).

Weber's conclusions quoted previously are not only a forceful expression of the social consequences of machine production, but also of its contradictions and limitations. There is no postulated technological fix nor assumption of the plasticity of the relationship of humans to their natural environment in Weber's analysis. On the contrary, machine production has the potential to take humans down the road to the degradation of the environment and the stripping of nature of its resources: to the moment when "the last ton of fossilized coal is burnt" (Weber 1930: 181). The "care for external goods" risks becoming, not "a light cloak," but instead "an iron cage" (Weber 1930: 181).

In Weber's argument, the consequences of values and social action can be quite paradoxical. He (Weber 1930) traced the ironic connection between the Protestant ethic (a religious ethic that among other things restricted the enjoyment of material goods) and the spirit of capitalism (a spirit that fostered the eventual development of a system based on the consumption and enjoyment of material goods). He demonstrated that Protestant asceticism led to a powerful dynamic of capital accumulation and hence paradoxically to secular materialism: "since asceticism undertook to remodel the world and to work out its ideals in the world, material goods have gained an increasing and finally an inexorable power over the lives of men as at no previous period in history" (Weber 1930: 181). The religious ethic of asceticism has, in other words, led to the secular spirit of enjoyment of material consumption.

The rest of the sequence, which Weber did not analyze, is no less ironic, resulting in the human consumption of nature, that is, the consumption of the very natural environment that brought humans into being and that has supported our continuous existence. This consumption of nature has unleashed hitherto unknown forces of nature that threaten the very basis of human existence. The pursuit of material goods through machine production has modified the relationship between humans and their dynamic natural environment in a way that could complete the vicious circle. The stripping of resources, the accumulation of waste, and in general the degradation of the environment risk producing an environment less capable of meeting human needs. Extending Weber's analysis leads to the following conclusion. Whereas the Puritan wanted asceticism, materialist humans (or their descendants) may be forced into asceticism because their transformation of nature's resources into waste and pollution has degraded the natural environment and diminished its future capacity to supply the resources necessary to produce material goods. Religious asceticism has led to secular materialism, which in turn threatens to lead to secular asceticism. Forced asceticism is already the fate of the poor in the Third World. The materialism of some has gone hand in hand with the forced asceticism of many and could possibly result, for ecological reasons, in the forced asceticism of all. As Beck (1992a: 22) puts it: "the unknown and unintended consequences come to be a dominant force in history and society."

The spirit of capitalism, that is, the pursuit of private profit, and its institutional expression in the development of transnational corporations, stock markets, trade agreements facilitating the development of the international market, etc., have been important elements in the promotion of technical and organizational efficiency, of the mastery-of-nature cult and plasticity-of-nature myth, and of the dynamic of waste accumulation and resource depletion. Thus, from an ecological point of view, the sequel to Weber's classic work *The Protestant Ethic and the Spirit of Capitalism* could be entitled *The Spirit of Capitalism and a Parasitic Disposition*. The development of capitalism has led science and technology to develop in a way that has been oriented towards the exploitation and degradation of the natural environment, that is, oriented towards the establishment and maintenance of a parasitic relationship between social action and the processes of nature.

This has been true of the legal system too. Laws have been made without the natural environment in mind. The resulting legal vacuum has permitted pollution and waste dumping, resource depletion, and environmental degradation. Since everything is allowed except that which is explicitly forbidden, the laws of the legal system have, by omission, been partial against the natural environment. And it is not only a question of legalizing environmentally parasitic practices, but also of lending legitimacy to them. Just as the lack of a law against rape would, by omission, indirectly condone and legitimize forcible sexual appropriation, so too the lack of laws against waste dumping, resource depletion, and environmental degradation indirectly condone and legitimize, by omission, those actions. For example, the absence of laws prohibiting the disposal of waste in rivers, lakes, and the atmosphere, and lack of laws requiring that land degraded by open-cast mining and clear-cut logging be returned to its original state, have set the rules of the market contest and of bureaucratic planning in a way that encourages a parasitic rather than symbiotic relationship between social action and the dynamics of nature. Moreover, whereas corporations have been treated in law as legal persons in order to enhance economic rationality, ecosystems have not received similar treatment in order to enhance ecological rationality. Class-action lawsuits to enforce restitution for damage to the environment, with a view to preventing further damage, have not been permitted.

The development and application of science has been the technical basis of ecologically irrational consequences. Furthermore, an insistence on rigorous scientific proof of causality for damage from pollution has been the defense strategy of polluters, allowing them to continue their pollution. In a context where there are many polluters, many causes, many ailments, and only partial understanding, lack of rigorous proof does not necessarily mean absence of harm but rather a deficiency in the means to document causal relationships. Thus the insistence on rational scientific criteria of proof has been the tactic used to continue the irrational practice of environmental degradation.

Capitalism has hitherto involved the development and application of science and technology by hierarchical, bureaucratic organizations whose relationships have been governed predominately by the principles of exchange on the market. It has consisted of rationality in the sense of planning by private corporations and public state agencies in terms of profit and loss, supply and demand, resource extraction and consumption. State socialism, or Marxist-Leninism as it has existed, has involved the development of science and technology by bureaucratic organizations whose relationships have been governed predominately by a strict structure of command. It has consisted of rationality in the sense of central planning by the hierarchical bureaucracy of the Communist Party. Marxist-Leninists have rejected the private property market but, despite lip service given to a theory of the withering of the state, they have in practice promoted its bureaucratic organization and, through it, resource extraction and industrialization. Socialism as it exists has been another variant of formal rationalization, in the sense that somewhat different goals have been pursued by the same means -- similar technology, factory discipline, and in general, hierarchical bureaucratic organization -- as under capitalism (Raynaud 1987: 196). From an ecological point of view, both capitalism and state socialism have been oriented toward the efficient mastery of nature, with little regard given to the harmful, irrational consequences of the accumulation of waste and the degradation of the natural environment.

The formal abolition of private property and the capitalist market under state socialism has not led to a symbiotic relationship between social action and the processes of nature either. The central planning by bureaucratic Communist Parties has also resulted in the despoliation of the natural environment. The centrally planned development of productive forces by one-party socialist states has been a system of bureaucratic career incentives for the same purpose (the exploitation of the environment) as the capitalist market system of profit incentives. The spirit of capitalism has consisted of, among other features, instrumental rationality that has underpinned socialism as it has existed as well. In this type of rationality the natural environment is perceived as a mere instrument for the efficient attainment of human projects. Both capitalism and state socialism have resulted in systems of economic and political rationalization that have led to ecological irrationality: the perverse, largely unintended consequence of the development of a parasitic relationship with nature.

The pursuit of the means of mastering nature, and of attempting to foresee and calculate consequences, have been important parts of the process of rationalization. But pursuit does not imply that the means of mastery have been completely found. Unforeseen side-effects have been encountered. New unknowns have appeared in the calculations. In the cumulative process of the discovery of scientific, technological, and organizational solutions to problems, further problems of increasing severity have accumulated as well: radioactive and toxic waste, pollution of the oceans and the atmosphere, high-technological accidents, increasingly destructive weapons systems, destruction of forests and depletion of resources, extinction of species, etc. These ecologically irrational consequences have magnified as rationalization has proceeded. The very successes of scientific, engineering, and organizational calculations have led to the unleashing of forces of nature that, paradoxically, could have incalculable consequences. These unintended repercussions -- which already have occurred on a small scale and threaten to occur on a larger, even planetary, scale -- are becoming dominant forces both materially and in terms of their impact on human consciousness. Max Weber's concept of "rationalization" grasps particularly well this late modern reality, produced by successful rationalization.[3]

Weber (1958: 147) also argued that "the various value spheres of the world stand in irreconcilable conflict with each other." By "value sphere" Weber is referring to an objective sphere of activity that has its own specific requirements and values. For example, the economic sphere requires that people be treated as a means to attain economic ends, the political sphere requires a willingness to use violence, the religious sphere values brotherliness, and, we might add, the ecological sphere attaches a high value to nature and requires a long-term symbiotic relationship between social action and the forces of nature. The process of rationalization has had the perverse consequence of increasing latent tension and conflict between these spheres through specialization and autonomization: "the rationalization and the conscious sublimation of man's relations to the various spheres of values, external and internal, as well as religious and secular, have then pressed towards making conscious the internal and lawful autonomy of the individual spheres;

thereby letting them drift into those tensions which remain hidden to the originally naive relation with the external world" (Weber 1958: 328).

One insidious, irrational, cultural consequence of rationalization is particularly important. If it is believed that "there are no mysterious incalculable forces that come into play" (Weber 1958: 139) in the rational, intellectualized structure of thought, "one need no longer have recourse" to magical means. But that is not all. Recourse has tended to be lost as well to the awareness that there remain natural forces that are still mysterious and incalculable and that cannot be mastered. A perverse effect of intellectualization and rationalization is that they have obscured the incompleteness of knowledge and the implasticity of the relationship of humans to their natural environment. Rationalization, and in particular intellectualization, have promoted the belief that reality can be reconstructed by human society, and hence led to the loss of the attitude that humans must adapt to nature. The premise behind both the pursuit of profit under capitalism and the central planning of the Communist Party under state socialism has not so much been that planet Earth has infinite resources, but rather that human rationalization and intellectualization are powerful enough to mold nature to suit human projects through science and technology, bureaucratic and market organization. Environmental problems have recently and increasingly called that premise into question. Referring to the development of recombinant DNA, Perrow (1984: 303) concludes that

> researchers in both the university and commercial laboratories seem to feel that we know all we need to know about the risks of the technology. In a personal communication, Sheldon Krimsky suggests that what has emerged is a type of orthodoxy that holds that 'genetic materials will either do what they are supposed to do when they are displaced, or do nothing at all.' From the vantage point of the systems examined in this book [those that have resulted in high-technology accidents], this assertion of confidence seems quite unrealistic.

The loss of the awareness of human ignorance and of the recognition that humans must adapt to nature has been a particularly irrational cultural consequence of rationalization. Only recently have ecological problems begun to rekindle awareness that nature remains in large part mysterious, incalculable, and unmasterable, and that social action must adapt to it. For example, Dryzek (1987: 23) contends that "should the ecosphere eventually show signs of failing to perform, it may well be too late by then to take corrective action. ... The difficulty in reaching any summary judgment as to how far we are currently from any [planetary] limits reflects the substantial human ignorance of the workings of the world's ecosystems."

Faith in the mastery of nature by technical and organizational means is no less a belief than magic and religion. It is often held even by those who do not possess such technical and organizational knowledge and are unaware of their limitations. In some ways, humans in formally rational societies know less than those in traditional societies about the conditions in which they live. For example, the long-term effects of chemical, biological, and nuclear weapons and of new chemicals put into today's food are often poorly understood, whereas individuals in traditional societies understood the effects of the simple weapons and natural food they and their ancestors had used for centuries.

Regis (1990) has shown that faith in the power of human reason to reshape and master nature is rooted in alienation from nature, which humans then hold in contempt. This alienation from the natural environment has been aptly described by Kai Millyard of Friends of the Earth: "We don't have much of a sense of belonging to ecosystems or being a part of the environment. We live amidst concrete and steel and glass and bring in all our food and energy" (quoted in Southam 1989: 21). Rational, industrial society has resulted in the ecologically irrational tendency of humans to be less sensitive (1) to the fact that they too are nature's construction and (2) to the necessity of adapting to the processes of nature for the maintenance of human life and of human reason.

Sociology has been part of the process of Western rationalization and has shared its ecologically irrational premises of the plasticity of nature and of dualism between humans and nature. Environmental problems and ecology movements have demonstrated that not only non-human animals but also humans are embedded in nature, living in ecosystems whose structures are predetermined by their biological and ecological equipment, and that the relationship between humans and their environment is less plastic than was assumed. "Accordingly, my ecological image of nature leads me to drastically redefine my conception of economics, sociology, psychology, and even socialism, which, ironically, advance a shared dualistic gospel of a radical separation of society from nature even as they rest on a militant imperative to 'subdue' nature" (Bookchin 1987: 71). The growing awareness that social constructions unleash dynamic processes of nature beyond human control that bear on social action has the potential of radically transforming the untenable premises about nature underlying much of contemporary sociology.[4]

Talk about "the destruction of nature" (Beck 1992a: 80), or worse still, the *mere* destruction of nature, is misleading. It is not nature, but humanity, that is vulnerable to the ecologically irrational consequences of formal rationalization. Humans are efficiently manipulating nature in a way that unleashes forces of nature that threaten to destroy the present human-supporting form of the natural environment on Earth and replace it with one that is not human-supporting. Of all the celestial bodies in nature, planet Earth is the only one yet discovered that supports human life, and rationalization as it has hitherto occurred has had the perverse effect of placing that rare type of natural environment at risk. Human action has rendered problematic the type of environment nature has created on Earth, but nature itself will continue to exist, even on our planet, regardless of human action. Humans do not need to protect nature. Rather they need to protect themselves, other living species, and their habitats from the ecologically irrational effects of human rationalization.

Along with the process of the formal rationalization of the relationship between social action and the natural system have come unforeseen and previously never experienced ecological irrationalities. For example, Perrow (1984) has documented the process by which the social and technical complexity needed to harness nuclear energy, chemical reactions, etc., leads to a certain level of what he calls "normal accidents." Similarly, acid rain, the depletion of the ozone layer, and the greenhouse effect have been the ecologically pernicious consequences of technical and social rationalization.

Rationalization is, however, not a static state but a process through which these irrational consequences -- natural or social -- are dealt with by means of further attempts at rationalization. And so the intensification of rationalization proceeds. It is not, none the less, a mechanical process, but one which involves choices and decisions, strategies and constraints. It is open-ended, yet Weiss (1985) argues that it is irreversible.

Environmental problems have begun to stimulate an increasing recognition that the goal of the mastery of nature and the premise of the plasticity of the relationship between humans and their natural environment are illusions, mirages that recede as humans believe they draw near. Those problems have thrown down a challenge to the population to develop new conceptions of its relationship with the natural environment, conceptions based on an awareness of the finite capacities of our planet to support the human population and its consumption desires, as well as on a recognition of the power of natural forces unintentionally unleashed by the human manipulation of nature.

A Weberian approach points us in the direction of searching for the irrational premises and irrational goals underlying the process of rationalization. "Weber was a sociologist of irrationality as equally as he was of rationality" (Albrow 1990: 145). The assumed plasticity of the relationship between the social and the natural has been one of those irrational premises supporting the pursuit of the irrational goal of mastering nature through the process of formal rationalization. Increasingly that premise is becoming recognized as fallacious and that goal as unattainable. This has not, however, undermined the intensification of formal rationalization *per se*. Rather the growing awareness of that fallacy and of the unattainability of that goal has begun to reorient the intensification of rationalization in terms of a different premise, that of the power of nature and hence respect for it, and of a different goal, that of sustainable development. Thus a movement is afoot to intensify rationalization in terms of greenness, that is, to attain a higher level of rationality: ecological rationality.

Notes

1. The Japanese novelist, Shusaku Endo (1992: A13), comes to a similar conclusion for Japan in 1992. "In its search for happiness, Japan developed as an industrial nation. But in the process, it paid a price; it lost the two things that had always sustained it: 'the family with its respect for the ancestors,' and 'nature'. ... But many Japanese -- especially the young -- are gripped with a sense of emptiness. One manifestation of this is the recent crop of new religions."

2. Albrow also studied, in terms of the intensification of rationalization, the regulation of the scientific and technological manipulation of human genetic material.

3. This expression comes from Beck (1992a: 22), but here it is turned right side up.

4. A critique of the field of sociology from an ecological point of view is being developed in a related paper presently in preparation.

3

Rationalization
Under the Premise of Greenness

One aspect of rationalization has consisted of the attempt to make social and economic organization more durable by having similarly trained, replaceable persons occupy standardized positions, by transcribing information through printed or electronic means in order to transcend the limitations of human memory, by ensuring sources of supply, etc. Sustainability has been an important element of formal, instrumental rationality. In terms of this criterion, it would hardly be rational if the efficient use of means to attain ends had the consequence of exhausting those means. The ultimate irrationality would be for the apparently rational industrial or post-industrial system to run out of gas or choke itself into extinction. Failing to renew renewable resources, depleting non-renewable ones, and destroying abundant resources through pollution and the accumulation of waste are, simply speaking, not rational means to ensure sustainability. There is mounting evidence that apparently rational social and technical constructions are unleashing forces of nature that threaten to destroy those social constructions over the long run. This is beginning to promote awareness that what has been taken to date to be rationalization has been superficial, short-term, and restricted. By not taking ecological factors into account, the development of rationalization has been inadequate in terms of durability.

Moreover, faith in progress is starting to be criticized as being a secularized religion based on nothing more than trust in the unknown, and people are beginning to lose such faith. Faith in progress constitutes

a type of consent in advance for objectives and consequences that remain unknown and unmentioned. Progress is a blank page as a political

program, to which wholesale agreement is demanded, as if it were the
earthly road to heaven. ... Progress is the inversion of rational action as
a 'rationalization process'. (Beck 1992a: 214)

In other words, naive faith in progress to solve problems we ourselves
create is not rational enough.

Reconciling Social Constructions
with Nature's Constructions

Environmental problems resulting from the accumulation of waste and
the degradation of the environment, together with the growing
recognition that humans have not mastered nature, are promoting the
emergence of new forms of relationship between social action and the
processes of nature, both on the level of culture and organization, values
and institutions. They are beginning to stimulate an effort to redirect
technology, formal organization, and the market so as to make them more
compatible with the requirements of the natural environment. The
process of rationalization is not forsaken by this change, rather it is
intensified in a new direction, that of greenness. The rational criticisms
of the process of rationalization are integrated into the process of
rationalization itself and lead, not to its abandonment, but to its
reformulation (Raynaud 1987: 175-6). In this transformation, the
assumption of the plasticity of nature is renounced. A new dimension of
rationality -- ecological rationality -- emerges as part of the process.
Ecological criteria are to monitor and control the instrumental
relationship between humans and nature.

Thus an important response to environmental problems, most likely
the predominant green one to date, has been the attempt to take into
account past and probable future consequences of human action on
nature in the planning of further social and technical action. For
example, the calculation of environmental impact assessments before
deciding to install production facilities has been proposed as a significant
element of ecological rationalization. An effort has also been started by
environmentalists to go beyond the prediction of short-term consequences
and to foresee those more distant in time.

This intensification of rationalization has also begun with respect to
space: environmentalists argue that consideration must be given to long-
range consequences as well as local ones. Hence the slogan of
environmentalists: think globally. For example, discussion of the distant
effects of deforestation, nuclear accidents, acid rain, the accumulation of
pollutants in the oceans, etc., has started. There is a growing realization

that the planet is one interdependent system: displacing polluting factories from the industrialized world to the developing world will fail to prevent the pollution from eventually spreading back to the industrialized world, the destruction of the shared ozone layer and the greenhouse effect will affect everyone, etc.

Far from opposing rationalization, this response constitutes an attempt to intensify and extend rationalization. It consists of the incorporation of ecological criteria into the conception and process of rationalization. For example, taking the harmful consequences of waste accumulation and resource depletion into account has resulted in efforts at recycling in order to render development sustainable. The three environmental Rs -- reduce, reuse, recycle -- are important elements of the rationalization of waste under the green transformation. Ecological rationality involves a dialectical relationship between social action and the processes of nature, in which the consequences of socially and technically acting on the natural environment are taken into consideration so as to improve ecologically the next stage of socially acting on nature (see Dryzek 1987; Albrow 1987: 175).

In this "garden" vision (Nash 1982) of the natural environment, humans carefully and prudently manage the planet in order to promote and/or sustain development in favor of humanity. During this development, "the humanization of Earth inevitably results in destruction of wilderness and of many living species that depend on it" (Dubos 1980: 1), but this is seen as an acceptable price to pay for such progress.

Many (but not all, as we shall see) environmental groups perceive their role as pressure groups having the goal of rationalizing the political process, the legal system, the state bureaucracy, private corporations, and the market in terms of preserving the human-sustaining natural environment. They perceive the fastest and most effective route to resolving urgent environmental problems to be the rationalization in environmental terms of the forms of social organization already in place, rather than having to invent alternatives to those organizations (see Davidoff in Davidoff, Foreman, and Bookchin 1991: 63-5). Increased control by the state, by the legal system, by world regulatory agencies, and even by private corporations has been the typical institutional proposal in this intensification of rationalization under greenness. Proponents of this world-view attempt to eliminate the irrational damage human social action has done to the natural environment and attempt to rationalize future social action so as to render it complementary to its human-sustaining natural infrastructure.

The work on sustainable development, neo-Malthusian research, and much of the environmental movement constitute attempts to deepen and enlarge the process of rationalization in order to render available on a long-term, sustainable basis the means to attain human goals. "It is clear that a low energy path is the best way towards a sustainable future. But given efficient and productive uses of primary energy, this need not mean a shortage of essential energy-services. ... The development of renewable sources will depend in part on a rational approach to energy pricing to secure a stable matrix for such progress" (World Commission on Environment and Development 1987: 201). The most influential attempt, and the one broadest in scope, to intensify in environmental terms the process of rationalization has been the push toward sustainable development.

Sustainable Development

The United Nations and other regulatory organizations at the world level are the closest institutions to world government that exist at the end of the Twentieth century. These world organizations, as well as individuals associated with them, have produced a series of studies of the environment (Daugherty, Jeanneret-Grosjean, and Fletcher 1979; Sachs 1980; Sachs 1981; Pirages 1977; Brown 1981; Glaeser 1984; Redclift 1987) culminating to date in the influential work on sustainable development of the World Commission on Environment and Development (1987) and the United Nations program for the environment (Tolba 1987, 1992; Tolba and El-Khaly 1992).

"Sustainable development is development that meets the needs of the present without compromising the ability of future generations to meet their own needs" (World Commission on Environment and Development 1987: 43). The Commission argued that there are two key elements in this definition: that of the needs of future as well as present generations, and that of limitations imposed by the state of technology, social organization, and the natural environment. It presented detailed arguments and evidence concerning the degradation of the environment on a planetary scale, advanced suggestions to make development sustainable, and related them to the need for development opportunities in developing countries.

The Commission argued that the complexity of coordinating increasingly specialized organizational sectors has had grave consequences for the natural environment: "impacts on forests rarely worry those involved in guiding public policy or business activities in the fields of energy, industrial development, crop husbandry, or foreign trade. Many of the environment and development problems that confront us have their roots in this sectoral fragmentation of responsibility. Sustainable development requires that such fragmentation be overcome" (World Commission on Environment and Development 1987: 63). This is a restatement in terms of environmental consequences of Weber's argument examined in the previous chapter that, in the process of rationalization, the different spheres of activity tend to drift apart and proceed according to their own specialized logic and values. The environmental irrationalities generated by this fragmentation of responsibility arise because of the organizational uncoupling of what is coupled in nature. The forces of nature "lock together environment and development, once thought separate; they lock together 'sectors', such as industry and agriculture; and they lock countries together as the effects of national policies and actions spill over national borders" (World Commission on Environment and Development 1987: 310). Hence the Commission recommended an intensification of efforts at rationalizing social and organizational coordination in terms of the requirements of the natural environment so that ecological irrationality be reduced and development become sustainable.

To a much greater degree than other studies, the analyses of sustainable development have been written with the needs of people in developing countries in mind. The common theme is the relationship between environment and development, in fact, some authors refer to their work as eco-development (Sachs 1980, 1981). An important characteristic of this work is its examination of the connection between environmental degradation and social inequality:

> these increased social inequalities have led toward a dual degradation of the environment by: (1) the small wealthy elite, wasting scarce resources in ostentatious consumption patterns (for which a very large and still growing part of the total national income has to be allocated); and (2) the poor, largely majoritarian segment of the population, overusing by necessity the few natural resources to which they have access. (Daugherty, Jeanneret-Grosjean and Fletcher 1979: 1)

Wealth is destructive of the natural environment through greed and overconsumption. Poverty is destructive of the environment through desperation and neglect. Thus the struggle against waste and environmental degradation necessarily involves a struggle against social inequality and poverty (Sachs 1980: 22).

If developing countries in the South follow the same path to development as industrialized countries in the North -- through deforestation, burning of coal, use of ozone-layer destroying CFCs for refrigeration and air conditioning, etc. -- then those industrialized countries will be environmentally affected because the already seriously degraded planet is one interdependent system, whose parts are connected by wind and water currents. The global village has come into being not only in terms of the development of new media of communication (McLuhan 1965), but also in terms of the global environmental consequences of social action. The systemic character of the planet results in the environment being a medium of interaction between the poor and the wealthy, even poor and wealthy countries. If "the medium is the message" (McLuhan 1965), then the message is clearly an environmental one of the deleterious effect of the present world system of social inequality.

This message has not been lost on developing countries. Potentially harmful environmental consequences of unsustainable development are now being used by countries in the developing world as a lever in an attempt to transform their terms of exchange with wealthy countries. This was evident at the conference on the environment in Rio in 1992. Our common dependence upon the natural environment binds all humans together and lays the basis for human solidarity in which the human chain will be seen as only as strong as its weakest link. It is hope in this principle that has been fostered by the work of the World Commission on Environment and Development.

Although it emphasized development possibilities for developing countries in the South, the work of the World Commission on Environment and Development, culminating in its elaboration of the concept "sustainable development," was largely an effort at consensus-building. This is suggested by the title -- *Our Common Future* -- of its principle publication. It attempted to offer something to everyone. To the poor and to developing countries it held out the hope of development and an escape from poverty. To the wealthy it fostered the expectation that the present level of development could be sustained if only environmental problems were dealt with instead of ignored. Most of all, it emphasized economic growth in the interests of both. "If large parts of the developing world are to avert economic, social, and environmental catastrophes, it is essential that global economic growth be revitalized. In practical terms, this means more rapid economic growth in both industrial and developing countries. ... The Commission's overall assessment is that the international economy must speed up world growth while respecting the environmental constraints" (World Commission on Environment and Development 1987: 89). Industrial countries must grow so that developing countries can sell their products and grow too. The Commission stressed technical efficiency as the means of reconciling the need for economic growth with the limits of planetary resources (World Commission on Environment and Development 1987: 196-202). This proposed convergence of interests emphasizing growth and efficiency came as a welcome suggestion indeed from a commission on the environment at a time when neo-Malthusian environmentalists were counselling reduced consumption and less growth.

The assumption of the convergence of interests between the environment and development, and between present and future generations, has been a common theme of professional, expert managers of natural resources in formal organizations, both public or private. And this has been true since the inception of the rationally planned conservation of natural resources in the nineteen forties. Thus in nineteen forty-seven Pinchot (1947: 261) wrote: "The first great fact about conservation is that it stands for development. There has been a fundamental misconception that conservation means nothing but the husbanding of resources for future generations. There could be no more serious mistake. ... The first principle of conservation is the use of the natural resources now existing on this continent for the benefit of the people who live here now." Using natural resources more efficiently has been a much applauded alternative in order to avoid the more painful process of diminishing human use of those resources. Conservation of the natural environment is a more sellable idea if associated with growth and development than with restraint and reduced consumption.

As an educational concept, "sustainable development" was immensely successful, impelling managers in government agencies and private enterprises, as well as journalists, to confront and discuss environmental problems in a way they had not done before. Who, after all, would be so irrational as to prefer unsustainable to sustainable development? Sustainable development presents advantages for everyone. "The sustainability movement encompasses mainstream and grassroots environmental organizations, scientists and political activists, and First and Third World concerns and peoples. It has the imprimatur of the United Nations at the top of the global hierarchy and the *campesino* to *campesino* movement at the bottom" (Merchant 1992; 232). The discussion of sustainable development succeeded in sensitizing many administrators, managers, and capitalists, as well as people generally, to environmental problems and raised their level of consciousness about the connection between environmental problems and social and economic problems.

The Limitations of the Sustainable Development Approach

The very basis of the rhetorical success of the concept "sustainable development" was, however, the basis of its intellectual inadequacy. It succeeded in sensitizing managers, administrators, and capitalists to environmental issues because it avoided attributing responsibility for environmental problems and avoided an analysis of the source of those problems. "It is not that there is one set of villains and another of victims. All would be better off if each person took into account the effect of his or her acts upon others. But each is unwilling to assume that others will behave in this socially desirable fashion, and hence all continue to pursue narrow self-interest" (World Commission on Environment and Development 1987: 47). Because no cause was uncovered and no responsibility attributed in this we-are-all-sinners approach, no way was found to raise the capital to clean up the accumulated waste and restore the environment to the state it was in before it became degraded. The argument that the present form of development is unsustainable, which is the basis of the proposal to move toward "sustainable development," glossed over the accumulation of capital that has occurred at the expense of the environment in the current process of unsustainable development. The proposal for sustainable development lacked the means -- the capital -- for carrying out its proposal because it failed to analyze the relationship between the production of pollution and the accumulation of capital, between contributors to environmental degradation and its potential victims, and between the degradation of the environment and economic development. In fact, it is not even certain that the discussion of "sustainable development" diminished the rate at which waste accumulated and environmental degradation occurred. The Commission did not pursue very far its promising departure point: the analysis of the relationship between the natural environment, development, and inequality.

The Commission did demonstrate how poverty pollutes and advocated giving priority to the needs of the poor. But this argument was not well integrated into the theory of sustainable development, leaving much room for readers to pick and choose whichever aspect of sustainable development suited their interests and predispositions. Sustainable development for all became easily translatable into sustaining unequal development, "our common future" became 'our future and theirs.'

Moreover, the Commission did not deal in sufficient depth with the ecological dilemma faced by developing countries. Although poverty in those countries may eventually produce environmental consequences harmful to industrialized countries, those consequences are likely to produce much more harm, sooner, in developing countries themselves (Leonard 1985). If environmental considerations are not taken seriously, the short-run development of the Third World will occur at the expense of its long-run sustainable development, as in the case of the destruction of tropical rainforests (Guimaraes (1991). The threat of contributing to global environmental degradation is a weapon developing countries are beginning to use in an attempt to transform their terms of exchange with wealthy industrialized nations, but it is a weapon that risks blowing up in the face of the user.

Although the World Commission on Environment and Development (1987) pointed to the necessity of examining the relationship between social inequality and the natural environment, and although it proposed many important recommendations, it did not analyze the impediments to the implementation of those recommendations. Hence its recommendations leave the impression of pius preaching. By not analyzing the relationship between the degradation of the environment and the world system of monopolization and closure, it has failed to examine what such commissions are up against. The acceptance of the theory of sustainable development by the beneficiaries of unsustainable development was directly related to its limitations as theory.

Furthermore, the proposal for sustainable development also glossed over the possibility that the world has already been transformed into a zero-sum struggle for development. The waste accumulation and resource depletion that have occurred may have degraded the environment to such an extent that the poor will only be able to consume more if the rich consume less. Sustainable development for latecomers (the poor, future generations) may now require that the present developed position of the rich earlycomers not be sustained. "To bring developing countries' energy use up to industrialized country levels by the year 2025 would require increasing present global energy use by a factor of five. The planetary ecosystem could not stand this, especially if the increases were based on non-renewable fossil fuels" (World Commission on Environment and Development 1987: 14). Increased technical efficiencies would be necessary to reconcile development with the needs of the environment, but as the Commission itself admitted, the implementation of those efficiencies would require massive restructuring.

> By using the most energy-efficient technologies and processes now available in all sectors of the economy, ... growth [could be achieved] ... regarded in this report as a minimum for reasonable development. But this path would require huge structural changes to allow market penetration of efficient technologies, and it seems unlikely to be fully realizable by most governments during the next 40 years. (World Commission on Environment and Development 1987: 173)

The Commission failed to resolve the contradiction between its documentation of the limits of the ecosystem and its rosy recommendation for the economy to grow (see Merchant 1992: 229). The very concept of sustainable development could prove to be a contradiction in terms. Next we will examine a powerful argument that the problem goes much deeper and finds its origin in growth itself.

Neo-Malthusian Research

Malthus (1798, 1801) was an early critic of technology, arguing that, rather than mastering nature and eliminating the problems inherent in the relationship between humans and their natural environment, technology has promoted growth, shifted those problems to a more global level, and merely postponed the "positive" checks on human population (famine, epidemics, war). His theory of an ecological crisis that is technologically held in abeyance but technologically enlarged can be generalized from the problems of food production and population -- the focus of Malthus's theory -- to include the problems of waste accumulation and resource depletion. Improvements in technological efficiency have hitherto resulted in humanity moving not only to a higher level of population but also to a higher level of consumption and perversely to a higher level of the accumulation of waste and an aggravation of the problem of resource depletion. If Malthus is right, the long wave of technologically deferred crisis during the two centuries since he published his work will have enlarged that crisis when it hits. The long, big boom risks being followed by a particularly big bust.

Environmental problems in the late Twentieth Century are forcing recognition that nature is not as malleable as was assumed over the last two centuries. Despite several limitations of his theory, the fundamental Malthusian insight into the relationship between social action and the processes of nature is now belatedly being elaborated. Researchers have begun to develop the view that the natural environment is limited in its capacity to sustain human population and its consumption desires, and that if these limits are exceeded, powerful forces of nature governing the availability of the means to satisfy basic human needs will provoke social crises.

Demographers have documented that the human population has grown at an exponential rate since the industrial revolution and development of science. Whereas it took all of human evolution until the year 1830 A.D. for the human population to reach one billion, the second billion was added in just one hundred years, the third in 30 years, the fourth in 15 years, and the fifth in the 9 years ending in 1985 (Vander Tak, Hamb, and Murphy 1979: 2, fig. 1; Myers 1984: 18).

As this exponential growth in population was occurring, technological development enabled the discovery and exploitation of new resources so that the standard of living increased in industrial countries. In those countries it appeared as if there were no Malthusian dilemma and in Third World nations it appeared as if the problem was solely one of maldistribution of unlimited resources.

Recently, however, there is increasing evidence that resources, including nutritional ones, are limited. One illustration involves the harvesting of the oceans, which seemed to be the promised solution if land crops ever became scarce for a large and growing population. The development of long-distance refrigerator boats with radar to locate schools of fish, and fine nets to vacuum them from the sea, enabled the catch to increase rapidly and the supply of fish on the store shelf to be abundant. But this was only a temporary abundance, because overfishing (and pollution and perhaps the greenhouse effect) led to declining fish stocks, the collapse of some fisheries, and eventually to a global decline in the fish catch. For example, overfishing resulted in the haddock catch in the North West Atlantic falling from 250,000 tones in 1965 to 20,000 tones in 1974 (Myers 1984: 82). This decline occurred because the oceans were treated as an unlimited resource, rather than seeking to anticipate the limits and, if unknown, erring on the side of prudence. Some of this decline could have been avoided with more rational management, that is, management with ecological limits in mind. The evidence is accumulating to support the neo-Malthusian argument that there are planetary limits on resources, in this case, fish. Similarly, increases in agricultural production are also becoming more and more difficult because of the limited supply of arable land and of water for irrigation, diminishing fertilizer response ratio (Myers 1984: 61), and the increased resistance developed by pests and weeds to pesticides and herbicides.

Neo-Malthusians argue that planet Earth has a finite "carrying capacity", not only a limited capacity to produce food, but also a limited supply of non-renewable resources and a limited capacity to absorb waste and pollutants. They have shown growth to be the source of the risk of running up against these limits: growth in terms of population increase (Ehrlich 1968; Ehrlich and Ehrlich 1972; Ehrlich and Pirages 1974; Hardin 1968; Hardin 1969; Borgstrom 1965; Borgstrom 1969) and in terms of industrial expansion (Meadows et al. 1972, 1992; Mesarovic and Pestel 1974; Dolman 1977; Lazlo et al. 1977; Botkin et al. 1979; De Montbrial et al. 1979; Giarini 1980; Catton 1980). The persistent quest for growth, whether in pursuit of private profit under market capitalism or of centrally planned bureaucratic aggrandizement under state socialism, oblivious of the limits of the natural environment and of ecological consequences, leads not to the greatest good for the greatest number but rather to the "tragedy of the commons" (Hardin 1968).

Lasch (1990) contends that progress conceived of in terms of growth has its destructive side and must be viewed with skepticism because the finite resources of our planet can not support an unlimited expansion of industrial civilization, Thus he argues that, for the planet to survive, the focus must be shifted from the assumption of the progressive reshaping of nature to the limits nature sets on such reshaping and on growth. Neo-Malthusians have examined not only the consequences of growth in different sectors and regions taken separately, but also the structured system of their interrelationships. The importance of studying cumulative effects can be understood through the analogy of the ten students who claimed they were innocent of murdering their professor because none had given sufficient poison to be fatal. When added together, though, the poison received by the professor was indeed lethal. The accumulation of human-produced toxins in the environment has led neo-Malthusians to predict that, if growth continues as it has, a planetary collapse can be expected in the not-too-distant future (Meadows et al. 1972, 1992). Technical development, previously assumed to be expanding the planetary limits, has been shown by neo-Malthusians to be increasing the race to the limits at an even greater rate.

Neo-Malthusians contributed the first systematically documented critique on a planetary level of the assumed human mastery of nature. They have drawn attention to the finitude of natural resources and of waste sinks on our planet, and have shaken the seemingly unshakable faith in the discovery of technical solutions to environmental problems. They accomplished this at a time when capitalists, bureaucrats, and, alas, sociologists, were still portraying the relationship between humans and their natural environment as plastic (Berger and Luckmann 1967), were still maintaining faith in the facility of technical discovery (Collins 1986), and were still constructing "social scare" theories of ecological problems (Fox 1991, Buttel et al. 1990, Buttel and Taylor 1992, Taylor and Buttel 1992) rather than seeing them as human-produced changes in the natural environment that in turn affect social action. Neo-Malthusians have, more than any other group of researchers, stressed the urgency of restraining growth and have exposed the problematic character of the relationship between social action and the processes of nature, between political economy and ecology. Although neo-Malthusians have been mistaken about the timing of some of the ecological problems, evidence has been accumulating in favor of their key concept of "limits to growth." Dissemination of their research has in turn influenced public attitudes. Half of the respondents to opinion surveys in the United States now agree with the affirmation: "Environmental protection should be given priority over economic growth" (Olsen et al. 1992: 162).

There are, none the less, substantial differences between neo-Malthusians concerning the means to be used to restrain growth rationally and to reconcile social action with the forces of nature. One variant of neo-Malthusianism explicitly promotes a predominant role for the market. Thus Boulding (1973) argues in favor of "stock maintenance," whereby estimates of the finite capacities of the closed system of planet Earth to provide resources, absorb waste, and sustain people would be calculated. Quotas of these stocks would be traded freely on the market such that stocks of resources would not decrease, stocks of waste would not accumulate, and the number of people would not exceed estimated carrying capacity. For example, quotas for the use of natural resources and the discarding of waste would be issued by the state and these quotas would then be traded on the market. Similarly, to restrain population growth, the state would issue licenses to give birth to children in proportion to replacement fertility, then the licenses would be sold and bought on the open market. Couples who want more than their share of children could buy childbirth licenses from those who do not want children.

These ideas are not just idle speculations. Rather they are a particularly clear expression of a way of thinking about environmental problems that has already been partly enacted in legislation. For example, the Chicago Board of Trade voted on July 16, 1991 to create a market for rights to emit sulfur dioxide (The Ottawa Citizen July 17, 1991: E1), a possibility in turn created by the American Clean Air Act of 1990 that gave polluters the chance to meet sulfur emissions standards by selling and buying quotas allotted by the Environmental Protection Agency to particular plants. This amounts to quotas of acid rain that can be bought and sold on the market.

Daly (1973) suggests in addition an element of distributive justice in terms of an upper and lower limit to wealth. He (Daly 1973: 157-8) states as follows his basic principle for reconciling social action and the processes of nature primarily in terms of market freedom. "In all cases the guiding design principle for social institution is to provide the necessary control with a minimum sacrifice of personal freedom, to provide macrostability while allowing for microvariability, to combine the macrostatic with the microdynamic."

Other neo-Malthusians have argued in favor of a greater role for government based on an "ecological contract" between humans promoting harmony between humans and nature (Ophuls 1977). Government would, according to this contract, limit the amount of mineral resources and fossil fuel used in production and limit the toxic waste discarded. Some forms of energy, such as nuclear, would be abandoned in favor of others, such as solar. The number of children per couple would be restricted. Government regulation would be more efficient at achieving ecological equilibrium than market forces. Neo-Malthusians tend to be favorably disposed to private property, but these neo-Malthusians recognize the need for government regulation so that private enterprise does not run out of gas or asphyxiate itself. "Nor need the right to own and enjoy ... property be taken away, only the right to use private property in ecologically destructive ways would be checked" (Ophuls 1977: 226).

Another variant of neo-Malthusian research (Brown 1972; Sprout and Sprout 1971; Peccei 1981) focusses on a still higher level of structured system, arguing that the very existence of nation states has fostered waste, duplication, and overconsumption:

> the cost of maintaining the existing system of independent nation-states is extremely high. It is largely responsible for spending more than $200 billion worth of the world's public resources for military purposes, and for the artificially high consumer prices for goods which are inefficiently produced behind the protection of national tariff walls. It is also responsible for a great deal of redundancy in scientific research. (Brown 1972: 351)

The standard of living could be improved using less resources and producing less waste if a more efficient, globally integrated system of world government -- in short, one big nation -- were created to replace present nation states.

One only has to think of the wastage involved in the two world wars compared to the potential efficiency of an integrated European community to understand the validity of the structure-of-nations level of analysis. National boundaries are not written in stone. It could even be argued that, despite temporary countertrends in the Soviet Union, Yugoslavia, and perhaps Canada, the long-term history of humanity has been a tendency toward larger groupings: from tribes to kingdoms to nation states to international blocks and the United Nations.

A further offshoot of the limits-to-growth perspective involves the investigation of the social consequences of resource scarcity and environmental degradation, particularly the inequitable distribution of their impact among social strata (Schnaiberg 1975, Morrison 1976, Unseld et al. 1979). This offshoot constitutes both an improvement of the limits-to-growth approach and a criticism of those neo-Malthusian proponents who have been class-blind.

The Limitations of Neo-Malthusian Research

Multinational Corporations and World Government

Brown (1972: 225-6) unfortunately combines, in a way that is characteristic of many neo-Malthusians, his insightful critique of the division of the world into nations with a hypernaive assessment of multinational corporations (MNC). "In its efforts to achieve the most efficient possible combination of productive resources, the MNC contributes to the creation of a more equitable world order. ... The net effect world-wide is to provide a higher level of living for a given use of resources and effort than would be possible without MNCs." On the contrary, it could reasonably be argued that multinational corporations have been the most prolific institutions in the production of inequity, in the wasteful use of resources, and in the degradation of the environment. They have replaced local, environmentally innocuous industries like wool and leather with new high-polluting ones such as acrylic fibers and plastics. Instead of cleaning up their act, they have often moved the dirtiest part of their operations out of countries that have enacted strict pollution control standards and into countries too poor to be strict. Their investment criteria have pitted state against state, making states that seek to attract investment reluctant to enact strong regulations concerning pollution control, concerning the renewal of renewable resources, concerning the use of non-renewable resources, and concerning repayment to clean up the pollution already caused by multinational corporations.

Multinational corporations have moved many of their production facilities out of countries where workers receive high wages to states where they can pay workers less. Their cheap commodities have rendered many small, local industries in developing countries uncompetitive, thereby increasing unemployment. They have certainly provided a higher level of living for their executives, for shareholders and for some of their workers, but the conclusion that their "net effect world-wide is to provide a higher level of living" remains dubious to say the least.

Multinational corporations would in all probability oppose a "world without borders" (Brown 1972) because an integrated world government would be able to set common rules concerning the use of resources, pollution control standards, minimum wage, formation of unions, etc., thereby diminishing the capacity of multinational corporations to play off one nation and group of workers against another. An integrated world government would also imply citizenship rights for all humans -- unemployment insurance, medical care benefits, pensions for the disabled and the aged, etc. -- that would reduce poverty and with it the birth rate, hence diminish the population pressure on the carrying capacity of the planet. To pay for these measures, taxes on multinational corporations would have to be increased substantially, another reason to expect their resistance to the idea.

Resistance to a continuation of the trend toward an integrated world government is liable to come also from the most developed states, which monopolize most of the world's wealth and would be reluctant to see their small populations outvoted in a "world without borders" by the larger ones of developing countries. National borders have hitherto enabled democratic principles to be applied within the borders while maintaining the exclusion of outsiders from the rights and benefits of insiders.

The Capitalist Market

Market coordination has been developed for private goods, but works poorly if at all in the case of common public goods. For example, the market has failed to coordinate the protection of the atmosphere, oceans, and rivers. There is no market for biotic diversity. The invisible hand of the market has hitherto maintained its invisibility by its absence in coordinating the protection of the commons. Human action following market principles has on the contrary amounted to a coordinated attack on the natural environment based on continual economic growth. Waste-reducing measures that might decrease profitableness have been greeted by threats from capitalists to diminish investment and hence employment. The claim that the market is best suited to coordinate a transition from growth of consumption to its decline, or more generally, from a parasitic relationship between humans and their natural environment to a symbiotic one, remains unconvincing (see Dryzek 1987: Chapter 7 for a detailed study).

Neo-Malthusians do not seem to realize how the market restricts personal freedom. For example, childbirth licenses sold on the market according to supply and demand could well bring into existence a holding company specializing in cornering the market on children, tempting the poor to sell their license, and pushing up the price of a license to have children. Similarly, a limited supply of tradeable licenses for consuming non-renewable natural resources and dumping waste would make it very profitable for companies to monopolize those licenses, rendering society even more dependent upon a small number of large companies than it now is. Worse still, companies that have hitherto accumulated capital by dumping their waste upon the commons and not paying for its benign disposal would be best positioned to buy up such licenses. Creating a system of licenses and quotas now, after capital has been accumulated through laying waste to the environment and depleting its resources, is a proposal that rewards the wasteful rather than making them clean up the mess they have made. It ensures an advantage to past wastefulness and renders permanent the power, wealth, and privilege created through environmental degradation. It would result in the sedimentation of stratification on the basis of unpaid waste cost, a concept I will develop in Chapter 6.

If on the other hand a check on the use of private property in ecologically destructive ways were implemented, it could well amount to a check on capitalism itself. Unregulated laissez-faire capitalism cannot be reconciled with an ecological contract in which the state forces checks on recalcitrant, ecologically destructive private enterprises. Limiting the amount of non-renewable resources used in production, requiring the reprocessing of waste, and ensuring that renewable resources are in fact renewed necessitates not only the setting by government of new ecological rules for the market contest, but also an adequate system of accounting for resources and waste in a way that ensures such information is not monopolized and concealed by those private enterprises. It requires affirmative action by government in favor of the environment, which, much like affirmative action in favor of minority groups, would result in government intervention not only in the market, but also in the private enterprise itself. "Legally responsible, governmental monitoring agencies and a risk-sensitive media publicity sphere begin to talk their way into and govern the 'intimate sphere' of plant management" (Beck 1992a 186). "Stock maintenance" and personal freedom require more state intervention than Boulding and Daly seem to realize. The political system that has the best track record, although far from a perfect one, for checking the use of private property in ecologically destructive ways appears to be the social democratic system. An ecological contract would in all probability require that laissez-faire capitalism be replaced by social democracy.

Central State Planning

A hierarchically administered state command structure, essentially what Weber referred to as a rational-legal bureaucracy, appears at first sight to be a logical social means to attain ecological rationality. Not only Marxian socialists (Stretton 1976; Mellos 1988) see this central planning and control as the social means for correcting the ecological problems of the laissez-faire capitalist market system under liberal democracy, but also many neo-Malthusian environmentalists (Hardin 1968; Weinberg 1972; Harman 1976; Ophuls 1977; Heilbroner 1980; Odum 1983). They are attracted to government fiats because compromise among diverse interests and more so consensus are slow, difficult processes. Whereas checks and balances can lead to political paralysis, the ecological crisis requires decisive action. This is usually the basis of arguments in favor of authoritarian solutions. Yielding to the temptation to use particularly dangerous technologies also creates pressure for an authoritarian, quasi-military power structure to diminish risks, pressure that has already come, for example, from the American nuclear industry (Perrow 1984).

There are two principal reasons for doubting that a centralized, hierarchical system of commands from government is the best way of establishing a symbiotic relationship between social action and the processes of nature. The first concerns the ecological conditions of social action. "Highly structured organizations are at a loss, though, when it comes to dealing with high degrees of uncertainty, variability, and complexity -- circumstances that are, of course, ubiquitous in the ecological realm. ... Signals from natural systems are subtle and ever-changing; the rigidity of a bureaucratic organization is a poor way to cope with them" (Dryzek 1987: 108).

The other reason why hierarchical forms of central administration tend to be ecologically irrational is that they depend heavily on the commitment of the dominant elite to ecological goals. They are particularly vulnerable to the displacement to other goals, such as serving the self-interest of the elite or preserving the bureaucratic status quo. Such displacement has been documented as a common occurrence in all hierarchical organizations (Odum 1983: 276). If mortals need to be coerced and supervised into establishing a symbiotic relationship between social action and the processes of nature, then so do the elite, mortals that they are. Who, in other words, is to control the controllers in the centralized hierarchy and how is this to be done?

The dismal record of states (both capitalist and socialist) concerning the environment strongly suggests that an integrated world-state, if it came into being, would need to be accompanied by stringent checks on its monopoly power. The capacity to use public state power (whether in the name of the people under capitalism or in the name of the proletariat under state socialism) in ecologically destructive ways has to be checked as much as private property. One of the fundamental weaknesses of neo-Malthusian analysis is that it fails to perceive that environmental problems have been generated by capitalism and bureaucracy and that its proposed solutions are based on one or both of these forms of social organization that have caused the problems in the first place.

In order to minimize the problem of deviation from ecological goals, an ecological contract promoting harmony between humans and nature requires accountability. Accurate accounts of the use of resources and the disposal of waste would have to be accessible to the people, not monopolized by either private enterprise or government. An early warning system of environmental problems and of violations of the ecological contract by either private enterprise or government requires a strong, independent press and independent environmental groups willing and capable of monitoring the ecological contract and disseminating the results. It requires a free flow of knowledge and information as well as a mobilization of the population to ensure that private and public organizations act in their interests and in the interest of their natural environment (see Chapter 7).

A Restricted View of Overpopulation

Neo-Malthusians have, much like Malthus himself, emphasized the problem of population growth exceeding carrying capacity. For example, Hardin (1968: 1245) goes so far as to claim that "the pollution problem is a consequence of population." However, eliminating half the population of the world would, if it were the poorer half, hardly put a dent in the rate of carbon dioxide emissions, in the accumulation of radioactive and chemically toxic waste, in the pollution of the oceans, and in the exhaustion of oil, coal, and mineral resources. A relatively small number of maxiconsumers has done more harm to the natural environment than a larger number of miniconsumers. Population growth is indeed a source of ecological problems, especially if the poor are to consume more, but such growth needs to be seen in its social class context rather than used as an ideological lever to shift the blame to the poor. High birth rates are at least as much an effect of poverty as its cause. Neo-Malthusians have tended to ignore the social preconditions of exponential population growth.

Poverty itself is ecologically destructive, not only in terms of its relationship to a high birth rate, but also in terms of the desperate measures destructive of the environment the poor need to take to survive (World Commission on Environment and Development 1987: 28-31). If the ecological contract is to be taken seriously, then it requires the elimination of poverty on a planetary scale. The ecological value of the proposed upper and lower limits to wealth suggested by Daly (1973) depend entirely on what those limits are and whether they are implemented globally or restricted to a few wealthy nations.

Other Weaknesses

Nor have neo-Malthusians grasped other economic and social implications of their ecological insights. If the relationship between humans and their natural environment is best characterized as one of the use of finite resources and limited carrying capacity, and if humanity is approaching those limits, as expressed in the sigmoid curve of neo-Malthusians (Ophuls 1977) with its terminal steady state of zero growth, and more sensationally expressed by the prediction of planetary collapse, then growth of any kind implies a zero-sum struggle for finite and rapidly diminishing resources. The first-come, first-serve system of environmental exploitation that has existed up to now threatens to deplete resources and pollute the environment before latecomers (developing nations, Communist states, previously Communist states, and future generations in capitalist states) are served. Even the accident of year of birth becomes a determining factor of position in the queue for rapidly depleting environmental resources. If latecomers are to be served in an increasingly zero-sum world where overall growth is to be restrained, this must come at the cost of shrinkage in the present developed capitalist world and in consumption by the wealthy. Neo-Malthusian discussion of limits of growth has not drawn attention to the issue of differential shrinkage between countries and social classes.

Moreover, it is not the finitude of resources that is important, as neo-Malthusians claim, rather the level of the finite. The sun, for example, is finite but so immense that it will support life on earth for what amounts to, in human terms, eternity. The level of the finite capacity of the Earth to provide resources and to absorb waste is not self-evident. It too will have to be estimated. "No one yet knows what is the optimum number for the human species. The analytic equipment needed to provide the answer is not yet assembled" (Lovelock 1979: 132). A definitive response to such a vast and fundamental question may be a long time coming. The estimation of the earth's finite capacities will not be unaffected by the interests of the various interest groups involved. State organizations are the primary institutions that have the means to attempt such an estimation, and they will be subjected to corporate pressures to provide estimates in line with the interests of those corporations.

Neo-Malthusians have tended to present the finitude of resources as a fixed limit set by nature. Rather than being determined solely by nature, the finite limits, and not just the estimate of their level, result from the relationship between social action and the processes of nature. Instead of conserving non-renewable resources, minimizing waste, and selecting renewable resources for use and renewing them, humans have used up non-renewable resources (fossil fuels rather than using solar energy), have dumped their waste in the water and the air to accumulate, and have failed to renew renewable resources (reforestation has lagged far behind deforestation, fishing grounds once thought infinite have been depleted by humans, agricultural land has been lost to the desert): "we collectively failed to notice the dramatic decline in what had complacently been called 'renewable resources'" (World Commission on Environment and Development 1987: 317). Failure to renew renewable resources is equivalent to transforming them into spent non-renewable ones. By laying waste to the natural environment in this way, social action is on a curve pushing the carrying capacity of our planet downward instead of upward. Humans are compressing the finite limits of the human-supporting natural environment.

Although Ophuls (1977) is probably correct to depict the growth curve of industrial civilization as sigmoid, it must be remembered that its slope, point of inflection, transition period, and level of terminal steady state are determined not only by the finite resources of the natural environment, but also by social choices concerning growth or restraint, recycling or dumping waste, use of renewable or non-renewable resources, renewal or non-renewal of potentially renewable resources, etc. Just as it is misleading to perceive only humans shaping a plastic natural environment, so too is it misleading to perceive only limits fixed by the natural environment determining its carrying capacity. Rather it is the dialectical relationship between social action and the dynamics of nature that is crucial in this regard.

The Green Transformation

Despite their deficiencies, both neo-Malthusian research and research on sustainable development have made important contributions to undermining (1) the taken-for-granted assumption of the plasticity of the relationship between humans and their natural environment, and (2) the prevailing goal of the social and technical reconstruction and mastery of nature. They have been a significant part of an emerging cultural transformation from a belief that nature is a weak force in the process of being mastered by humans to a recognition that nature is a powerful force in the process of being unleashed by humans. This transformation has been based upon a growing awareness of the difference between the fragility of the human-sustaining natural environment and the power of nature in a more general sense. It has constituted a recognition that reality cannot be reduced to its humanly constructed fraction and that nature can be manipulated, but has not been mastered, and hence must be adapted to. This has been the basis of the emerging cultural transformation in which thought about the relationship between social action and the processes of nature, structured by the ideas of plasticity and mastery, is beginning to be replaced by those of respect and greenness as master concepts (Cotgrove 1982; Dunlap and Van Liere 1984; Olsen et al. 1992). The dominant ideas of the mastery of nature and of the plasticity of the relationship between humans and nature have resulted in social action, the environmental consequences of which have laid waste to the material foundation of those ideas, and provoked the rise of usurpatory movements that have begun to undermine those dominant ideas and practices.

This green transformation is, however, far from being a fait accompli based on an inevitable, predestined or mechanical process. On the contrary, it is just emerging. The conception of the relationship between social action and the processes of nature is still predominantly structured by the notion of plasticity and by faith in the capacity of human reason to master nature and reconstruct it. The green transformation remains largely a potential transformation opposed by powerful classes benefiting from the prevailing assumption of plasticity and prevailing goal of mastering nature. The proposed changes threaten, to a lesser or greater extent according to the specific proposal, to usurp the present distribution of power, and hence encounter stiff resistance.

Just as there has been struggle between proponents of a plastic and a green conception of the relationship between social action and the processes of nature, so too there is struggle between advocates of different emerging green conceptions who attempt to define the cultural and institutional direction the green transformation will take. The intensification of rationalization under greenness is but one of several alternatives in a broader movement toward a green transformation. The other alternatives are more revolutionary, renouncing not just the assumption of a plastic relationship between social action and the processes of nature, but in addition the form and process of rationalization itself as it has occurred in industrialized countries. The accumulation of waste and the degradation of the natural environment have led to an ecological critique of bureaucratic organization, market capitalism and of formal, instrumental rationality itself. The remaining variants of greenness -- the emerging master concept governing the proposed new relationship between social action and the processes of nature -- resulting from these critiques will be examined next.

4

Rerationalization

At the beginning of the Twentieth Century, Weber suggested several possibilities concerning the direction in which the process of rationalization was heading. One particularly bleak possibility was toward a cage of "mechanized petrification."[1]

> No one knows who will live in this cage in the future, or whether at the end of this tremendous development entirely new prophets will arise, or there will be a great rebirth of old ideas and ideals, or, if neither, mechanized petrification, embellished with a sort of convulsive self-importance. For of the last stage of this cultural development, it might well be truly said: 'Specialists without spirit, sensualists without heart; this nullity imagines that it has attained a level of civilization never before achieved'. (Weber 1930: 182)

New prophets are indeed arising and old ideas and ideals are indeed being reborn at the end of the Twentieth Century as an alternative to the threat of the intensification of rationalization -- both plastic and green -- becoming an ecological cage of "mechanized petrification".

Social Ecology

Murray Bookchin, described on the cover of his books (Bookchin 1987) as "the prophet of the green revolution", draws a distinction between environmentalism and social ecology.

> 'Environmentalism' tends increasingly to reflect an instrumentalist sensibility in which nature is viewed merely as a passive habitat ... that must be made more serviceable for human use irrespective of what these

uses may be. ... 'Environmentalism' does not bring into question the underlying notion of the present society that man must dominate nature; rather, it seeks to facilitate that domination by developing techniques for diminishing the hazards caused by domination. (Bookchin 1980: 58-9).[2]

By environmentalism Bookchin is referring to what I have called the intensification of rationalization under greenness, namely, the work of neo-Malthusians and proponents of sustainable development. "Environmentalism advances the goal of using these resources efficiently and prudently, with minimal harm to public health and with due regard to the conservation of raw materials for future generations" (Bookchin 1980: 107).

Dobson (1990: 13) refers to this distinction as the difference between "light green" reform environmentalism and "dark green" radical ecologism. Bookchin argues that reform, at best, slows down but does not stop the degradation of the environment, and at worst, lulls us into a false sense of security. "To the extent that European environmentalists have entered into national parliaments seeking state power as greens, they have generally attained little more than public attention for their self-serving parliamentary deputies and achieved very little to arrest environmental decay" (Bookchin 1991: 77).[3]

Bookchin has developed a critical analysis that opposes the intensification of rationalization under either plasticity or greenness, hence opposes environmentalism, as a solution to environmental problems. His analysis, which he refers to as "social ecology", points to the capitalist market and hierarchical, bureaucratic organization as the social causes of contemporary ecological problems. This social ecology "is avowedly *rational* ... [and] is revolutionary, not merely 'radical'. It critically unmasks the entire evolution of hierarchy in all its forms ... It is rooted in the profound eco-anarchistic analyses of Peter Kropotkin" (Bookchin 1988: 26). Such a social ecology repudiates the intensification of rationality as it has hitherto developed, but not rationality as such. It pursues a new cultural and institutional direction for rationalization. Hence it can be referred to as rerationalization.

Although Bookchin calls his approach "social ecology," anarchist social ecology is a term that would describe its critical focus on hierarchy more precisely and would distinguish it from other possible forms of social ecology: "my emphasis on achieving a new totality between humanity and nature is part of a larger endeavor to transcend all the divisions on which hierarchy has been reared for centuries" (Bookchin 1980: 28). Bookchin (1980: 92; 1991: 131) himself accepts the label "ecoanarchist" with eagerness. It is also important not to confuse this social ecology with human ecology, which has a long tradition in American sociology, but does not share the influence of anarchist theory. Neither should anarchist social ecology be equated with the scientific discipline of ecology, even though the latter is clearly a source of inspiration for anarchist social ecology. And anarchist theory does not refer to anarchy in the popular sense of disorder, rape, and murder.

Anarchist social ecologists argue that the roots of the ecological crisis lie not in technology itself, but rather in the social conditions that result in harmful technology. "What humanity needs is not a wholesale discarding of advanced technologies, but a sifting, indeed a further development of technology along ecological principles that will contribute to a new harmonization of society and the natural world" (Bookchin 1980: 37). Similarly, population growth is seen only as effect, not as cause of the environmental crisis (Bookchin 1980: 37-8). Where birth rates have exceeded death rates, Bookchin argues that this has not so much been because developments in medical care and sanitation have reduced the rate of mortality. Rather the birth rate has risen because the development of the factory and the destruction of the traditional way of life, of village institutions, and of the pre-industrial family farm led people to take refuge from a life of toil not only in alcoholism but also in sexuality and the begetting of children. This same process exists in Latin America, Asia, and Africa today, according to Bookchin.

Bookchin (1980: 15) argues that "man's domination of nature stems from man's domination of man," which he (Bookchin 1980: 304) sees as a reversal of the Marxian formulation. Thus Bookchin (1987: 67) states that "hierarchy exists today as an even more fundamental problem than social classes, that domination exists today as an even more fundamental problem than economic exploitation." The ecological crisis has resulted from centralization, hyperspecialization, large-scale impersonal forms of social organization and technologies that are incomprehensible to most individuals, in short, from hierarchy and social domination. Replacing nuclear energy and fossil fuels with huge, space-age solar collectors and high tech wind mills run by transnational corporations or state bureaucracies would solve nothing. Moreover, man's domination of man has led to a prevailing Western image of nature as mute, blind, cruel, stingy, competitive, and necessitarian (Bookchin 1987: 55, 71).

Bookchin (1980: 271-2) perceives ecology, on the contrary, as

an outlook that interprets all interdependencies (social and psychological as well as natural) non-hierarchically. Ecology denies that nature can be interpreted from a hierarchical viewpoint. ... all life forms have their place in a biosphere that becomes more and more diversified in the course of biological evolution. ... Ironically, ecology more closely realizes Marx's vision of science as dialectics than any other science today, including his own cherished realm of political economy. ... the ecological outlook sees unity in diversity as a holistic dynamic totality that tends to harmoniously integrate its diverse parts, not as an aggregate of neutrally co-existing elements.

Even Marxism is seen, not just as failing to go far enough, but "as the historic essence of counterrevolution, indeed, of counterrevolution that has more effectively used every liberatory vision against liberation" (Bookchin 1980: 197) because it consists only of a critique of social class, not hierarchy itself. The workers movement, according to Bookchin (1980: 13), is dead. The proletariat "shares actively in a system that sees its greatest threat from a diffuse populace of intellectuals, urban dwellers, feminists, gays, environmentalists -- in short, a trans-class 'people' that still expresses the utopian ideals of democratic revolutions long passed" (Bookchin 1980: 196-7). The locus of potential revolutionary change has shifted to these other groups that Bookchin describes in a variety of ways. "The 'new classes' we now deduce are united more by cultural ties than economic ones: ethnics, women, countercultural people, environmentalists, the aged, the *déclassé*, unemployables or unemployed, the ghetto people -- all defy the economistic 'class analyses' that underpinned Marx's scientific socialism. ... Let us call this remarkable *déclassé* phenomenon by its real name: the reemergence of 'the People'" (Bookchin 1987b: 152).

Bookchin (1980: 21-2) proposes "direct action ... [whereby] individuals and individuated communities *could take the social realm directly into their own hands* -- an authentic public guided by ethical considerations ... [and] affinity groups ... [that] provide the intimate, human-scaled, decentralized forms" of organization. "Direct action is merely the free town meeting writ large. ... it is the means whereby individuals take control of society directly, without 'representatives'" (Bookchin 1980: 48). The affinity group is a permanent, intimate community of around a dozen adults. Recallable delegates would coordinate activity between affinity groups: "within the affinity groups structure of an alliance, power actually diminishes rather than increases at each ascending level of coordination" (Bookchin 1980: 49). These affinity groups would be the basis of the municipality, which "forms the bedrock for direct political relationships, face-to-face democracy, and new forms of self-governance by neighborhoods and towns" (Bookchin 1987: 40). He then proposes "the replacement of the nation-state by the municipal confederation" (Bookchin 1987: 160).

Thus the solution he (Bookchin 1980: 26-9; 1987: 36) proposes to solve environmental problems consists of decentralization, face-to-face democracy, participation, and small-scale forms of social organization and of technology, for example, small solar collectors and wind mills built and run by small communities in order that local communities and the individual understand and control their organization and technology.

> No longer would people be separated from the means whereby they satisfy their material needs by a suprahuman technology with its attendant 'experts' and 'managers'; they would acquire a direct grasp of a comprehensible ecotechnology and regain the power over everyday life in all its aspects which they lost ages ago to ruling hierarchies in the political and economic sphere. Indeed, following from the attempt to achieve a variegated energy pattern and an ecotechnology scaled to human dimensions, they would be obliged to decentralize their cities as well as their industrial apparatus into new ecocommunities -- communities that would be based on direct face-to-face relations and mutual aid. ... They [the means by which we acquire the necessities of life] would be restored to the everyday world of the familiar, of the *oikos*, like the traditional tools of the craftsman. (Bookchin 1980: 92-3)

Society would be stateless (Bookchin 1987: 72). In this moral rather than market economy, "services and provisions are available as needed, with no 'accounting' of what is given and taken" (Bookchin 1987: 92). Eliminating the domination of man over man would lead to the elimination of the domination of man over nature and to a new ecological image of nature as "creative, mutualistic, fecund, and marked by complementarity" (Bookchin 1987: 71).

Bookchin seeks to maintain both instrumental and value rationality but base them on ecological and egalitarian ethics. He aims to do away with the present organizational forms of rationality, namely, private corporations in a capitalist market and hierarchical state bureaucracies. In order to rationalize society better than could be done through hierarchical forms of organization, small-scale organizations would be developed and joined in a cooperative federalism. Present society is, in other words, not rational enough because it is based on the irrationalities of the capitalist market system of production and of bureaucratic organization that have resulted in the degradation of the natural environment.

Dryzek's "rational ecology" follows Bookchin in proposing radical decentralization that is non-hierarchical, small-scale, and involves local autonomy. "Any radically decentralized system may also be described as anarchical. Anarchy means, quite literally, the absence of a state, and therefore of state authority. ... A pure anarchy, then, may be defined as a social system in which there is no concentration of force and no political specialization" (Dryzek 1987: 216). Order is maintained ideally by means of a culture of community cooperation, reason, and common socialization, but if necessary also by ostracism, ridicule, and fear of violent conflict.

Bookchin rejects the return to an earlier way of life as a solution to ecological problems and proposes instead post-scarcity anarchism.

> However much a hunting band may be in equipoise with its primitive tool-kit and its limited needs, it remains primitive and limited nevertheless. ... 'Post-scarcity' denotes a free society that can reject false, dehumanizing needs precisely because it can be substantially free of need itself. ... A 'post-scarcity' society, in effect, would have to be a libertarian communist society that possessed enough material resources to limit growth and needs as a matter of choice, not as a matter of need. (Bookchin 1980: 25)

Hence Bookchin (1980: 25) assumes the falseness of the neo-Malthusian "myths of depleted or shrinking resources" as well as the falseness of the Marxian premise that nature represents the "realm of necessity" and that humans must forever "wrestle with nature."

Bookchin (1980: 286) argues that there must be a complete elimination of the domination of some humans by other humans in order to achieve the elimination of the domination of nature by humans: "there can be no compromises with contradictions -- only their total resolution in a new ecological society or the inevitability of hopeless surrender." In his view the total elimination of hierarchy in all its forms is required both as a goal in itself and in order to re-establish the harmony between humans and nature.

> We must eliminate not only bourgeois hierarchy, but hierarchy as such; not only the patriarchal family, but *all* modes of sexual and parental domination; not only the bourgeois class and propertied system, but *all* social classes and property. ... Unless the ecology movement encompasses the problem of domination in all its aspects, it will contribute *nothing* toward eliminating the root causes of the ecological crisis of our time. (Bookchin 1980: 42-3)

Reforms in pollution control and conservation constitute mere environmentalism, and will not do.

Bookchin's revolutionary proposal is based on a faith in the capacity of the human mind to transcend radically present conditions by imagining an ideal world. Rather than limiting humans to what is, anarchist ecology proposes a revolutionary alternative in order to expand the possibilities of choice and hence the scope of what might be. It is in this sense that Bookchin's project is prophetic and counterfactual. Bookchin (1988: 28) argues that natural evolution has conferred on human beings the capacity to form a 'second' or cultural nature out of 'first' or primeval nature. Natural evolution has not only provided humans with the *ability*, but also the *necessity* to be purposive interveners into 'first nature', to consciously *change* 'first nature' by means of a highly institutionalized form of community we call 'society'.

The Limitations of Anarchist Social Ecology

Ecological problems transcend the local area and are typically global in scope. Even Dryzek (1987: 228) admits that the "question of coordination above the local level therefore looms large, and this is the point where decentralizing theory is at its weakest." In an ecological crisis demanding global solutions to global problems, coordination of action is at a premium; yet coordination of the small-scale communities proposed by Bookchin, which would be enormous in number because of their smallness, is precisely the weak point of his anarchist proposal.

The attractiveness of Bookchin's alternative is achieved by remaining intentionally vague (Bookchin 1980: 189-90) concerning the conceptions of community and needs: "the *polis* must be large enough to meet its material needs and achieve self-sufficiency, but small enough to be taken in at one view" (Bookchin 1980: 103). In an age when people perceive a need for airplanes to transport them across oceans, it is difficult to imagine each community large enough to be self-sufficient in the production of transoceanic airplanes, yet small enough for members "to know each other's personal characters" (Bookchin 1980: 103). Reconciling material needs with smallness of scale, with non-expert technology, and with non-hierarchical organization is accomplished with facility in the theorist's imagination, but with difficulty in practice. Bookchin's proposal would most likely necessitate a dramatic reduction in the perception of material needs requiring complex means for their satisfaction: adieu to the transoceanic airplane.

And who is to distinguish true from false needs in the case of disagreement? Bookchin's proposal fails to take into account the full force of value conflict, merely wishing it away in a utopian consensus. "Weber was convinced that the value spheres were inevitably based upon conflicting premises, and that the development of any one value was bound to generate conflict with another. Each value had its own autonomy and the pursuit of this necessarily involved individuals in bitter choices and conflicts within themselves and with others" (Albrow 1990: 239). Is the distinction between true and false needs to be made by an elite of expert ethicists? Hierarchy would then re-enter anarchist ecology through, not the back door, but the front door of anarchist ethics. Behind the anti-hierarchical veil, capitalists and bureaucrats would be replaced by the highpriests of anarchist ethics. Here too the difficult realities of the world collide with the anarchist's imaginary paradise, leaving it just that: imaginary.

Furthermore, small-scale autonomous community life has not led to the absence of hierarchy and domination. Jonestown was an example of a small-scale autonomous community being dominated by a particularly authoritarian leader who, despite his rhetoric of equality, imposed his will on the community to the extreme of ordering the collective suicide of its 913 members. The illustrations of direct democracy cherished by Bookchin did not result in a libertarian society free from domination either. The Puritans in colonial America held their town meetings, and the result was harsh, Puritanical, patriarchal asceticism. Even Bookchin (1980: 104, 140) has to admit that the local direct democracy of Athens went hand in hand with patriarchy, slavery, and class domination. A strong argument could be made that small communities are as apt to smother freedom as to enhance it. Moreover, small-scale production does not necessarily use fewer natural resources and produce less waste. It may, by failing to take advantage of economies of scale and coordinated action, have the opposite effect. Greater local control over some matters of local concern may be an important means to resolving specific ecological problems and increasing certain liberties, but as a panacea it is thoroughly simplistic.

In Puritan colonial America and in ancient Greece "man's domination of man" existed, yet humans were not degrading their natural environment the way they are today. These illustrations, indeed all of pre-industrial history, demonstrate that the degradation of nature by humans results not from "man's domination of man" as such -- that has occurred for millennia -- but from a fundamental transformation of the character of that domination and of the means used to achieve it. The degradation of the natural environment results from a modern, rationalized form of domination of both humans and nature quite distinct from traditional, pre-industrial forms of "man's domination of man." Such degradation has been the perverse, unintended consequence of the systematic manipulation of nature in order to produce goods not produced by nature (automobiles, airplanes, air conditioners, nuclear bombs, etc.) so as to satisfy human material desires. Moreover, since the manipulation of nature yields more efficient means of dominating humans (e.g., so-called smart bombs), it is as correct to state that "man's domination of man" stems from man's attempted domination of nature as it is to state the reverse. Bookchin's theory of anarchist social ecology has captured only one side of the dialectical relationship between the two.

Bookchin's fundamental premise -- that ecology is based on the absence of hierarchy and competition -- is highly questionable. His defense of that premise constitutes a particularly unconvincing element of his work. That a queen bee doesn't know she is queen, that an alpha male baboon's status drops when the baboon troop moves from the plains to the forest, that patriarchal harems of red deer cannot be equated with the expulsion of elephant bulls when they reach puberty and, in short, that "'dominance' and 'submission' mean very different relationships depending upon the species" (Bookchin 1987: 65-6) does not demonstrate the absence of dominance and submission in the ecology of nature. Claiming, as Bookchin (1987: 66) does for animals, that a hierarchical relationship of domination and submission is merely "asymmetrical," has been the typical strategy for justifying hierarchical relationships among humans too.

The ecological emphasis on symbiosis is a welcome corrective to the overemphasis of hierarchy and competition in Darwin's theory of evolution, in Social Darwinism, and in Human Ecology. The premise of anarchist ecology that hierarchy and competition do not exist in the ecology of nature is, however, as incorrect as would be the opposite claim that symbiosis does not exist. Darwin is not completely wrong, nor Bookchin (1987: 56) completely right.

Similarly, Bookchin's argument -- that the image of nature as cruel, stingy, and necessitarian is responsible for the environmental crisis, which can be solved by an alternative image of nature as fecund -- is simplistic, to say the least. Present environmental problems have resulted from the naive assumption that reason can, with impunity, enable humanity to make nature more fecund and escape the limits and necessities of nature. Fertilizers can be developed to grow more food, insecticides and herbicides to eliminate competing species of insects and plants, fossil fuels can be used in motors so that humans are propelled through the air faster and further than the swiftest birds, over the water than the strongest fish, and over land than the fleetest animals. The pollution and other perverse consequences resulting from the use of fertilizers, insecticides, herbicides, and fossil fuels have, however, demonstrated the limits of the human attempt to make nature even more fecund. The premise of the fecundity of nature and the assumed escape from the necessities of nature by means of reason, far from being part of the solution to ecological problems, have been and continue to be part of the problem. An ideology of nature as fecund, and failure to appreciate the necessities of the human-supporting natural environment, can only intensify the consumption ethic. On this important point, anarchist ecologists join hands and minds with think-tanking futurists assuming the plasticity of nature. They are further from an ecologically sound theory than neo-Malthusians emphasizing the limits to growth and than Marx was in postulating that humans must forever wrestle with nature.

Hence there is danger in Bookchin's apparent belief that the anarchist approach, internally coherent though it may be, has *all* the truth. The complexity of ecological matters, and social matters as well, make pragmatism preferable to dogmatism. That the town meetings of colonial America so admired by Bookchin were Puritan meetings may not be intellectual coincidence. He presents a simple but extremely strict basis for non-hierarchical and ecological ethics. His ecological parallel of Puritan religion could appropriately be characterized as dogmatic puritan ecology.

Bookchin (1988: 28) at times flirts with an anarchist version of the mastery-of-nature argument and of faith in the plasticity of the relationship between humans and their natural environment. Thus he has been accused of having a "Faustian ambition to seize control of evolution" (Manes 1990: 160) and dominate nature. Because knowledge of nature is incomplete, new life-forms fostered by the human manipulation of nature -- life forms thought to be valuable -- sometimes prove to be lethal. Peculiarly human capacities -- intellectual, communicative, and social -- are plagued by their own contradictions. They enable humans to manipulate nature, with consequences that can be destructive. Human reason has led to the accumulation of waste, depletion of resources, extinction of benign non-human species, in short to the degradation of the natural environment, more than it has led to the furthering of new and ecologically valuable life-forms. It has led more to biotic uniformity than to biotic diversity. Even with the best of intentions, human knowledge of natural processes is incomplete hence its application involves risks, and intentions are often not the best. Bookchin lacks a conception of the limitations of reason and a conception of nature as an overpowering force that humans sometimes unintentionally unleash with catastrophic consequences. His analysis amounts to a denial of the complexity of nature.

Bookchin's anarchist agenda seeks to use the environmental crisis to destroy hierarchies among humans: "until we undertake the project of liberating human beings from domination and hierarchy -- not only economic exploitation and class rule, as orthodox socialists would have it -- our chances of saving the wild areas of the planet and wildlife are remote at best" (Bookchin 1991: 131). Unfortunately, environmental problems are too urgent to be used in this way. If the solution to environmental problems must await the elimination of human hierarchies, then the accumulation of waste and the degradation of the environment could produce a planetary catastrophe before dehierarchization is achieved because of the resilience of hierarchy and the tendency of hierarchies to be replaced by other hierarchies. Although Bookchin (1980: 54) is not worried about being ineffective, humanity may not have the luxury of fecklessness in solving environmental problems.

The anarchist solution has not been implemented in any country: not under Lenin, nor Mao, nor Castro. Revolutionaries give at best lip service to anti-hierarchical notions to combat their enemies higher up the hierarchy, then consolidate their power by constructing their own bureaucratic hierarchy. The bureaucracy subsequently becomes increasingly oppressive, despite claims that it will eventually whither. One does not have to go back as far as the "Paleolithic shaman, in reindeer skins and horns" (Bookchin 1988: 19) to find the predecessor of Stalin. He has been found in Lenin and Marx (Castoriadis 1977). The ease with which a revolutionary doctrine can be "slowly reworked as it has been so often in history, into a social hierarchy" (Bookchin 1988: 19) should lead to prudence concerning such doctrines, including anarchist theory, and especially idealist doctrines that provide no plausible theory of transition to a non-hierarchical society nor of the maintenance of such a society. Bookchin (1987: 124) himself admits that "socialism and even canonical anarchism ... can be as deceptive in forming a new consciousness as the conventional ideologies of ruling elites." Even anarchists themselves cannot agree on where libertarian ethics end and domineering canons begin.

One problem is that hierarchies have been found useful to combat other hierarchies. The control, discipline, and specialization of hierarchical organization, as well as experience in office, give rise to certain efficiencies, which in turn reinforce hierarchy. Thus organizations, such as trade unions and socialist and communist parties, which have been developed to oppose particular hierarchical organizations, have typically become profoundly hierarchical themselves.

Non-hierarchical, direct participation is onerous, especially if power is to be shared by a large number of people. Furthermore, hierarchy is generated through participation at assemblies, whereby those with rhetorical skills ridicule into submission those with less inclination or capacity to ridicule. As Crozier (1964, 1970) has shown, refusal to participate in a meeting that demands conformity can be a strategy to enhance autonomy. These problems inherent in utopian attempts at mass non-hierarchical participation have rendered them like houses of cards that have been blown over by the slightest puff of hierarchical organizations.

Three-quarters of a century ago Weber analyzed the socialist solution as follows.

What is decisive is that in socialism, too, the individual will under these conditions ask first whether to him, personally, the rations allotted and the work assigned, as compared with other possibilities, appear to conform with his own interests. ... in short, appropriation processes of all kinds and interest struggles would also then be the normal phenomena of life. ... it would be the interests of the individual, possibly organized in terms of the similar interests of many individuals as opposed to those of others, which would underlie all action. The *structure* of interests and the relevant situation would be different, and there would be other *means* of pursuing interests, but this fundamental factor would remain just as relevant as before. It is of course true that economic action which is oriented on purely ideological grounds to the interests of others does exist. But it is even more certain that the mass of men do not act in this way, and it is an induction from experience that they cannot do so and never will. (Weber 1968: 203)

The history of socialism during the three-quarters of a century since Weber drew this conclusion has tended to confirm it. Anarchist idealism suffers from the same naivete as socialist idealism. Self-interest cannot simply be wished away; hierarchy *per se* has shown itself to be particularly resilient. It would be wise to share Weber's wariness regarding the fallacious "belief that the perfection of ideas would produce the perfect society" (Albrow 1990: 279).

Anarchist social ecology has been strongly influenced by the ideas of Rousseau (1950: 94) concerning the need for direct action, hostility toward representation, and an uncompromising stance: "Sovereignty ... does not admit of representation: it is either the same, or other; there is no intermediate possibility." In anarchist social ecology there is no room for compromise: "there can be no compromises with contradictions -- only their total resolution in a new ecological society" (Bookchin 1980: 286). The proposal of anarchist social ecologists for an attempted total solution in which all forms of hierarchy and domination are to be eliminated, instead of weighing the benefits and risks of less sweeping changes, itself presents both benefits and risks. The attractiveness on paper of total solutions is not in question, rather it is their tendency in practice to fail to live up to their rhetorical appeal. If the historical record is to be used as an indication, theories of total solutions have been not only mirages, but also the basis of totalitarian forms of domination.

At a time when hierarchical corporations and state bureaucracies abound, and when biological diversity is being decreased as a result of human action, Bookchin has the same idealized view of the social -- natural relationship as he does of social relationships. "The fact that people can consciously change themselves and society, indeed enhance that natural world in a free ecological society" (Bookchin 1988: 18) does not explain why they will do so. Bookchin advances no explanation suggesting why social relationships and social -- natural relationships as they exist will change to his ideal relationships. Luke's (1988: 90) critique of deep ecology applies rigorously to anarchist ecology as well. "As a utopia, it presents alluring moral visions of what might be; at the same time, it fails to outline practicable means for realizing these ecologically moral visions. ... Like many revolutionary programs, deep ecology lacks a 'theory of transition'."

The rosy blush of Bookchin's utopian fantasy leads him paradoxically to tear technology out of the social context in which it developed, and to universalize and reify technology. "In ever-growing numbers they [people by the millions] sense that society has developed a technology that could completely abolish material scarcity and reduce toil to a near vanishing point" (Bookchin 1980: 251). Present technology has produced an unprecedented material abundance that has removed scarcity as a rationale for domination, thereby making "post-scarcity anarchism" possible (Bookchin 1980: 256; 1986). Technology as it exists has, however, been developed by and for a hierarchical society. That it would have developed or would even function in a non-hierarchical society, or that an alternative technology could be developed in a non-hierarchical society to "reduce toil to a near vanishing point" and to "completely abolish material scarcity" for a growing population whose 'needs' have increased in proportion to technological development, this is nothing but a decontextualized wish. Bookchin's "social ecology" curiously fails to take seriously the social embeddedness of technology and of its development. If Bookchin (1980: 298) can criticize Gorz's proposals as a "Gorzutopia", then it is at least as appropriate to conclude that Bookchin's proposals are nothing more than a Bookutopia, unlikely to exist anywhere other than in Bookchin's books.

Although Bookchin and Weber share a critical focus on hierarchy and domination as central elements in the analysis of the process of formal rationalization, they differ as to the value of proposing utopias. Alport argues that Kant, Marx, Habermas, and we could add Bookchin, proposed utopias that Weber would have regarded as naive.

> Weber stood poles apart from the radical interpreters of the Kantian tradition, from Marx to Habermas. Far from a true social science revealing the potential for liberation, distilling the utopia from the accidentals of life, it began by imposing even greater order on the world than the confused aspiration of individuals could manage, and ended by showing just how chaotic life really was. Weber offered understanding where others offered vain hopes. (Alport 1990: 157)

Weber was skeptical about utopias proposed by intellectuals because he took power and coercion seriously in his analysis. The "social order was not a product of pure reason but more of an arbitrary imagination which could be shaped and directed willfully by those with power. ... Time and again underlying the posited common appeal of collective concepts was a reality of coercion" (Albrow 1990: 165). Assuming that humans will become non-dominating angels adds nothing to our understanding, nor does it enhance the potential for liberation. For example, liberation from ecological problems requires going beyond utopian assumptions to a struggle, based on an understanding of the difficulties involved, to transform values and institutions in an ecological direction.

Ecology and Feminism

After an analysis of Weber's work, Bologh (1987: 155) concludes that "Weber rejected servility and the social relations that produced it, whether these were the patriarchal relations of the family or the patriarchal relations of the welfare state. Thus he supported the women's movement of the time; in fact he was an outspoken feminist." She (Bologh 1987: 151) argues that this was because of "his sensitivity to situations of dependence and powerlessness."

Women have often been at the forefront of efforts to improve the quality of the local environment and to document the effects of toxic wastes. This is "partly because they are the chief health arrangers for their families, and partly because they are more concerned than men with local environmental issues" (Brown 1992: 276). Although many women -- from Rachael Carson to the Love Canal activists to those in the Chipko "tree-hugging" movement in India -- are frequently concerned about their natural environment without holding any explicit overarching social theory, two alternative perspectives in the women's movement have had sufficient influence to merit examination.

At the present time there is a raging debate among feminists concerning the relationship between feminism and the natural environment, with feminists divided into opposing camps. The first perceives the institutional structure of rationalization, but not rationalization *per se*, as the source of environmental problems. This Enlightenment feminism seeks to rerationalize society so that women can participate fully and equally with men as rational citizens and both can eliminate ecological irrationalities. The second, to be examined in the next chapter, sees rationalization itself and associated patriarchal Enlightenment as it developed in the West as the source of environmental problems and aggravator of gender inequality. Hence it leads to suggested solutions of derationalization.

Enlightenment Feminism

On one side of this debate among feminists are those who argue that "despite its many abuses, western culture does have emancipatory legacies ... legacies of democracy, of reason, and of the project of scientifically understanding much of the natural world as part of a radical liberatory movement" (Biehl 1991: 1-2). Biehl (1991: 135) argues that liberatory communities could not now exist had it not been for the heritage of the Enlightenment stressing the importance of the individual. Environmental problems were engendered by the instrumentalization of societies in which science developed, rather than by science itself. Rejecting science would amount to pouring out the baby with the bathwater. Biehl, who defines herself as a feminist in the ecology movement developing anarchist social ecology, states decisively: "I deeply value my power of rationality and seek to expand the full range of women's faculties. I do not want to reject the valuable achievements of Western culture on the claim that they have been produced primarily by men" (Biehl 1991: 7). Among those achievements are its majority-minority democratic tradition and conception of universal freedom that transcends the blood tie of tribal life and opens up the public sphere to women and to individual and collective dissent (Biehl 1991: 136-57). Kinship societies are caring only in the sense of looking after their own kin, hence are exclusive in their very essence. Democratic politics is, on the contrary, expandable to all citizens of a territory who share the human capacity for rationality, the basis of political equality. The ideal of democracy is to lift the barriers to all excluded groups, in particular women, and to resolve conflicts through reasoned argument rather than mutual slaughter.

This current of feminism had its origins in the work of De Beauvoir (1949) and Friedan (1963). The former showed that women could transcend what seemed to be biologically set roles as reproducers and participate fully in society. The latter argued that contraceptive technology could be one of the bases of women's liberation. Feminist social ecologists state that "women's lives are no more determined by biology than are men's. ... The human capabilities for reason, consociation, and ethical behavior are as female as they are male" (Biehl 1991: 127-8). And they are not fixed, rather they evolve. "Human beings, by virtue of their potentiality to choose different social roles, transcend the more rigidly biological sexual differences among nonhuman beings.

The emergence of second nature thus initiates a new dialectic in which men and women can have interchangeable roles in all realms of human life without losing their sexual distinctiveness" (Biehl 1991: 129). Women can go beyond the household and beyond traditional women's roles and develop all their human capacities. This version of feminism is unashamedly humanist and egalitarian (see also Ferry 1992: 221). Since environmental degradation poses a threat to both men and women, it "is the potential of the ecology movement to become a *general* interest that crosses gender lines" (Biehl 1991: 155-6).

Equality for women is seen as the key to sustainable development, with family planning being "one of the most important investments because it represents the freedom from which other freedoms flow" (Rodda 1991: 71). Women have traditionally been placed on a "reproductive treadmill" (Rodda 1991: 69) that endangers their health, often in order to give birth to sons rather than less-valued daughters. Women, in Third World countries as well as developed ones, want to get off that treadmill but are prevented from doing so by the attitude of men, by religious barriers, and by lack of information on alternatives. "According to the World Fertility Survey, of the 38 countries included, 23 showed that more than one-quarter of the women would prefer smaller families, and up to a half of women aged 40-49 did not want their last pregnancy" (Rodda 1991: 69). Thus the study found that "if women who wanted no more children had the choice there would be a 38% reduction in births and a 29% drop in maternal deaths worldwide" (Rodda 1991: 70). It also found that 75% of women in Latin America not planning their families would like to do so and that up to 90% of women in 10 African countries have not heard of modern methods of contraception (Rodda 1991: 70). Rodda (1991: 72) concludes that women want fewer children but children who will be better fed, dressed, cared for and educated, and that solving problems of population, lack of development in the Third World, and environmental degradation requires the empowerment of women so that they hold as much power as men.

Feminists argue that nature and women have been associated, devalued, and dominated. Menstruation, pregnancy, childbirth, and nursing have been interpreted as women's closeness to nature, whereas their absence for men has been seen in Western societies as the basis of freedom from nature enabling men to develop culture. Women have been characterized as nurturing, personal, emotional, and intuitive, men as calculating, impersonal, rational, and abstract.

Biehl argues that these characteristics are "personality traits that patricentric society assigns to women" (Biehl 1991: 3) and "mystifications of oppressive patriarchal stereotypes" (Biehl 1991: 7). They freeze women in particular roles and prevent them from developing their potential, especially their potential for rational action. The male-derived 'woman = nature' image has excluded women from "the important liberatory legacies of Western culture - its democratic tradition, its quest to understand how nonhuman and human nature interact, its high regard for the individual, its fight against superstition, its high ideals of rationality" (Biehl 1991: 27). Enlightenment feminists suggest the immediate elimination of this arbitrary labelling of women and men in terms of alleged personality differences that have been used to oppress women. They suggest the development of an ecological society in which nurturing and caring would be characteristic of both men and women.

Warren (1990) describes the logic of patriarchal domination as follows. (1) Women are identified with nature and men with the realm of the mental. (2) Whatever is identified with nature is inferior to whatever is identified with the mental. (3) Thus women are inferior to men. (4) Whatever is superior is justified in subordinating whatever is inferior (the logic of domination premise). (5) Thus men are justified when they subordinate women (patriarchy). Hence she argues that there is a logic of domination that sustains the twin dominations of women and nature, with the parallel of sexism being naturism. Because feminism attacks the very logic of domination, it has to be reconceived as a movement to end not just sexism but all forms of domination, including the domination of nature.

Enlightenment feminists would decisively attack assumption #1 in the above schema, and the remaining house of logical cards sustaining patriarchy would promptly fall apart. Warren is noncommital about assumption #1, simply describing the split between feminists who deny it and those who assert it. Hence although her work has elements in common with social ecology, namely its critical focus on all forms of domination, it also shares much with ecofeminism to be discussed in the next chapter.

Enlightenment feminists who propose a utopian vision of the elimination of all forms of hierarchy are in effect proposing a feminist version of anarchist social ecology. This is particularly evident in Biehl's (1991) work. Thus the criticisms of social ecology presented earlier apply as well to utopian total solutions of the abolition of all hierarchies advanced by Enlightenment feminists, and will not be repeated. One additional *caveat* none the less: Western democracy shaped by the Enlightenment has proven compatible with many forms of hierarchy and domination, in particular, class hierarchy.

Notes

1. Mommsen (1987: 41) argues that Weber's prediction is best interpreted as a "self-denying prophecy" to promote the struggle against its realization.

2. Bookchin is in error, however, when he postulates a belief by environmentalists in the passivity of nature. Such a belief is more characteristic of non-environmentalists who assume a malleable, masterable natural environment, that is, of proponents of the intensification of rationality under plasticity. Environmentalists seek, on the contrary, to benefit from nature on a sustainable basis by adapting to its active processes and they emphasize the limits of human attempts to dominate nature.

3. The infighting among the opponents of the degradation of the natural environment is well illustrated by Bookchin's statement, as well as by the internal problems of the Green Party in Germany and many other environmental groups. This suggests the importance of probing further the basis of such divisions.

5

Derationalization

One interpretation of the work of Max Weber claims that he is not only questioning what has been taken to be human progress, nor just examining the limitations of the process of Western, formal, instrumental rationalization (Brubaker 1984), although he does all this, but also that he suggests the limits of reason itself to bring about progress (Raynaud 1987: 172-3, 189, 205). "There were limits to reason for him, in the natural world, in human emotion, in intuition and faith. Reason itself could not found reason" (Albrow 1990: 7). As rational as the previously discussed paradigms might appear to their adherents, their conceptions of the relationship between social action and the natural world all involve elements of emotion, intuition, and faith. In Weber's view, "the grounds of human behavior were themselves always ultimately irrational and that could never change, however much rationality advanced. That was axiomatic, built into the basic assumptions of Weber's thought and method. The key question was where the boundaries were located" (Albrow 1990: 187). There are ecological currents of thought that not only dispel the plasticity-of-nature illusion and go beyond the intensification and/or reorientation of rationalization, but also suggest the limits of human reason to bring about a better world.

"It was a fundamental tenet of Weber's view of the world that those who maintained an intimate relation with the organically prescribed cycle of natural life experienced meaningfulness at the level of the unconscious, prior to even conceiving meaning to be a problem at all" (Albrow 1990: 75). Paradoxically, the development of human culture, that is, the sphere of meaning, has fractured this intimate relation and with it the meaningfulness of life: "all 'culture' appears as man's emancipation from the organically prescribed cycle of natural life. For this very reason culture's every step forward seems condemned to lead to an ever more devastating senselessness. The advancement of cultural values, however, seems to become a senseless hustle in the service of worthless, moreover self-contradictory, and mutually antagonistic ends" (Weber 1946: 356-7). The deep structure of Weber's pessimism apparent in this quotation, concerning the state of affairs he observed, has none the less to be balanced against his opposition to determinism, leaving open the possibility of a cultural return to nature at a later stage of development. "Human culture was always a roundabout way of leaving the self-evident nature of life only to return at a later stage. Culture ... could only make sense as a whole in relation to natural existence" (Albrow 1990: 76). It is precisely a culture based on a return to nature that is developing at the present time.

Ecofeminism

Ecofeminists agree with Enlightenment feminists that the context of Western patriarchal society has resulted in the value judgement that traits associated with women, such as caring, nurturing, intuitiveness and closeness to nature, are inferior, whereas those associated with men, including reason itself, are superior.

> In all the senses of rationality, the 'rational' side of the contrasts is the more highly regarded and is part of the ideal human character. Women, to the extent that they are faithful to the divergent ideals of womanhood, emerge as inferior, impoverished or imperfect human beings, lacking or possessing in a reduced form the characteristics of courage, control, rationality and freedom which make humans what they are, and which, according to this view, distinctively mark them off from nature and the animal. The ideals of the rational sphere therefore give us a masculine ideal of the human. (Plumwood 1992: 8)

Ecofeminists (see Plant 1989 and Diamond and Orenstein 1990) perceive, unlike Enlightenment feminists, the traits associated with women as their authentic characteristics. In particular, women inherently have a privileged and closer relationship with nature than men. The oppression of women results not from these characteristics as such, but rather from the devaluation of such characteristics. Masculine rationality has led it to hate the irrationality of emotions. Feminine connectedness with nature and passivity towards it have been devalued, whereas masculine disconnectedness from nature and domination of it have been overvalued, and this masculine model has been misrepresented as a "human" model (Plumwood 1992: 9). The apparent human-centeredness of culture is in fact male-centeredness: scratch its anthropocentric surface and androcentrism is found beneath.[1]

Even Enlightenment feminists are labelled feminists "of uncritical equality" typical of the 1960s and 1970s (Plumwood 1992: 110) and are criticized for attempting to integrate women into institutions and values created by men, rather than recreating new institutions and values in terms of feminine visions. For example, Shiva (1988: 49) criticizes de Beauvoir in the following terms:

> Women's liberation is prescribed as the masculinisation of the female. The emancipation of the 'second sex' lies in its modelling itself on the first; women's freedom consists in freedom from biology, from 'bondage to life's mysterious processes'. ... The liberation that de Beauvoir conceives of is a world in which the masculine is accepted as superior and women are free to assume masculine values. The process of liberation is thus a masculinisation of the world defined *within* the categories created by gender-based ideology.

Integration of women into the masculine model constitutes shallow feminism whereas esteem for feminine characteristics, in particular women's connectedness with nature, constitutes deep feminism. "Only a shallow feminism could rest content with affirming the 'full humanity' of woman without challenging this model" (Plumwood 1992: 9).

Furthermore, "behind the view that there is something insulting or degrading about linking women and nature stands an unstated set of assumptions about the inferior status of the non-human world" (Plumwood 1992: 9). If women disavow their connectedness with nature in order to be accepted into the masculine model of humanity, a model claiming that reason results in man's pre-eminence over animals, this, Plumwood argues, amounts to a put-down of non-human nature comparable to the frequent insistence of upwardly mobile people that they be disassociated from the despised group out of which they have ascended.

The assumed dualism between humans and nature, reason and emotion, etc., is criticized by ecofeminists as an important source of the problems associated with the domination of nature and of women by men. Plumwood (1992: 10) argues that "the entire development of the dominant culture and its relationship to nature has been affected by male and other forms of dominance, expressed in the dualism of nature and reason."

Shiva (1988: 193) concludes that the desire to tame and control nature is the product of the "masculinist mind." The way to solve environmental problems and to end the domination of women is through respect for life in nature and society, which she (Shiva 1988: 223) refers to as the "feminine principle." "Maldevelopment is seen here as a process by which human society marginalises the play of the feminine principle in nature and in society" (Shiva 1988: 48). Ecofeminists propose instead the positive valuation of these feminine traits: closeness to nature is to be valued (particularly from an ecological point of view) whereas remoteness from nature has led men to a domineering culture of arrogance toward nature, nurturing leads to caring (in particular, for nature), etc. Françoise d'Eaubonne (1974) coined the term "ecofeminism" in her call for women to lead an ecological revolution that would consist of new relations between humans and nature as well as new gender relations between women and men. Ecofeminists argue that the issue of 'rights' needs to be enlarged well beyond its restricted Enlightenment usage. "The rights of the land, the rights of nature, and women's rights are all part of human rights" (Merchant 1992; 205).

There are none the less differences among ecofeminists. Some -- paradoxically referring to themselves as "cultural ecofeminists" -- claim that women's and men's characteristics are determined biologically (Spretnak 1989), and that "only a society in which women can limit or control the number and influence of men will be free of aggressiveness and the destruction of nature" (Plumwood 1992: 10). Others (King 1989) argue that those characteristics have been socially constructed, for example, through the long history of the domination of women by men.[2] Whatever the reason, women are seen as having a superior relation to nature than men. Just as militants opposing racism emphasized that 'Black is beautiful,' whether it be biologically based black skin color or Black culture developed in a context of oppression, so too ecofeminists stress the superior value of characteristics associated with women, whether these are biologically based or social constructions created in a context of oppression.

Ecofeminists argue that in ancient and early modern times "nature was contrasted with art (techne) and with artificially created things. It was personified as a female-being, e.g., Dame Nature. ... In both Western and non-Western cultures, nature was traditionally feminine" (Merchant 1980: xix). The Enlightenment replaced this notion of a nurturing earth depicted as female with the cartesian metaphor of nature as a machine to be controlled and improved upon by human rationality. Such mastery was to be accomplished by male-developed science and technology. Ecofeminism reacts against this change. "Often stemming from an anti-science, anti-technology standpoint, cultural ecofeminism celebrates the relationship between women and nature through the revival of ancient rituals centered on goddess worship, the moon, animals, and the female reproductive system" (Merchant 1992: 191).

Although most ecofeminists are not "cultural ecofeminists" and do not go as far as "goddess worship" and "feminist paganism" (Plumwood 1992: 10), the anti-Enlightenment reaction runs deep in ecofeminism. For example Shiva (1988: xiv) begins her influential book as follows.

> The Age of Enlightenment, and the theory of progress to which it gave rise, was centred on the sacredness of two categories: modern scientific knowledge and economic development. ... Throughout the world, a new questioning is growing, rooted in the experience of those for whom the spread of what was called 'enlightenment' has been the spread of darkness, of the extinction of life and life-enhancing processes. A new awareness is growing that is questioning the sanctity of science and development and revealing that these are not universal categories of progress, but the special projects of modern western patriarchy.

She argues that the attempted mastery of nature by man was closely associated with the domination of women by men. "The domination of nature by western industrial culture, and the domination of women by western industrial man is part of the same process of devaluation and destruction that has been characterised in masculinist history as the 'enlightenment'" (Shiva 1988: 219). Plumwood (1992: 13) contends that, notwithstanding diversity within ecofeminism, "a basic assumption common to all ecofeminist positions is the rejection of the assumed inferiority of women and nature and of the superiority of reason, humanity and culture."

The Limitations of Ecofeminism

Ecofeminists like Shiva underscore the worst aspects of the Enlightenment but gloss over the problems of gender relations in traditional societies. In non-Western patriarchal systems they mistake women's niches under a system of male domination for women's freedom. Ecofeminism's critique of democratic institutions resulting from the Enlightenment tends to obscure the fact that alternatives have typically been less democratic and even more dominated by males. Women have typically been most excluded from the public sphere in societies where the Enlightenment's rationality has made the least impact and where traditional values are strongest. The domination of women occurred long before the Enlightenment's attempted domination of nature began. In the West the women's movement developed as the attempted domination of nature intensified, which contradicts the simple hypotheses that the domination of nature and the domination of women are connected through the rationality of the Enlightenment.

Ecofeminism has a very partial view of Enlightenment rationality. The development of science, technology, and a scientific worldview were important aspects of such rationality, but democracy and the ideals of liberty and the equality of all humans were also essential features of this growing emphasis on reason. The ideal of equality of humans led to the demand for equality for women in the public sphere, to changes in the role of women, and to the women's movement, even as the development of science and technology promoted the attempted mastery of nature. Environmental problems are only now beginning to lead people to become conscious of the need to enlarge rationality to take ecological rationality into consideration. Only now has the questioning of the domination of nature joined the questioning of the domination of women in an intensification of the rationality begun during the Enlightenment.

Ecofeminism at times indulges in a dangerous appeal to collective unity based on common answers (Estes 1989) that has so often in the past been the euphemism to dispose of minority dissent. This call for unity contradicts the ecofeminist value of diversity, with the two being reconciled easily in the abstract but with great difficulty in practice. Biehl (1991: 16) speaks of "the passage in recent decades from a struggle for women's liberation to assertions of mere female chauvinism in ecofeminism." Illustrations are not difficult to find: "the standard of inclusiveness does not exclude the voices of men. It is just that those voices must cohere with the voices of women" (Warren 1990: 140).

Although ecofeminists advance generalizations that have a nice ring to them, they are vague about what those assertions would mean in practice: "ecofeminism is quintessentially anti-naturist. Its anti-naturism consists in the rejection of any way of thinking about or acting toward nonhuman nature that reflects a logic, values, or attitude of domination" (Warren 1990: 141). But what is being rejected? Are ecofeminists dominating nonhuman nature when they pick flowers, since flowers are unable to fight back and pick ecofeminists? Rejecting the domination of nonhuman nature is just an empty assertion unless it is given a precise referent. Similarly, valuing diversity in the abstract contributes little to the discussion since fascism, patriarchy, and fundamentalism, for example, add to the diversity of social organization but would hardly be valued by ecofeminists. Who is to determine the "rights of nature" and how are they to be balanced against human projects?

If the ideology of women's closeness to nature has been socially constructed by men to oppress women, rather than biologically based, then it is paradoxical that ecofeminists would want to maintain and even celebrate it. Good intentions of ecofeminists notwithstanding, there is danger that their approach will reinforce gender stereotypes (Prentice 1988). "I believe this unexamined attraction to a care ethic is related to a general veneration of 'feminine values' that informs much ecofeminist thought, and that such veneration promotes, rather than dismantles, a logic of domination" (Cuomo 1992: 352). It is one thing to argue that the problem consists of humans distancing themselves from nature, that is, a cultural flaw of the male-led Enlightenment that sought to master nature. It is quite another to claim that women are intrinsically more caring and closer to nature. Ecological injury has resulted from an environmentally damaging tendency among most men, and perhaps many women.

Women exhibit a variety of traits: some women are more caring, some more calculating. The same is true for men. There may well be underrepresentation or overrepresentation, but branding women as a whole (and men) rather than speaking of under and over-representation only reinforces stereotypes. Ecofeminists such as Plumwood criticize dualism, then reinforce dualism by labelling closeness to nature as a feminine trait and remoteness from nature as masculine.

The biological version of ecofeminism is based on an emphasis on the differences between men and women, and a neglect of all that they share. Men are also embedded in nature. Like women, they proceed through nature's processes of birth, growth, puberty, aging, and eventually death, all of which affect social constructions they participate in. Men need to breath clean air, drink unpolluted water, have an ozone layer to protect their immune system and skin from ultraviolet rays, just as women do. Apparent differences are often the specific effects of the same process of nature on the male and female body: men develop prostrate cancer, women breast cancer. The lives of women are no more determined by nature than the lives of men. Perhaps men have lost sight more than women of their embeddedness in nature's processes and dependence on nature, but that is not the same as claiming they *are* more remote from nature than women.

If an ethic of caring is determined by the biology of sexual difference, how could any man ever develop it? Any woman without it (perhaps Margaret Thatcher would serve as an example) would refute such a theory.

Both the biological and social constructivist interpretations of ecofeminism lead to the conclusion that only women can resolve the environmental crisis because only they have not become disconnected from nature. According to ecofeminism women are to play the historic revolutionary role of leading society to the promised ecosystem, much like the proletariat was to play the historic revolutionary role of leading society to the promised socialist land in Marxist theory. Both have proven to be rather simplistic tales. Furthermore, assuming that women are the special custodians of nature because of their closeness to it can only reinforce the irresponsibility of men toward nature, leaving it as women's work.

Some ecofeminists attempt to evade these problems by claiming that most men have an underdeveloped feminine side (closeness to nature, emotions, intuitiveness, etc.). But why not refer to these traits more precisely by their names, without the misleading label 'feminine'? After all, we do not refer to tallness as masculine and shortness as feminine just because the median is different. The argument that African-Americans have also developed a care ethic as a result of their oppression (Stack 1986, Collins 1989) contradicts the female centeredness of caring. There is nothing intrinsically feminine about caring, nor anything intrinsically masculine about rationality, only empirical associations at particular points in time. Human potentialities along these lines are as male as they are female. All humans have an interest in rationally caring about their shared natural environment. The human stake in the planetary ecosystem is non-gendered, whereas a feminine principle as non-gendered is a contradiction in terms.

"Weaving together the many strands of the ecofeminist movement is the concept of reproduction construed in its broadest sense to include the continued biological and social reproduction of human life and the continuance of life on earth" (Merchant 1992: 209). The paradox for ecofeminists is that this broad conception of reproduction may well be compatible only with reduced human reproduction in the narrower demographic sense of human fertility. The two concepts seem to be inversely related. Humans have continually overshot (Catton 1980) the reproduction of the human population to such an extent that human reproduction is one of the factors threatening the conditions that make possible non-human and even human life. There is tension between production and reproduction in the broad sense, as Merchant (1992: 9) argues, but there is also tension between the broad and narrow senses of reproduction. Reproduction in the sense of human fertility has a very different referent than reproduction in the sense of sustaining the conditions that make possible human life and that of other species. Conflating the two meanings only muddies the conceptual waters.

The identity of women, like the identity of men, has been socially constructed as above and superior to other species, as sharing a culture unattainable by nonhuman species, as controllers of nature partaking of the benefits of such mastery. "Women, especially members of industrial and technological societies, have contributed to the oppression of the nonhuman world, and must admit to this complicity so that they can create alternatives" (Cuomo 1992: 356). Feminism, including ecofeminism, is woman-centered, hence anthropocentric. There is another approach claiming that anthropocentrism, in whatever form, is the source of environmental problems.

Deep Ecology

There are many different currents of thought within the ecological movement, but the one that has articulated its concerns in the starkest fashion and brought an ecological consciousness to its furthest conclusion is that of "deep ecology" or "ecosophy" (Leopold 1949; Naess 1973, 1983, 1986, 1988; Devall 1979, 1988; Sessions 1981, 1985, 1987; Devall and Sessions 1985; Tobias 1985; Sale 1980, 1985, 1988, 1991; Fox 1990). It has provided inspiration for resistance against nuclear weapons, nuclear power, military bases, new dams and logging operations and is closely related to activist groups such as Greenpeace, Earth First, Friends of the Earth, and Green political parties (Foreman 1985, 1987, 1989, 1991a, 1991b; Manes 1990; Capra and Spretnak 1985; Porritt 1985). Even one of its critics admits that "deep ecology has cast itself as one of the primary theoretical forces behind many popular social movements' efforts to defend the quality of everyday life from further rationalization by the state and transnational commerce" (Luke 1988: 65-6).

"Thinking Like a Mountain"

Deep ecology perceives environmental problems to be the result of industrialism's instrumental rationalization since the Enlightenment. Unlike other approaches that seek to intensify or redirect Western rationalization, deep ecologists have set themselves the task of "reversing the trend of five centuries of Western civilization" (Sale 1988: 675). Foreman (1991: 45) contends that the anthropocentric rationalization summarized in Chapter 1 amounts to "stark, raving insanity. ... I don't believe in reforming the system any more. I believe in monkeywrenching it, thwarting it, and helping it to fall on its face by using its own stored energy against itself." He advocates a "return to the Pleistocene" (quoted in Chase 1991: 21). Deep ecology sees itself as being "anti-modern and future primitive" (Blea 1986: 13-4). It consists of "a systematic negation of the 'Enlightenment schema'. ... Deep ecologists want to overthrow this dictatorship of Enlightenment, returning human consciousness back to a re-enchanted world, an animate resubjectified Nature, and more mythic modes of knowing to overcome man's alienation from and domination of Nature" (Luke 1988: 72, see also 83). Bookchin (1991: 60) calls deep ecology's anti-Enlightenment mood "anti-rational."[3] It can be referred to as derationalization, rejecting the values and process of rationalization as it has occurred in the West and seeking a return to an identification with nature characteristic of primal peoples.   Deep ecology constitutes derationalization with respect to Western rationalization, but it is rational in its own value terms: terms entirely different than those of the other approaches to the environment.

Humans are not seen as being separate from nature mastering or even protecting it, rather they are perceived as part of nature.   Humans protecting forests is equivalent to humans protecting themselves through ecological action.   "'The thousands of years of (imagined) separation are over and we begin to recall our true nature.   That is, the change is a spiritual one, thinking like a mountain, sometimes referred to as deep ecology'" (John Seed, quoted in Devall and Sessions 1985: 199).[4]   The connection between deep ecology and ecofeminism is evident in the response of   (Doubiago 1989): "Women have always thought like mountains."

Anthropocentric Rationalization as Human Monopolization of Nature's Habitats

Deep ecologists (Devall and Sessions 1985; Sale 1988) argue that environmental problems have resulted from the intensification of rationalization:

> increasingly intensive management produces a host of unintended consequences which are perceived by the managers and the general public, and especially by the environmental/ecology movement, as real and severe problems.   The usual approach, however, is to seek ever more intensive management, which spawns even more problems.   And each of these problems is seen as separate, with separate experts and interest groups speaking to each other across a chasm of different technical vocabularies, hidden agendas and very narrow ideas of their own self-interest. (Devall and Sessions 1985: 146)

Environmental degradation is, according to deep ecologists, an inherent characteristic of an industrial economy (Luke 1988: 68), capitalist or socialist, because of its emphasis on economic growth and anthropocentric instrumental rationality and because of its disenchantment of the world (Devall and Sessions 1985: 45).   "While primal peoples lived in sustainable communities for tens of thousands of years without impairing the viability of ecosystems, modern technocratic-industrial society threatens every ecosystem on Earth" (Devall and Sessions 1985: 127).   The world of culture has developed an oppressive relationship with the world of nature. "The ultimate value judgment upon which technological society rests -- *progress* conceived as the further development and expansion of the artificial environment necessarily at the expense of the natural world -- must be looked upon from the ecological perspective as unequivocal *regress*" (Devall and Sessions 1985: 48).

The dominant worldview consists of "that ideology which sees Nature as material for human use, consumption and development. Nature is primarily a storehouse of natural resources for humans. The intrinsic value of Nature, or the spirit of a place, has no sanction in this ideology" (Devall and Sessions 1985: 115). The goal has not been to sustain the biosphere, rather to sustain the development of human society and to manipulate the biosphere to that end. The attempt can be made to correct unintended harmful consequences to the natural environment in a subsequent stage of rationalization, but such further rationalization only leads to more unexpected harmful consequences because it collides with the dynamic processes of nature and especially because nature is viewed only as a means not as an end with intrinsic value.

Thus the origin of environmental degradation is to be found in our anthropocentric culture, namely, humans treating the natural environment as a resource to be monopolized and used to their ends, to the exclusion of the needs of other forms of life. The "outcome is to consider other species as just genetic resources whose DNA can be frozen and stored in gene banks for manipulation by scientist-technologists at the command of corporations or government agencies" (Devall and Sessions 1985: 136). Ecology that accepts the idea that other species and resources exist for the use and enhancement of the species that regards itself as superior -- humans -- is shallow ecology, in contrast to deep ecology "which regards the human strictly as an equal participant in the biosphere" (Sale 1988: 670). Predation itself is not the problem, since mutual predation to satisfy basic needs is a biological necessity of life found among all species. The problem is the extent and kind of predation, namely, the monopolization of planetary resources by the human species as well as human interference in the processes of nature.

Deep ecologists therefore attack the basis of biospherical inegalitarianism, that is, the inequalities among different species of life. "I am deeply concerned about what is happening to people all over the world. Yet, unlike much of the left, I'm also very concerned with what's happening to a million other species on the planet who haven't asked for this eco-catastrophe to happen to them" (Foreman 1991: 40). Just as Marxists perceive the bourgeoisie exploiting the proletariat, and feminists perceive men dominating women, and theorists of racism perceive whites oppressing blacks, and dependency theorists perceive the developed world exploiting the Third World, deep ecologists perceive humans dominating and exploiting non-human forms of life. "Man-over-nature ... is the same mind-set as Americans over Vietnamese, or men over women, or managers over workers, or whites over blacks" (Aitken Roshi 1985 : 233). The focus of deep ecologists, resulting in the originality of their contribution, is on the exploitative relationship between humans and the rest of the biosphere. Not only those other forms of life, but also their habitats, have hitherto been treated as resources to be efficiently exploited, with the resulting extinction of species (Ehrlich and Ehrlich 1983; Myers 1979; Ehrenfeld 1976) as habitats are destroyed by humans to serve anthropocentric ends. Humans have monopolized nature's resources, and closed off resources from other species. Rationalization has amounted to the establishment of the empire of humans over non-human forms of life. It has resulted in this most basic imperialism, this most basic hierarchy.

The growth of the human population is one indication of the rise of this empire, and the focus on the "the carrying capacity" of the planet solely in terms of carrying humans -- irrespective of the diminished numbers or disappearance of other species -- is a sign of an anthropocentric worldview. Deep ecologists oppose "the utilitarian principle of the 'greatest good for the greatest number' of humans" (Devall and Sessions 1985: 135) because that principle excludes nonhuman species.

The focus of deep ecologists on the human exploitation of other species has led them into a tense relationship with leftist theories and with the working class.

> I have some big problems with how the left tends to romanticize workers and only see them as victims. ... Too many workers buy into the worldview of their masters that the Earth is a smorgasbord of resources for the taking. Indeed, sometimes it is the hardy swain, the sturdy yeoman from the bumpkin proletariat so celebrated in Wobble lore who holds the most violent and destructive attitudes towards the natural world (and towards those who would defend it). (Foreman 1991: 51)

Anthropocentric culture is characterized by an overriding faith in human rationality and in human civilization, a faith that "humans will continue to dominate Nature because humans are above, superior to or outside the rest of Nature" (Devall and Sessions 1985: 43). But since humans in fact remain part of nature, dependent on non-human forms of life and on Mother Earth -- Gaia -- in an ecologically interdependent system, anthropocentric rationality that exploits and lays waste to its partners sows the seeds of its own destruction. Deep ecologists are deeply skeptical about the possibility of human rationality, based on "the Resource Conservation and Development ideology," improving on or even matching the value of the environment nature has created. "There was a growing suspicion of the ability of technologists to manage natural systems successfully" (Sessions 1981: 392). This is because science and technology have been partial to controlling nature solely in the interests of humans and because they yield only very incomplete knowledge. "Modern technocratic societies have pinned their hopes for increased production and efficiency on technologies based on partial, and in many cases, inadequate theoretical scientific models. There is no reason to believe that scientific theories and models will ever capture the full intricacy of natural ecosystem functioning" (Devall and Sessions 1985: 151). Thus deep ecologists reject the garden vision according to which human reason renders nature more bounteous and beautiful, preferring instead to emphasize a wilderness vision (Nash 1982). They place their faith in Commoner's (1972: 37) third law of ecology -- "nature knows best" -- rather than in the rational planning of manipulations of the natural environment by humans. They argue that "'the biotic mechanism is so complex that its working may never be fully understood,' thus undercutting the possibility of its total successful domination and control by humans, and thereby also stressing the essential mysteriousness of the biotic process" (Devall and Sessions 1985: 86). The emphasis on "the essential mysteriousness of the biotic process" is the polar opposite of the assumed absence of mysterious, incalculable natural forces in the intensification of rationality under the premise of a plastic natural environment discussed in Chapter 1.

Deep ecologists have made an important original contribution. Research on sustainable development and neo-Malthusian research, both promoting the intensification of rationalization under greenness, have demonstrated from an anthropocentric perspective the long-term irrational consequences for humans of accumulating waste and depleting natural resources on this planet. Deep ecology has demonstrated, from a broader biocentric perspective, irrational consequences in terms of the effects on non-human species and in terms of the intrinsic value of nature. It has exposed in striking fashion the extreme anthropocentric bias of human culture and demonstrated the problems inherent in the assumption that humans can improve on nature. It has increased awareness that other species and nature in general are not mere instruments to attain human goals and human pleasure, rather they have intrinsic value of their own.

Living As If Nature Matters

The way out of the environmental crisis is to challenge economic growth and development and cultivate an ecological consciousness: "we may not need something new, but need to reawaken something very old, to reawaken our understanding of Earth wisdom" (Devall and Sessions 1985: ix). Deep ecologists propose "turning back to ancient Indian land ideas, to the Indian understanding that we are not outside of nature, but of it" (Stuart Udall, quoted in Devall and Sessions 1985: 59), and to a sense of equality with other living species rather than mastery over them. Non-human species and the natural environment must be seen more as ends and less as means. This requires a total change in human culture, not just isolated conversions leading to a few, solitary, deep ecological saints (Devall and Sessions 1985: 14) in an otherwise anthropocentric human society. Deep ecologists attempt to usurp the human monopoly of resources and rights. They seek to include other species and ecosystems among organisms having intrinsic value and substantive rights.

The criticism by deep ecologists of anthropocentrism and of the growing human exploitation of the planet and its other species have led them to propose the ultimate dehierarchization and the ultimate equality: interspecies (biocentric, biospheric) equality.

> Biocentric equality is intimately related to the all-inclusive Self-realization in the sense that if we harm the rest of Nature then we are harming ourselves. ... the insight draws us to respect all human and non-human individuals in their own right as parts of the whole without feeling the need to set up hierarchies of species with humans at the top. The practical implications of this intuition or norm suggest that we should live with minimum rather than maximum impact on other species and on the earth in general. (Devall and Sessions 1985: 68)

A low material standard of living is counselled as consistent with a deep ecological view (Devall and Sessions 1985: 205-6). Deep ecologists suggest (1) replacing the consumption/production ethic with a simplicity-of-wants-and-therefore-of-means ethic, (2) replacing present centralized bureaucracies with decentralized, nonhierarchical, democratic, small-scale communities, and (3) replacing government regulation with self-regulation. As in primal societies, "the best management is, in principle, the least management" (Devall and Sessions 1985: 152). A "bioregional vision" is proposed in which food, energy, and resources would be produced, distributed, and recycled locally. "The city would have to be as fully rooted in the earth, as close to the natural processes, as the farm and the village" (Sale 1991: 28).

Deep ecologists seek to re-enchant local communities with environmental rituals. Models of ecological consciousness and practice are to be found through identification with primal peoples, such as American Indians (Sale 1988: 671). Deep ecologists do not reject technology per se, rather they seek easily understandable, unobtrusive (to nature) technology that serves vital needs and fosters individual autonomy in nonhierarchical communities.

Deep ecologists propose the zoning of the world to safeguard wilderness areas. Thus Foreman (quoted in Scarce 1990: 66) would declare fifty North American wilderness areas, covering over 716 million acres, "off-limits to industrial human civilization as preserves for the free-flow of natural processes." Then he would proceed to expropriate additional large tracts of privately owned and developed land, which would be restored to a wild state. Nature would reign in these big wilderness areas, because deep ecologists would permit

> no human habitation (except, in some cases, indigenous peoples with traditional life-styles); no use of mechanized equipment or vehicles; no roads; no logging, mining, water diversion, industrial activity, agriculture, or grazing; no use of artificial chemical substances; no suppression of wildfires; no overflights by aircraft; and no priority given to the safety and convenience of human visitors over the functioning of the eco-system. (Manes 1990: 74)

This "wilderness" vision is quite different from the "garden" vision (Nash 1982: 379-88) discussed previously. In order to protect and expand wilderness areas, deep ecology activists argue in favor of direct action, including the need to "illegally monkeywrench and sabotage wilderness-destroying projects" (Foreman 1991: 70).

Although deep ecologists deny any similarity between their approach and that of neo-Malthusians (Sale 1988: 672), there are certain logical affinities, such as their contention that "human population has long ago moved into a dangerous phase of the 'boom-bust' cycle of population growth and decline" (Devall and Sessions 1985: 47; see also Catton 1980) and that "the longer we wait [for population stabilization and reduction] the more drastic will be the measures needed" (Devall and Sessions 1985: 72). Deep ecologists perceive, however, the population problem as wider in scope than Malthus's focus on food for humans, and wider in scope than even the neo-Malthusion conception of strain on all the planet's resources available to humans. They focus on the resources available not just to the human species, but to all living species, hence on the growing human population depriving other species of their share. Deep ecologists seek a level of human population that would enable other species to prosper. Thus they suggest much deeper cuts in human population than neo-Malthusians. "In deep ecology, we have the goal not only of stabilizing human population but also of reducing it to a sustainable minimum without revolution or dictatorship. I should think we must have no more than 100 million people if we are to have the variety of cultures we had one hundred years ago" (Arne Naess, quoted in Devall and Sessions 1985: 75-6). The presently increasing human population on planet Earth should be reduced to less than one-fiftieth of its present size, that is, to less than the present population of Japan.

Is Deep Ecology Shallow?

Replacing government regulation with self-regulation presupposes that all humans will want what deep ecologists propose, and that none will need to be regulated against their will. Hence it assumes as unproblematic a global cultural conversion to deep ecological thought, which is particularly problematic. Even deep ecologists (Sale 1988: 674) admit they have failed to show how their proposed changes, such as population reduction, are to be done "without revolution or dictatorship," and without bringing greater suffering to the poorer, more vulnerable segments of the human population. The rare concrete suggestions to promote population reduction made by some deep ecologists (described by Sale 1988: 675) have been particularly callous ones, such as letting people in Ethopia starve, or depicting AIDS as a welcome development because it affects only humanity and not other species. In reaction to our anthropocentric culture, some (not all) deep ecologists have gone to the opposite pole of misanthropy.

Thus, although deep ecology consists of both an explanation of what exists and a vision of what should be, it does not go far in suggesting practical means for realizing that vision. It lacks a theory of transition from the present state of affairs to the achievement of its vision. The vision of deep ecology therefore remains largely a utopia or "ecotopia" that risks blinding its proponents to the character of their world at the present time. For example, the local focus of bioregionalism has some merit as a desired goal, but factually wind and water currents have always contradicted it, and human action -- from shipping to the development of ozone-layer depleting CFCs -- have had the effect of breaking down bioregionalism and reinforcing global ecosystemic features.

Furthermore, who is to be the spokesperson for species incapable of speaking for themselves, who is to interpret the requirements of the biosphere, and will the interpretation be partial to the interests of the interpreters? One critic (Luke 1988: 85) has even suggested that "deep ecology provides the essential discursive grid for a few enthusiastic ecosophical mandarins to interpret Nature and impose its deep ecological dictates on the unwilling many." This issue can, however, be raised concerning any critical, utopian theory. For example, communist parties have demonstrated the ease with which Marxism can become partial to the interests of its theoretical and bureaucratic interpreters.

Deep ecology's quite valid critique of rationalization and the Enlightenment has unfortunately led it to obscure their accomplishments. It tends to romanticize, on the other hand, the past and the rituals of aboriginal peoples as the reason for the symbiotic relationship with the natural environment in previous ages. Thus deep ecology tends to degenerate into the promotion of a reactionary, anti-scientific, anti-Enlightenment way of thinking that "is potentially quite dangerous. Anti-rational, anti-humanist, supernatural, parochial, and atavistic moods are a frightening foundation on which to build a movement for a new society" (Bookchin 1991: 60).

The most basic, and the most contentious, proposition of deep ecologists is their "refusal to acknowledge that some lifeforms have greater or lesser intrinsic value than others" (Devall and Sessions 1985: 71). The goal of biocentric egalitarianism cuts against the grain not just of Western civilization but of human history in general. It is doubtful that the equality of all species has ever been accepted by humans. Primal peoples might have had an attachment to species useful to them, and a respect for species dangerous to them, but that does not mean primal peoples believed and acted as if those species were their equal. Some of the techniques they used, such as the age-old method of slash-and-burn agriculture (Merchant 1992; 213), were hardly respectful of the habitats of other species and were sustainable only because high mortality kept down the population using that technique. Interspecies respect and interspecies equality as practised by primal peoples -- to the extent that there was respect and equality -- were based at least in part on the absence of the means to dominate and exploit other species. The development of those means has transformed interspecies respect and relative equality from a matter of unintended necessity to a matter of intentional choice.

The very concept of interspecies equality is particularly ambiguous. Among humans, equality means at the most elementary level that we do not eat one another: cannibalism as the ultimate expression of domination is forbidden. In what sense, then, are the Irishman and the pig he eats, or for that matter, the potato, equal? If a virus has the human body as its sole habitat, would interspecies equality not require that we meet the needs of that species as much as our own?

The struggle against an extreme anthropocentric bias and against the increasing human exploitation of our planet and its other species does not have to be based on the goal of biospheric equality. The cumulative dynamic of evolution resulting in the inequality of species produced by nature does not have to be denied. The difference between (1) humans with their power of reason, (2) animals having a central nervous system experiencing pain, and (3) the amoeba, can be recognized as inequality. All species use their habitat as a source of resources and modify it to serve their needs according to the means they have developed. The basic inequality between humans and non-humans is founded upon the fact that only humans have developed scientific and technological means to transform their habitat. Hence only humans are confronted with the necessity of having to choose how those means will be used. Humans will necessarily perceive and interpret nature from the point of view of humans. Hence there will necessarily be an anthropocentric foundation to the social action of humans. Biospheric disrespect -- an extreme form of anthropocentrism, such as that which exists at the present time -- occurs when humans fail to take into consideration the intrinsic value of nature and its other species. Whereas biospheric equality is unattainable, biospheric respect can be achieved. Biospheric respect is a more logical and promising basis than biospheric equality for struggling against the increasing exploitation of nature and its other species, that is, for mitigating anthropocentrism.

Luke (1988: 82-3) argues that deep ecology implies not an impossible "biocentrism" but rather a "soft anthropocentrism ... [making] more limited anthropocentric claims against the ecosphere ... befitting a minimal pressure on the Earth." The presentation of deep ecologists suggests, however, that it is more likely that a hard anti-anthropocentrism and true biocentrism are intended. If the soft-anthropocentric interpretation were correct, then, far from being a criticism of deep ecology, as Luke claims, this would indicate a sensible thrust of deep ecology: replacing the present savage anthropocentrism -- savage in terms of its effects on other species and on the natural environment -- with a soft anthropocentrism respectful of the intrinsic value of those species and of nature.

The focus on the human domination and exploitation of other species has led deep ecologists to a shallow theory of domination within the human species. The discovery and use by private corporations and state bureaucracies of the knowledge of how to manipulate nature, whether to produce consumer commodities or military weapons, constitutes the discovery of the means to dominate humans through the peaceful struggles of market competition and bureaucratic planning or the violent struggle of military confrontation. The pursuit of such knowledge and technology for these ends has been the dynamic propelling the human exploitation of nature. It is this pursuit of the means of domination and of the class monopolization of nature's resources that has been an important element steering culture in the direction of extreme anthropocentrism and away from a culture of biospheric respect. Deep ecology has not gone far toward explaining the dynamic by which the social classes that make up the human species contribute to and benefit from the exploitation of nature in a particularly unequal way. Its homogeneous, almost classless conception of humanity has not deeply penetrated the socio-economic basis of the ecological crisis. Since this is a problem common to most analyses of environmental issues, the next section of the present book will analyze in detail this issue of the political economy of nature.

Collision or Harmonization?

Derationalization does not necessarily mean irrational. It can also refer to a value rationality that is very different from Enlightenment rationality in its goals, priorities, and potential institutions. That is the case for ecofeminism and deep ecology.

The proponents of the three green options -- the intensification of rationalization under greenness, rerationalization, and derationalization -- struggle not only with the proponents of the intensification of rationality under plasticity, but also with each other. This is because ecological goals are not the only goals: they conflict not only with instrumental rationality but also with other goals for primacy. The instrumental / value rationality conflict is but one part of a larger conflict that includes conflict between value rationalities. Competing rationality claims vie for endorsement.

The intensification of rationalization under greenness attempts to balance off ecological goals against the goal of a high material standard of living for humans. It pursues ecological rationality in terms of sustainable development through a reform of the bureaucratic, market, and legal structure of society. Rerationalization subordinates ecological goals to the anarchist goal of eliminating social hierarchies, and in the case of Enlightenment feminism, particularly the hierarchy of men over women. Derationalization is the only perspective that criticizes the Enlightenment focus on human reason, with ecofeminism promoting emotion, intuition, and the special connection between women and nature, and deep ecology advancing an anti-anthropocentric view arguing for the intrinsic value of nature as a whole. Rationalization under plasticity or under greenness, rerationalization, and derationalization are fundamental lines of cultural conflict concerning the natural environment in the contemporary world.

The intensification of rationalization -- based on the profit and investment cycle of capitalism, associated with an impetus to constant technological innovation (Giddens 1980: 887-8), and on bureaucratic and legal rationalization and on the development of scientific knowledge -- constitutes one systemic and structural dynamic. The dynamic processes of the ecosystem of nature constitute another. Whether these two dynamics will continue to collide or will be brought into harmony depends on the choices of human agents making their world. "Not ideas, but material and ideal interests, directly govern men's conduct. Yet very frequently the 'world images' that have been created by 'ideas' have, like switchmen, determined the tracks along which action has been pushed by the dynamic of interest" (Weber 1958: 280).[5] Human agents choosing the "switchmen" of world images -- mastery of nature, sustainable development, limits to growth, non-hierarchical participation, Enlightenment feminism, ecofeminism, or biocentric equality -- will determine whether rationalization will be intensified in terms of plasticity or greenness, or take the direction of rerationalization, or go along the tracks of derationalization. The collision or harmonization of the two great dynamic forces -- of human rationalization and of the processes of nature -- depends on these creative human choices.

Notes

1. Although they share a great deal, ecofeminism and deep ecology differ on this point, as indicated by the title of Salleh's (1984) ecofeminist critique "Deeper than Deep Ecology: The Ecofeminist Connection."

2. Attributing biological determinism to an author, then criticizing her for it, has become a rhetorical weapon of choice for attacking one's opponents. Thus Shiva (1988: 49) claims, against the interpretation of most readers, that de Beauvoir's work "is based on the acceptance of feminine and masculine as biologically established, and the status of women as the second sex as similarly determined." Birke (1986: x) argues that the opposition between biological determinism and gender as a social construction is itself a social construct, one that has had dire consequences for feminism and the Left leading to the neglect of biological experiences and of the specificity of women's oppression.

3. Deep ecology seeks to probe deeper than Bookchin's anarchist ecology, which it now perceives as just one more, old paradigm, leftist ideology that has failed to develop an authentically ecological philosophy (Devall 1988: 136).

4. The "thinking like a mountain" metaphor was first used by Leopold (1949) and has often been repeated by deep ecologists. See also Flader (1974) and Devall and Sessions (1985: 199). Its ambiguity also makes it a favorite target for critics of deep ecology (see Bookchin 1988).

5. Weber has often been interpreted as belonging to the human agency, motivation, ideas approach rather than to the structural or systemic approach. That is an oversimplification of his work, which is concerned precisely with the relationships between agency and system, motivation and structure, ideal and material interests: "the whole of Weber's work is concerned to explore the relations of action and structure" (Albrow 1990: 213-4).

PART TWO

The Sociology of
Environmental Degradation

6

The Political Economy of Waste

The best starting point for the analysis of exploitation, of the price of commodities, and of the accumulation of capital is that of Marx (1967: especially I, Chapters 7-9; II, Chapter 6; III, Chapter 9, 17; and 1969) and subsequent Marxists (Gough 1972; Mandel 1975; Cuneo 1978 and 1982; Varga 1935; Varley 1938; Corey 1934; Vance 1970; Wolff 1975, 1977, and 1979; Wright 1977). In the Marxian model, raw materials are bought by the capitalist, then transformed by variable capital (workers) using constant capital (machinery) into commodities that are exchanged on the market. If the commodity has an exchange value greater than the sum of the cost of the raw materials, of the machines, and of the wages paid to the workers, then this surplus value consists of the unpaid labor of the workers who added value to the raw materials by transforming them into commodities. Surplus value results, in other words, from the exploitation of the workers: the appropriation of their unpaid labor by the capitalist. This surplus value can be consumed by the capitalist, but it can also be reinvested in more constant capital with a view to accumulating even more surplus value in the future. Thus we have the dynamic of the accumulation of capital. Although the price of commodities is not identical in Marxian theory to their exchange value, nor profit to surplus value, almost all Marxists (Marx 1967: I. 219-20; II. 129, 135; III. 166; Burawoy 1977: 14; Mandel 1975: 174-5; Vance 1970; Cuneo 1978 and 1982; Varga 1935; Corey 1934) use price as the best indicator of exchange value and profit as the most appropriate indicator of surplus value. Hence this model describes the central dynamic of the accumulation of monetary capital as well.

The Missing Element in Political Economy

The foundation of this model is the idea that raw materials are transformed into commodities, and this would seem to be the most acceptable and widely shared aspect of it. But something is missing. Waste in the process of production is ignored. The model is constructed as if raw materials were transformed into commodities with perfect efficiency. But this in fact never occurs. Processes of production always operate at less than 100% efficiency. It is not only saleable commodities that are produced in the process of production. Waste is also produced. In the nuclear-power system, for example, "Uranium ore goes in and electricity, highly radioactive waste, and the waste heat inevitably emitted by any power plant come out" (Commoner 1976: 89).

As early as 1824 Carnot (1824) demonstrated that even an ideal heat engine has an absolute upper limit to its efficiency because, inherent in its operation, it loses to the environment some of its input energy as waste heat. Carnot's work is not obscure research of little importance. On the contrary, it constituted the basis for the establishment of one of the pillars of physics: the Second Law of Thermodynamics. If waste is inherent in the operation of even ideal engines, then it is a fundamental aspect of real engines and of the process of production. Schumpeter (1961) is one of the few people to even allude to this when he argued that industrial production presupposes creative destruction.

It might be argued that this is a trivial matter, since waste has been dumped (into rivers, into the air, etc.) at no cost to the capitalist. But that is precisely the point. It is only now, after the accumulated effects of dumping waste over a long period of time (since the advent of industrial engines and the industrial revolution) as well as the development of particularly dangerous technologies, that people are becoming more and more conscious of the fact that such dumping has indeed a cost that someone, or the environment itself and therefore everyone, must pay. The development of the means of production has stimulated an increasing extraction and use of raw materials, and generated an increasing production and accumulation of waste. This basic observable fact and looming environmental crisis have now been perceived by most natural and social scientists, even those who have quite different theoretical perspectives (Bookchin 1971; Borgstrom 1965, 1969; Brown 1972; Brown 1979; Carson 1962; Commoner 1971, 1976; De Montbrial et al. 1979; Dolman 1977; Egginton 1980; Ehrlich 1968; Ehrlich and Ehrlich 1972; Ehrlich and Pirages 1974; Gorz 1980; Hardin 1968, 1969; Lagadec 1982; Lazlo et al. 1977; Lovelock 1979; Meadows et al. 1972, 1992; Mellows 1988; Mesarovic and Pestel 1974; Ophuls 1977; Peccei 1981; Perrow 1984;

Sprout and Sprout 1971; World Commission on Environment and Development 1987).

Although waste can be measured in different ways, any measurement leads to the conclusion that it and its consequences are significant. "From Second Law [of thermodynamics] efficiencies it appears that about 85 percent of the work available in the energy presently consumed is not applied to the work-requiring tasks of the production system -- it is wasted. The extremely high proportion of waste in the use of energy greatly intensifies demand" (Commoner 1976: 216). The industrial editor of the *New Scientist* stated in 1973 that the "best modern power stations recover only about 30 to 40 per cent of the heat in the fuel as useful work. The rest is lost in the intermediate steps. ... A great deal of waste heat (from condensers, where spent steam is condensed) is discharged, usually in the medium of cooling water, into waterways" (Hamilton 1973: 132-3). He specified the waste emitted in the form of pollutants as follows.

A large coal-fired power station of 350 MW emits each day about 75 tons of sulphur dioxide -- a heavy, colorless, corrosive gas -- 16 tons of nitrogen oxides (another potentially harmful gas) and 5 tons of ash particles. ... The fluid fuels, though they do not give rise to much grit -- if any -- do liberate combustion gases often containing large amounts of sulphur dioxide. Car and lorry engines emit, among other things, unburnt petrol or diesel fuel, sulphur dioxide, carbon monoxide (a deadly poisonous gas), oxides of nitrogen, and traces of compounds added to the fuel to give it anti-knock or other desirable properties. (Hamilton 1973: 139)

The damage as a result of dumping waste has been enormous. For example, Uranium mining companies in the American Southwest dumped their radioactive mill tailings, which then entered the water reservoirs behind large dams.

On June 16, 1979, one of these dams broke at Church Rock, New Mexico, and released 93 million gallons of contaminated liquid and 1,100 tons of hazardous solid waste into an arroyo. The toxic materials then flowed through an Indian Reservation, on to Gallup, New Mexico, and then on into Arizona. ... Measured contamination extended over 100 miles of river bottom beyond Church Rock. But some experts testified during a congressional hearing that unmeasured contamination will extend further and eventually contaminate ground and lake waters. Some of the contamination sank 30 feet into the soil and eventually is expected to reach the food chain. (Perrow 1984: 241)

Radioactive and nuclear waste is accumulating at a rapid rate, yet no safe storage solution has been found. Sulphur and nitrogen emissions into the atmosphere have enormous consequences. "Europe may be experiencing an immense change to irreversible acidification, the remedial costs of which could be beyond economic reach. ... Studies place damage costs due to material and fish losses alone at $3 billion a year, while damage to crops, forests, and health are estimated to exceed $10 billion per year" (World Commission on Environment and Development 1987: 180-1).

The accumulation of waste and the degradation of the natural environment no longer have only local consequences.

> Modern man's despoliation of the environment is global in scope, like his imperialism. It is even extra-terrestrial, as witness the disturbances of the Van Allen Belt a few years ago. Today human parasitism disrupts more than the atmosphere, climate, water resources, soil, flora and fauna of a region: it upsets virtually all the basic cycles of nature and threatens to undermine the stability of the environment on a worldwide scale. (Bookchin 1971: 59-60)

The sigmoid growth curve of industrial civilization suggested by neo-Malthusians (Ophuls 1977) implies that annual production, and with it waste that will be dumped annually (unless a fundamental change occurs), will reach their maximum level even in the terminal steady state of zero growth. Edelstein (1988) and Peck (1989) have shown that there are social and psychological effects of toxic exposure in contaminated communities.

Waste is too important to be ignored in the sociology of the productive process. It can be taken into account by analyzing the social relations that (1) govern the degree to which real engines deviate from ideal engines by failing to minimize the waste produced, (2) govern what happens to the waste (dumping, recycling, reusing, purifying, etc.), and (3) govern responsibility for waste. In order to begin such an analysis I will develop the following hypothesis. The dynamic of capital accumulation has been closely related to waste accumulation with all its environmentally destructive effects. The accumulation of surplus capital has been based upon the accumulation of surplus waste.

Unpaid Waste Cost

Without denying the exploitation of the proletariat, we can add the missing element in the answer to the question: where do surplus value and profit come from? They come in part from the exploitation of the environment and of humans and other species who are dependent on that environment. Surplus value and profit come into being in the process of production, not only through the unpaid labor of workers, but also by not paying the costs of waste reduction, waste purification, and resource renewal, that is, by degrading the natural environment (Commoner 1971, 1976; Perrow 1984: 339-42). This entails the victimization and exploitation of particular environmental classes, to be examined in Chapter 8.

Waste is produced in the process of producing commodities, in the process of using the commodities (e.g., gas), and in the process of disposing of the commodities after use (e.g., aerosol cans). Thus in addition to having an exchange value and a use value, a commodity also has what could be called a waste cost. This refers to the cost of purifying production waste or the commodity itself during or after use so as to render it benign to the environment, of renewing the environmental resources used, of recycling the commodity or its components, and of other means to bring the environment back to the state it was in before the commodity was produced.

Although Marxian theory is a good starting point for the analysis of the accumulation of capital, the exclusive focus of its labor theory of value on the exploitation of the proletariat renders it a very restrictive and misleading end point. Marx ignored waste and its victims in his theory of the production of surplus value, even though *local* air and water pollution resulting from industrial production were horrific in his day. Profit is a function of the capacity of capitalists not only to keep labor costs down, but also selling price up, cost of raw materials down, and cost of waste disposal down. The first involves exploiting the proletariat in the Marxian sense, the second exploiting the consumer (see Murphy 1988: Chapter 5), and the third and fourth exploiting the natural environment as well as humans and other species who depend on it.

Marxian theory is valuable as an important first step toward a more comprehensive approach, but it has frequently lost its value by being used as a bonanza of tautological possibilities (Smith 1991). To prevent the analysis from degenerating into quasi-Thomistic questions concerning the transformation problem (of exchange value into prices, of surplus value into profits), it will have to remain on the level of directly or indirectly observable phenomena such as prices, profits, and wages.

Unpaid waste cost is in principle an observable phenomenon -- observable in its effects -- even though it is in practice difficult to quantify because waste-cost accounting procedures have not been developed. Waste cost refers to the cost of preventing pollution and environmental degradation from occurring, of cleaning up and paying for damage that has occurred, and of renewing resources. If the introduction of new commodities or technologies produces a source of new profits and a degradation of the environment (whether foreseen or not), then the cost of reversing the degradation -- of bringing the environment back to the state it was in before the new commodities or technologies were introduced -- constitutes the waste cost of those commodities or technologies, and is directly related to the profits. Since the effects of unpaid waste cost are only experienced in the future, such cost has to be estimated from environmental degradation that has already occurred.

It is possible that the production of a commodity is so harmful to the environment -- its waste cost is so high -- that the cost of producing it will exceed its selling price. It will be produced only if its waste cost goes unpaid. This is another way of stating that the inclusion of waste cost in the price would stop the production of commodities and development of technologies that are particularly harmful to the environment. Nuclear energy has already been suggested by Perrow (1984) as an example; the high cost of safely disposing of nuclear waste is one reason why Monroe and Woodhouse (1989) speak of the demise of nuclear energy.

The key question in determining the environmental cost of producing commodities is the following. How much would it cost to restore the environment to what it was before production and use began, including the cost of recycling the commodities or their components and renewing resources so as to use such resources at the same rhythm as they are created by nature? This question underscores the significant impact the production and consumption of commodities has on the environment. The question is posed in reverse mode, as a restoration cost, in order to facilitate the development of indicators of the environmental cost of dumping and accumulating waste.

After carrying out the most extensive empirical study to date of accidents involving high-risk technologies, Perrow (1984: 339-42) concludes that they can be best understood as "externalities": the social costs of an activity (pollution, serious accidents, injuries) that are not included in the price of the activity and are typically borne by those who do not even benefit from it.

> Externalities are important in the case of high-risk systems because of, for example, the costs of cleanup from toxic substances, or of rebuilding after a dam failure. The price of electricity from nuclear power plants does not reflect the very large government subsidies, nor the costs of the unsolved problem of long-term waste storage, nor even the unknown costs of dismantling reactors after their forty allotted years, if they run that long. Had all these been properly considered in the 1950s and included in the cost, this book would have not been written because no utility would have

ordered a plant. The externalities of coal-fired power plants without proper scrubbers are enormous, and the externalities drift over several states and the Canadian border. (Perrow 1984: 341)

Economic growth has had environmental costs that became social costs. These have been treated as externalities, and left unpaid.

Perrow uses a term -- "externalities" -- already used by economists (Baumol and Oates 1975; Kapp 1971). Economists tend, however, to treat "externalities" as a fringe phenomenon, rather than having been at the heart of the determination of prices and of the accumulation of capital. The concept of "externalities" embedded in economic theory fails to bring out the fact that past and present accumulation of capital has been closely related to an accumulated environmental debt of unpaid waste cost left to be dealt with in the future. Economic theory tends on the contrary to discount the future (Clark 1974; Page 1977; Dryzek 1983). "Without discounting [the future], the calculations at the heart of economic rationality become indeterminate" (Dryzek 1987: 56). The concept of "unpaid waste cost" embedded in a theory that focusses on present indebtedness to future generations captures better the depth of the economic -- ecological cleavage than the concept of "externalities" embedded in an economic theory that tends to discount the future.

Dials and Moore (1974) have estimated that returning strip-mined land to a vegetated state would add $1 to each $20 of coal. Another way of putting this is that one-twentieth of strip-mined coal income (which would account for a sizeable chunk of the profit of such coal companies) is based on the unpaid cost of reclaiming land degraded by strip mining. The resistance of coal-burning companies to paying the high cost of scrubbers necessary to reduce air pollution and acid rain, and their preference for directly pumping their waste into the atmosphere, have reflected a worry about the profitability of their industry if they had to pay their waste costs. This worry is an eloquent testimony to the fact that their accumulated profits have been based on unpaid environmental costs and damage. Perrow (1984: 171) has studied the "substantial" yet hidden costs of marine freight transport accidents "to the consumer who pays the cost of accidents in higher prices, to the seamen who pay it with their lives, and most of all to the people of the earth who suffer the risk of toxic spills, gigantic explosions, and massive pollution." By not paying the environmental cost of their profit-making activities, capitalists exploit the people who suffer the environmental damage. Capitalists have had the power to profit from using the environment shared by all living species, that is, "the commons" (Hardin 1968), as a waste dump in order to accumulate capital.

The chain of production of commodities, hence accumulation of capital, and the chain of unpaid waste cost, hence accumulated environmental degradation, are linked together.   For example, the automobile, whose gas pollutes the atmosphere during its use and whose unrecycled components after use pollute dumping areas, consists of an assembly of the products of different producers.   The automobile company receives its raw materials from steel, aluminum, rubber, and plastics companies. These in turn receive their raw materials from energy companies, etc. Just as there is an accumulation of profit and capital based on the value added at each stage of the productive process, so too there is an accumulation of unpaid waste cost at each stage in the production of commodities. Like a value-added tax entering invisibly into government coffers, the unpaid cost of the environmental damage resulting from pollution is invisibly added to the profits of capitalists.

The pollution of the early industrial period has been well documented. Since then, companies have become more efficient, not so much at eliminating or purifying their waste, as at dumping it further afield. Instead of solving the problem, this merely globalizes it as the waste accumulates.

> Measures taken by many industrialized countries in the 1970s to control urban and industrial air pollution (high chimney stacks, for example) greatly improved the quality of the air in the cities concerned. However, it quite unintentionally sent increasing amounts of pollution across national boundaries in Europe and North America, contributing to the acidification of distant environments and creating new pollution problems. (World Commission on Environment and Development 1987: 178)

In the dynamic of accumulation there has been not only an internationalization of capital but also an internationalization of waste. Dryzek (1987: 16-20) argues that what has appeared to be solutions to the problems of pollution have merely been displacement of those problems: displacement in space, displacement to another medium (apparently solving water pollution by a technical process that results in greater air pollution), and especially displacement to the future.

With the internationalization of capital and of waste, the unpaid waste cost is being borne more and more by the people of impoverished countries. The World Commission on Environment and Development (1987: 83-4)) estimated that wealthy nations saved $14.2 billion in pollution control costs (not including resource depletion costs) in 1980 by importing commodities from Third World countries that had lax pollution control laws. These environmental "costs continue to be borne entirely domestically [in the Third World], largely in the form of damage costs to human health, property, and ecosystems" (World Commission on Environment and Development 1987: 83). It concluded that "the prices of commodity exports do not fully reflect the environmental costs to the resource base. In a sense, then, poor developing countries are being caused to subsidize the wealthier importers of their products" (World Commission on Environment and Development 1987: 81).

If the producing enterprise had paid its environmental cost, for example, paid to purify its waste instead of dumping, paid to minimize the depletion of resources through recycling its products, reforestation, etc., then its costs would have risen. "If and when the problem of carcinogenicity is taken into account in the design of coal-conversion and shale-oil plants -- so that the plant work force, the people who live nearby, and everyone who uses these products are not exposed to this hazard -- the plants' already high costs are likely to increase appreciably" (Commoner 1976: 76-7). Increased costs would have led to specific consequences. Either the profit of the enterprise would have been reduced, which would have meant a reduction in the capital it could accumulate and reinvest. Or it would have passed on the cost to the consumer, the higher prices having as a result that the consumers with reduced buying power would be unable to purchase as many of its commodities, which would likewise reduce its potential for capital accumulation. Companies would have less capital to use to pursue new technologies and governments would have a reduced tax base and be less able to develop new military technologies. Having to pay the waste cost as production proceeds would result in a pricing system in line with sustainable development and a stable, rather than degrading, natural environment. It would result in pressure to redirect technological development toward technologies partial to, rather than against, the environment. Instead, though, the environmental waste cost has been left unpaid and appropriated privately as profit.

The monopoly position of companies in some industries enables them to pass on, with impunity, costs to the consumer for a long time. For example, Perrow (1984: 101-2) found in the nuclear power industry that "short of catastrophic accidents that would close all plants overnight, accidents by and large only generate costs that can be passed on to ratepayers. It takes something really large, such as TMI [Three Mile Island accident], to even effect stockholders." However, when accidents such as those at Three Mile Island and Chernobyl demonstrate that an industry is particularly dangerous, resulting in pressure on it to have higher safety standards and to dispose of its waste safely, the necessary price increases can destroy the viability of the entire industry. Thus the American and Canadian nuclear industries are in serious difficulty because of safety and waste disposal problems. This shows that the economic viability of those industries has been predicated upon their unpaid waste cost.

Ozone-destroying aerosol cans and radioactive-waste producing nuclear reactors have an immediate use value, but one that diminishes the capacity of the environment to meet human needs in the long run. The exchange value / use value distinction is not particularly helpful in developing a sociology of the environment. A more significant distinction is between high and low waste cost, that is, between environmentally costly (or wasteful) commodities and environmentally cheap (or benign) ones. For example, whereas pesticides, herbicides, and inorganic fertilizers used in the production of foodstuffs have long-term deleterious effects on the natural environment, organically grown food has very little if any waste cost, integrating positively into nature's life cycle. Commodities and their productive processes have varying degrees of environmental waste cost.[1]

Surplus is appropriated not only from the workers in the factory producing a particular commodity but also from other parties through an appropriation, not of their labor, but of their common environment. Public rivers, lakes, oceans, and the atmosphere have been appropriated as a dump for the purpose of accumulating private profit and private capital. Unpaid labor is but one element in the accumulation of capital. Unpaid waste cost resulting in the degradation of the natural environment is another. The accumulation of surplus is therefore more complex than Marx thought. There are, none the less, all-too-rare phrases in Marx's work in which he admits the superiority of an enlarged ecological conception of exploitation and appropriation: "all progress in capitalistic agriculture is a progress in the art, not only of robbing the laborer, but of robbing the soil; all progress in increasing the fertility of the soil for a given time, is a progress towards ruining the lasting sources of that fertility" (Marx 1959: 505-7). Unfortunately this crucial insight has not been incorporated into Marxian theory. On the contrary, it has a contradictory relationship with the cornerstone of Marxian theory -- the labor theory of value -- which is based on "only of robbing the laborer". Unpaid waste cost is, moreover, a missing element not just in Marxism. Other sociological approaches have ignored environmental exploitation as well.

Interest on the Environmental Debt

Capital has been accumulated in the production of commodities, not through a costless use of the environment, but rather by borrowing on the environment. Ignoring the accumulating environmental debt has meant seeing only the benefits side of the ledger, and failing to perceive the cost side. The accumulation of capital has been based on the process of cumulating an environmental debt in terms of the postponed payment of the cost of cleaning up the waste that has been dumped, and of the postponed renewal of the resources that have been depleted. Thus a book on the political economy of environmental abuse has been appropriately entitled *Divesting Nature's Capital* (Leonard 1985). The environmental debt has been left to the public, and especially to future generations, to pay. "They draw too heavily, too quickly, on already overdrawn environmental resource accounts to be affordable far into the future without bankrupting those accounts. They may show profits on the balance sheets of our generation, but our children will inherit the losses. We borrow environmental capital from future generations with no intention or prospect of repaying" (World Commission on Environment and Development 1987: 8).

Waste left to accumulate becomes more difficult and more costly to eliminate than if it is dealt with at the time it is produced. For example, Canada's pulp and paper industry has laid waste to the country's forests, with the result that those companies must go further afield in search of timber and suffer higher transportation costs at a time when reforestation is needed. Sweden, on the other hand, has to a greater degree than Canada reforested as it cut, and thereby avoided the higher transportation costs at a later date. Paying the environmental cost at the time of production, although it adds to the immediate cost of production, results in a lower accumulated environmental debt, and a more sustainable basis of production in the long run. Hence there is something analogous to interest that accumulates on the environmental debt making it advantageous to pay off as quickly as possible in order to prevent it from accumulating.

For example, if emissions that cause acid rain are not purified -- such as by scrubbers -- at the point of production then the environmental waste cost will eventually include not only the scrubbers but also the forests and lakes that have been killed, the fishermen who must be compensated, etc.

> By the late 1960s, when some industrial countries began to mount significant environmental protection programs, they had already incurred heavy economic costs in the form of damage to human health, property, natural resources, and the environment. After 1970, in order to roll back some of this damage, they saw expenditures on environmental pollution measures alone rise from about 0.3 per cent of GNP in 1970 to somewhere between 1.5 per cent and, in some countries, 2.0 per cent around the end of the decade. Assuming low levels of economic growth in the future,

these same countries will probably have to increase expenditures on environmental protection somewhere between 20 to 100 per cent just to maintain current levels of environmental quality. (World Commission on Environment and Development 1987: 335)

I am not arguing that capital can only be accumulated by laying waste to the environment, nor that the capital accumulated is necessarily equal to the accumulated environmental cost, nor that protection of the environment implies lack of development. Merchant (1992: 226) quotes a study that estimated that extraction of products from the Amazonian rain forest would be twice as profitable per hectare as burning or clear-cutting followed by cattle ranching. Rather I am arguing that historically a large part of accumulated capital -- how much varies from company to company, industry to industry, and country to country -- has been based on accumulating an unpaid environmental cost. This environmentally exploitative path to capital accumulation has brought immediate competitive advantages but long-term problems of environmental degradation.[2] An example of the differences from country to country is in the development of DNA, where according to Perrow (1984: 301-3), the United States has had less rigorous standards of protecting the environment than Japan in order to gain a competitive edge.

Development in terms of immediate payment of the environmental waste cost is more expensive in the short run, yet not excessively so. A six per cent increase in the price of electricity dedicated to pollution control would cut in half sulphur and nitrogen emissions into the atmosphere (World Commission on Environment and Development 1987: 181). It would result in less environmental degradation and more sustainable development over a long period. Fire extinguishers are costly to install in buildings, but replacing what has been destroyed by fire is much more costly. Similarly, preventing an environmental debt from accumulating by paying the waste cost at the time of production and use is in the long run the least costly solution to environmental problems.

The Uncoupling of Capital and Waste Cost

Capital has hitherto been seen as positive, and is transferable from one form to another, from monetary capital to machinery, even to cultural and scientific capital (Bourdieu 1966, 1981; Bourdieu and Passeron 1970). Waste is the negative side of productive capital. The creation, circulation, and accumulation of capital has brought in its train the creation, circulation, and accumulation of waste, much like sunshine brings in its train shadows. Unlike sunshine and shadows, however, the circulation of waste has been uncoupled from the circulation of capital.

It is instructive to compare the present society with a pure model of coupling between commodities and the waste entailed in their production. If the circulation of waste were coupled to the circulation of commodities, because the production of waste is coupled to the production of commodities, the owner of the commodities produced would also bear responsibility for the waste produced in the process. Ownership would apply not just to the commodities resulting in the production of waste, but also to the waste itself. And this waste cost would circulate along with the commodities, influencing their price. One of the components of the price of commodities would be the waste cost entailed by their production and use, waste cost being the cost of bringing the environment back to its pre-production state, whether that involve pollution-control measures, recycling, renewing resources, etc.

In the asymmetrical situation of society as it exists, however, the ownership of the commodities produced, and hence of the capital exchanged for them, has been uncoupled from ownership of the waste produced in the creation of those commodities. Ownership of commodities has not been conditional upon ownership of the waste that is produced. The exchange only of commodities, stripped of responsibility for the waste that went into their production and use, enables the unpaid waste cost to accumulate as profit and/or reduces the price of the commodities. This not only results in the accumulation of private capital, but also it stimulates consumption of environmentally harmful commodities and enables them to compete on the market as if they were environmentally harmless. Capital has been accumulated through the radical uncoupling of the two results of production: commodities that are owned privately and exchanged on the market for capital that is then accumulated, and waste that is dumped upon the commons and accumulated publicly. This uncoupling and ensuing dynamic of capital accumulation has resulted in the environmental component of what Galbraith (1984: xxii) has aptly referred to as "the coexistence of private affluence with public squalor."

The Survival of the Filthiest

Commoner (1976: 205) advances the argument that an industry can be very inefficient in terms of capital and energy, yet be very cost effective and hence profitable if its labor productivity (value-added per man-hour) is high. "Thus, although the petrochemical industry is very inefficient in its use of fuel and capital, it is remarkably efficient in its use of human labor, and therefore highly profitable." Such industries can keep their cost per unit of a commodity low only if they produce enormous quantities (for example, of plastic commodities), hence they tend to flood the market, drive out competitors because of lower price or/and higher profitability, and monopolize a market niche.

Despite its insightful contribution, there is a missing link in Commoner's (1976: 205) explanation of the "remarkable tendency for energetically inefficient petrochemical products to push energetically efficient competitors out of the marketplace." If the petrochemical industry is so inefficient (read wasteful) in its use of energy -- using only a small proportion of the energy of energy-laden material thereby lighting up the sky with huge torches over refineries -- then how is it that such wastefulness and inefficiency in the production of acrylic fibers, astroturf, and plastics can result in lower costs than more energy-efficient competitors like wool, natural sod, and leather? Why did the competitors not achieve high labor productivity and produce enormous quantities? Enlarging the scale of production, far from solving the puzzle, only extends it.

The dilemma is solved and the missing link found when it is realized that the costs of energy-inefficient and hence wasteful industries are kept down because their waste costs go unpaid, whereas their competitors have used more expensive labor-intensive techniques that minimize waste and environmental degradation. If the former industries had to pay for the effects caused by (1) the accumulation of their effluents in rivers, oceans and the atmosphere during production and transportation, (2) the accumulation of waste in those nondegradable commodities after use, and (3) the wastefulness inherent in the inappropriate use of an energy-laden substance, then the cost per unit would rise no matter what the scale, their profitability would decrease, and they would have much greater difficulty driving out energy-efficient competitors. Their low unit cost, hence competitiveness (or capacity to carve out a monopolistic niche) and profitability, are to be explained by the fact that their waste cost has gone unpaid and their waste has contributed to environmental degradation. For example, the plastics industry has succeeded in monopolizing niches of the market because, by not paying its waste costs and dumping its waste in the public domain to accumulate, it was able to maintain high profits yet at the same time undercut its less-wasteful competitors.

Although he does not explicitly draw attention to unpaid waste cost, it is implicit in Commoner's argument. "If most plastics were withdrawn from the marketplace and their functions were restored to the products that they have displaced, we would experience appreciable reductions in air and water pollution and in trash accumulation; known and potential risks of cancer and other diseases would be reduced; there would be appreciable savings of fuel" (Commoner 1976: 208).

Companies that avoid paying the environmental cost of their operations have a competitive edge in the market over companies that pay such cost. Instead of paying the environmental waste cost, the former can convert that amount into profit and reinvest it to accumulate still more capital, or/and the former can reduce their prices in order to increase their market share by undercutting competitors. There has been, in other words, a dynamic in the market in favor of the survival of the filthiest and most wasteful. The filthiest has been the fittest for market competition. Capitalists are very much aware of this survival-of-the-filthiest dynamic in the market, although they express it in more euphemistic terms. "If one of us steps out in front and is much more competitive environmentally and less competitive otherwise, you know who the customer goes to? The one that's the cheapest" the President of Husky Oil said in an interview (Southam 1989: 15).

For example, in 1971 a freighter with 25 tons of mercury compounds sank off the coast of Uruguay. Since the cost of recovery was greater than its salvage value, it was not raised. In 1978 it broke up, killing thousands of marine animals and some people and polluting beaches (Lagadec 1982). The logic of the *laissez-faire* market pushes companies, in order to reap profit and maintain or increase their share of the market, to avoid paying the cost of disposal of their waste (and of commodities after use when they too become waste) in an environmentally benign way. Throwaway bottles and disposable cans eliminated the cost of returning and cleaning the used containers, but it promoted the accumulation of litter, the centralization of bottling plants, the elimination of local ones, and the increase in the amount of energy used to deliver beverage (Commoner 1976: 220-1).

These market dynamics contradict the fond enunciations of capitalists that "market forces are the best hope to finding solutions to environmental problems" (Southam 1989: 14. See also Boulding 1973; Daly 1973; Beckerman 1974; Maddox 1972). Companies under market pressures cannot be counted on to pay voluntarily their environmental waste costs, because those that don't will be at a competitive advantage over those that do, at least in the short run. Experience has demonstrated that if the market as a whole is not structured by the legal and political systems so as to ensure that the environmental waste cost of production is paid by the producing company, it will be left unpaid to accumulate.

By playing one state against another, filthy companies put pressure on states not to implement waste-control legislation, taxes on pollution, etc. For example, the London Brick Company successfully resisted attempts in the early nineteen-eighties to diminish its air pollution by threatening to close its operation and move to another location (Blowers 1984). Filthy companies make for filthy states. The internationalization of capital and the internationalization of waste, together with weak collaboration among states, have resulted in the waste cost generated by polluting producers left unpaid.

The 'survival of the fittest' aphorism captures a fundamental truth, not in that survivors are more intelligent or morally superior than others, but in that survivors tend to fit their context to a greater degree than non-survivors. 'Fitness' can only be understood in terms of the context: a capitalist company is not 'fit' under state socialism; the Communist Party is not 'fit' for capitalism.

The context is not, however, static. The accumulated consequences of social relationships and of relationships with nature change the context. For example, production that pollutes the spring making it silent (Carson 1962) transforms the context and hence the requirement of what is fit. At an early low point on the waste accumulation and environmental degradation curve, fittest is closely related to filthiest as illustrated above. As corporations and states proceed higher on that curve -- as they pollute their own nest and lay waste to their own resources as well as to those of everyone else -- a reaction is provoked on the part of victims and potential victims. To the extent that organizational capacity and communicative action are not monopolized, pressure is brought to bear on government and companies to change their wasteful ways, for example, through consumer boycotts, lobbying, and electing politicians to enact environmentally friendly legislation (such as forcing companies with smelters to use scrubbers to control emissions and forcing newspaper companies to use recycled paper). If this pressure is successful, companies that have not adapted to the new context are no longer as fit and have trouble surviving. They are stuck with inappropriate technology that appears primitive. Perversely, though, it is precisely those corporations and states most filthy in the previous context that have accumulated the most capital to make the transition to appropriate technology in order to become most fit in the new context.

The effect of production on the natural environment determines waste cost, whereas social struggle determines the part of waste cost that companies are forced to pay at a particular place and time. Companies pay little of their waste cost if the environmental consciousness of the population and the organization of the environmental movement are weak, just as companies pay low wages if competition for labor and the labor movement are weak. The strength of environmental consciousness and of the organization of the environmental movement are in turn related to location on the curves of waste accumulation and capital accumulation, although there are also other contingent factors. This location affects the predisposition to support or to oppose environmentally sound practices.

Note that a country's positions on these two curves are not necessarily identical. Transnational companies centered in one country, for example Switzerland, can accumulate capital in that country yet export the dirtiest part of their operations to another country, for example Italy, and contribute to the accumulation of waste in the second country. That is precisely what the Swiss drug company Hoffman-Laroche did in Seveso, Italy (Perrow 1984: 295-6). Thus the accumulation of capital has been related to the accumulation of waste, even in those cases where there appears to be little association between the two within particular countries.

The Diminishing Productivity of Capital

There is reason and evidence to believe that human action on the natural environment has resulted in a diminishing productivity of capital. Coal and oil are first skimmed from easily accessible deposits. As these are exhausted, more difficult to find or less accessible deposits are explored, thereby increasing costs per unit of energy produced and requiring greater technological knowledge. With the introduction of antipollution equipment

> there is no corresponding increase in the amount of merchandise produced. ... The falling rate of profit is thus aggravated; the productivity of capital encounters *physical limits*. ... [With] the exhaustion of the most accessible mineral deposits *industry consumes more for its own needs*: it delivers fewer products to the final consumer than it used to. Its efficiency has diminished; its physical costs have increased. (Gorz 1980: 25-6)

Similarly,

> the productivity of nitrogen fertilizer -- the crop produced per pound of nitrogen applied -- has been declining as the rate of application has increased. This reflects a basic biological fact: that there is a limit to the amount of growth that a plant can sustain. ... as insect pests become more resistant to the new pesticides, the amounts of these chemicals used have also risen faster than agricultural output. (Commoner 1976: 169)

As safety problems are discovered in nuclear power plants and as radioactive waste accumulates, the cost of dealing with them also results in increased cost of nuclear energy.

Hence a law of diminishing returns to capital appears to be at work, but it is a contingent law, not an absolute general law. It is true for coal, oil, and nuclear energy, but not true for solar energy.

> In every conventional energy source, the productivity of capital -- the energy produced per dollar of capital invested -- has fallen sharply with increased production. In contrast, the capture of solar energy can be continuously expanded with no decrease in capital productivity because the production of one unit of solar energy in no way makes it more difficult or costly to produce the next. (Commoner 1976: 153)[3]

The diminishing productivity of capital is contingent mainly upon the non-renewability of resources and of waste sinks. "Because the present energy sources are non-renewable and technologically complex, they demand progressively more capital" (Commoner 1976: 216. See also Commoner 1976: 212). The non-renewability of certain resources (coal, oil, Uranium), and hence the need to exploit increasingly inaccessible deposits, results in the diminishing productivity of the capital invested in them, whereas the renewability of other resources (solar energy) holds the law of diminishing returns at bay. A third category of resources can also be distinguished: renewable resources that have not been renewed, for example, forests that have been cut by pulp and paper companies but not reforested, or farms that have used inorganic fertilizer and pesticides in such a way that the land requires increasing quantities to reach the same level of production. This too results in the diminishing productivity of capital.

Thus the diminishing productivity of capital is not a deterministic law, rather it has its present force because non-renewable resources (coal, oil, Uranium) have been selected over renewable ones (solar energy) and because renewable resources have been treated non-renewably. This selection and treatment have resulted in a secular tendency for the productivity of capital to diminish, that is, increasing amounts of capital have been needed over time to produce the same output in the non-renewable energy and resource sectors, in sectors highly dependent on them, and in sectors where renewable resources have been treated non-renewably.

One consequence of the diminishing productivity of capital is the increasing difficulty of latecomer enterprises and states (see Laxter 1988) to develop because the earlycomers have used up or monopolized the easily accessible resources. The first enterprise or state that develops is the best served because at that point the productivity of capital is highest. Those beginning their economic development later are confronted with higher capital requirements per unit output because the easily accessible non-renewable resources have been exhausted. They run a higher risk of not being served at all. There has been a tendency toward the monopolization of non-renewable natural resources within a system of competition formally open to all because only earlycomers have accumulated the capital necessary to accomplish the more difficult task later of accessing less accessible resources.

The observation of the diminishing productivity of capital must not be equated with the Marxian assumption of the diminishing rate of profit. In some areas it can even be the opposite. "It seems clear, then, that the profitability of the different modes of transportation -- which governs the extent to which they are developed -- tends to be associated with a low productivity of energy and capital" (Commoner 1976: 188). Similarly "it has become apparent that the energy industry's own income will not meet its need for capital [to develop continued sources of energy], even though the price of energy and the industry's profits have sharply increased in the last few years" (Commoner 1976: 214). The need for more capital per unit of production promotes high prices and high profits in order to raise the needed capital (see Commoner 1976: 212-4).

The diminishing productivity of capital is also different from the Marxian conception of the diminishing rate of profit in that it is not an absolute relationship but a contingent one. It tends to hold true for non-renewable but not for renewable resources. It is also contingent on particular technical developments. Certain technical innovations, especially micro-electronics, have provoked a rise in both capital productivity and profits, thereby mitigating the diminishing productivity of capital and the diminishing rate of profit.

> Micro-electronics (of which robots are one applied example) has the previously unheard-of characteristic of making it possible to economise not just on human labour, but on *labour and capital at the same time*. They allow you, if you are an employer, to replace nine-tenths of your workforce with machines - while paying less for these ultra-efficient machines than for the ones you used previously. (Gorz 1982: 126-7)

The diminishing productivity of capital in the non-renewable resource sector is also different from the Marxian conception of the diminishing rate of profit in that it would confront socialism as well.

If waste cost is left unpaid to accumulate and environmental degradation to continue, the diminishing productivity of capital will become a long-run secular tendency because of the increasing cost of cleaning up the environmental mess and because of the decreasing accessibility of raw materials. If, on the other hand, waste cost is recoupled to production and paid, then, although there will be a drop in profits and level of consumption (due to higher prices passed on to the consumer), the diminishing productivity of capital over the long term will relent and development will be more sustainable. Recoupling waste cost and production would push development towards a reorientation in favor of renewable resources and toward technology partial to the environment instead of against the environment. And the resolution of environmental problems almost certainly requires a decrease in the rampant consumerism in industrialized capitalist states.

Who Will Pay the Unpaid Waste Cost?

Some authors claim that the very functioning of the capitalist market will prevent waste cost from ever being paid. Bookchin (1980: 293-6) argues that capitalist competition is based on the unrelenting exploitation of nature and on a grow-or-die law that will prevent it from assimilating ecological needs as technical restraints: "capitalist -- and hierarchical [including socialist as it has existed] -- society are utterly incompatible with a viable biosphere." Hence he contends that capitalism is the cancer of society that produces not so much an economic crisis as an ecological crisis destructive of society. "If there are any 'limits' to the growth of capitalism, they are to be found not in any of its so-called internal contradictions, such as economic breakdown or class wars between the workers and bourgeoisie as so many radical economists tell us, but in the destruction of that host we call 'society', the host which this cancer parasitizes and threatens to annihilate" (Bookchin 1987: 30).

Marx argued that humans transform themselves by transforming nature, but he had something more positive in mind than the self-destruction of the human race. Humans are transforming their natural environment such that the environment threatens to become unable to meet their most basic material needs. Nature will continue to exist, but humans may no longer be part of it. Maintaining nature's capacity to meet human needs on a sustained basis will require a costly reorganization and control of production, consumption, and waste to prevent future accumulation of waste and prevent further environmental degradation, as well as a costly program of restoration to correct damage that has already occurred. Who will pay? Where will the capital come from to undertake these tasks?

The 'Polluter Will Profit' Principle

Take a specific example. In February 1990 a massive fire started at a dump site containing fourteen million used tires in Hagersville outside

Toronto, Canada. Toxic fumes were released into the atmosphere polluting the air. Oil leaked into the soil, threatening the contamination of the water table and hence the water supply of surrounding communities. Farmland was threatened. Enormous expense was incurred putting out the fire. Hundreds of families had to abandon their homes. A costly clean-up operation had to be undertaken. The owner of the dump site, a high school dropout who began as a tire sorter in the mid-1960s, did not have sufficient funds if he were sued to pay even a fraction of the cost of all this damage. In 1988 an Environmental Appeal Board overturned a 1987 government order that he sort his mountain of tires into smaller piles because compliance would likely bankrupt him (The Ottawa Citizen February 25, 1990: A4). Journalists assumed that the government, hence the taxpayers -- the people -- would have to foot the bill.

There is, however, another source of capital with a direct connection to the origin of the problem, namely, the accumulated capital of the tire companies. The tire companies have profited from unleashing a commodity on the market that has resulted in the degradation of the environment, yet they are detached from bearing their share of the responsibility. Capital has been accumulated by tire companies at one end, and a used commodity (tires) that has proved lethal to the environment has accumulated as waste at the other end, but the two have been radically uncoupled. The fact that eight million tires are discarded annually in the Canadian province of Ontario alone (The Ottawa Citizen February 25, 1990: A4) gives an indication of the magnitude of the problem.

Liability for the consequences of the commodities unleashed on the market has not been a requirement for profiting from the production and sale of those commodities. The cost of rendering a commodity compatible with the natural environment has been uncoupled from the capital that has been accumulated on the basis of the production of that commodity. It is this uncoupling -- the fact that waste costs of commodities have been left unpaid -- that has enabled capital to be accumulated so quickly by the producing companies.

The accumulation of capital on the basis of accumulated unpaid waste cost constitutes a process of empowerment of the companies involved. It makes society economically dependent on the companies for its supply of capital and gives to them the means to struggle politically against recoupling the accumulated unpaid waste cost they have generated with the capital they have accumulated. Those companies are in a strong position to lobby governments not to implement the 'polluter must pay' principle, but instead measures that polluters can profit from.

As the President of a Canadian oil company put it: "Tax breaks and other incentives could be used to make it profitable for companies to produce environmentally sound products using clean technology" (Southam 1989: 15). The industrial editor of the *New Scientist* has suggested a solution to the problems of pollution based on ignorance, that is, on ignoring the source of the pollution. "The goal of reducing air pollution is a social -- and not an immediately profitable -- one. There has to be some form of inducement to provide the necessary boost" (Hamilton 1973: 175). Polluting companies are now in an excellent position to profit from the need to clean up the environment. "Ian Smyth, president of Canadian Petroleum, estimates that the worldwide cost of addressing the greenhouse effect could reach $45 billion a year by 1995. Reforestation could also produce some handsome profits. By 1995, Smyth estimates it could grow into a $6-billion-a-year industry worldwide" (Southman 1989: 15). Dow Chemicals, Westinghouse, General Electric, etc., constitute "a whole industrial complex for manufacturing and installing pollution control systems, made up essentially of those firms whose activity is at the source of the worst pollution" (Castells 1978: 157).

The 'Polluter Must Pay' Principle

The cost of repairing the accumulated environmental damage resulting from a commodity could alternatively be paid by retrieving that amount from the capital accumulated by the companies that have produced the commodity. Recovering from those companies the capital necessary to clean up the waste and return the environment to the way it was prior to the production of the commodity would amount to paying belatedly the waste costs inherent in its production. It would return rivers, lakes, oceans, the atmosphere, etc., to the state they were in before companies appropriated them as waste dumps in order to accumulate profit and capital. The surplus privately appropriated would be diminished and profits decreased, but so would the accumulation of pollution and the degradation of the public environment. Recuperating the waste cost from the producing companies would provide the means to enable the natural environment to recuperate.

The tire illustration referred to in the previous section is pertinent in regard to the 'polluter must pay' principle. The tire tax introduced in the May 1989 Ontario, Canada budget constitutes a belated and timid initial recognition of the need to recoup the cost of environmental degradation provoked by a commodity to the production and sale of the commodity, a recognition that as yet has no counterpart in most if not all of the other provinces in Canada, in Canadian federal taxation that shares jurisdiction in this area, or for other commodities. Moreover, the issue goes deeper than a tax that absolves the producing company of future responsibility. It involves the integration into the value structure and the legal system of the idea that the company producing a commodity is responsible for its harmful effects on the environment, even if those effects are only felt much later and even if the company has partially paid for the consequences in the form of a tax.

It is essential that responsibility for waste cost include the entire cost of the effects of the waste produced, of environmental degradation, and of resource depletion involved in the production, use, and disposal of a commodity. If it does not reflect the complete cost of returning the environment to its pre-production state, then polluting commodities will merely become environmentally harmful luxury goods, purchased and used by the wealthy, but whose consequences are suffered by the environment and the remainder of the population.

Laws ensuring such environmental responsibility would have the advantage not only of providing a source of capital for restoring the environment, but also of inciting companies to foresee the environmental impact of commodities they introduce on the market, and take measures to avoid a negative impact. "Were externalities [social costs] built into the price of the product, the consumer of electricity, defense, or motorcycles could make a better choice" (Perrow 1984: 341). The price and the sale of environmentally malignant commodities would be affected in proportion to their malignancy towards nature. Such laws would ensure that it does not pay to pollute, that a competitive advantage is not given to the filthiest. A significant benefit of the 'polluter must pay' principle is that it would push society away from dangerous, and environmentally costly, commodities and technologies. Unlike an indiscriminate tax that makes everyone pay to clean up the mess made by polluters, the 'polluter must pay' principle targets the cause of the waste and makes it the immediate economic interest as well as the long-term ecological interest of everyone to avoid waste. Environmental choices would be made more visible, and those choosing them more accountable to the population, if the environmental cost of waste and accidents were included in the price of commodities. In this way the technology of organizations, and its coupling with other systems, would better reflect the environmental impact of human activity.

Furthermore, companies are bought and sold like any commodity. Capitalists purchasing polluting companies would realize that they are buying not only the benefits -- the accumulated capital -- but also the accumulated environmental debt of the polluting company. Let the buyer beware. Recoupling unpaid waste cost to accumulated capital would tend to slow down artificial profiteering through turnovers of cash-rich but environmentally indebted companies.

The foregoing analysis leads directly to the 'polluter must pay' principle and provides a logical support for it. That analysis constitutes a recognition that polluters have been the principal beneficiaries of their pollution. The defense that polluting companies would be wiped out financially, if they had to pay for the environmental damage their waste and their commodities have caused, is merely a defensive formulation of the fact that the accumulated profit and capital of polluting companies have in large part been the result of the unpaid cost of waste disposal resulting in environmental degradation.

It is true that the producing companies have not been the sole beneficiaries of unpaid waste cost in the production of commodities. In particular, the consumer has had the benefit of their use and has paid a lower price than if waste cost had been included in the price. Recoupling the cost of environmentally safe waste disposal and environmental regeneration to the accumulated capital of the producing companies and to the price of commodities would ensure that the burden of cleaning up the environment will fall on the consumer as well as on the producer. Fear not: the producing company would, as much as it could, pass on the waste cost to the consumer through a higher price for commodities.

Innocent Intentions and Consequential Relationships

Ignorance has been as partisan to vested interests as has been knowledge. Companies and states attempt to absolve themselves of responsibility by making the argument that they were ignorant of the harmful effects of their waste on the environment. This might have been true a long time ago for the global consequences of industrial and commodity waste, such as the destruction of the ozone layer, the greenhouse effect, etc. However, even for these exotic phenomena there was an important element of turning a blind eye away from the available evidence. For example, scientists were warning about the impending greenhouse effect as early as 1938 (Hare 1989). The less exotic consequences, for the immediate vicinity, of waste emission from the process of production have been all too evident for a very long time. The harmful effects of industrial pollution have been visible since the beginning of industrialization. Furthermore, even after the dangers of acid rain, radioactive waste, aerosol containers, etc., became well known, companies profiting from the production of the offending wastes continued their production and mounted lobbies to prevent their regulation and control. The claim of ignorance of ecological laws, like the claim of ignorance of the laws of the legal system, is no excuse.

The argument of this chapter is not that capitalists have intentionally damaged the natural environment, rather that their introduction of certain commodities and technologies have had that consequence, whether intended or not. Their accumulation of capital has been directly related to their degradation of the environment, even if they did not intend it to be so. Hence the capital necessary for the environmental clean-up can be drawn from the capital that was accumulated as a result of the wastage of the environment. The question is one of objective consequences and relationships, not of subjective intentions. Capitalists do not have to intend that workers be injured during the process of production for workers to receive compensation for their injuries, because the injuries were consequences of work necessary for capitalists to make profit and accumulate capital. So too capitalists do not have to intend that their production of commodities injure the natural environment to have laws ensuring they pay compensation for the damage their products have inflicted on the environment.

That no one in the past had foreseen many of these environmental problems is beside the point.[4] What is at issue is whether capital has been accumulated on the basis of environmental degradation. The consequences of the production and use of new products are difficult to foresee and will remain so in the future. Laws ensuring that companies bear the consequences, bad as well as good, of introducing new products would maximize foresight.

Notes

1. Humans themselves eventually become waste, but so far at least, are only toxic to the natural environment while alive.

2. Note that I am defining the exploitation of the environment in terms of its degradation. If it is not degraded, as for example in organic farming where waste re-enters the cycles of nature as benign and useful elements, then the environment is not exploited. Thus the natural environment can be used in production without its exploitation, on condition that the waste costs are paid and it is not degraded.

3. Unfortunately, Commoner (1976: 153) draws unwarranted egalitarian conclusions about solar energy. "No giant monopoly can control its supply or dictate its uses." Although the sun is available to all, the technical means of harnessing its energy, such as photovoltaic power plants and cells, are not readily available to everyone and can be monopolized like any other technical means of production.

4. Knowledge of the harmful consequences of dumping waste must not, however, be underestimated. Such consequences were at times foreseen, but the practice of dumping waste on the commons continued none the less.

7

Accounting for Waste
and
Accountability for Waste

The development of accounting has an important place in all theories of capitalism, modernization, and rationalization, but nowhere does it have a more central role than in Weber's analysis of these phenomena. Weber "accorded enormous significance to the development of money as a formal means of exchange and to the rise of double-entry bookkeeping as a means of calculating profit" (Albrow 1990: 180). The elaboration of accounting practices was seen as crucial for the development of capitalism and formal rationality.

> Weber went on to give rational capital accounting pride of place as the main defining characteristic of modern capitalism, and it was calculability which was the bonding element in his list of further features; trading on the market, a technology which could be reduced to calculation, law on which the trader could calculate, free labour so that costs of employment could be calculated, and the development of instruments of exchange which could facilitate commercialisation. (Albrow 1990: 120)

As economic rationalization proceeded, more and more elements became calculable in greater detail: prices of commodities, labor through wages and salaries, raw materials, intermediate materials, machinery, value-added taxes, companies themselves, and even consumer tastes through market surveys.

In the economic sphere, accounting constituted the very definition of formal rationality for Weber.

The term 'formal rationality of economic action' will be used to designate
the extent of quantitative calculation or accounting which is technically
possible and which is actually applied. ... A system of economic activity
will be called 'formally' rational according to the degree in which the
provision for needs, which is essential to every rational economy, is
capable of being expressed in numerical, calculable terms, and is so
expressed. (Weber 1968: 85)

The Exchange of Waste

Waste has been an important, albeit often unrecognized, element of
market exchange. In the past, managers of polluting factories were not
so concerned about dissimulating the waste component of the exchange
between themselves and their workers as they are today. They would
bluntly tell workers who complained about pollution that if their
community wanted the jobs and wages it would just have to put up with
the pollution.[1] Wages have typically been exchanged, not only for labor,
but also for pollution. This wage-waste exchange has been accepted,
however grudgingly, by workers, communities, regions, and entire
countries because of the need for a livelihood. Waste was exchanged in
a particularly dramatic way by the capitalists and managers of Union
Carbide to the people living near the plant at Bhopal, by the socialist
bureaucrats at Chernobyl to the people in the surrounding Ukraine and
Byelorussia, and by the owners of the Exxon Valdez tanker to the people
of Alaska. And it has been demonstrated that these spectacular accidents
are much less important contributors to the production, exchange, and
accumulation of waste than routine forms of pollution (Perrow 1984).
The documentation in the previous chapter of unpaid waste cost also
documents how waste has been a more or less covert element, and yet an
integral element, of exchange. The unwanted waste has been exchanged
by capitalists and bureaucrats to "the commons" (Hardin 1968) in return
for jobs and commodities. Just as the production of waste has been the
dark side of production, so too the exchange of waste has been the
unmentionable side of exchange.

Money has been developed as a formal medium of exchange, enabling
the monetary quantification of the value of the elements exchanged:
commodities, resources, labor, skills, inventions, companies, workplace
injuries, defective merchandise and accidents resulting therefrom, etc.
The fact that the effects of waste have not been incorporated into the
money market, the dominant means of exchange under capitalism, has
stunted the development of accounting procedures for waste. Although
de facto an integral part of exchange on the market, waste and unpaid

waste cost have gone unnoticed in the market. The invisible hand of the market has cloaked unpaid waste cost in its invisibility, transforming it into the phantom of the market.

Just as forcing employers to document and pay for injuries suffered by workers led to improvements in work safety, and forcing automobile companies to pay for injuries suffered in defective automobiles led to recalls, repairs, monitoring of defects and greater quality control, so too accounting for waste emissions and financial responsibility for their effects would lead to less waste. Only recently has a new dimension of exchange emerged as victims of pollution forcibly extract through the political system or legal system some compensation from the producers of pollution and waste.

A more insidious type of waste trade has also begun, in which capitalists or states avoid expensive waste reduction or treatment by buying dumping privileges for their most toxic waste, for example PCBs, in Third World countries with lax environmental laws or feeble enforcement. This constitutes merely a dumping fee that fails to monetize the effects of such dumping. It is the polar opposite to incorporating the effects of waste production into the money market. The latter would place waste on a par with defective products, in which the producer of waste that proves harmful would be required to recall it and pay damages for its noxious effects.

The Undeveloped State of Accounting for Waste

Environmental degradation stemming from industrial development has resulted from decisions to develop particular technologies and commodities as the means to comforts, conveniences, and power. Unlike natural disasters of the past, present environmental problems have been caused by the social and technical constructions of humans. Humans are responsible for them, some humans more than others, and can be held accountable. "For with the origin of industrial risks in decision-making the problem of social accountability and responsibility irrevocably arises, even in those areas where the prevailing rules of science and law permit accountability only in exceptional cases. People, firms, state agencies and politicians are responsible for industrial risks" (Beck 1992b: 98).

There is a great deal of evidence to show that, whereas accounting procedures have been highly developed for flows of capital, raw materials, commodities, and labor, they have not been developed for the other major aspect of production and exchange: waste. Schnaiberg (1980: 321; see also 419 and Schnaiberg 1977) concludes for the United States that there has been poor ecological accounting even in many environmental impact statements. "Underdevelopment of impact sciences and impact research findings provides far less documentable ecological impacts than are likely to exist" (Schnaiberg 1980: 322). In Canada in 1989 no one knew where 50% of the PCBs had gone. In Ontario, Canada, it was only in 1989 that the government began to require cement companies to monitor their effluent to find out what they were dumping into rivers. From Germany Beck (1992a: 45) concludes: "No records are kept on entire families of chemicals out of consideration for the economic consequences [job loss and profit decline]; they do not exist legally and can be freely circulated for that very reason." A system of environmental accounting, as efficient as the existing system of accounting for capital and commodities, is lacking and badly needed. "It is particularly important that consumers, especially large commercial and industrial agencies, obtain professional audits of their energy use. This kind of energy 'book-keeping' will readily identify those places in their consumption patterns where significant savings can be made" (World Commission on Environment and Development 1987: 197-8). Accurate procedures for the calculation of money spent to repair environmental degradation, and more so of money that needs to be spent, have yet to be developed: "figures are not available on the level of expenditures made to rehabilitate lands and natural habitats, re-establish soil fertility, reforest areas, and undertake other measures to restore the resource base" (World Commission on Environment and Development 1987: 335). Accounting procedures, calculation, and quantitative measurement of waste, resource depletion, and environmental degradation resulting from human production and consumption have been left wanting.

At the international level, the World Commission on Environment and Development (1987: 325) found that the data base necessary to account for waste and resource depletion is weak. It concluded that "the data collection, assessment, and state of the environment reporting functions (Earthwatch) of UNEP need to be significantly strengthened as a major priority. ... The UNEP voluntary funding base of $30 million annually is too limited and vulnerable for an international fund dedicated to serving and protecting the common interests, security, and future of humanity" (World Commission on Environment and Development 1987: 321-2).

The deficiencies of environmental accounting and the unwillingness to take seriously the meager accounting that does exist can lead to disastrous results. In June 1979 a dam burst in New Mexico, releasing 93 million gallons of radioactively contaminated liquid and 1,100 tons of hazardous solid waste into an Indian reservation and then into Arizona.

The company's own geologists had warned of bedrock problems and the need for continuous inspection; the company agreed to put in sensors but didn't; the company's design called for buttressing the dam structure, but they did not do it; some cracking in 1977 occurred and should have given warning, but the State Engineering Office was not even informed, contrary to an agreement; and the dam did not incorporate all the necessary protections that the company's engineering consultant had advised. ... A Nuclear Regulatory Commission official testified that cracks appeared in January of 1979, a few months before the failure, giving 'significant' warning. (Perrow 1984: 242)

The Monopolization of Information in the Global Village

The scientific and technological discoveries that enabled the invention and development of the telephone, radio, television, fax, and especially the computer, have led to the present age being characterized as the information age (McLuhan 1965, Toffler 1984). There is a circulation of information and ideas on a much broader scale than ever before. Hamilton (1973: 150) states that the "amount of accumulated knowledge in the world is doubling every fifteen years or less, as one generation hands on its recorded findings to the next." He (Hamilton 1973: 316) argues that for "the first time in history, everyone is reasonably well informed about the life, work and conditions of his fellows on all sides. ... Mass communication allows everyone to be organized together."

This technological potential for communication has, however, been actualized in particular directions. The content of the information -- and misinformation -- that are being circulated, as well as the information not in circulation, are geared to particular interests. For example, Dryzek (1987: 5) showed that the data required to demonstrate the causes and consequences of acid rain, as well as the long-term trend data, do not exist and argued that "as long as responsibility for pollution damage cannot be established, traditional legal remedies are unavailable." This as well as the previous illustrations raise suspicions that the undeveloped character of environmental accounting as compared to capital accounting is not just a matter of technical difficulty or lack of awareness. They suggest that it may in large part be a matter of malign neglect.

Manufacturers themselves have a good idea of the danger of their operations. Their technology and capital have enabled them to monopolize knowledge of the environmental risks of their operations. They have effectively excluded others (the environmental movement, the public, and even the state in certain instances) from gaining access to that knowledge. Transnational companies, often in complicity with state organizations, have overestimated the safety of their factories in order to convince the public to allow them to pursue their search for profit.

Hooker Chemical Company knew of the danger of the toxic waste they buried at Love Canal. The Swiss drug firm, Hoffman-Laroche, in LaRoche was well aware of the danger of dioxin contamination in their plant in Seveso, Italy, and indeed plant officials were instructed to readily reimburse their neighbors for dead farm animals that continued to appear. Knowing that dioxin was a by-product of the pesticide the plant produced, they would not allow production to take place in clean little Switzerland, where their headquarters were, but instead had it produced in dirty northern Italy. When the chemical reactor exploded one weekend when no one was attending it, the safety device protected the plant by allowing the poison to blow up into the air through a stack, from where it drifted over the neighboring community. Plant officials avoided a panic by simply not informing the community. (Perrow 1984: 295-6).

Thus Perrow (1984: 296) concludes that such accidents "are presumably not only anticipated, but carefully calculated risks as well."

A Consolidated Edison nuclear plant thirty-five miles up wind of New York City developed a dangerous leak and was shut down. "Contrary to an agreement with federal and state officials to notify them immediately of any trouble at the problem-plagued plant, nothing was done until 3:20 that afternoon. ... [Three days later] Con Ed waited another day -- five all told -- before it informed local officials and the public of the leak" (Perrow 1984: 46). When the public has been informed, it has typically been at the last possible moment.

Commoner (1976: 35) reported on discrepancies concerning the availability of petroleum products in the United States during the 1973 oil crisis. "When Congressional committees tried to investigate such discrepancies, they discovered that nearly all the original information about the production and availability of petroleum was in the hands of the oil companies and their organizations. Few hard facts about the oil situation reached the arena of public debate in a form that could be understood by the participants." Thus he concluded as follows. "Even now the government -- and the people of the United States -- must depend on the industry for most of the information about fossil-fuel resources, much of which is Federal property" (Commoner 1976: 269-70). The dependency of less wealthy and less powerful states on information from the oil industry can be easily imagined.

Perrow (1984) documented that the petrochemical industry was very reluctant to review accidents in a public, accessible form. "My efforts with companies and trade and technical associations were generally met with the statement that, 'We do not want to wash our dirty linen in public'" (Perrow 1984: 103). Other industries -- nuclear power plants, airline, railroad, and marine transportation, mining companies, companies constructing dams, and space agencies -- only conduct a public review when required by a government review agency. Referring to a survey of vapor cloud accidents in petrochemical plants, Perrow (1984: 113) concluded as follows. "The author of the article is associated with the insurance industry, and thus has access to all the published data on such events. Yet 42 percent of the accidents noted, including some large and catastrophic ones, are referenced only as 'private communication'. ... it is unfortunate that full technical discussions appear to be available only on a private basis."

Even government-funded reports are extremely difficult to obtain.

> In response to my first inquiries I was told that there was no such thing as a Subpanel IX report. ... His [Senator James Abourezk of South Dakota] efforts also failed. ... When the White House, at Senator Abourezk's request, asked the AEC for the Subpanel IX report, all that supremely powerful institution (Mr. Nixon was President at the time) received and sent on to Senator Abourezk (and eventually to me) was only another copy of the 'Futures' report to add to my own. Finally, like a genie materialized by the appropriate incantations, the report's existence was confirmed. (Commoner 1976: 142-3)

If scientific researchers and senators face these exclusionary barriers to gaining access to environmental information, then the monopolization of such information excludes all the more the general public from developing an informed opinion on environmental matters.

In 1972 the Teton Dam was constructed in eastern Idaho. When construction was well underway, geologists from the U.S. Geological Survey wrote an internal memorandum stating that they had found evidence of five earthquakes in the region in the last five years, that dam reservoirs cause earthquakes, and concluded that a failure of the dam would cause catastrophic flooding. Because so much had already been spent on constructing the dam, the geologists were pressured to redraft their memorandum and tone it down, and their warning was subsequently ignored. In 1976 the Teton Dam burst, killing eleven people, leaving thousands homeless, destroying towns and 100,000 acres of farmland, killing 16,000 head of livestock, and resulting in property damage of over $1 billion (Perrow 1984: 233-9). A similar withholding of warning information occurred in Italy before the Vaiont Dam burst in 1963. "The Italian government, acting on findings by a technical board, held that the disaster was a direct result of 'bureaucratic inefficiency, muddling, withholding of alarming information, lack of judgement and evaluation and lack of serious individual and collective consultation'" (Perrow 1984: 239).

The question of military nuclear waste has been treated as a national security matter and hence closed to public examination (Goodin 1982: 228-9). On the civilian side in the USA until 1974, "all nuclear issues were the preserve of a tight and exclusive 'iron triangle,' which, as part of its pro-nuclear ways, managed to keep the waste question out of the limelight. This triangle was composed of the Joint Committee on Atomic Energy of the US Congress, the federal Atomic Energy Commission (AEC), and the nuclear industry" (Dryzek 1987: 112).

When dissenting information does surface, it is quickly rooted out at its source. "Dr. Gofman and his colleague Dr. Arthur Tamplin have challenged the over-optimistic approach of the AEC to radiation hazards in a remarkable series of scientific analyses carried out while they were employed by the AEC. For this courageous and important service to society, they were rewarded by losing their positions" (Commoner 1976: 282). Thus Schnaiberg (1980: 302) argues that "those who may be most knowledgeable about the state of the art and prospects for change are the most entrapped in the industrial sphere they can observe." Beck (1992a: 223) concludes that everyone "else -- even the most responsible and best informed people in politics and science -- more or less lives off the crumbs of information that fall from the planning tables of technological sub-politics."

Not only is information about safety problems monopolized by the companies and branches of government involved in high-risk technologies, but also they disseminate their own partial information. Cover-ups are all-too-frequently part of the process (Bertell 1985). When an accident did occur, Perrow (1984: 351) found "rampant attribution of operator error to the neglect of errors by the Great Designers and the Centralized Managers." Perrow (1984: 350) has also documented some of the monies spent by the pro-nuclear lobby in the United States that feels insecure because of its failures.

The embarrassment caused by accidents in high-risk systems has led to pressure for even greater monopolization of information. "The centralized design for nuclear plants recommended by most (but not all) regulatory and industry personnel ... calls for a wartime, military model in a peacetime civilian operation. A military model reflects strict discipline, unquestioning obedience, intense socialization, and isolation from normal civilian life styles" (Perrow 1984: 335). The tightly controlled organization used for the operation of naval nuclear submarines would be extended to all high-risk technologies on the assumption that the public is poorly equipped to participate in decisions concerning risk. The commission of inquiry into the Three Mile Island nuclear accident did not argue in favor of keeping the local population informed about safety problems. Even the "sociologist on the commission, Professor Cora

Marrett, said 'it would be ridiculous' for the utility to provide information on everything that happened that might be counter to safety, thus defending the utility's right to secrecy" (Perrow 1984: 336).

The democratic political system "is caught in the unpleasant dilemma of either failing in the face of systematically produced hazards, or suspending fundamental democratic principles through the addition of authoritarian, repressive 'buttresses'" (Beck 1992a: 80). Ecological dangers could lead to the legitimation of totalitarianism or to precisely the opposite: the development of environmental accounting and the improvement of accountability.

Risk Analysis and Environmental Accounting

As it becomes more and more evident that the social fabric is at risk (Short 1984), impact assessments and environmental risk analyses are belatedly beginning to be developed (Dietz 1987; Dietz et al. 1989; Whipple 1987; Freudenburg 1986, 1988; Sjoberg 1987; Gould et al. 1988; Edelstein 1988; Stern et al. 1990; Lambert 1990; Krimsky et al. 1988; Beck 1992a and 1992b; Viscusi 1992). However, although future impact assessments and risk forecasts are important, the partiality of knowledge, both in the sense of its incompleteness and in the sense of its orientation according to particular interests (Fischhoff et al. 1981) and cultures (Douglas and Wildavsky 1982; Johnson and Covello 1987; Mazur 1987), results in the uncertainty of predictions concerning the future (Covello et al. 1984; Thompson 1986; Morgan and Henrion 1990; Von Furstenberg 1990; Yearley 1991).

Such forecasts tend to be constructed using weak data bases (Levi 1980, Schrader-Freschette 1985), extrapolation, and most importantly, have to do with dynamic processes of nature whose complicated interactions remain beyond human knowledge, hence these forecasts are quite speculative. Projective estimates are based on past effects, but documentation to pinpoint the extent and causes of past effects has been almost nonexistent. "When data on past externalities cannot be found in the literature, they are excluded from concern" (Schnaiberg 1980: 331-2). Hence "the range of impacts to be included is always an underestimate" (Schnaiberg 1980: 329). The requirement of strict scientific proof of risk, rather than of absence of risk, stacks the deck in favor of risk taking over risk avoidance. The absence of means to prove the existence of risks is mistaken for the absence of risk and legitimates risk taking. Acceptable levels are set for individual chemicals without knowing the effect of the accumulating combination of human-produced chemicals in the environment. Environmental forecasts also tend to be biased toward underestimating risk because they are often calculated by people linked with private or state enterprises with an interest in downplaying risk to promote products (Levi 1980).

Furthermore, a standard feature of risk analysis consists of discounting the future, whereby projects with immediate benefits and distant costs will be favored, and those with long-term benefits and short-term costs will be ruled out (Schnaiberg 1980: 342-4). This political criterion systematically biases risk analysis against the environment, since many symbiotic projects fall into the latter category. Not taken into account either are potential victims of environmentally degrading constructions who are distant in space or in time or other species that are endangered. Some aspects of risk, such as the danger that nuclear, chemical, and biological technologies will be shifted from civilian to military uses, are not factored into risk calculations at all. Risk calculation as it has so far been done is inadequate.

Underestimation of risk, and false estimates of minimal risk where no estimate is possible, only serve to legitimate the imposition of dangerous risks on the population: "under the surface of risk calculation new kinds of *industrialized, decision-produced incalculabilities and threats* are spreading within the globalization of high-risk industries. ... *Along with the growing capacity of technical options grows the incalculability of their consequences*" (Beck 1992a: 22).

It is not just a matter of society deciding the amount of health that must be sacrificed for particular amounts of wealth (Douglas 1985), rather the terms of that equation have been left largely as unknowns. In fact, healthful approaches -- both for individuals and the environment -- may even lead to greater wealth in the long run, for example, the Swedish reforestation programs in place since 1903 have resulted in a more sustainable source of wealth than the traditional Canadian cut-and-run approach to producing pulp and paper.

Accounting for waste, unlike risk analysis, is concerned with the present. It would provide a documentary base for pinpointing the source of harmful effects (Edelstein 1988), if such effects occur in the future. It would, in short, enhance accountability. Thus Schnaiberg (1980: 326) distinguishes such retrospective accounting from projective estimates. Risk projections are to environmental accounting what loss projections are to capital accounting. Just as the rights of shareholders are grounded in accounting and accountability for actual profits and losses rather than in projections, so too the environmental rights of humans are grounded in waste accounting and environmental accountability instead of in predictions of risk. Futurology is less persuasive than history. Risk analysis yields only before-the-fact guesses whereas accounting makes possible after-the-fact accountability.

The perverse consequence of the lack of environmental accounting is that it amounts to *de facto* no-fault pollution, that is, lack of accountability for environmental degradation. Schnaiberg (1980: 334) argues that projects should be required to have a monitoring component so that excuses of ignorance will no longer be available. Protection against unpredictable environmental degradation could be attained through mechanisms already in place in some domains, such as insurance policies for automobile accidents. Where negligence is involved, retribution could be made through mechanisms similar to those existing in other areas, such as lawsuits and criminal prosecution in the case of negligent physicians. Human creativity could invent new mechanisms to deal specifically with environmental risks. Environmental accounting is necessary to provide the documentation for these pollution control mechanisms, and to distinguish between unforeseen accidents and negligence.

The critique of present risk analysis and of existing environmental accounting practices has to be done in terms of bias, lack of accounting, and the deficiency of current accountability rather than in terms of a broad-brush critique of expertise and science as such. "Chemical formulas and reactions, invisible pollutant levels, biological cycles and chain reactions have to rule seeing and thinking if one wishes to go to the barricades against risks" (Beck 1992: 72). Removing the means of accounting for environmental degradation, which is implied by a critique of science and expertise *per se*, would be the best way to obfuscate ecological risks and prevent accountability.

Environmental accounting is closely tied to accountability for present and past consequences, whereas risk analysis is not, even though the latter is important in its own right for deciding possible courses of action. Risk analysis without environmental accounting threatens to become public manipulation based on wilful ignorance and the withholding of available information, whereas environmental accounting keeps risk analysis honest by making documentation available and eliminating the excuse of ignorance: "what matters is whether risks and threats are methodically and objectively interpreted and scientifically displayed, or whether they are downplayed and concealed" (Beck 1992a: 158). Knowledge of past environmental effects is a crucial element of risk projections. Stated inversely, the "history of unawareness of ecosystem impacts of sociocultural production imposes severe restrictions on contemporary impact research" (Schnaiberg 1980: 278). Although they are both important, environmental accounting is more fundamental than risk analysis for developing a symbiotic relationship between social action and the processes of nature. Furthermore, the development of environmental accounting raises a further question: accounting to whom and for whom?

Environmental Accounting and Accountability
Under Capitalist Liberal Democracy

Accounting has been a partial science, both in the sense of being incomplete and in the sense of being partial to the interests of those for whom it has been developed. It has been left undeveloped in particularly important areas, such as monitoring and accounting for waste. "Why have we been able to mobilize our social intelligence to expand high-technology production, but not to understand the environmental effects of this production?" (Schnaiberg 1980: 278). Clean air and pure water are among the most basic needs of humans. The capability has not, however, been developed to express the provision of needs such as these in numerical, calculable terms, or stated inversely, the means have not been developed to express quantifiably the erosion of the capacity of the natural environment to provide for these needs. Waste has been left out of the development of the rational calculus of accounting for the elements of production and exchange. It has similarly escaped monetization. The contrast is striking between the extensive development of rational accounting for capital and the lack of development of a system for the rational accounting for waste and its effects on the environment and on the provision of human needs. The problem of the accumulation of waste was not seen until its effects became catastrophic because its producers didn't look, and didn't want to look for fear of being held accountable for it.

Calculation and prediction of consequences are, as Weber stated, what make capitalism and formal organization more efficient than other forms of organization. But calculation and prediction of consequences have hitherto been limited to prices, movement of capital, of labor, and consumer desires. They have not been extended to the environmental impact of commodities and their production. Calculation and prediction of consequences have been, not too extensive, but too limited. Accounting has been thoroughly developed for capital, yet accounting for waste has remained undeveloped. This is closely related to the fact that accountability for waste has remained undeveloped as well. Environmental problems have resulted, not so much from the development of quantitative measurement techniques *per se*, as from the fact that those techniques have been constructed as the means to exploit the environment rather than to harmonize the relationship of humans to it. The capacity to calculate and to foresee the consequences of social action has been developed for the goal of rationally appropriating resources from the environment, not for the goal of rationally creating a symbiotic relationship between social action and the processes of nature. Rationalization has hitherto been institutionally truncated.

The development of partial accounting practices and the monopolization of knowledge about waste dumping and environmental dangers are not just traits of individual bureaucratic organizations, private or public. They are also characteristics of the larger system within which they are found. Under capitalist liberal democracy, shareholders have a legal right to an accurate accounting of profit and loss, of input of resources and output of commodities, and of foreseeable consequences of planned future courses of action of the corporation in which they hold shares. Humanity, however, as shareholders in the commons -- nature's legacy to all humans -- does not yet have the recognized legal right to an accurate accounting of the waste cost of production and of the foreseeable environmental consequences of the development of new commodities and technologies of production. The state enforces through the legal system accurate accounting procedures to minimize financial risks for shareholders of corporations and render managers accountable, yet the state does not enforce accurate accounting procedures to minimize environmental risks for the shareholders of the natural environment and render polluters accountable. The assessment of the environmental impact of production and consumption, and the channels to disseminate this information, have been poorly developed. Where they do exist, accounting practices for waste cost as well as environmental accountability have not yet been institutionalized and the channels of communicating this information to the public at large tend to be blocked. Capitalist liberal democracy has been deficient in environmental accounting practices and public accountability.

Access-to-information legislation is an important potential wedge to develop an open society. A great deal of financial resources and knowledge are, however, necessary to make use of access-to-information legislation. Such access is at present so narrowly circumscribed (typically applying only to government information) one could conclude that information is more closed off than accessible. Because of its restricted functioning, access-to-information legislation has operated as a safety valve maintaining the general tendency of the monopolization and closure of information and of barriers to its accessibility.

Monopolizing information, covering up problems, and glossy public relations campaigns are inadequate means for establishing a relationship of trust. These strategies can suppress "the *perception* of risks, but only the perception, not their reality or their effects; risks denied grow especially quickly and well" (Beck 1992a: 45). The monopolization of information prevents the population from developing an informed opinion on environmental problems, and from even perceiving the problems, until an all-too-evident catastrophe occurs that cannot be hidden. Trust is thereby undermined. Gould et al. (1988: 136) found that risk perceptions were closely related to the judgment of people concerning the adequacy of safety regulations. Monroe and Woodhouse (1989) concluded that the lack of democratic control of nuclear energy and hence lack of responsiveness to the preferences of the public led to its demise in the United States, as indicated by the fact that no new nuclear plants have been constructed there since 1980.

The relationship of trust concerning environmental matters between on the one hand, private enterprises, states, and political parties, and on the other, the population, has been badly damaged by failed assurances. "People suspect the unsaid, add in the side effects and expect the worst" (Beck 1992a: 169). Even if a perfect method were developed to decontaminate toxic waste, the 'not in my backyard' syndrome would now still prevail. This 'NIMBY' response is, however, inadequate because of the global consequences of the accumulation of waste. The planet as a whole has become everyone's backyard.

An important element in the formation of a relationship of trust is transparency to public scrutiny and criticism, and therefore the institutionalized free access to information by critics, so that the public knows that nothing is being held back from public scrutiny. Perrow's (1984: 306) study of accidents using high-risk technologies led him to the following conclusion concerning the need for ecological openness: "Above all, I will argue, sensible living with risky systems means keeping the controversies alive, listening to the public, and recognizing the essentially political nature of risk assessment. Ultimately, the issue is not risk, but power; the power to impose risks on the many for the benefit of the few." Therein lies the basis of distrust.

In order to have institutions accountable to the public who run the risks, the development of a precise, rigorous system of environmental accounting for waste and for environmental degradation is required. The United States National Environmental Policy Act of 1969-70, not adequately implemented even in its own domain according to Schnaiberg, 'specified that all federal government agencies had to specify the total environmental impacts of federally sponsored construction and production projects. What I am calling for is an extension of this logic to all societal production operations, both private and public" (Schnaiberg 1980: 26). Such accounting is needed just to comprehend environmental problems.

Environmental accounting is the documentary basis of accountability: the means to make problems visible and connect social cause to environmental effect. In a field situation this can, however, only be accomplished in a probabilistic way. Demands for the rigor of laboratory controls upon which scientific proof is usually based, when these controls are not possible, only serve to mask the causal relationships as unproven. The availability of documentary evidence can nonetheless be the means to remove such masks and establish accountability. Cigarette companies argued that there was no rigorous scientific proof connecting smoking and lung cancer, but the documentation of the correlation between their product and that disease eventually proved persuasive. Similarly, Japan has taken statistical correlations between measures of pollution and particular sicknesses as entailing legal responsibility, and sentenced firms to make large payments to victims (Beck 1992a: 63-4). This demonstrates the feasibility of the polluter-pays principle for dealing with environmental risks.[2] If the accumulation of pollution proves toxic, then legal responsibility can be defined in terms of contributing to that buildup, rather than having to prove that the pollution coming from that particular factory was lethal for that particular person. Furthermore, the present burden of proof -- the requirement to prove that a product introduced into the market, or waste dumped into public waters or air, is toxic -- has to be shifted, in order to achieve ecological rationality, to proving that it is safe.

Accountability also demands a political system that has sufficient independence from economic institutions to set ecologically sound rules for the economy. It is equally important to have a legal system with the capacity to maintain its autonomy from economic and political institutions in order to enforce those rules. And it is particularly important to have a media whose function is to pursue information and knowledge independently of the economic, political, and legal institutions (see Sandman et al. 1987). "The risk society is in this sense also the *science, media, and information* society" (Beck 1992a: 46) in that knowledge and the media become more important. The assumption cannot be made that these institutions are already autonomous under capitalism as it presently exists. Studies of organizational elites in different institutional spheres (Porter 1965; Domhoff 1967, 1970, 1972, 1979, 1980; Clement 1975, 1977) have found that they are under a great deal of common control.

The relationship of states to the natural environment has been a mixed blessing. On the one hand, only the state has the resources necessary to force information out of private companies and to set and enforce the rules needed to ensure that knowledge is not monopolized. For example, only the state has the power to enforce a "waste audit" on companies, industries, and institutions, as is being discussed in Ontario, Canada (The Ottawa Citizen 22 November 1990: A5). Only it has the capacity to legislate laws governing the association of humans and their natural environment. States are tools that could be used to promote a less exploitative relationship between human social action and the rest of nature. Yet on the other hand the experience of states has not been an ecologically happy one. States have participated in the degradation of the natural environment, and have covered up that participation, through their own monopolies of knowledge and power.

It is true that the "individual or corporate group cannot be entrusted with the freedom to define private goals and proceed to achieve them unhampered by any external authority" (Mellos 1988: 28). But it is equally true that the state, or more precisely the bureaucratic class that dominates it, cannot be entrusted with the freedom to define public goals and proceed to achieve them unhampered by any external authority either. The state and legal apparatus are important tools for checking the power of corporate monopolies to degrade nature, but the power of the state itself to participate in such degradation cannot go unchecked.

It is equally indispensable, therefore, to have formal and informal checks on the power of the state. A formal legal system, a press, and opposition political parties that are independent of the ruling state political party are essential components of such checks on the power of the state. So too are social movements, such as the environmental movement, that struggle to ecologically transform the state. "The state can only cease to be an apparatus of domination over society and become an instrument enabling society to exercise power over itself with a view to its own restructuring, if society is already permeated by social struggles that open up areas of autonomy keeping both the dominant class and the power of the state apparatus in check" (Gorz 1982: 116). It is crucially important to have a strong ecology movement to push the economic, political, and legal institutions into a symbiotic relationship with the natural environment. "To be effective, given the politically sensitive nature of many of the most critical risks, intergovernmental risk assessment needs to be supported by independent capacities outside of government" (World Commission on Environment and Development 1987: 324). Not just "supported" but more importantly pushed in an ecological direction.

> Only when medicine opposes medicine, nuclear physics opposes nuclear physics, human genetics opposes human genetics or information technology opposes information technology can the future that is being brewed up in the test-tube become intelligible and evaluable for the outside world. ... This institutionalization of self-criticism is so important because in many areas neither the risks nor the alternative methods to avoid them can be recognized without the proper technical know-how.[3]
> (Beck 1992a: 234)

If an informed populace is to be a better judge of its interests than a monopolistic dominant class, and if the state and corporations are to be held accountable to that populace, then litigants are needed who will demonstrate to the populace, using the strongest possible arguments and evidence, the ecological consequences of social action.   Open environmental accounting has an important role to play in stimulating consciousness and political demands among environmentally exploited classes, "with official legitimation of their grievances through the benefit-cost analysis. This assumes, of course, that such analysis is made public" (Schnaiberg 1980: 339).   Thus Beck (1992a: 227) argues that "political action gains influence in parallel to the *detection and perception* of risk potential.   Risk definitions activate responsibilities and create zones of *illegitimate* systemic conditions, which cry out for change in the interest of the general public. ... risk definitions *open up* new political options which can be used to win back and strengthen democratic parliamentary influence."

Environmental Accountability Under State Socialism

At the time these lines are being written, soviet socialism in eastern Europe is in ruins, and some observers contend that state socialism as a whole is dying.[4] It must be remembered, however, that state socialism directed by the central planning of the Communist Party is still the form of government in China, that is, for almost one-quarter of the world's population.   And the formally organized central planning of state socialism will continue to have appeal as an alternative to the deficiencies of the invisible hand of the capitalist market. It is important, therefore, to learn from the experience of three-quarters of a century of state socialism in eastern Europe. Like capitalism, the problematic feature of state socialism is that of accountability, and hence of the concentration of power.   The issue of public accountability goes to the core of the relationship of state socialism to the natural environment.

The Promise of Socialism

Marxists explain the ecological crisis in terms of private property and the pursuit of profit. "The source of the [ecological] crisis rather lies in the privatisation of the surplus product as private property.   In the relation of private property lies the propulsion for expansion of profitable commodity production" (Mellos 1988: 158). The solution to the ecological crisis is therefore to replace the capitalist market with socialism.

> In theory, the superiority of socialist society lies in the fact that the outcome of multiple activities is not, as in market societies, a random result which can only be corrected after the event either by the state or by individuals themselves, with all the waste, delay, duplication and error that this entails. The specificity of socialism lies in the fact that the results of social activity are determined in advance as an objective chosen by the collectivity, so that each person's activity is adapted, regulated and programmed as a function of this collective goal. (Gorz 1982: 77)

Central planning will, according to this argument, facilitate coordination and maximize foresight. It will eliminate the anarchy of the market and the electoral paralysis of competing groups tugging in different directions in liberal democracies. By abolishing the profit motive and private property, socialism promised to be superior to capitalism, especially for collective concerns as opposed to the private individual accumulation of wealth. Hence socialism should have a particularly good record for matters such as protecting the common environment of all humans (Rothman 1972: 33; Sherman 1972: 355).

At the time state socialism began in the Soviet Union in the first quarter of the Twentieth Century, Weber pointed out the Achilles heel of the central planning argument, namely, its bureaucratic character, which would promote the development of a dominant bureaucratic class. He argued that it is an illusion to believe that the abolition of private property and of the pursuit of profit in the market and their replacement by central socialist planning in a one-party state would have a liberating effect. This would only enlarge the sphere of instrumental rationality while destroying the formal principles that limit bureaucratic action: "socialism would, in fact, require a still higher degree of formal bureaucratization than capitalism" (Weber 1968: 225), for example, to carry out its central planning. The theory of socialism also underestimates the effects of modern technology as a constraint in production (Weber 1968: 223-4; Raynaud 1987: 170). Furthermore, "all economic activity in a market economy is undertaken and carried through by individuals acting to provide for their own ideal or material interests. ... In an economic system organized on a socialist basis, there would be no fundamental difference in this respect" (Weber 1968: 202). The self-interest of the dominant class does not vanish by utopian theoretical fiat.

Thus, although Weber did not comment on socialism as a solution to ecological problems, his analysis leads to caution because, under socialism too, self-serving bureaucratic domination has the potential to monopolize knowledge of imminent environmental problems resulting from its commands. Socialism based on central planning fortifies the capacity to hide the failures of the bureaucratic dominant class of central planners. Rather than enhancing accountability to the people, concentration of power in the hands of central state planners is a system that constitutes a threat to public accountability on environmental matters, and other matters as well.

State Socialism and the Environment

The environmental record of state socialism confirms Weber's critical analysis rather than the lavish pretensions of socialist theorists. The German Democratic Republic and Czechoslovakia, while they were still communist countries, were two of the four highest emitters per capita of carbon dioxide pollution in the world (the other two were the United States and Canada). Socialist states have been no better than capitalist ones at developing environmentally benign solar energy. Before the nuclear accident at Chernobyl, Perrow (1984: 40) found that the Soviet Union "is far less concerned about the chance of large accidents, so they did not build containment structures for their early reactors, nor do they yet require emergency core cooling systems. Had the accident at Three Mile Island taken place in one of the plants near Moscow, it would have exposed the operators to potentially lethal doses, and irradiated a large population." The promise of the nuclear reactors at Chernobyl, installed at the command of the central planners, was of a cheap source of energy that would hasten the full development of productive forces and economic growth. The worst nuclear accident on record resulted, instead, in the contamination of the environment and of people in it and had a wide-ranging social impact (Marples 1988).

Production pressures and cost cutting are not peculiar to the capitalist pursuit of profit. An explosion in a Hungarian liquid carbon dioxide plant (when Hungary was a state socialist society) froze five workers instantly and seriously injured others. Among the causes of the explosion and deaths were improper preheating procedures, the use of below-grade steel, and faulty safety valves (Voros and Honti 1974). In his study of technological accidents, Perrow (1984) concluded that state socialist countries have behaved in much the same way as capitalist ones. "They pollute, ignore the long-run costs, and in at least the Soviet sphere, enfeeble workers much more than capitalist societies do (because the workers cannot fight back). Production pressures appear to be as high or higher in some socialist countries" (Perrow 1984: 340). Thus he concluded that, although the capitalist pursuit of profit is part of the explanation of technological accidents, the source of the problem goes well beyond, and is much deeper than, profit-making capitalism.

Under capitalism there are production pressures due to the pursuit of profit that lead to pollution, environmental accidents, resource depletion, etc. Under state socialism there are production pressures resulting from the centrally planned, hierarchical, bureaucratic command structure in which production goals are set. The least costly path to meet these goals in the short run is through waste dumping, pollution, shoddy safety measures and hence accidents, and resource depletion. The invisible hand of the market under capitalism has its parallel under socialism in faceless bureaucrats. The pursuit of profit under capitalism is analogous to the pursuit of bureaucratic careers under state socialism. Furthermore, many technical production pressures are common to both capitalism and socialism: "under the production pressures generated by a huge facility standing idle waiting for tools or hydrogen or pipes we can expect forced errors" (Perrow 1984: 111).

Production pressures under socialism stem directly from the core of Marxian theory, namely, its commitment to an economic growth ethic and centrally planned control.

> But, whereas some ecocentrics might disapprove of growth *per se*, Marxists do not. In the first place they see that the 'full development of modern productive forces' is necessary before socialism can be established. The division into classes is regarded as an inevitable feature of societies which have insufficient production, so growth towards a sufficiency is needed before people will begin to think of their future society rather than just immediate need satisfaction. (Pepper 1984: 170)

Marxists tend to dismiss the problems of finite resources and of the limits to growth as unimportant (Sandbach 1978). Dryzek (1987: 89) observed with respect to the pre-Gorbachov era in the Soviet Union that if ecological proposals "obstruct production, they will almost certainly be set aside. This situation is typical of that obtaining throughout the Soviet block, where Marxist materialist dreams of productive cornucopia through rational direction of the forces of science and technology die hard."

Marxian theory has in this way provided the ideological justification under state socialism for the development of productive forces at the expense of the natural environment, and this is precisely what occurred in the Soviet Union, eastern Europe, and China (Singleton 1976; Fullenbach 1981; Goldman 1972). Communist academics (Ryabchikov 1976) provided the cover up of environmental degradation under state socialism, the extent of which was only revealed after the Gorbachov *glasnost* movement. And many Western academics (Pryde 1972) were naively taken in.

The central planning of the Communist Party under state socialism, like capitalist market planning, has furthered capital   accumulation through a process that has resulted in the accumulation of waste and the depletion of resources. The centrally planned goal of providing massive energy at Chernobyl had as a consequence the radioactive contamination of Bylorussia. The centrally planned goal of augmenting rice production in the Soviet Union through irrigation and river diversion had as a consequence the degradation of the Aral Sea. Under both the demands of the capitalist market and the commands of state socialist central planning, respecting the environment and adapting to it have had low priority.

State socialism imposes, however, more fetters on the development of the forces of production -- fetters such as demotivation, problems of centrally planning a system of coordination, etc. -- with resulting shortages not only of luxury goods but also of food, shelter, clothing, transportation, and other items for satisfying basic needs. Hence it has had a less detrimental effect on the environment as an unintended consequence to the extent that it has failed to become a society of abundance. State socialism has not been an environmentally less wasteful path to development, rather it has been environmentally less wasteful in some ways only because it has been a less successful path to development.

Commoner (1976) concludes that capitalism should be replaced by socialism in order that humans live in harmony with their natural environment, yet his (Commoner 1976: 183, 194) concrete proposals -- such as high-speed trains to replace planes and automobiles -- have been developed, not under state socialism, but under European and Japanese capitalism. In contradiction with his proposal, the actual results of Commoner's (1976) study favor welfare-state capitalism and social democracy over both laissez-faire capitalism and state socialism as it has existed.

Although Commoner argues in favor of socialism replacing capitalism, he (Commoner 1976: 259) criticizes business leaders for promoting the ideology that Americans must consume less in order to raise the capital necessary for costly energy projects. The restriction of working-class consumption in order to accumulate the surplus and capital necessary to undertake industrial development projects has, however, been one of the key characteristics of state socialism as it has existed. And it has been a permanent restriction on consumption by the working class, but not on consumption by the Communist Party *apparatchik* (Lane 1967; Matthews 1978; McInnes *et al.* 1978).   A low level of consumption, including necessities of food and lodging, by the working class and "the failing supply of capital" (Commoner 1976: 260) have been more characteristic of state socialism as it has existed than of capitalism, and still state socialism has severely degraded the natural environment.

Commoner has limited his investigation to the study of the "poverty of power" under capitalism, in fact, under American capitalism. Had he also investigated power under socialism as it exists and the degradation of its natural environment, the "poverty of power" under socialism and the deeper roots of environmental problems could not have escaped him. State socialism as it has existed has amply demonstrated that the abolition of private property and of the pursuit of profit do not result in the elimination of environmental degradation. The roots of environmental problems are to be found in monopoly power itself -- whether private power in pursuit of profit in the capitalist market or Communist Party power in pursuit of bureaucratic domination and privilege -- and in an anthropocentric, exploitative relationship with nature. Learning from socialism as it has existed is as necessary as learning from capitalism as it has existed.

Ironically, there is evidence that there has been more ecological planning in capitalist nations than in state socialist ones. Before the Gorbachov revolution Dryzek (1987: 88) argued that it remains

> paradoxical that there is currently more in the way of administrative planning for environmental goals in the Western world than in the Soviet bloc. For, while the capitalist world has made substantial use of environmentally oriented administrative agencies such as the Alkali and Clean Air Inspectorate in Great Britain and the Environmental Protection Agency in the USA, little beyond lip-service has generally been paid to ecological goals by the governments of the Soviet bloc. (Dryzek 1987: 88)

The explanation of this apparent paradox is not hard to find. Tight bureaucratic control results in an increased capacity to monopolize and conceal knowledge of environmental problems, and eliminates the means whereby the bureaucratic elite is pushed into being held accountable to the population at large, such as elections, an independent press, and an independent environmental movement. Whether in China or in pre-*Glastnost* Soviet Union, East Germany, Czechoslovakia, Bulgaria, etc., there was an accumulation of pollution and environmental degradation, but there was no independent environmental movement.

Environmental degradation can not be explained by only private property, the pursuit of profit, and private acquisition, that is, by market capitalism. It has also resulted from social systems where capitalism has been officially abolished, namely, state socialist systems based on central planning and collective acquisition and accumulation in the name of the public and the proletariat. Environmental degradation is related to anthropocentric values that have given priority to human projects at the expense of the natural environment and to a monopolization of channels of communication and power such that the population is excluded from consciousness of environmental problems until a disastrous accident makes everyone aware. "Consequently, administered systems often effectively conceal and hence perpetuate their errors. Two of the worst examples of this syndrome are the cover-up of a massive nuclear accident in the Urals in 1958 by the Soviet hierarchy (Zile 1982: 203), and the less successful denial, first of occurrence and then of severity, of the 1986 near-meltdown of a nuclear reactor at Chernobyl" (Dryzek 1987: 101).

The Communist Party has been one mammoth bureaucracy monopolizing the disposition of surplus, expertise, the setting of priorities, and information concerning environmental matters. As a total institution affecting all aspects of public life, it has completed the circle of monopolization thereby abolishing ecological accountability to the public. The history of state socialism only underscores the need for independent groups (opposition political parties, media, environmental groups, etc.) to uncover information about pollution, environmental accidents, and resource depletion and bring it to the attention of the people.

The high ecological cost of state socialism for a low level of basic need satisfaction (as illustrated by the scarcity of lodging) is the result, not only of a cultural priority valuing production (however inefficient) over the natural environment, but also of an institutional shortcoming: the command hierarchy of a one-party state with its central planners. "Would planners choose to promote ecological values? Or would they pursue other ends? Should we rely on the good intentions of an elite of planners?" (Dryzek 1987: 86). The sad ecological experience of state socialism teaches a great deal not only about state socialism but also about the probable results of authoritarian ecological solutions under capitalism.

Bookchin argues that Marxian socialism has been and will continue to be an ecological failure. "We must either choose between ecology, with its naturalism, its anarchistic logic of decentralization, its emphasis on humanly scaled alternate technologies, and its non-hierarchical institutions, or socialism, with its typically Marxian anti-naturalism, its political logic of centralization, its emphasis on high technology, and its bureaucratic institutions" (Bookchin 1980: 18).

Critical Theory Versus Euphemistic Theory

Commoner (1976: 261) argues that "there appears to be nothing in basic socialist theory that *requires* the establishment of a totally centralized economy, or of political repression to enforce it." But wonderful things have also been said about capitalism "in theory" (Smith 1776), including its reconciliation with the natural environment (Boulding 1973; Brown 1972: 225-6; Daly 1973). The focus on the theory of socialism instead of learning from the experience of socialism is a common limitation of neo-Marxian analyses. Just as the Pope dismisses criticism that the Roman Catholic Church has been tried and found wanting by claiming that it has not really been tried, so Marxian apologists pretend that socialism has not been found wanting by claiming that it has not yet been tried. Soviet society, for example, would only have been socialist if air had been pure, water clear, and dreams became reality. Thus Burgess (1978) claims that the "'a priori' acceptance of Soviet society as socialist has a theological quality to it which leads to some rather interesting contradictions ... the polluted air of the Don Basin and the black waters of the Volga ... both are excellent indices of the distance between the Soviet and socialist reality" (Burgess 1978). The "theological quality" has, however, more to do with giving 'socialism' the same conceptual status as 'paradise' -- out of reach of any possible observation and criticism -- than with examining how the Marxian theory of socialism has degenerated into the observed practice of Marxist socialism. It consists of dogmatically equating "socialist reality" with socialist theory instead of investigating the problems resulting from the three-quarter century imposition of Marxian socialist ideology on big and powerful states. The former can be referred to as euphemistic theory, and amounts to a glossy advertisement for a social system. The latter could be called critical analytical theory, and is, on the contrary, a verifiable analysis of that system as it exists and as it has originated in euphemistic theory. The difference between the two is as important to grasp as the difference between ornament and substance.

André Gorz is one of the rare Marxists who finally admits that central planning, which appears in theory as the superiority of socialism, has in practice been the source of its deficiencies leading it to be no better than market capitalism.

> From the point of view of the individual, the plan has no advantage over the market. ... From being 'soldiers of production' in the capitalist economy, individuals end up as soldiers permanently mobilised to serve a plan presented to them as the emanation of 'the general will'. As long as the protagonists of socialism continue to make centralised planning (however much it might be broken down into local and regional plans) the linchpin of their programme, and the adherence of everyone to the 'democratically formulated' objectives of the plan the core of their political doctrine, socialism will remain an unattractive proposition in industrial

societies.   The source of the theoretical superiority of socialism over capitalism is thus the source of its practical inferiority. (Gorz 1982: 78-9)

Socialist theory has led to a military model that imposes the preferences of the dominant socialist class and perceives everyone else as mere soldiers mobilised to adhere to its plan. Thus socialism in the Marxian sense fails to satisfy a crucial ecological imperative, namely, the dissemination of knowledge of ecological problems, including those engendered by the dominant elite of central planners, to the people by an independent environmental movement and an independent press free to criticize and oppose the ruling elite. The euphemistic theory of socialism itself is deficient in that its promotion of central planning gives rise to a practice of socialism characterized by inadequate institutionalized means of accountability of the elite to the people.

The theory of socialism has repeatedly given birth to a practice of socialism that bears little resemblance to the pretensions of its progenitor, but the theory gave birth to the practice none the less. The history of socialism has demonstrated that the monopolization of power by the Communist Party leads to an overwhelmingly centralized system and to political repression. The "general will" has been the will of the generals of the Communist Party, and the "democratically formulated objectives" have been the objectives formulated by the dominant socialist class. This leads to the degradation of the environment because of the deficiencies of the institutionalized means of accountability to the rest of the population who must suffer the ecological consequences and because of the inadequacy of checks on power. The capacity to cover up pollution problems and the repression of criticism of error makers in positions of power promote waste by making no one accountable for it.   Tight coupling of institutions, as under state socialism, leads to an overloading of the political bureaucracy and to an overbearing capacity to hide the harmful ecological consequences of bureaucratic decisions.   As it has existed, socialism has consisted of the exploitation of the proletariat and of the environment (Shabad 1979) for the benefit of its Communist Party bureaucrats.

Accountability for Environmental Degradation

Ecological problems have had a somewhat different character under capitalism and state socialism because of the presence or abolition respectively of private property (and presence or abolition of the pursuit of profit). A common, deeper source has, however, produced ecological problems in both these systems. That deeper source consists of the fact that both market capitalism and state socialism are planned bureaucratic systems of production based on the exploitation of the environment. Marxists such as Mellos leave bureaucratic relations of the Communist Party outside the scope of their explanation of the ecological crisis. Theirs is a restricted theory, failing to perceive that the source of ecological problems includes but is deeper and broader than "the privatisation of the surplus product as private property" (Mellos 1988: 158). Although capitalism is a particularly important element in generating environmental degradation, it is but one element. States that have abolished the capitalist market, private property, and the pursuit of profit have also created serious environmental problems because another element -- bureaucratization -- has filled the void.

Gorz (1982: 58) has given the following apt description of how bureaucrats, private or public, maintain the mechanisms of domination yet avoid accountability.

> In the state apparatus as in the giant firm, power is an organigramme. ...
> The elimination of personal power to the benefit of the functional power
> inherent in an anonymous organigramme has profoundly changed the
> implications of class conflict. Power in both society and the firm is now
> *exercised* by people who do not *hold* it, who are not personally answerable
> for their actions and take refuge behind the functions which answer for
> them. Since they are executants or servants, bureaucrats are never
> responsible. The predefined obligations inherent in their function relieve
> them of all personal responsibility and decision and enable them to meet
> protest with the disarming reply: 'We haven't chosen to do this. We're
> only enforcing the regulations. We're carrying out orders.' Whose orders?
> Whose regulations? One could go back indefinitely up the hierarchy and
> it would still be impossible to find anyone else to say, 'Mine'.

Gorz has drawn attention to the passing of the buck up the hierarchy, which is the characteristic way subordinates, even high level ones such as Adolf Eichmann in the case of the Nazis, avoid responsibility for their actions. The buck is also passed down. Superiors avoid responsibility by monopolizing information, covering up errors and problems, and by shifting responsibility to subordinates. The captain of the tanker Exxon Valdez claimed he gave the correct orders, but that they were not followed, and the oil spill resulted from the disobedience of his orders. Perrow (1984) has shown that the typical defense of managers involved in high-technology accidents is to claim that it was operator error, not bad management nor the system, that caused the accident.

Environmental problems unleashed by humans have resulted from a system of class domination in which no one has been held responsible for laying waste to the environment. The bureaucratic logic of centrally planned economic development under socialism as it has existed, like the market logic of economic development through the pursuit of private profit under capitalism as it has existed, have propelled the degradation of the natural environment. In both cases there has been an uncoupling of the production of waste from responsibility for its production. The channels of information and communication concerning environmental degradation have been closed, and accountability successfully avoided.

The development of values, consciousness, and culture favorable to the natural environment is a necessary but not sufficient condition for solving ecological problems. Values tend to be reinterpreted according to interests and thereby usurped. It is necessary in addition to institutionalize accounting and accountability practices in order to assess and control the effect of social action on the natural environment. "What is needed to recognize toxic substances in the air, the water and food, is not so much established values as, rather, expensive measuring instruments and methodological and theoretical knowledge" (Beck 1992a: 177). The development of environmental accounting, of the social and political means to communicate widely the results of that accounting, and of accountability for environmental degradation constitute checks not only on the exploitation of the natural environment but also on social systems of dominating humans. "Toxic substances and pollutant emissions, which were first considered 'latent' and then 'unavoidable' side effects, are gradually related under the observation of the scientists to the decision-making party concealed in them, and reconnected to the conditions of their controllability" (Beck 1992a: 175).

After an extensive analysis of what he calls the predominant social choice mechanisms, Dryzek (1987: 114) concludes that, with respect to the environmental consequences of the use of nuclear energy, "polyarchy out-performs both markets and administration on this issue. No pure market system (even if it *did* produce nuclear power) would possess any plausible means of coping with high-level wastes. Administered systems have succeeded only in denying the problem's existence" (Dryzek 1987: 114). By polyarchy (Dahl 1971; Lindblom 1977) Dryzek is referring to what is commonly known as electoral democracy. Furthermore, Dryzek (1987: 115) concludes generally, and not just with respect to the nuclear issue, that, in spite of some severe failings, polyarchy has greater ecological rationality than either the market or hierarchical administered systems. "While no polyarchy has wholeheartedly embraced ecological values, progress toward rectifying environmental abuses has been more pronounced in polyarchies than in any other kind of extant and widespread form of social choice" (Dryzek 1987: 120). Given the greater failings of the alternatives, polyarchy has an essential role to play in the establishment of a symbiotic relationship between social action and the processes of nature. Moreover, the implication of my argument in this chapter is that the failings of even the best performer -- polyarchy -- are related to inadequate public accountability, that is, to the tendency for information and power to be monopolized.

The weakness of the American system of checks and balances is not so much that it is wrong as that it has been limited to the state. Private companies have been very imperfectly checked and maintain an unbalanced relationship with the state, with labor, and with the environmental movement. Whereas in totalitarian regimes, the monopoly held by a political party and its control of the state has had disastrous environmental consequences, under capitalism the unbalanced power of private enterprise, and in particular its lack of environmental accountability, has produced disastrous ecological consequences.

The application to environmental issues of Weber's conception of economic rationality quoted at the beginning of this chapter implies that deficiencies in accounting for the provision of needs (or for the erosion of such provision through environmental degradation) amount to deficiencies in rationality itself. These environmental accounting deficiencies, as well as the monopolization of information, knowledge, and channels of communication, lead humanity to postpone its confrontation with environmental problems until they are aggravated, and to an irrational ordering of priorities. Formal rationality has consisted of tunnel-vision rationality and has itself been irrational in broader ecological terms of its failure to develop accounting methods to calculate the ecological impact of its actions. The problem is not that there has been too much calculation, rather that there has been too little, in particular, of environmental degradation. Accounting for waste -- and for its effects on the provision of needs -- in numerical, calculable terms, and accountability for waste, are the missing elements in the intensification of rationality in the economic sphere.

The environmental crisis that is requiring payment to restore a polluted environment and to replenish resources has the potential to increase accountability for environmental degradation, that is, to enhance the transparency of responsibility for waste and environmental degradation. "The consequence for politics is that reports on discoveries of toxins in refuse dumps, if catapulted overnight into the headlines, change the political agenda. The established public opinion that the forests are dying compels new priorities. When it has been scientifically confirmed on the European level that formaldehyde has carcinogenic effects, the previous chemical policy is threatened with collapse" (Beck 1992a: 197-8). Hence environmental problems have the potential to promote the retrieval of the capital necessary for paying the unpaid waste cost of pollution from the class that appropriated it in the first place and that contributed most to the degradation of the environment. Accounting and accountability are important elements in the struggle to determine how the waste cost will be paid, in particular, on which class the burden will fall. The social class basis of conflict over the environment will be examined more closely in the following chapter.

Notes

1. The present author was told precisely that in the nineteen-sixties when, at a summer job in a pulp and paper mill, he inquired about the pollution. If owners and managers for their part expect to receive the profits of production, why do they not have to put up with paying the environmental costs of their operations?

2. Beck's (1992a: 63-4) illustration refutes his own argument on this point. Furthermore, Beck (1992a: 65) argues that the problems lie in the concessional character of pollution laws, rather than in the outrageous character of the concessions. This frames the pollution issue in terms of an all-or-nothing choice that will prove unpalatable. For example, if Beck believes his no- concessions, no-toxins-at-all argument, then at the present time his sole means of transportation would be a horse. Similarly his (Beck 1992a: 175) argument against end-of-pipe remedies, such as catalytic converters for automobiles, that only fight symptoms rather than removing the causes of pollution (e.g., fossil-fuel propelled automobiles) has a nice ring to it. In the transition to the removal of causes (e.g., the change to solar energy) there is, however, a role for end-of-pipe remedies, unless Beck succeeds in putting everyone back up on a horse.

3. Unfortunately Beck (1992a: 231-5) puts all his hopes in the basket of self-criticism, and does not pay sufficient attention to the development of institutionalized means of environmental accounting upon which criticism by self and by others could be based and promoted.

4. By state socialism I am referring to the monopolization of power by the Communist Party in one-party states, such as in China and as existed across eastern Europe until the nineteen-nineties. Communist Parties and Socialist Parties operating under capitalism, under electoral democracy, and in a context where there is a press and an environmental movement independent of the dominant political party, are quite different phenomena. Except for this part of this chapter, which examines the ecological consequences of lack of accountability in one-party socialist states, the present book focuses on the capitalist variant of the planned exploitation of the natural environment.

8

Environmental Classes
and
Environmental Conflict

Recently the environment has become a popular subject of discourse. Reporters describe the state of the environment. Editors and journalists give their opinions concerning what should be done. Politicians talk about how much they are doing for the environment and will do. The environment has even become a theme used in commercials to promote the sale of commodities. Yet waste continues to be dumped into rivers, lakes and oceans and pumped into the atmosphere, accidents and wars that contribute to the degradation of the environment become more numerous and catastrophic, and the human population that the planet must support continues to climb. Communicative action has not yet led to substantive action to put an end to environmental degradation. Who is responsible for the continuing accumulation of this environmental debt, who are the beneficiaries, and who are its victims?

Environmental Classlessness?

"Until now Man has plundered, pillaged and polluted his planet with careless abandon, thinking only of his short-term gain" (Hamilton 1973: 262). The blame for planetary plunder, pillage and pollution is attributed in this way of thinking to generic Man, that is, spread over the entire human population. "'It's not industry that's out there taking the plastic ring off the six-pack [of beer] and dumping it in the ocean,' says the chief executive officer of Cominco Ltd., a Vancouver-based mining and smelting firm ... [whose] huge zinc smelter at Trail, B.C. emits 24 tonnes of sulphur a day into the air" (Southam 1989: 14). A constant refrain of corporate leaders is that all of society has benefited from and contributed to the exploitation of the environment, hence all of society is responsible for it, and all of society must clean up the mess. "'There is no one enemy out there. We are all part of the problem, and we all have to be part of the solution,' says Thomas d'Aquino, president of the Business Council on National Issues, a lobby organization for 150 of Canada's largest corporations" (Southam 1989: 15). Everyone is seen as answerable for environmental problems: not only entrepreneurs pursuing profits but also workers pursuing high-paying jobs and consumers pursuing low-cost, high-quality commodities.

According to this argument, consumption that was previously reserved for the privileged few has been made accessible to the masses, hence the masses because of their consumer demands are liable for the degradation of the natural environment. "The blame cannot be placed upon any small section of the community but belongs quite definitely to the main 'consumers', the proletariat. The more we proceed towards a fair division of the spoils the greater blame accrues to the 'common people'" (Alsopp 1972: 93). Environmental responsibility is proportional to the size of the group: the proletariat is more responsible for environmental degradation than entrepreneurs because workers are more numerous than capitalists.

Similarly, generic Man has been seen as the victim of environmental exploitation. "Whatever the consequences, Man can no longer escape. He is a prisoner of technology on a small planet of limited resources and limited capacity. He has to live with his wastes. ... It is unlikely that Man can adapt with sufficient rapidity" (Hamilton 1973: 265). Just as there is no differentiation of the contribution to environmental degradation nor of the benefits from it in this classless view of Man, so too there is no conception of differences in victimization resulting from such degradation.

As Albrow (1990: 224) points out concerning structures that regulate outcomes, Weber argued that all "individuals who orientate to them contribute to their continuity and change, even if it is an unthinking acquiescence to the *status quo*. ... everyone, as an individual, bears some modicum of responsibility, however small, for the maintenance and change of the structures in which they participate." But the key questions are: what is the contribution and how small, or how large, is the responsibility? Thus Weber held that "the possessor of power in a social relationship holds the vital resource for creating the conditions for communication, namely being able to define what is or is not a fact, in practice and in the daily experience of the parties" (Albrow 1990: 225).

Although everyone bears some modicum of responsibility for structures that degrade the environment and communication about them, the powerful bear a great deal more than the powerless.

Even though there is truth to the claim that most everyone as workers and consumers is responsible for environmental problems to some extent, the assumed homogeneity of responsibility in the above statements obscures crucial differences in contributions to, benefits from, and responsibility for environmental problems. It brackets out of view the origin of the vicious circle: "monopolistic control over resources can drive those who do not share in them to excessive exploitation of marginal resources" (World Commission on Environment and Development 1987: 48). It also ignores crucial differences in victimization. "When urban air quality deteriorates, the poor, in their more vulnerable areas, suffer more health damage than the rich, who usually live in more pristine neighbourhoods. When mineral resources become depleted, late-comers to the industrialization process lose the benefits of low-cost supplies" (World Commission on Environment and Development 1987: 49). Schnaiberg (1980: 337) argues that because of their powerlessness, the poor "who have suffered the most (both economically and ecologically) are most vulnerable to being saddled with future costs and minimal benefits." Schnaiberg (1975), Schnaiberg et al. (1986), Morrison (1976), Unseld et al. (1979), Hare (1981), and Bullard (1983, 1990) have shown the inequitable distribution of the consequences of environmental degradation and resource limitations among social strata and minority groups.

In his study of technological accidents, Perrow (1984) discovered that the air traffic system has had relatively few accidents whereas accidents abound in the marine freight transport system. The air traffic system has operators (pilots) and clients (business persons) with abundant resources who have forced the system to pay compensation through lawsuits, media campaigns, etc., and hence forced it to be safety conscious. The marine freight transport system has, on the contrary, impoverished operators (seamen) and anonymous and unpredictable victims (fishing villages, the ocean) and can hide the human and environmental damage more easily. "Systems that have high-status, articulate, and resource-endowed operators are more likely to have the externalities brought to public attention (thus pressuring the system elites) than those with low-status, inarticulate, and impoverished operator groups" (Perrow 1984: 341). Social class is significantly related to the functioning of systems of transportation, production, and distribution, and hence to environmental issues. Furthermore, many of the assumptions underlying the hypothesis of environmental classlessness -- for example, that the proletariat and the common people are the main consumers and that we have proceeded "towards a fair division of the spoils" -- are questionable, to say the least.

The 'we-are-all-sinners' discourse has always been used by big sinners to mask the disparity between themselves and little sinners. If everyone is responsible for degrading the environment, then no one in particular is accountable. If everyone is hurt equally, then there are no groups that could be referred to as victims. Such discourse camouflages the differences in contributions to environmental degradation, the differences in benefits accruing from that degradation, and the differences in environmental victimization. These differences would confirm the conclusion that the principal benefits of the exploitation of the natural environment have been appropriated by the few at the expense of the many.

The key question that must be uncovered from beneath the 'we-are-all-sinners' rhetoric is: which groups are the principal contributors to environmental exploitation and the main beneficiaries of it, which groups are lesser beneficiaries, and which groups are the principal victims? The focus on the shared responsibility of everyone has hidden the existence of environmental classes, that is, a social relationship (acting through nature) in which the environment has been exploited principally for the benefit of some humans at the expense of others. Responsibility for environmental problems is shared to a degree, but some are much more responsible than others.

Marx made visible one part of the invisible hand of the market by showing how the exploitation of workers at the point of production by capitalists is related to the accumulation of capital. Locked in step with this accumulation of capital by capitalists is the accumulation of unpaid labor. This division of society into classes with the exploitation of one by the other provokes class conflict between labor and capital. Thus the exploitation of workers, that is, unpaid labor, is in Marxian theory the *raison d'être* and basis of class conflict.

In Chapter 6, I attempted to make visible another part of the invisible hand of the market by showing how the unpaid waste cost of environmental degradation during the processes of production, circulation, use, and disposal of commodities is related to their price and to the accumulation of capital. Locked in step with the accumulation of capital by capitalists is a growing debt to the environment in the form of its degradation. Groups in society differ in terms of their contribution to, benefits from, or victimization by this double-edged cumulative process. The exploitation of the environment by one group to the detriment of other groups constitutes (1) the exploitation of the latter, and (2) the division of society into environmental classes. It provokes social conflict over their shared natural environment upon which all humans depend.

Environmental Classes Defined in Terms of
Social Conflict over the Environment?

The degradation of what has been called "the commons" (Hardin 1968) -- the human supporting natural environment -- is the basis of an emerging multi-faceted social conflict that takes place on many fronts: between polluting companies and environmentalists, between workers protecting jobs and conservationists attempting to keep the natural environment as it is, between loggers and indigenous peoples, between native trappers and fur boycotters, between oil transportation companies and fishing villages or tourist areas, between regulating bureaucrats and those affected by their regulations or lack of them, between politicians and those on both sides of the environmental question, and between developed and developing nations. As resources are depleted and waste accumulates, the resources and unspoiled environment that remain become all the more precious and the object of more bitter struggle. The temptation is great, therefore, to define environmental classes in the simplest possible way, namely, in terms of overtly conflicting groups.

Overt conflict over the environment does not, however, provide an accurate guide to contributors, beneficiaries, and victims of environmental degradation. The most seriously victimized are often not in a position to lead or even to participate in the struggle against their victimization. The most vociferous anti-environmentalists are frequently mere cheerleaders whose role is quite modest compared to the behind-the-scenes contributors to environmental problems. The principal beneficiaries are usually removed from the overt conflict and are absentee contributors to environmental degradation.[1]

For example, the directors of an oil company and the workers who clean their offices may both seek to protect their jobs by supporting oil companies and hence the burning of fossil fuels, yet the benefits they receive from the release of carbon dioxide into the atmosphere as well as the contributions they make to such pollution differ not only in degree but also in kind. Although the benefits workers earn from their polluting companies are crucial to the maintenance of their life style, they are microscopic compared to the benefits their employers appropriate. Unions of workers in environmentally degrading industries, such as forestry companies and coal mining companies, have joined with capitalists to oppose environmental protection for fear of losing their jobs, yet their benefits and their decision-making power to dispose of capital in an environmentally injurious manner can not be compared to that of the managers and controlling shareholders of the company that employs them.   Coalitions are formed in which employers and workers in polluting industries both support the continuation of environmental degradation, but they do so for very different reasons: one for substantial profit, the other for a subsistence salary. Focussing only on overtly conflicting groups obscures fundamental differences between allies in the struggle over the environment.

This can be expressed in motivational terms: the degradation of the environment can be motivated by either necessity or greed. Whereas alternatives must be provided to those acting out of necessity, reparations must be made by those acting out of greed. 'Workers against the environment' may make sensational press and a public relations bonanza for the companies that employ them, but it deflects attention away from groups with real power to determine the relationship between social action and the natural environment.

The side of environmental conflict a group appears to be on, concerning a particular issue at a particular moment in time, can be a misleading indicator of overall contribution to, benefits from, and victimization as a result of environmental exploitation. For example, fractions of classes that have benefitted the most from the accumulation of capital due to unpaid waste cost can, by lobbying for government incentives to promote environmental restoration, profit a second time by having taxpayers pay them to clean up the mess they themselves have created. This profit-oriented environmentalism can occur while the parent company has other branches still contributing to the degradation of the environment.

Subjective attitudes are also misleading indicators of contributions to, benefits from, and victimization as a result of the exploitation of the environment. Only the most foolhardy of capitalists can fail to perceive that it is against the long-term interests of their children and perhaps themselves to destroy the ozone layer, to contaminate oceans and the atmosphere through pollution, to accumulate radioactive and chemically toxic waste and to deplete natural resources at the present rate. Everyone has an interest in oxygen on Earth. Groups that have accumulated capital by damaging the environment, but have shifted to a more environmentally friendly stance, are prone to a posture of moral superiority toward subordinate groups (workers, minority groups, poor countries and poor regions within countries) that, because of their greater economic vulnerability, continue to support the maintenance of their jobs that damage the environment. Paradoxically, the latter groups are often the most victimized in the long run by environmental degradation because of local pollution and dangerous working conditions. The disdainful posture of the accumulators of capital towards others rings hollow as long as they have not paid their environmental debt upon which their accumulation of capital was partly based.

It is instructive to examine how Weber conceived of social class. Even though he is renowned for his emphasis on values, intentions, and conflict, Weber avoided defining class in terms of subjective attitudes or overt conflict, preferring instead a conception based on objective life chances.

> 'Class situation' means the typical probability of 1. procuring goods 2. gaining a position in life and 3. finding inner satisfactions, a probability which derives from the relative control over goods and skills and from their income-producing uses within a given economic order. 'Class' means all persons in the same class situation. ... A 'social class' makes up the totality of those class situations within which individual and generational mobility is easy and typical. (Weber 1978: 302)

This shared probability of benefits, and hence interests, deriving from the objective control (or its absence) of goods and skills is one of the elements, but only one, influencing class-conscious organization and conflict. Other elements include: (1) the immediacy of opponents, for example, workers see themselves as a class more easily vis-à-vis visible managers than vis-à-vis unseen stockholders; (2) the number of persons in a similar class situation; (3) the technical ease of organizing a class, for example, its concentration in a workshop community; and (4) the capacity of an intelligentsia from outside the class to propose to them understandable goals and thereby lead them (Weber 1978: 305).

Weber disentangled the objective probabilities of benefits and the control of goods and skills (that is class) from subjective attitudes and overt conflict so that the former could be used as a significant part (but only a part) of the explanation of the latter. Objective class position is an important basis of conflict, even when that conflict takes the overt form of struggle between religious groups (Northern Ireland), races (United States, South Africa), language groups (Canada), ethnic/national groups (USSR, Yugoslavia), etc., rather than the form of direct struggle between classes. Although class position is part of the explanation of consciousness and conflict, they cannot be reduced to class, nor class to consciousness and conflict. Class was not equated with consciousness and conflict by Weber so that, instead of degenerating to tautology, it could be one of the elements explaining consciousness and conflict.

Social practices are not limited to overtly conflictual relationships. They consist also of relationships of domination, appropriation, and victimization that do not appear as overt conflict but that shape the character of such conflict. Often the boundary lines of overt conflict give a false impression of victims, contributors, and beneficiaries. It is, none the less, the underlying dynamic of victimization, contribution to environmental degradation, and benefits from it that is the source of environmental problems and of social struggle concerning them. Hence an analysis of environmental classes must go beyond the battle lines to that underlying dynamic. Rather than conceiving of environmental classes in terms of conspicuously conflicting groups or groups with particular subjective attitudes, important as these are, it is better to conceive of them in terms of the structured relationships that lie beneath these manifest conflicts and attitudes.

The Natural Environment as a Medium of Interaction Between Contributors/Beneficiaries and Victims

Weber (1968: 303-4) also disentangled different dimensions of social class, namely, property classes determined by the monopolization of wealth and capital, and commercial classes determined by the monopolization of management and skills. In a similar fashion, another emerging dimension -- environmental classes -- can be distinguished by examining (1) differences in the power to manipulate nature and appropriate the benefits of such manipulation, and (2) differences in suffering the harmful effects of this manipulation. Environmental classes are based on the objective probabilities of benefiting from, contributing to, and victimization as a result of waste accumulation and environmental degradation, that is, they can be distinguished by perceiving the natural environment as a medium of interaction between contributors/ beneficiaries and victims of environmental degradation.[2]

Principal contributors to environmental degradation and beneficiaries from it on the one hand, and victims on the other, are involved in a social relationship, but it is not a simple one of face-to-face interaction. It is a social relationship at a distance, even in some cases distant in time, and the medium for the social relationship is the natural environment itself. The natural environment carries the social relationship between contributors to and victims of environmental degradation like space carries the gravitational relationship between the Sun and planet Earth. Both involve action at a distance. Just as money is a medium for a social relationship between the Japanese capitalist class in Tokyo and the Mexican working class laboring in a Toyota assembly plant in Mexico, so too the natural environment is a medium for a social relationship between environmental classes. "There was a rapidly emerging awareness that increased population, pollution, resource depletion, nuclear radiation, pesticide and chemical poisoning, the deterioration of the cities, the disappearance of wildlife and wilderness, decreases in the 'quality of life,' and continued economic growth and development under the rhetoric of 'progress' were biologically interrelated" (Sessions 1981: 392). The biological medium, and more generally the ecological medium, transmits a social relationship between environmental classes.

There are two variants of this social relationship. The first occurs when contributors and beneficiaries do not know or intend that anyone be victimized. Even in this case there is a social relationship because the actions of contributors and beneficiaries -- oriented to some goal, for example profit -- have as an objective consequence a harmful effect on victims. The shareholders and managers of Union Carbide did not intend the accident at Bhopal, but their pursuit of profit by their chosen means had as an objective consequence the victimization of the people living near the plant by a poisonous cloud of their toxic chemicals. The executives at Exxon did not intend to spill oil in Alaska, yet the system of transportation they organized in order to keep costs down spilled their oil into the ocean thereby degrading fishing grounds. Wind and air currents carried the unintended radioactive consequences from the centrally planned system of nuclear industrialization at Chernobyl to victims in other parts of the Ukraine, Byelorussia, Poland, Sweden, etc. Environmental accidents such as these are only the most spectacular occurrences of a more subtle and broader process of the victimization of some humans through the medium of the environment as a result of the planned pursuit of benefits by others. The routine emission of chemicals into the atmosphere through low-cost smokestacks has resulted in acid rain, which undermines the livelihood of those who live off lakes and forests. The routine disposal of waste in lakes and rivers has likewise contaminated drinking-water supplies and fish, with the victimization of people, such as indigenous peoples, who depend on those supplies. Future generations run the risk of becoming the principal victims as a result of the impending consequences of the accumulation of waste dumped on land, in water, and in the atmosphere.

Thus social action has unintended consequences (Weber 1930, 1958, 1978) and perverse effects (Boudon 1977). The pursuit of profit and production by one class has resulted in the accumulation of waste and the degradation of the environment, whether intended or not, and this has affected the life chances of other classes. The environment is the medium through which the class of contributors to and beneficiaries of environmental degradation exploits, even if they would never admit to such an intention, the class of environmental victims. The planet Earth is a global medium for the action of some humans on other humans. Toxic chemicals produced in Southern Canada, the United States, and even Europe have been found in the food eaten by the Inuit of the Arctic. Oil from ships flushed out using ocean water has polluted beaches and contaminated fish upon which the livelihood of people in fishing villages is based. The depletion of the ozone layer and the greenhouse effect provoked by one generation threaten to become burdens to be borne by the next.

The degradation of the natural environment constitutes not only the exploitation of nature, but also the exploitation of humans who depend on that environment. This is the answer to the question: how could there possibly be a social relationship between contributors/beneficiaries of environmental degradation and remote victims, especially those who do not even live at the same time? The unpaid waste cost (pollution) generated by the former but whose consequences have been left to be borne by the latter is, like unpaid labor in Marxian theory, the basis of a social relationship of exploitation. Whereas capital accumulation generated by the unpaid labor of workers constitutes direct exploitation, capital accumulation generated by unpaid waste cost to be borne by other humans constitutes indirect exploitation. The exploitation of the environment is an indirect form of exploitation of humans whose needs are not as well met by a degraded environment and/or who will have to pay the cost of reversing environmental degradation.

The second variant of the relationship mediated by the natural environment between contributors/beneficiaries and victims occurs when the harmful consequences are known but denied. This variant is much more prevalent than contributors/beneficiaries would have victims and potential victims believe. For example, in the nineteen-eighties polluting companies pushed the American government to fly in the face of the best available evidence on acid rain and to steadfastly refuse to enact legislation to diminish pollution. Similarly, cigarette companies did all in their power to camouflage the connection between smoking and lung cancer, as did asbestos companies concerning the dangers of asbestos. The most hazardous factories, which produce profits for their distant owners, are intentionally placed in poor areas, hence factory-produced environmental accidents, such as at Bhopal, have devastated the poor and left the wealthy hitherto untouched.

In addition, the medium of the natural environment propagates, as a result of social action, future expectations. Exxon's promises about the safety of oil transportation were proven false by the Exxon Valdez spill; the nuclear industry had its Chernobyl and Three Mile Island, the chemical industry its Bhopal, and so on. The consequences of the past action by enterprises and governments with respect to the natural environment, rather than their glossy words, have created a set of expectations in the population concerning the willingness and capacity of such organizations to enter into a symbiotic relationship with nature. Past consequences of social action have led the population to react in anticipation of similar future environmental degradation to be suffered by themselves, their offspring, and humanity in general.

In short, environmental classes can be defined by, on the one hand, their contribution to the degradation of the environment and accumulated benefits appropriated from this degradation, and on the other, the human victimization resulting from such environmental exploitation. Environmental classes consist of a relationship between humans in which some are victimized by the actions of others, and the basis of this victimization is the exploitation of their shared natural environment. The environment is the carrier or bearer of a social relationship between humans.

The Difficulty of Specifying Environmental Classes

Exploited environmental classes (indigenous peoples, victims of pollution and of environmental accidents), which Weber would have called negatively privileged, can be distinguished from positively privileged environmental classes (those who have built careers, acquired power, and amassed fortunes through the degradation of the environment). To a certain extent, however, the victims of environmental degradation also benefit from unpaid waste cost, for example, through jobs or lower prices for commodities, and the beneficiaries of unpaid waste cost are victimized by environmental exploitation, for example, they too must live in a degraded natural world. A sense of proportion must none the less be kept in mind. Some classes contribute to environmental exploitation and benefit from it a great deal more than others, and some are victimized by it much more than others.

A precise specification of environmental class boundaries would require an exact assessment of the environmental consequences resulting from the actions of particular groups, and an exact assessment of which group suffers those consequences. Although such an assessment could be done in principle, it is difficult in practice. This is especially because companies have not been required to measure and give annual accounting statements of the impact on the environment and on particular human groups of the operation of their production facilities and of the commodities they have unloaded on the market. The result is underdeveloped means to detect who does what to the environment, and ultimately to whom. Accounting has been developed only for capital and commodities, not for the impact of production on the natural environment and on the victims of environmental degradation. This limits the possibility of specifying environmental classes with precision.

Moreover, in most capitalist societies, government and virtually every enterprise have hitherto contributed to and/or benefitted from environmental degradation, albeit to different degrees. Many of today's environmentally friendly companies have been able to modernize their primitive technology because of their prior accumulation of capital using that wasteful and environmentally degrading technology. Other clean enterprises profit from relatively cheap inputs of energy and raw materials provided by dirty enterprises or by environmentally degrading state companies. Some have displaced the dirty part of their operations to developing countries, so that their remaining operations in modern capitalist countries are relatively benign to the environment. The pervasiveness among enterprises and state organizations of the short-term benefits of unpaid waste cost and of an accumulated environmental debt aggravates the problem of detecting environmental class differences. The connections among organizations and their directors also make it necessary to conceive of environmental classes not in terms of this or that particular factory, but globally.

As in so many areas of science, first approximations must be made as a starting point, with a view to refining the approximations as better methods are developed. The first approximation to environmental classes that follows is advanced in order to stimulate effort to develop better methods for the detection of the contribution to, benefits from, and victimization by environmental degradation. Distinctions between enterprises and between states in terms of their contribution to such degradation, like the "polarizations between capital and capital" referred to by Beck (1992b: 111), can be added later, as an improved second approximation, when the tools of accounting for waste and its effects become more refined and as enterprises and states that pay their accumulated environmental debt begin to differentiate themselves from enterprises and states that do not.

The Human Victims of Environmental Degradation

The main division between environmental classes is that between the principal contributors to environmental degradation and beneficiaries of it on the one hand, and their victims on the other. The victims are not, however, a homogeneous class. Four types of human victims of high technological accidents have been distinguished by Perrow (1984: 67-70) according to their participation in the organization. His valuable distinctions can serve as the departure point for the development of a first approximation to environmental classes on a more global level.

First-party victims are the operators of the factory, petrochemical plant, nuclear reactor, airplane, or oil tanker under consideration, ranging from those actually running the system to those in attendance on a regular shift, such as laborers and assisting personnel. They are most immediately affected by pollution or accidents, for example,

> 'jumpers' or the 'glow boys' in the nuclear industry, temporary help who dash into a radioactive area to make repair, will be hired for two or three weeks' work, at only six dollars an hour, even though they can receive high doses of radiation in the few minutes they are in the core. ... Textile workers are not compensated for brown lung disease, nor are chemical plant workers compensated for cancer showing up ten or twenty years after exposure. (Perrow 1984: 68)

First-party victims are also the ones most frequently blamed for accidents, in terms of 'operator error', by owners and managers seeking to avoid responsibility for failures of design, planning, and safety measures.

These first-party victims typically live in communities near the factory, and are victimized there as well. They and their families often have to live with polluted water and insalubrious air in their homes surrounding the factory. "Property values near a chemical plant are likely to be low because of odors, fumes, and fire and explosion risks. When an accident takes place, the damage to the environment is calculated in terms of values already depressed because of the accident potential" (Perrow 1984: 310).

Second-party victims are "those associated with the system as suppliers or users, but without influence over it. ... To some extent they 'choose' to participate in the system, and thus elect to share at least some of the risk" (Perrow 1984: 68). Examples are passengers on ships, trains, airlines, cars and buses that have accidents, and office personnel or truck drivers delivering goods when an explosion hits. Second-party victims get more and worse than they bargained for, but they do voluntarily accept risk to some extent by participating in the system.

Third-party victims are innocent bystanders who have no involvement in the system. Perrow (1984: 68) gives the following example: whereas airline passengers killed in a crash (second-party victims) accepted the risk of flying, innocent bystanders on the ground killed by the airliner's crash did not and are therefore third-party victims. Another example he gives is of people living downstream from dams that burst.

Fourth-party victims are fetuses and future generations. They include children stillborn or deformed because of exposure to radiation or toxic chemicals, people who will be contaminated in the future by residual substances that become concentrated as they move up the food chain, and those who must pay for their care.

Perrow (1984: 69-70) argues that "fourth-party victims potentially constitute the most serious class of victims. Chemical or radioactive contamination of land areas could have far-reaching effects upon the health of future generations. ... Future generations carry the burden; the present generation reaps whatever rewards there may be from the activity." His assessment becomes even more true when, along with high-technology accidents, routine pollution and waste dumping are taken into consideration. In the past when pollution was localized, first-party victims of pollution were the principal victims, with a few cases of second-party victims, very rare third-party victims, and no fourth-party victims. The accumulation and globalization of pollution have transformed third and especially fourth parties into potentially the most victimized in the modern world. The accumulation of capital through the exploitation of the environment and attendant accumulation of an unpaid environmental debt is resulting in new classes of human victim.

This valuable distinction between victims of high-technology accidents suggested by Perrow does none the less have a few weaknesses, and must be somewhat modified before it can be used for the analysis of environmental classes in general. For example, Perrow defines the distinction between first and second-party victims in terms of the former having some influence over the system not possessed by the latter. Laborers do not, however, have more influence over nuclear reactors, petrochemical plants, etc., than do deliverymen. Textile workers who developed brown lung disease and chemical plant workers who developed cancer had only a trivial influence over their textile and chemical plants. Rather than characterizing first-party victims as having influence over the system, it would be better to characterize them in terms of their participation as salaried workers. They receive benefits in terms of jobs, salaries, and pensions from the operation of the facility, and this is an important element shaping how they feel about its operation. The coal, oil, and automobile companies primarily responsible for carbon emissions into the atmosphere are among the major employers in many countries. Forest products companies so destructive of forests employ a significant proportion of the population in other countries.

Perrow's distinction between second and third-party victims is also imprecise. Passengers on ships that sink and planes that crash are users and, as such, second-party victims. But who are the second-party user-victims of nuclear reactors, petrochemical plants, dams, etc.? Are consumers of gas, oil, and electricity (produced by coal-burning generators, nuclear reactors and dams), as well as consumers of plastics produced by petrochemical plants, to be considered as users involved in the system as consumers and clients? I would argue that, in terms of a broadly based conception of environmental classes, they should be. Second-party victims are those victims who participate as users, consumers, or clients of environmentally degrading commodities, resources, or services, and as such stimulate demand for them. Their desire for an air-conditioned automobile to take them from their air-conditioned house to their air-conditioned office has resulted in the use of chlorofluorocarbons, which ultimately victimizes them, their offspring, and other humans by destroying the ozone layer. They are like cigarette smokers who get lung cancer, alcohol abusers who develop cirrhosis of the liver, and drug users who suffer drug-related problems in that their consumption practices contribute to their problems.

In Perrow's previously quoted illustration, the person on the ground hit by the crashing plane may have been a frequent flyer, thereby accepting the risks of flying more than the person on the plane making his or her first flight. People living downstream from dams that burst, unless they use no electricity, participate in the creation of the demand for energy sources such as dams. "Nuclear plants exist near all densely populated areas in the United States; there is simply no practical means to avoid being within 50 miles of one" (Perrow 1984: 68-9). Why? Because the people in those densely populated areas demand a cheap source of energy. They are in the line of fire because of their own consumption desires. Although consumers are indeed bystanders, their "innocence" is suspect. They are better perceived as second-party victims who stimulate a demand for the commodity or service that proves to be dangerous.

The distinction between second and third-party victims is best understood in terms of (1) users of environmentally degrading commodities or services and hence stimulators of the demand for their production and (2) non-users and hence truly innocent bystanders. People who fly are second-party victims of plane crashes; people who don't and who are hit on the ground by a crashing plane are third-party victims. People who use ozone-layer-destroying commodities are second-party victims; people who don't are third-party victims.

When applied to the social system as a whole, rather than to individuals or their communities, second-party victims are those who make high consumer demands on the environment, whereas third-party victims are those who make low consumer demands. There is a whole class of people who fall into the latter category of truly innocent bystanders: the aboriginal peoples and the poor in developed countries, and particularly the poor in developing nations. These third-party victims are unlike second-party victims in that their low patterns of consumption stimulate little demand for the production of commodities that damage the environment. These victims of environmental degradation are very different from the high consumers whose demands promote the production of waste and environmental degradation, even though the latter or their offspring will be victims too. The distinction between third and second-party victims can be used to capture this important difference.

Third-party victims -- innocent bystanders -- are also unlike first-party victims in that they do not receive the benefit of a job and salary from the production of environmentally degrading commodities. For example, Indians and Inuit have not been part of the proletariat laboring to produce surplus value in exchange for a wage. Profit and capital have, however, been accumulated as a result of unpaid waste cost at the expense of these groups through the degradation of their natural environment. A particularly tragic example of third-party victims was the Indian band of the Grassy Narrows Reserve in Canada, whose traditional fishing grounds were contaminated by the effluent from a paper mill and whose members were thereby poisoned by mercury-contaminated fish. They had neither the benefit of jobs in the mill nor that of the consumption of products of such mills. The same happened in Minamata, Japan, from which Minamata disease takes its name. The time has long passed since factory workers and their families living near the factory were the sole victims of industrial pollution. For example, the Inuit of the Arctic have been found to have levels of PCBs in their blood and in the milk of mothers five times higher than people in the industrialized temperate zones (The Ottawa Citizen 30 June 1991: E3). The PCBs were brought from those zones by air and water currents, then became concentrated in the Arctic food chain. Receiving neither jobs nor consumer comforts, the Arctic Inuit have been the innocent victims of the actions of the contributors to, and beneficiaries of, environmental degradation.

Present contributors to environmental degradation have reaped the benefits at an early stage of borrowing on the environment. Future generations (fourth-party victims) will live at a later stage of higher accumulated environmental debt and will be forced to bear the cost. "We borrow environmental capital from future generations with no intention or prospect of repaying. They may damn us for our spendthrift ways, but they can never collect on our debt to them. We act as we do because we can get away with it: future generations do not vote; they have no political or financial power; they cannot challenge our decisions" (World Commission on Environment and Development 1987: 8). The conflict of generations in the future risks being based, not just on some dubious psychoanalytic premise, but on laying waste by one generation to the natural environment needed by the next. Olsen et al. (1992: 75) have already documented that younger people hold ecological beliefs and values more extensively than their elders. Each generation is handing on its accumulated pollution, radioactive and toxic waste, its contribution to the depletion of the ozone layer, and its addition to the means of nuclear, chemical and biological warfare to the next generation. Each group and class, each nation, and especially each generation is therefore being judged more and more according to the question: is it passing on a planet more degraded than the one it inherited?[3] The struggle between generations over the environment increasingly revolves around the posing, the repression, and the answer to that question.

This conception of environmental victims brings into focus two new exploited classes, innocent bystanders (third-party victims) and future generations (fourth-party victims), which have come into existence as victims as a result of the cumulative unpaid waste cost and growing environmental debt. These two new exploited classes result from social relationships unique to environmental degradation. The accumulation of capital through the degradation of the environment has brought with it new classes of human victim.

Following Perrow (1984), by workers I am referring to workers in industries that degrade the environment. Workers in other industries who none the less consume environmentally harmful commodities are consumers as far as environmental degradation is concerned. First and second-party victims, that is, workers and consumers, are to some extent beneficiaries of environmental degradation and contributors to it, whereas third and fourth-party victims, namely, innocent bystanders and future generations, are not.[4] This fourfold distinction referring to the victims of environmental exploitation is at the same time an incomplete distinction between those who benefit from or contribute to such exploitation and those who do not. The distinction is incomplete because it only deals with minor beneficiaries and minor contributors. The principal beneficiaries and the principal contributors must also be brought into the picture.

The Principal Contributors to Environmental Degradation and Beneficiaries of It

The difference between the above victims on the one hand, and the principal contributors to environmental degradation and beneficiaries of it on the other, constitutes the main cleavage between environmental classes. The principal contributors to the accumulation of unpaid waste cost and environmental degradation are those committees (because almost without exception they involve bureaucracies, public or private) that decide to introduce products that degrade the environment or to use wasteful production processes. These principal contributors are typically among the principal beneficiaries. The consequences of their decisions consist in an accumulation of waste and a depletion of resources, hence a degradation of the natural environment in which the victims must live. Their decisions and actions to exploit the natural environment have unleashed unforeseen dynamics of nature that have led to perverse effects on the life-sustaining natural environment and on humans. Rare have been the occupants of these gatekeeper positions who have kept shut the gates to pollution in order to be good stewards of the natural environment. On the contrary, they have hitherto opened wide the pollution gates and thereby degraded the environment. Profits and bureaucratic careers have been tied to the accumulation of an environmental debt, which has victimized the aforementioned parties.

The Private Sector

In private companies the principal contributors in the above sense have been the top managers and major shareholders who hold controlling interest. It is they who determine or approve the way the accumulated capital of the enterprise will be used in the pursuit of profit. They are also the principal beneficiaries of the operation of the company, as measured in terms of capital gains, dividends, and/or salaries and fringe benefits (Poulantzas 1978; Wright 1976, 1977; Clement 1975, 1977; Domhoff 1967, 1970, 1972, 1979). Under capitalism, the private accumulation of profit and capital by corporations has been directly related to an increasing public debt in the form of pollution and resource depletion.

The principal contributors and beneficiaries of unpaid waste cost and environmental degradation include the top managers and controlling shareholders not only of polluting companies, but also of their assisting corporations. For example, bankers, trust company owners and managers, and financiers of all sorts contribute to the accumulating environmental debt and benefit from it by lending money to and investing capital in companies whose production processes and commodities degrade the environment. By failing to take the integrity of the natural environment into account in their key investment decisions, they have contributed to its degradation. In the light of the strong connections between companies, a good first approximation would be that, in the private sector, the capitalist class as a whole has hitherto been the principal contributor to the degradation of the natural environment and the principal beneficiary of it.

Owners and managers typically take credit for the success of their businesses, arguing that success results from their 'entrepreneurship.' Hence it is only logical that they take responsibility for the environmental consequences of that financial success. Parallel to the financial concept of 'entrepreneurship' (managing the operation of the company to attain a positive impact on the company's finances) is the environmental concept of 'stewardship' (managing the operation of the company to avoid a negative impact on the natural environment). Entrepreneurship has, however, not been coupled to stewardship in the training of entrepreneurs and managers in schools of business and administration. This lack of coupling has been particularly detrimental to the environment. Decisions have been made to produce and promote commodities without consideration of the harmful effect on the environment. The result has been a *de facto* negative coupling, whereby successful financial entrepreneurship has been attained through a neglect of environmental stewardship on the part of the principal contributors to environmental exploitation and principal beneficiaries of it.

As the cumulative effects of environmental pollution and resource depletion become increasingly severe, pressure is mounting on companies to pay for pollution control equipment and to pay the cost of restoring the environment they degraded. Corporations attempt to pass the cost on to the consumer. But that strategy runs the risk of commodity substitution: if the pollution-control cost of producing commodities is included in the price, consumers will substitute commodities that are intrinsically less polluting (e.g., grass instead of astroturf, leather rather than plastics). In order to avoid reducing their sales and profits, enterprises prefer to foist the environmental costs of their waste onto government to be paid by all, even by people who have had nothing to do with their commodities. If this strategy is successful, capital is accumulated privately whereas attendant waste cost is accumulated publicly to be paid by the state.

The State Sector

In the state sector as in the private sector, the principal contributors to environmental exploitation are those who set the agenda of environmentally injurious practices. In the state sector these key decision-makers consist of the top managers, administrators, and politicians. It is they who determine legislation and government policy. They are also among the principal beneficiaries within the state sector, as measured in terms of careers, salaries, fringe benefits, post-government consulting and post-government private directorships (Clement 1975).

States typically participate in environmental degradation in two ways. The first is by commission, by directly accumulating an unpaid environmental debt of their own. For example, most states pursue inexpensive sources of energy in order to give a competitive edge to enterprises producing within their borders. States have formed their own hydroelectric, nuclear, oil, and coal companies to make available an abundant and cheap source of energy in order to attract private enterprise. To the extent that this energy production results in the degradation of the environment -- through the accumulation of radioactive waste, the air pollution of coal-burning generators, and the methane released into the atmosphere by the massive flooding necessary for hydroelectric power generation -- it constitutes an unpaid environmental cost and part of the accumulating environmental debt. It is in part because this environmental cost goes unpaid that a saving is made and the supply of energy made available by the state to private enterprise is cheap. The proportion purchased by private enterprise indicates the proportion of the unpaid environmental cost that it profits from. Since the degree of profitability of these enterprises is directly related to access to this cheap source of energy, their profits, their accumulated capital, and the price of their commodities are connected to this unpaid environmental cost transferred to private enterprise by the state in order to attract them to operate within its borders. This is the energy path through which the degradation of the environment by the state is closely related to the accumulation of capital by private enterprises.

The second way states participate in the accumulation of an environmental debt is by omission, for example, by failing to ensure that private enterprises pay the environmental cost of their operations. Failure by governments to ensure that the environmental costs of commodities are included in their price -- if the environmental costs are ignored as in the past and in most cases the present, or if the government picks up the tab -- amounts to encouraging the consumption and production of environmentally injurious commodities. States that pay clean-up costs after the fact, instead of enacting laws ensuring that the full environmental cost of the production and use of commodities is included in the price, are subsidizing the degradation of the environment. "The division of labor thus leaves the industries with the primary decision-making power but *without* responsibility for side effects, while politics is assigned the task of democratically legitimating decisions it has *not* taken and of 'cushioning' technology's side effects" (Beck 1992a: 213).

An environmental debt has also been accumulated by the military apparatus of states and by other parapublic organizations. "Externalities [social costs] are found in both profit-making and governmental activities.

The Corps of Engineers is not a profit-making organization, but the possible externalities of dam failures are not included in the budget they request. The published figures on our weapons systems do not include money set aside for broken arrow accidents" (Perrow 1984: 341). The Persian Gulf war was an illustration of the cost to the environment of military conflict.

Nations that have accumulated the most capital are typically those that have run up the greatest environmental debt. Despite the concern about the potential destruction of the Latin American, Asian, and African rain forests, it is the European, North American, and Japanese countries that have savaged their forests and pumped the most carbon dioxide and other pollutants into the atmosphere, rivers, lakes, and oceans. It has been estimated that the industrialized world still dumps on an annual basis -- the cumulative proportion is probably even greater -- 80% of the carbon dioxide (the worse cause of the greenhouse effect) into the atmosphere of the planet (Southam 1989: 11) and that it generates about 90% of the world's hazardous wastes (World Commission on Environment and Development 1987: 226). Since the media of water and the atmosphere carry pollutants from one country to another, states that contribute to and benefit from environmentally damaging processes of production victimize other states.

Dominant classes and wealthy states have accumulated capital in part on the basis of unpaid environmental cost. Those who accumulated capital during the environmental *laissez-faire* and *laissez-aller* period are in an advantageous position even as rules are implemented to protect and restore the environment. Other classes and less developed states have now to compete without this accumulated capital resource and thus are placed at a disadvantage. For example, economically developed states, whose initial industrialization and accumulation of capital were based on the burning of coal, now claim that the world's atmosphere is too polluted for countries that are developing later to burn coal, such as China and India with their abundant coal resources. Developed countries have at least as much responsibility to pay their environmental debt, that is, to clean up the waste they have generated and left to accumulate on the planet, as developing countries have not to travel down the same wasteful path to development.

There have always been groups in society that do its dirty work and receive minor benefits, yet are looked down upon by those in positions of power who receive the principal benefits. In feudal society kings and popes could remove themselves from the mundane world and surround themselves with works of art and the spirit, while basking in material opulence. The dirty work of killing was done for them by soldiers, of commerce by merchants, of farming by peasants, etc. Similarly today, the future King of England and the Commonwealth speaks nice words about the environment, yet he and his Royal household have inherited a position of prestige and wealth based on the dirty work of past and present polluters. Small local companies that own and manage tire dumps do the dirty work for transnational tire corporations; whereas the latter accumulate the capital, the former receive the criticism. Computer companies and high-tech corporations tend to develop an environmental superiority complex with respect to companies in environmentally primitive, polluting sectors such as coal, oil, and nuclear energy. The former typically benefit none the less from environmentally degrading inputs, such as low-cost energy from dirty coal, oil, or nuclear sources. It is not just the owners and managers of polluting companies who are the principal beneficiaries of pollution. The latter also includes the arms-length principal beneficiaries of a polluting society that has laid waste to the environment. Hence the positively privileged environmental class closely parallels the positively privileged social class in today's society.

Environmental Classes and Environmental Conflict

Victimization as a result of the degradation of the environment has typically occurred in inverse proportion to the contribution to its exploitation and benefits received from that exploitation. This is because the benefits appropriated by not paying waste cost can be used to purchase the means to become somewhat less vulnerable to the consequences of environmental degradation, which is another feature of the 'polluter will profit' principle. The relationships of contributing to, benefiting from, and victimization as a result of environmental exploitation provoke conflict between environmental classes (or fractions thereof). The set of environmental class relationships described above constitutes a structured field within which conflict over the environment occurs. It is a field that has engendered not only the rise of the environmental movement as a reaction against potential victimization, but also the constraints it faces because of divisions among victims.

The organization and consciousness of environmental classes are problematic and are influenced by many contingent factors, notably economic booms and recessions, but it would be erroneous to perceive these classes as nothing but conceptual artifacts. They constitute instead aggregates facing particular dilemmas. Their relationships to each other and to the natural environment lead them to have specific predispositions toward environmental problems, which can result in the formation of cohesive associations. "While environmentalism is no more middle class than most moral protest movements and even many class movements, the dominant emphasis in this book is that some class-consciousness and class-action is necessary to change the production treadmill" (Schnaiberg 1980: 389-90).

Although the four classes of environmental victims are drawn together by their common environmental victimization, they tend to react to environmental issues in somewhat different but patterned ways. For example, third and fourth-party victims -- innocent bystanders (such as native peoples) and future generations (the closest approximation being the young) -- tend to be predisposed in favor of the ecological side of conflict over the environment. This is because they have not contributed to the degradation of the environment and have received few if any benefits from that degradation, yet are its victims or potential victims. The barriers that have excluded innocent bystanders, such as native peoples, from integration into the labor market and the consumption market have reinforced their status as innocent bystanders who resent being victimized by the degradation of their environment. It is only when they are beneficiaries of or contributors to the exploitation of the environment that they oppose environmentalists. Thus the principal exception to the support given by native peoples to the environmental movement has hitherto consisted of their participation in the fur trade. Their traditional practices of hunting, trapping, and exchanging furs have led them to part company with environmental groups on this issue. Young people are the closest approximations to future generations, and Olsen et al. (1992: 75) documented that "ecological beliefs, values, and the overall [ecological] paradigm are most extensively held by younger people." And not just by young people who are unprepared for modern technical, scientific society. Beck (1992a) argues that it "is predominantly young people *interested* in technology who see and speak of these hazards." In general, as society proceeds further along the cumulative environmental degradation curve, the classes of innocent bystanders and future generations are, in the light of the growing evidence of their potential victimization, increasingly drawn into the environmental movement and its struggle against environmental degradation.

Even when these two environmental classes are not organized as such and do not appear to have an environmental consciousness, environmental problems tend none the less to predispose them to particular practices. Large parts of the developing world, e.g. Haiti, are suffering severe environmental degradation (World Commission on Environment and Development 1987). The poor in these countries, who are largely innocent bystanders profiting little from jobs or consumer benefits that degrade the environment, are propelled into becoming ecological refugees under the guise of political refugees or economic migrants. In general, environmental degradation comparisons with developed countries have the potential to   aggravate North-South conflict on all fronts, led by the young and fed by the frustrations of the poor.

At an earlier stage of environmental degradation second-party victims, that is, consumers, enjoyed the benefits of not paying for pollution-control measures in the production of commodities, namely their low price. As the world proceeds further along that curve -- as accidental environmental catastrophes become more frequent, as acid rain, river, lake, and air pollution are experienced, and as forecasts of impending environmental problems come to be felt -- second-party victims are increasingly made aware that the short-term benefits of unpaid waste cost threaten to become outweighed by the harmful consequences of environmental degradation. Hence consumers are torn between their desire for cheap commodities maintaining a life style of mass consumption and their actual or potential victimization as a result of intensifying environmental degradation.

Of the four classes of principal victims, it is especially workers in polluting industries, first-party victims, who are anti-environmentalist, precisely because they fail to see why they should suffer the severest consequences of paying the environmental debt -- loss of their livelihood -- when they did not enjoy the greatest benefits from its accumulation. The way these workers earn their living is particularly vulnerable to being undermined by the need to stop environmental degradation, because their employers have failed to develop environmentally friendly production. Workers in companies that have degraded the environment tend to react as real groups defending their jobs when that livelihood appears to be threatened by the environmental movement. The threat of loss of jobs as a result of the need to protect and restore the environment and pay the environmental debt is the basis of an anti-environmentalist alliance (see Schnaiberg 1980: 372) that workers in polluting industries enter into with their employers: workers for jobs, managers and professionals for careers, and capitalists for profits. Beck (1992a: 53) formulates this principle as follows: "Risk consciousness and activism are more likely to occur where the direct pressure to make a living has been relaxed or broken."

Moreover, many of the potentially harmful consequences are not immediately and directly experienced. Some familiarity with scientific knowledge, through reading, listening to serious radio and television, or association with knowledgeable people, is required to be even aware of the dangers of DDT, PCBs, CFCs, formaldehyde, etc. Beck (1992a: 53) states this dependence on knowledge dramatically: "in class positions being determines consciousness, while in risk positions, conversely, *consciousness (knowledge) determines being*." Although Beck understates the effects of environmental experiences on consciousness, there is a tendency for those with less education to have less awareness of the long-term dangers that are invisible to the naked eye.

Yet these workers too are adversely affected by unpaid waste cost and its degradation of the environment. When the pollution of their local community becomes serious, especially as a result of environmental accidents, workers and their union attempt to push their employer to change to a cleaner, less primitive technology. Workers in polluting industries are, however, in a perilous position to attempt this, because if they push too hard they subsequently face threats from their employer of the loss of their livelihood. Workers in polluting factories are torn between their need for a job and salary, and their need for clean air, pure water, and the maintenance of a healthy environment for themselves and their families. They are attracted to environmentalism if and only if they do not have to bear more severe consequences to restore the environment than other groups.

Hence both first and second-party victims, workers in polluting industries and consumers, tend to be favorably disposed to technical fixes that promise to maintain their jobs and consumer benefits while diminishing their environmental risks. As the great difficulty of discovering technical fixes for cumulative environmental damage, which is global in scope, becomes increasingly evident, and as it becomes apparent that catastrophic accidents are the normal result of the use of complex and dangerous technologies (Perrow 1984), technical fixes come to be seen more and more as false promises. Thus conditions are developing that challenge consumers to modify their lifestyle by adapting it to the requirements of nature and that make workers more aware of the harmful effect of their production facilities on the natural environment. But the transformation from a salaried, consumer orientation to an ecological orientation is a difficult one, since consumers and workers are still attracted by the short-term consumer and salary benefits of unpaid waste cost.

This conception of a differentiated class of environmental victims brings out the complexity of social relationships involving environmental issues, with individuals being tugged in different directions by material needs and desires. First and second-party victims are in a position similar to what Wright (1976) referred to as a "contradictory class position." Workers in polluting industries are pulled in the opposite directions of their salaried job and the environment, and consumers are pulled between low prices and the environment. Conflict occurs not only between environmental classes, but also within the individual member of those classes. The division of society into environmental classes constitutes the basis upon which the struggle for consciousness and organization concerning environmental issues is waged. The environmental and ecological movement becomes an important mobilizing force in society to the extent that it (1) overcomes differences between victims (which means going beyond rather than ignoring them) by drawing attention to what is shared -- the victimization of these four environmental classes as a result of the degradation of their common environment -- and (2) draws attention to the principal contributors to that degradation and principal beneficiaries of it.

Beck (1992a: 91-102) argues that class consciousness is disappearing and is being replaced by individualization as a result of a rising standard of living, education, the welfare state, etc. He claims that class society is being transformed into the "risk society." His argument is, however, an oversimplification. Environmental risks produced by humans and knowable through science have emerged from class society. They modify that society, but do not dissolve it. Risk society remains a class society. Far from melting away, class influences the way risks are experienced. New environmental risks in turn reshape the way class is experienced. Environmental risks threaten to reduce the standard of living, to subvert the apparent democratization of consumption and styles of living, to diminish the accessibility of education, and to destroy fiscally the welfare state because belated payment of the environmental debt results in excessive payment and less money for other forms of welfare. Hence environmental risks undermine the affluent society, impede individualization, and throw people back to old solidarities (racial, ethnic, religious, gender, national and class identities) as well as create new ones. Although the privileged classes contributing most to environmental problems and benefiting most from environmental exploitation remain much the same, victims are no longer the homogeneous proletariat specified in Marxian theory. They are instead divided in terms of workers in polluting factories, consumers, innocent bystanders, and future generations. Battle lines in this emerging conflict depend on specific environmental problems, but general cleavages already making their appearance tend to consist of owners, managers, and workers in polluting factories against the young and native groups, with consumers deciding the issue through their response to consumer boycotts and parliamentary votes.

A social movement to protect the natural environment consists of the creation of an ecological coalition that is militantly against its victimization or potential victimization. It struggles through Green political parties to transform the environmentally degrading processes that threaten to victimize it. It pushes science and technology in the direction of developing new accounting procedures to document pollution and the effect of pollution on the environment (Greenpeace,

Pollution Probe). This militant environmental alliance has come into existence and has tended to grow as society has proceeded up the cumulative curve of unpaid waste cost and environmental degradation, that is, as cases of victimization through environmental accidents, pollution, etc., have become more numerous and as the potential for further victimization increases.

The principal opponents of environmentalism and the ecological movement consist of the principal contributors to the accumulation of an environmental debt and principal beneficiaries of it, especially the owners and managers of companies and administrators of state organizations that degrade the environment or assist in environmental degradation. They have not paid their waste cost and have lobbied governments to maintain lax laws permitting them to continue to pollute long after the harmful environmental consequences of their operations have been pointed out. They also refuse to pay reparations for, or even to see, the connection between their present accumulated capital and their past pollution practices. Is it possible, from this present social field of environmental classes, to go beyond the parasitic degradation of the natural environment to a symbiotic relationship with nature? That important question will be examined in the next section.

Notes

1. See Murphy (1988: Chapters 6 and 7) for a more general discussion of these issues with respect to social class and power.

2. The Weberian conception of social class refers to overall life chances, which is shaped by private property and commercial practices under capitalism, as well as by status-group forms of monopolization based on race, ethnicity, gender, nationality, etc. (see Murphy 1987). I am arguing that the medium of the environment carries another element influencing overall life chances, increasingly so as the accumulation of waste, depletion of resources, and degradation of the human-supporting natural environment make themselves felt. Thus environmental classes constitute an emerging additional dimension of overall social class, not an alternative to it.

3. The French translator of Barry Commoner's *Science and Survival* chose that central question as the French title for Commoner's book: *Quelle terre laisserons-nous à nos enfants?*

4. The tiny fraction of people in future generations who will inherit the accumulated capital of their wealthy but waste-producing forebears will be among the principal beneficiaries, but they will also live during

a period of greater accumulated waste and environmental debt, and hence at a time of more severe environmental crisis.

PART THREE

Toward a Symbiotic Relationship with Nature

9

Science and Applied Science as Partial Knowledge

The legitimacy of science and applied science in the eyes of the population has been based in large part on the successful manipulation and promised mastery of nature. "For centuries, it has been argued that science deserves support because of the promethean gifts it brings to mankind" (Merton 1977: 109). Abstract theories that cannot be understood by non-scientists appear to be proven by their technological applications in a way that can be understood by everyone. "Readiness to accept the authority of science rests, to a considerable extent, upon its daily demonstrations of power" (Merton 1968: 597).

The manipulation of nature by means of science and technology has transformed the relationship between it and humans.

> Tribes could remain in equilibrium with their habitat only so long as their curiosity did not come up with a new way of exploiting their natural world. But when they did, the equilibrium was bound to be broken. This is what distinguishes human ecology from that of any other species. From the moment we discovered fire we have been breaking through each successive state of ecological equilibrium. (Ignatieff 1992)

As Polanyi (1992: 133), winner of the Nobel Prize for chemistry in 1986, argues, the rate of breakthrough has accelerated because of scientific development. "The Renaissance represented a modest transformation compared with that which science and technology have brought about in recent decades. We scientists [are] in the center of the cultural stream that is presently reshaping the global landscape."

The global consequences of scientific relandscaping have not, however, been only positive. As the manipulation of nature led to the increasing degradation of the natural environment and as mastery proved in an ecological sense to be the pursuit of a mirage, science and applied science have begun to appear more and more illegitimate. The threatening consequences of science and technology have undermined the credibility of not only scientists but also the endeavor they are engaged in and its institutions. What humans have done to their natural environment by means of science and applied science has provoked the growing criticism of those means as the ultimate source of environmental problems. If science accepts credit for the achievements of applied science, then science must accept blame for the harmful consequences of its development. Scientists have, unfortunately, shown little consciousness of the risks they have produced.

> The origin of risk consciousness in highly industrialized civilization is truly not a page of honor in the history of (natural) scientists. It came into being against a continuing barrage of scientific denial, and is still suppressed by it. To this day the majority of the scientists sympathize with the other side. Science has *become the protector of a global contamination of people and nature*. In that respect, it is no exaggeration to say that in the way they deal with risks in many areas, the sciences *have squandered until further notice their historic reputation for rationality*. (Beck 1992a: 70)

Thus Polanyi (1992: 130) worries that young people are turning against science and attempting to terminate or slow down the whole enterprise of science. "And that seems like a very sad response to our predicament. Human dignity is ill-served by the wearing of a blindfold." Environmental problems have added a new dimension to the debate about science initiated by the development of weapons of mass destruction and of automation-engendered unemployment, a debate that has been framed in terms of science: for or against?

Capitalism and state socialism are both different from traditional societies because of their development and use of science and technology. These have been the means by which the mass consumption explosion under capitalism, the attempted industrialization under state socialism, and the human population explosion in the Third World have been produced. Are science and applied science therefore the operative elements common to both capitalism and state socialism that are responsible for environmental degradation, and does a symbiotic relationship with nature require their eradication? In examining how the parasitic relationship between human rationality and the processes of nature can be transformed into a symbiotic one, it is crucial to analyze the role of science and applied science.

The Specificity of Science and Applied Science

What is science? The predominant conception of science has been one of impartial, objective knowledge of nature accumulated by disinterested scientists (Braithwaite 1953; Popper 1960, 1963; Giere 1988). In this view as enunciated by scientists themselves, the bottom line of science and built-in check on its validity is its "success in uncovering the truth. In addition to that, it involves uncovering the most powerful truths in the minimum time with the expenditure of the least possible amount of money. ... Real criteria of effectiveness exist and are applied. The staggering achievements of science in the present century attest to the reality of these criteria" (Polanyi 1992: 128). Attempts to direct science have failed because the "questioning mind requires the freedom to pursue the truth wherever it leads. ... we can only compromise success by adding extraneous criteria of choice derived from seat-of-the-pants judgements about the ultimate utility and beneficence of understanding that is yet to be achieved" (Polanyi 1992: 128-9).

This conception of science as the discovery of factual knowledge has been associated with an image of science as conflictless and interest-free and with a distinction between science as the reflection of nature versus ideology as a distorted representation of reality resulting from the interests of dominant groups (Mitisavljevic 1978: 315; see also Woolgar 1983). "There may be something here of the sentiment that science remains the more pure and unsullied if it is implicitly conceived as developing in a social vacuum" (Merton 1968: 586).[1] What scientists do, if they "can steal a sufficient degree of freedom, is to pick those discoveries of the largest size, secure in the belief that they will put the greatest power into mankind's hands" (Polanyi 1992: 129). No thought is given to which hands, of all the hands of "mankind," the power goes. Scientists absolve themselves of the issue of the constructive or destructive consequences of that power by distinguishing sharply between pure and applied science. "Whether, as a society or a species, we use that power ill or well is a separate question" (Polanyi 1992: 129). Beck captures nicely the way in which the initiators of change deny responsibility for it: "Businessmen and scientists, who occupy themselves in their everyday work with plans for the revolutionary overthrow of the present social order, insist with the innocent face of objectivity that they are not responsible for any of the issues decided in these plans" (Beck 1992a: 224)

In reaction to this conception, contemporary studies in the sociology of science have drawn attention to the way scientific knowledge is *socially* constructed and to the relative rather than absolute character of that knowledge (Ashmore 1988, 1989; Chubin 1981; H. M. Collins 1975, 1981a,

1981b, 1981c, 1982, 1985; H. M. Collins and Cox 1976, 1977; H. M. Collins and Pinch 1979, 1982; Barnes 1974, 1977; Cooley 1976; Fleck 1979; Garfinkel 1967, 1982; Garfinkel, Lynch, and Livingston 1981; Gieryn 1982; Knorr 1977; Knorr-Cetina 1981, 1982; Knorr-Cetina and Mulkay 1983; Latour 1987; Latour and Woolgar 1979; Laudan 1982; Law 1977; Lynch 1982a, 1982b; Mulkay 1979, 1980, 1985; Mulkay and Gilbert 1982, 1984; Nowotny 1973; Pfohl 1977; Pickering 1980; Shapin 1982; Travis 1981; Wallis 1979; Woolgar 1988a, 1988b).

In their attempt to emphasize the social construction of reality, many of these studies in the sociology of science have tended to obscure the dynamic processes of nature that underlie science: "the natural world has a small or non-existent role in the construction of scientific knowledge" (H. M. Collins 1981b: 3). The thrust of their argument is "that scientific knowledge originates in the social world *rather than* the natural world" (Woolgar 1983: 244). Some of these studies even claim that, instead of capturing the real world of nature, science produces real consequences only because people believe the fictional accounts of scientists. "Constructivists claim that 'reality' is a fabric of fictions and narratives, and that the most convincing fictions such as natural science produce 'reality effects'" (Kelly 1990: 302). In his critique, Trigger (1989: 786-7) demonstrates that this social constructivist theory of science dissolves into hyperrelativism that "takes the form of arguing that science cannot be objectively distinguished from magic and other forms of popular belief."[2]

Science and applied science are not just arbitrary social constructions under the guise of usefulness (see also Baber 1992). What arbitrariness there is resides in the goals determining their development and use, not in whether they are useful means to attaining those goals. The convenience of microwave ovens and the prestige of being a nuclear superpower are arbitrary goals, but knowledge of physics is a necessary means to attaining those goals. Conceiving of science and technology as social constructions like magic has obscured the difference between factual and spurious knowledge of nature. It has led to an underestimation of the importance of science and its applications, as well as of their danger, and to a misunderstanding of their power as monopolizable resources. To conceive of science and applied science as ideology is, paradoxically, to ignore the basis that enables them to function ideologically. Thus Biehl (1991: 113) argues that "physical science is quite simply true in its own sphere of competence." It is a circumscribed truth upon which the imperialistic ideology of 'scientism' has been constructed.

Although the social constructivist approach initially showed promise as a welcome corrective to the one-sidedness of the previous conception of science as impartial, it has degenerated into a one-sided conception of its own, but from the other side. For example, Woolgar (1983: 252) perceives "a recurrent refrain in the social study of science: there is nothing in nature itself which gives rise to accounts of nature." The sociological representation of science as a social construction has tended to obscure the discovery of the properties of nature and the effect such discovery has on social action, to ignore that nature itself is a crucial element in the scientific determination of what will be taken as factual knowledge, and to gloss over the manipulation of nature and attendant environmental repercussions.

The constructivist approach has had a pernicious effect on the sociology of environmental issues, leading some authors (Fox 1991, Buttel and Taylor 1992) to play down human-induced changes in the natural environment and the effect these have on social relationships, which in turn unintentionally props up an anti-environmental ideology (see the critique by Dunlap and Catton 1993b: 11). Lack of perfect consensus is characteristic of "frontier knowledge" (Cole 1992) in science, and much of scientific ecology is at the frontier. Constructivists, like polluting entrepreneurs, have all too often used lack of perfect consensus among scientists to blind readers to the difference between assertions that are more plausible and those that are less plausible according to the weight of the available evidence, and blind them to the difference between ecologically prudent and ecologically reckless activity.

Although Weber emphasized the importance of social constructions, he did not lose sight of the autonomy of nature and the material world. "They can be shaped and interpreted by reason, but their source is from elsewhere" (Albrow 1990: 125). Science is not just any social construction, rather its specificity consists in learning about natural processes. It is a social construction having a peculiarly crucial relationship with nature, in fact, it is grounded in nature. The unique learning curve of science gives it its utility, and also its danger. "It is only since science has learned to replicate complex physical, chemical, and biological processes in the laboratory that its actions have been so consequential for the eco-system" (Perrow 1984: 296).

It is important to develop a conception of science and applied science that does not reduce them to either pure reflections of nature or to pure social constructions like any other (Benton 1991, Dunlap and Catton 1993b, Cole 1992), that is, it is important to capture their specificity. Science and applied science are the means by which distinctive relationships between the social system and the natural system are established. In this holistic conception, social factors would be seen as mediating between the processes of nature and scientific knowledge such that science is the result of the interaction between social action and the dynamics of nature.

Science does not consist of fixed knowledge, but of a rough-and-ready struggle to determine what will provisionally be taken as factual knowledge. The struggle over the discovery of the structure of DNA (Watson 1968) was a good illustration of the usually more routine conflict over the development of scientific knowledge. The controversy concerning cold fusion was an even more sensational illustration. The relationship between nature and science is mediated by the interests of dominant groups, as shown by the directions in which science is promoted through public and private funding of science. Strategic funding decisions are typically based more on goals of military power, national prestige, and profitability than on the search for truth. Even pure science is often funded in proportion to hoped-for applications. Not only the use to which science is put, but also the particular branch of pure science selected for development by the wider society and the level of support provided are related to values, interests, and power in that society and of that society. These social factors influence the formation of conceptions of nature, including the scientific conception, and steer the technological manipulation of nature. They intervene between the processes of nature and scientific description and theory.

There is none the less a structural dynamic to the development of science and applied science in which the discovery of certain phenomena and their applications facilitate the discovery of further phenomena and further applications. Science and applied science are important resources in the struggle to monopolize power and privilege precisely because of their utility in monitoring and manipulating nature. "The physical sciences are able to predict transformations of matter and energy in a precise, quantified manner and have been able to construct increasingly elaborate theoretical structures that have the capacity to transform humanity's relations to the natural world to a substantial degree" (Trigger 1989: 787). A conception of science and applied science as partial knowledge would, without assuming their impartiality, capture their specificity as formidable yet dangerous resources of empowerment.

Science and Applied Science as Partial Knowledge

Science and applied science are based neither on impartial, disinterested knowledge nor on social constructions like any other. Science and its applications are social constructions the specificity of which involves the discovery and accumulation of a potentially utilitarian knowledge of nature and the development of the capacity to manipulate nature. A concept that takes into account the quality of science and applied science as social constructions, yet does not obscure their quality as factual knowledge of nature, is the concept of partial knowledge. Science and applied science are partial in two senses.

(1) Incompleteness

Science is an incomplete form of knowledge: what is known consists of only a part of the processes of nature. The very notion of discovery attests to the incompleteness of scientific knowledge. So does the typical result that the more scientists learn, the more they find other puzzles they had previously ignored, which reinforces the conclusion of the immenseness of what remains to be learned. "The empirical and provisional basis of scientific knowledge -- its apparent strength -- can readily be re-formulated as an *uncertain* basis" (Yearley 1991: 137).

Ecological science is an area where uncertainty (Cramer 1987), "factlessness" (Yearley 1991, 1992), very imperfect understanding and technical difficulty of monitoring nature (Nicholson 1987: 54) are all too apparent. Scientists have not been able to balance their carbon dioxide spreadsheets: more is emitted than they can find and they do not know where it is going (Pearce 1989). Knowledge about the consequences of production facilities on large-scale ecosystems, particularly the long-term consequences of waste accumulation in the environment, is even more incomplete than knowledge about the workings of specific nuclear and chemical plants: "the chains of interrelationships in an ecosystem are so complex that the results of such studies [environmental impact studies] are usually tentative and inconclusive" (Devall and Sessions 1985: 135). The unexpected and poorly understood coupling between human-made systems and very complex natural systems, such as between automobile emissions and the atmosphere, can and does lead to eco-system degradation. The President of the U.S. National Academy of Sciences admitted that for "many of these troubling transformations, data and analyses are fragmentary, scientific understanding is incomplete, and long-term implications are unknown" (quoted in Silver and DeFries 1990: iii).

Applied science also constitutes incomplete knowledge. Thus Perrow (1984) argues that complex technological processes, such as nuclear reactors, chemical transformations, space missions, and recombinant DNA, as well as the iron and steel production of the past, are only partly understood leading to what he calls "normal accidents": "recall that the nuclear scientist who advised Governor Thornburg of Pennsylvania during the accident [Three Mile Island] had asserted three years before in a scientific journal that there could be no problem with a zirconium water reaction -- the process was well understood. Yet precisely this problem produced the hydrogen bubble" (Perrow 1984: 85). These applications of science "were often discovered through trial and error, and what passes for understanding is really only a description of something that works" (Perrow 1984: 85; see also 119).

The knowledge of some of the workings of nature and the resulting capacity to manipulate it is a central resource in social constructions and negotiations. But that knowledge is incomplete, fallible (Yearley 1991: 132), and runs up against its own contradictions. Partial knowledge enables advances in technology to occur, but it also makes possible technological mishaps, even catastrophes. "The frequency of unintended interventions in the eco-system are likely to increase as the keys to more natural processes are discovered" (Perrow 1984: 296).

> When the century began, neither human numbers nor technology had the power to radically alter planetary systems. As the century closes, not only do vastly increased human numbers and their activities have that power, but major, unintended changes are occurring in the atmosphere, in soils, in waters, among plants and animals, and in the relationships among all of these. The rate of change is outstripping the ability of scientific disciplines and our current capabilities to assess and advise." (World Commission on Environment and Development 1987: 343)

Thus Beck argues that techno-scientific development must not be encumbered with the insupportable burden of infallibility. Instead it must be based on an alternative hypothesis confirmed many times over: *"that of the entrapment of human thought and action in mistakes and errors"* (Beck 1992a: 177).

(2) Favoring Some More Than Others

The part of knowledge that is selected for further scientific development, for technologies of production and destruction (war), and that constitutes the basis of formal educational credentials, is chosen according to the dominant predispositions and "habitus" (Bourdieu 1977) in society that is itself shaped by the interests and ideologies of dominant classes. "Apparently 'objective' knowledge is often only partial knowledge, meaning structures that come from and legitimate the most powerful elements of a society" (Apple 1977: 111). Even Merton (1968: 589), who is not usually seen as questioning the impartiality of science, argued that there is "not the least paradox in finding that even so rational an activity as scientific research is grounded on non-rational values."

Many illustrations can be given of the partiality of applied science in this second sense. "There is no technological imperative that says we *must* have power or weapons from nuclear fission or fusion, or that we *must* create and loose upon the earth organisms that will devour our oil spills. We could reach for, and grasp, solar power or safe coal-fired plants, and the safe ship designs and industry controls that would virtually eliminate oil spills" (Perrow 1984: 11). Elites holding power in society have steered the development of applied science according to their own interests, for example, towards nuclear reactors and dangerous chemical transformations: "elites have decided on highly risky technologies that will inevitably have system accidents. ... People -- elites -- *decide* that certain technological possibilities are to be financed and put into place" (Perrow 1984: 339). For example, "the military value [of aviation] was quickly seen, as Europe prepared for war. By 1913, just ten years from the first powered flight, France had 1,400 military airplanes, Germany 1,000, Great Britain 400, and even Russia had 800. The United States, which was not preparing for a war, continued to lag, with only 23" (Perrow 1984: 125). The geneticist Suzuki (1990) argues that the Human Genome Project to decode the exact sequence of DNA will be oriented toward recovering its huge cost, hence toward applications based on market principles of capacity to pay. Schnaiberg (1980: 301) concludes that "it is virtually impossible to carry out research by recruiting petroleum engineers with *no* ties to the oil industry" and that "an oil company releasing a top petroleum scientist or engineer [for blue-ribbon, public-interest committees] anticipates that energy-research policies arising from participation will diminish environmentalist pressures and provide incentives for energy production" Schnaiberg (1980: 281). Scientific studies that imply criticism of products face serious publishing problems that discourage further studies. For example, Graham (1970) has documented the threatened lawsuits the publisher of Rachel Carson's book, *Silent Spring*, faced from the agrichemical industry and even the threatened withdrawal of advertising faced by journals publishing favorable reviews of it. "Dismissal, demotion, and sustained attacks on 'scientific integrity' help maintain such structured ignorance" (Schnaiberg 1980: 290).

Research and development tend to be focussed on projects in line with the interests of countries and corporations that finance it.

> The technologies of industrial countries are not always suited or easily adaptable to the socio-economic and environmental conditions of developing countries. To compound the problem, the bulk of world research and development addresses few of the pressing issues facing these countries, such as arid-land agriculture or the control of tropical diseases. ... Most technological research by commercial organizations is devoted to product and process innovations that have market value. Technologies are needed that produce 'social goods', such as improved air

quality or increased product life, or that resolve problems normally outside the cost calculus of individual enterprises, such as the external costs of pollution or waste disposal. (World Commission on Environment and Development 1987: 60)

When knowledge is incomplete, gaps tend to be filled according to interests and ideologies. For example, ecologists "felt pressed to come up with clear answers. ... They achieved this by evaluative steps which were largely coloured by political and ideological premises" (Cramer 1987: 62).

On the surface one might think that, although applied science is partial in this second sense, pure science is not: it is pure. Differences between pure science and applied science must not, however, obscure a fundamental similarity between them. They are both social constructions influenced by values, interests, and power in society. Although pure science may be, in principle, less partial in terms of favoring some interests more than others, it does not attain impartiality either.

Pure science has been an essential element in the construction of applied knowledge slanted in particular directions in that, without pure science, there would be no applied science. Without research on the atom, there would have been no atomic bomb dropped on Hiroshima or Nagasaki. The development of science has hitherto had, through technological applications, the consequence of manipulating and degrading nature rather than adapting to it. Pure science is a prerequisite for applications that are oriented in terms of society's values, interests, and power.

Pure science is also slanted in particular directions in the still stronger sense of its own development: "science itself is variously dependent on the social structure. ... there was first the emergence of Nazi Germany with its dramatic impact upon the nature, quality, and direction of the science cultivated in that country" (Merton 1968: 586). Even pure science is steered by society through funding decisions, with society (or more precisely those in positions of power) more favorably inclined to some scientific research than to others (Benton 1991: 16-8). For example, the possibility of developing nuclear weapons promoted the development of nuclear physics, and in general, the arms race has been a crucible of scientific discovery oriented according to military priorities (Hamilton 1973). The potential of weapons in space (as well as national prestige) during the Cold War between the USSR and the USA acted as a catalyst to channel funds to NASA and promoted scientific research slanted toward the discovery of knowledge about space. It was this, rather than the goal of confirming the intriguing Big Bang theory of the origin of the universe, that had the side effect of confirming that cosmological theory (tentatively at the time this is being written). "Even a limited roster of scientists expressly linking part of their scientific work to military applications would include the most illustrious names in the annals of science" (Merton 1977: 110). The lucrative potential of DNA research has pushed the development of biology and chemistry in that direction. Powerful enterprises and states promote scientific research in directions they judge strategic to their interests through their laboratories and funding policies. Schnaiberg (1980: Chapter 6) argues that our socioeconomic system has hitherto emphasized "production science" to the detriment of "impact science." Heims (1991) has documented how research on the practical problem of developing automatic weapons led to more fundamental research on cybernetics, thereby demonstrating a spiral relationship and cross-fertilization between fundamental and practical research rather than a one-way flow from pure to applied science.

The often ill-formed boundary between science and applied science as well as the partiality of their development in both senses -- incomplete and directed in the interests of dominant groups (corporations, states, professions) that have power over their development -- are well illustrated by recombinant DNA research. Attempts are being made to patent genetic material that seems to control the development of the human brain, even though the functions in a more precise sense of those DNA fragments remain unknown. Individuals and companies are also in a race to monopolize through patents hitherto unknown forms of life that can be produced as a result of discoveries in genetics, without knowing in any complete way what those forms of life really do.

> The potentials here for human benefit appear to be more extraordinary than all the other technologies put together. The potentials for human disaster are equally unprecedented, and rival that of nuclear holocaust -- if there can be a question of rivals where extinction is involved. With breakneck speed we (that is, primarily the oil companies) are proceeding down a thoroughly unknown path without brakes, without headlights, in search of undreamed amounts of private profits. (Perrow 1984: 258)

The peculiarly intimate relationship between science and nature has become increasingly coupled to the capitalist market and bureaucratic organization. In the past, scientific discovery meant intellectual excitement and personal recognition. Now more and more it also means lucrative prizes, patents and commercial development. Extrinsic monetary incentives for scientific discovery are overwhelming intrinsic incentives and are steering research in particular directions. Perrow's conclusion regarding DNA research is true for a growing number of scientific fields. "The rush to develop the field may have less to do with the intellectual excitement of the subject matter than with the incredible economic incentives that are now apparent. It appears that research in the field is more and more coming to be perceived as an economic competition rather than a scientific one" (Perrow 1984: 302). In her study of AIDS research, Haritos (1993) refers to this distinction as "salesmen or entrepreneurs of science" selling a product linked to royalties and patents as opposed to "scholars of science" pursuing the truth.

The purity of pure science is suspect. The idealized notion of pure science does not fit the reality of its development. Even the development of pure science is context driven. The partial science thereby elaborated is only a part of the knowledge that could have been sought and is partial to the interests of particular groups. It may or may not benefit other groups. It is, none the less, factual knowledge of nature.

These two aspects of the partiality of scientific knowledge are at times linked together so that dominant groups can profit from the incompleteness of scientific knowledge, particularly concerning ecological matters: "the authorities used the lack of certain knowledge that acid rain (and in particular British acid rain) was responsible for the death of trees and the acidification of lakes in Europe as a justification for continuing with power station emissions" (Yearley 1991: 139). Beck (1992a: 59) concludes that "sometimes with the clear conscience of 'pure scientific method', sometimes with increasing pangs of guilt -- the sciences become the *legitimating patrons* of a global industrial pollution and contamination of air, water, foodstuffs, etc."

The Double Determination of Science and Applied Science

Conceptions that perceive science and applied science as *either* impartial factual observations of nature (and discovery of the principles governing nature) *or* social constructions grounded in values, interests, and power are conceptions based on a false opposition, regardless which side of the dichotomy one claims allegiance to. Science and applied science are social constructions the specificity of which is the discovery of factual phenomena and explanatory principles concerning the natural world, hence they constitute the development of the capacity to understand, monitor, and manipulate nature. The facts and principles are, however, partial in both of the above senses. The discoveries of science and applied science are mediated by values, interests, and power, but they are discoveries of nature's processes none the less.

The ideas of science and applied science have an internal sequence of development based on the characteristics of nature, but the particular paths in that sequence chosen for further development result from social dynamics external to science and applied science. Science and applied science are underdetermined by logic and evidence, but they are also underdetermined by ideological influences. The content of science and applied science is not determined solely by nature's dynamics nor solely by social processes. Rather it is doubly determined: by external social powers that select and direct it, and internally by the characteristics of the natural world that is the object of study. Their development cannot be reduced to a social construction unrelated to nature, which distinguishes it from other social constructions, nor can it be reduced to pure impartial knowledge of nature. This is summarized by stating that science and applied science constitute partial knowledge.[3] The ecological consequence of this partiality is that "the ecological impact of human reason, science, and technology depends enormously on the type of society in which these forces are shaped and employed" (Bookchin 1991: 32).

Empowerment by Means of Science and Applied Science

Science and applied science are social and intellectual constructions whose relationship to nature is very different from traditional constructions of religion, magic, parapsychology, etc. Science and its applications have a factual relationship to nature that other forms of social and cultural constructions do not have, even though they share the quality of being oriented by particular values, interests, and power. A recognition that science is partial, rather than impartial, knowledge does not eliminate the difference between it and non-scientific knowledge. Scientific knowledge entails a factual possibility of understanding and manipulating nature that is not characteristic of non-scientific knowledge. This feature of science and its applications render them major means of empowerment in contemporary society.

Weber was well aware of the importance of science as a monopolizable resource and of the dialectical relationship between the accumulation of scientific knowledge and the accumulation of capital.

> Now the peculiar modern Western form of capitalism has been, at first sight, strongly influenced by the development of technical possibilities. Its rationality is to-day essentially dependent on the calculability of the most important technical factors. But this means fundamentally that it is dependent on the peculiarities of modern science, especially the natural sciences based on mathematics and exact and rational experiment. On the other hand, the development of these sciences and of the technique resting

upon them now receives important stimulation from these capitalistic interests in its practical economic application. (Weber 1930: 24)

Many of today's most important social relations are formed on the basis of a relationship with nature. For example, it is precisely by monopolizing control over a technology of transforming the raw materials of nature into commodities that capitalists and bureaucrats empower themselves and accumulate capital. Manipulating nature has become the means to accumulate power by humans, whether in terms of the pursuit of profit by private capitalist corporations operating in the market, or in terms of the pursuit of careers in powerful public bureaucracies under capitalism or socialist bureaucracies under state socialism, or in terms of the pursuit of military power by both. Scientific and technological knowledge empowers its possessor with the capacity to manipulate nature, which is an important resource in the pursuit of rewards, prestige and power, even if it has not resulted in the mastery of nature in an ecological sense.

Japan is a good illustration of how the technological manipulation of nature to one's advantage through the application of science -- for example in the production of color televisions, sound systems, cameras, watches, automobiles, motorcycles, laptop computers, and robots -- has resulted in the accumulation of capital and the construction of an economically powerful society in a strong negotiating position vis-a-vis other societies. The Japanese novelist, Shusaku Endo (1992: A13) put it this way. "Technology, technology, industry, industry -- these constituted the direction for the new Japan. ... Industrialization, with happiness as its goal, progressed. Japan produces cars and TVs; it also possesses them in abundance."

It is true that humans exercised power in an earlier age with clubs just as they do today with nuclear bombs. Such a focus on continuity should not, however, obscure the importance of a marginal theory of the means of exercising power.   The group monopolizing the accumulating knowledge of the means of domination -- and therefore a marginally superior technology of power -- can dominate other groups. Merton (1977: 111) put it bluntly: "the atomic bomb had demonstrated, beyond all measure, that knowledge really was power." The superior technology of coercion monopolized by minority whites in South Africa enabled them to have power over the majority blacks for a long period of time. The superior technology of destruction held by the Gulf allies in the war of 1991 forced Saddam Hussein of Iraq to leave Kuwait.

A fundamental change has occurred, based on the discovery of tools for construction, production, and destruction quite different from those that existed in the past. Such tools result from the accumulation of a partial understanding of nature and how to manipulate it. Although human values are not necessarily nor typically transformed by the development of new means to manipulate nature, the age-old struggles for power and interest are thereby re-equipped. This re-equipping process changes the relationship between social action and the processes of nature as well as the relationships between humans.

Scientific knowledge is not always directly and immediately useful (often it is), but it is an important building block of a type of knowledge that has demonstrated its utility in the everyday lives of people, in their transportation and communication, the technologies of housekeeping and entertainment, the cure of disease, warfare, etc. In a formally rational, utilitarian society, this tends to legitimate science in the eyes of both the dominant class and the population, rendering it a potent resource in political struggle. The development of the knowledge of how to manipulate nature provides fertile ground for specialization, for the development of niches upon which others are dependent, and for carving out positions of prestige, rewards, and power. Paradoxically even the dangers created by applied science are knowable only through science. They constitute hazards that are "invisible and yet all too present -- and they now call for experts as sources of answers to the questions they loudly raise" (Beck 1992a: 54).[4] The development of these new knowledge resources -- ones that are eminently monopolizable -- constitutes a significant part of formally rational closure (see Murphy 1988).[5]

The capacity to manipulate nature based on an understanding of some of its laws is a resource of central importance in social negotiations, but the principal beneficiaries are not the professions, such as scientists and engineers, with immediate hands-on control. Rather the principal beneficiaries are the second-order, arms-length controllers -- capitalists and administrators (Collins 1979) -- who control the hands-on controllers. A two-tier structure of control has typically developed whereby the manipulators of nature are controlled by the manipulators of humans, with the main benefits of the knowledge of how to manipulate nature accruing to those who have ultimate control over the development and use of such knowledge. The development and application of science tend to be controlled by the enterprise or bureaucracy that hires the scientist or engineer or that holds the patent, thereby monopolizing control over such knowledge. This closure over the development and use of knowledge has, in an ecological sense, particularly serious consequences, as specified in Chapter 7.

The Facility of Scientific and Technological Discovery?

The belief that humans, rather than nature, now construct reality is often associated with an assumption of the facility of discovery, invention, and innovation: "innovation is relatively easy, as far as the production of new ideas is concerned. ... It follows that whenever there is the social pressure to innovate, solutions will always be found" (Collins 1986: 115-6).[6]   When referring to science and applied science, assumptions like this are expressions of the plasticity-of-nature premise that often underlies the pursuit of the goal of mastering nature. "Technology can achieve practically anything today if we spend enough on it. It gives Man unprecedented powers over his environment and over himself. ... There are few technological barriers left in the way. Virtually everything is possible for those with the money and the will. The barriers are political, economic, social" (Hamilton 1973: 41). Even the problems caused by the use of technology are assumed to have technological solutions. "When one has wealth and technology without worrying about how to use them, problems are created. But the moment that serious concern arises over their actual and potential uses, the problems can usually be alleviated or prevented" (Kahn 1979: 74-5).

The husbands, wives, children, and parents of those who have died of cancer during the past century know the error in the assumption of the facility of scientific discovery. Contrary to this assumption, new ideas, discoveries, innovations, and solutions are particularly difficult to come by. Even with great resources and social pressure, solutions often are not found: "the breeder [reactor] was assigned $2.844 billion in research funds in the hope (now abandoned) that it would contribute 21 percent of electrical demand in the year 2000" (Commoner 1976: 145).   Where great social pressure and resources to innovate produce the desired results, they typically come with great difficulty. "The space missions illustrate that even where the talent and the funds are ample, and errors are likely to be displayed before a huge television audience, system accidents cannot be avoided. ... The weapons systems have hardly been starved for funds or engineering talent either, but accidents abound" (Perrow 1984: 257).

Apparent solutions to problems have often proved to be pseudo-solutions that only enlarge the scope of the problem. This is especially true in ecological matters. Dryzek (1987: 16-20) has shown that what has appeared to be solutions to pollution problems has frequently been merely the displacement of those problems in space (e.g., taller smokestacks), to another medium (the procedure used to reduce water pollution increases air pollution), or to the future (nuclear power gives energy now but radioactive waste later). Most ecologists (Ophuls 1977) have concluded that, no matter how much social pressure there is to find technological solutions to the environmental problems of resource depletion and pollution, adequate solutions cannot be found. Hence they advocate restraint on growth as more feasible than the pursuit of technological remedies.

The argument that innovations come easily if there is enough social pressure to innovate is clearly tautological. If a discovery has not been made -- if cancer has not been solved despite the enormous investment of capital and creativity of so many researchers in the most affluent nations over the past century -- then it could simply be argued that the failure resulted from not opening the resource tap even further, that is, from insufficient social pressure. Since the amount of resources and social pressure necessary for the discovery of solutions is evaluated by the discovery of solutions, the argument turns in a merry circle.

There is of course a tendency for the probability of discovery to increase if more social pressure is exerted and more resources are provided. But it is precisely the enormous quantity of resources needed that makes possible the monopolization of discovery, innovation, ideas, and solutions. This is also what makes innovation so important a resource for further struggle. The crucial question is: are the financial, knowledge, and organizational resources necessary for an innovation so enormous that most people and groups are excluded from attempting such an endeavor (discovering an oil well, exploration of space), or so modest (opening a small store) that the innovation is easily accessible to most everyone?

The opposite hypothesis -- the great difficulty of the creative discovery new ideas, of invention, and of innovation -- provides a more accurate description of the relationship between social action and nature's processes. "The brand-new $64-million reprocessing plant [for plutonium] built by General Electric at Morris, Illinois, is a total failure. After several years of trying, the company has concluded that the plant simply will not work" (Commoner 1976: 107). Enormous expense, twenty-five years of planning, and much publicity went into the production of the Hubble space telescope, yet scientists were incapable of focussing it correctly once it was launched into orbit. Although geological knowledge increases the chances of finding oil, it remains an enormously difficult and economically risky task. "In the United States at present, even after the best available geophysical exploration, about eight out of every ten exploratory wells are 'dry holes'. ... [Furthermore] only part of the oil actually located can be brought to the surface, or 'produced'" (Commoner 1976: 44-5). Similarly, discovering suitable drugs is a process that involves many dead ends for each drug that is found. "For every successful compound there are on average 5000 others discovered or created that finally have to be discarded because they are unsuitable in some way" (Hamilton 1973: 293). Krieger (1992) concludes that nature is recalcitrant and full of surprises for physicists studying it. Ecological knowledge is particularly difficult to acquire: "a scientifically authoritative interpretation of the greenhouse effect is still far from us; in some respects, we even seem to become less certain the more we study it. Knowledge about the oceans is hard to come by" (Yearley 1991: 136).

It is this difficulty that makes discoveries, and the science and applied science underlying them, so precious when they are found. It explains why their monopolization by professions, by capitalist corporations, and by states constitute such important resources in the pursuit of profit, privilege, and power. For example, if it were not for the great difficultly and huge resources needed to develop solar energy, the South -- the Third World -- would have long since turned its geographical position to an advantage as a source of solar energy in its struggle with the North. The limits imposed by nature on the social construction of reality present empowering resources to those who control the expansion of those limits by manipulating nature through a knowledge of some of its laws.

Science, Applied Science, and Ecological Irrationality

Manipulation but not Mastery of Nature

It is evident that there has been a tremendous development of science and applied science. Natural forces remain, however, beyond the control of humans. Science and its applications have resulted in an unprecedented capacity to observe, understand, and manipulate nature, but they have not led to its mastery. Nature has reacted to such manipulation through high-technology accidents, the creation of pesticide-resistant and drug-resistant species, atmospheric change, etc. The capacity to construct automobiles on a mass scale has improved transportation and empowered the possessor of that capacity (the automobile companies) with an important resource in the pursuit of rewards, but those automobiles subsequently pollute the air, degrade the environment, and render it less responsive to basic human needs in the long run. Domination of some humans by others by means of nuclear weapons instead of clubs results in a fundamental transformation in the possibility of extinction of human life on this planet, because of the secondary effects even a limited nuclear war would unleash. Nature reacts to human constructions that manipulate nature, such as automobile-based transportation and nuclear weapons, in unexpected ways that come back to haunt its manipulators.

The Big Bang theory of the origin of the universe is a striking example of the capacity of humans to understand nature. Confirmation by satellite informs scientists they are on the right track, thereby distinguishing theories that fit nature from those that do not, and directing further theoretical reflection in particular directions, such as that of 'cold dark matter.' The Big Bang theory is also, however, a striking reminder of the power of nature that humans will never master.

The Wastefulness of Science and Applied Science

It is paradoxical that postmodern states and enterprises, apparently oriented toward efficiency, are so enormously wasteful that they are placing the life-sustaining natural environment of our planet in peril. Waste, as Commoner (1976: 38) points out, is the converse of efficiency. The accumulation of scientific and technological knowledge has been closely related to the accumulation of waste, the opposite of efficiency. The use of science and applied science to manipulate nature has hitherto led, not to too much efficiency, but to too little, that is, to too much waste. The assumption that science and technology have resulted in efficiency is simplistic, to say the least. Science and its applications have been part of the problem of the human production of waste and degradation of the environment.

For example, Japanese industry is highly regarded as the epitome of efficiency. Yet the Japanese novelist Shusaku Endo (1992: A13) argues that in the pursuit of happiness by means of technology and industry "we Japanese divorced ourselves from nature, with which for so long we had so closely identified. ... We ended up destroying it instead of controlling it ... we were probably one of the first nations in the world to suffer environmental problems as a result of our destruction of nature. Fish no longer inhabit the rivers; the lakes are foul; many people still suffer from terrible diseases as a result of the effluent discharged from factories."

Even John Polanyi, winner of the Nobel Prize for chemistry in 1986 and a critic of those who would halt or slow down scientific research, admits that the power of science to transform the world has been a significant component (indeed a necessary condition) generating the explosive environmental crisis.

> What we now realize, however, is that the power of modern science has transformed the world in a much more extensive way than is represented by the emergence of weapons of mass destruction. There is another highly explosive situation, namely the intolerable and increasing inequities deriving from the expanding population of the world (one more China per decade gives a measure of the rate of increase), escalating energy

consumption and depleted resources. Hidden in that statement is the fear that we may now be doing irreversible damage to our habitat -- and the certain knowledge that we must act without delay if we are to stand a chance of avoiding irreversible damage in the future. (Polanyi 1992: 133)

The Connection Between Partial Science and Catastrophes

One of the most suggestive analyses of the harmful consequences of the manipulation of nature by humans through the means of science and applied science is Perrow's (1984) investigation of what he calls "normal accidents." After his extensive empirical study of high-technology accidents (nuclear, chemical, biological, aviation, marine, etc.), Perrow (1984: 330) concluded that they became particularly destructive, inevitable, and normal because of three characteristics of present high-technology systems.

First, the system transformed potentially explosive or toxic materials of nature or existed in hostile natural environments. For example, a valve on an oil tanker was mistakenly left open for half an hour, with the result that twenty-two miles of beaches in Bantry Bay, Ireland, were coated with oil (Perrow 1984: 198).

Second, invisible complex physical, chemical, and biological interactions resulted from designs that were required by the dangerous conditions. When minor failures occurred, the interactions of multiple failures defeated or went around designed-in safety devices and produced further unexpected and incomprehensible failures.

> No one dreamed that when X failed, Y would also be out of order and the two failures would interact so as to both start a fire and silence the fire alarm. ... The problem is just something that never occurred to the designers. Next time they will put in an extra alarm system and a fire suppressor, but who knows, that might just allow three more unexpected interactions among inevitable failures. (Perrow 1984: 4)

The problem of complex interactions was aggravated by efficient designs serving multiple functions. "For example, a heater might both heat the gas in tank A and also be used as a heat exchanger to absorb excess heat from a chemical reactor. If the heater fails, tank A will be too cool for the recombination of gas molecules expected, and at the same time, the chemical reactor will overheat as the excess heat fails to be absorbed" (Perrow 1984: 72). The attempt to manipulate nature by means of applied science has unleashed unintended complex interactions of nature because nature is a dynamic system, not just a static, malleable object or limiting condition.

An important element of instrumental rationalization consists of the attempt to foresee the probable consequences of human action. Paradoxically, even the attempt to foresee possible consequences can trigger the forces of nature to act in an unforeseen manner. For example, the solution to potential failures -- safety devices -- typically consists of more components and more complex designs, which ironically leads to more items that can fail in more complex ways. Critics are beginning to suggest that the problem is complexity itself (Hagen 1980, Perrow 1984). Furthermore, safety devices often have a perverse effect in that they encourage the pushing of the dangerous system further or faster.

Third, the system was tightly coupled, hence there was little or no time to recover or to contain the problem and the failure was quickly propagated to other parts of the system, other subsystems, and to the entire system. Small, often trivial, and very normal (in that they occur in all production processes and organizations) component failures in design, equipment, procedures, operators, or materials were thus magnified by the nature of the system itself into a major catastrophe.

To prevent accidents, systems having these characteristics require error-free operation: heroic operators, exemplary design, flawless procedures, and perfect equipment and materials. But since nothing is perfect, failures do occur, and they are amplified by the systemic properties of unexpected complex interactions and tight coupling into major disasters. "This is an expression of an integral characteristic of the system, not a statement of frequency. It is normal for us to die, but we only do it once. System accidents are uncommon, even rare; yet this is not all that reassuring, if they can produce catastrophes" (Perrow 1984: 5).

The tight coupling of such systems leaves too little time for operators to react in emergencies, hence coping strategies must be planned by the designer in advance. But the unexpected complex interactions require, on the other hand, a creative response from the operators. These dangerous, complex, and tightly coupled systems are characterized by a built-in contradiction between the need for both centralization and decentralization.

Perrow (1984) documented "normal accidents" in large-scale eco-systems resulting from the use of dangerous materials, complex interactions, and tight coupling. "With eco-system accidents the risk cannot be calculated in advance and the initial event ... becomes linked with other systems from which it was believed to be independent. ... Eco-system accidents illustrate the tight coupling between human-made systems and natural systems. There are few or no deliberate buffers inserted between the two systems because the designers never expected them to be connected" (Perrow 1984: 296), or did not know how to seal them off or did not want to.

Environmental Degradation as Gradual
War by Humanity Against Humanity

Perrow's analysis needs to be generalized from sensational accidents to the routine process of environmental degradation. Perrow admits as much himself. "This routine and mostly conscious contamination of the planet [by pollutants from industrial plants] probably has more serious long-term consequences than any accident we shall consider in this book, other than military accidents, but it is beyond the scope of our concern" (Perrow 1984: 69). For example, of the pollution produced by oil tankers, only 10 percent has been caused by accidents, the remaining 90 percent has resulted from routine wastage: leaks, washing out tanks, and defective loading and unloading (Clingan 1981).

Production by means of applied science routinely takes raw materials that are relatively benign in nature because of their form or location and transforms them into waste that is toxic for living organisms and for the human-supporting natural environment. Coal enclosed in the ground is dug out and converted in the process of producing energy into carbon dioxide, which subsequently results in air pollution, acid rain and the greenhouse effect. Fissile but rare Uranium-235 does not attain an explosive critical mass in nature; when culled and concentrated by humans it can, however, be induced into a nuclear reaction and transmute plentiful but non-fissile Uranium-238 into the synthetic element plutonium, which is used in nuclear bombs and is a radiological poison because of its absorption in bone marrow. Chlorofluorocarbons are produced in petrochemical plants and subsequently destroy the ozone layer when released as waste into the atmosphere. Whereas the equilibrium constructed by nature has rendered raw materials relatively benign to living species, the materials produced by humans in their transformation of nature are potentially explosive or toxic.

The degradation of the environment results not only from spectacular accidents, but also and especially from the interaction between routine systems of production (and distribution) -- which transform benign raw materials into toxic waste -- and the eco-system of nature. The unwanted consequences of dangerous materials, complex interactions, and tight coupling described by Perrow can be generalized from accidents in high-technology systems to routine pollution of the environment by many of the applications of science.

Accidents and ecologically harmful wars are thus part of the broader phenomenon of the production of waste and the depletion of resources.

Whereas waste dumping has constituted the routine, gradual process of interaction between social systems of production and the natural system, accidents and wars have constituted a non-routine waste discharge. Technological accidents and modern warfare typically result in an instantaneous massive accumulation of waste in the environment. For example, nuclear reactor accidents quickly contaminate the environment with radioactive waste, so would nuclear warfare. Oil spills and chemical explosions produce huge accumulations of waste in the environment within very short periods of time. So did the 1991 Gulf War. There is symmetry around the instantaneous -- gradual axis between accidents and wars, on the one hand, and routine pollution, on the other, that allows the relationship to be expressed as well the other way round. Routine pollution by humanity of the human-sustaining natural environment with toxic and radioactive waste has occurred as if the human race were slowly waging chemical and nuclear war against itself.

Objectified Intelligence Leading to a Shell of Bondage?

In his critique of bureaucratization Weber (1978: 1402) wrote the following haunting passage.

> An inanimate machine is mind objectified. Only this provides it with the power to force men into its service and to dominate their everyday working life as completely as is actually the case in the factory. Objectified intelligence is also that animated machine, the bureaucratic organization, with its specialization of trained skills, its division of jurisdiction, its rules and hierarchical relations of authority. Together with the inanimate machine it is busy fabricating the shell of bondage which men will perhaps be forced to inhabit some day, as powerless as the fellahs of ancient Egypt.[7]

Mommsen (1987: 41) calls the latter prediction a "self-denying prophecy" presented in order to mobilize action against the ominous side of this development. Weber's prophecy constitutes a very real danger in an ecological sense. The shell of bondage fabricated by objectified intelligence in the form of machines and bureaucratic organizations may well, if humans do not change their ways, consist of the degraded natural environment they will be forced to inhabit some day because of the objects, notably waste, their intelligence has indirectly produced.

The manipulation of nature by means of science and applied science gives capitalists and bureaucrats power, but it also, through the accumulation of waste, provokes the degradation of the natural environment and stimulates social conflict concerning the environment. The contradictions, namely the experience of the harmful ecological consequences of such manipulation and knowledge of those consequences, have been the impetus to new negotiations and nascent social constructions, particularly in the form of the environmental movement, that take into account the needs of a natural environment capable of sustaining human society and other forms of life.

Social relations are not constructed upon the base or infrastructure of a constant, plastic natural environment. Rather social relations are constructed in large part by acting upon a dynamic natural environment, and being acted upon by the processes of nature. Through environmental problems and the ecological movement, humans are now confronted with the question of their willingness to go beyond the erroneous assumption of the plasticity of nature and the illusory goal of its mastery to an understanding of the embeddedness of social action in the dynamics of nature and of the need for a symbiotic relationship between the two.

Is the Choice Between Science and Anti-Science?

The plausibility of Merton's (1968: 588) argument from the 1950s to the effect that the "social consequences of the present employment of science [referring primarily to the development of weapons of mass destruction and of unemployment resulting from automation] are laying the groundwork for a revolt against science" has been reinforced by recent environmental problems. If high-technology accidents are normal in the sense of inevitable, as Perrow (1984) argues, does it not follow that the elimination of technology and indeed science is the only way to avoid such accidents and to avoid an ecological shell of bondage consisting of an environment degraded by pollution? Is the only choice that between either environmentally destructive science or anti-science, either mastering nature or being mastered by nature, either exploiting nature or retreating to the past?

The exploitation and attempted mastery of nature by means of science and its applications have led to the accumulation of toxic waste and the degradation of the human-sustaining natural environment. An anti-scientific, anti-technological program would, however, render impossible the economic development necessary to raise the quality of life to an acceptable minimum for the present human population of developing countries and to motivate a decrease in that population. Scientific and technological knowledge is also needed to understand the ecological consequences of past human action, as well as present and future action:

"scientific rationality without social rationality remains *empty*, but social rationality without scientific rationality remains *blind*" (Beck 1992a: 30). Without scientific knowledge, humans would be ignorant of the dangers of their constructions. Environmental protection and clean-up measures, environmental impact assessments, environmental accounting, and environmental accountability would not be possible. Nuclear waste, toxic chemicals, and polluted lakes, rivers, oceans, and atmosphere have been brought into existence by humans and require action. Scientific knowledge and its applications are with us, and it is difficult to see how the elimination of science could be other than a chimera. Scientific amnesia is particularly unlikely. Thus reacting to the degradation of the natural environment by humans in terms of an either/or choice -- either present scientific and technological development and all the environmental problems they have entailed, or an anti-scientific, anti-technological ideology leading to stagnation in the midst of an environmental crisis -- limits the possibilities to a very poor choice indeed. "It is this very crisis of scientific authority which can favor a general *obfuscation of risks*. Criticism of science is also *counter*-productive for the recognition of risks. ... A solid background of faith in science is part of the paradoxical basic equipment of the critique of modernization" (Beck 1992a: 72). This dilemma explains why the environmental movement has been characterized by a great deal of ambivalence about science (Yearley 1992).

If science and applied science constitute partial knowledge, then there exists another alternative: redirecting science and its applications such that they become partial to the life-sustaining natural environment. Recognizing the partiality of science leads to the possibility of going beyond either accepting science and technology as they have been or rejecting them. It opens up the possibility of reorienting them so as *both* to adapt to nature *and* benefit from it. The recognition that science and applied science are not impartial leads to an awareness of the necessity of carefully choosing partialities. Human action has provoked environmental problems, and human action will be part of the solution, with science and applied science being an important element of human action in both cases. "If the path of an ecologically conscious agriculture is chosen, it too will require support from research, but of a different sort" (Beck 1992a: 179).

Science and its applications can be and have already begun to be part of the solution to environmental problems by making humans more aware: (1) of those problems (for example, the invisible-to-the-unscientific-eye depletion of the ozone layer and greenhouse effect, the lengthy time needed by nature to repair damage to the ozone layer), (2) of the error of an assumed plastic relationship of humans to their natural environment, and (3) of how nature reacts against the attempts of humans to manipulate it (e.g., how pests develop resistance to pesticides, how bacteria develop resistance to antibiotics). "Scientific groups and NGOs (Non-Governmental Organizations) have played -- with the help of young people -- a major part in the environmental movement from its earliest beginnings. Scientists were the first to point out evidence of significant environmental risks and changes resulting from the growing intensity of human activities" (World Commission on Environment and Development 1987: 326). Scientists established that toxic pesticides accumulate in the food chain (Moore 1987). It was science that demonstrated in detail how the chain of life binds human needs to those of other species in a profound ecological sense, thereby showing the potential of science to render human culture less anthropocentric and more partial in favor of nature. "Had not the scientific base of ecology and conservation been already so sound, the successful [policy change] agreement with the [agrochemicals] industry could not have been concluded" (Nicholson 1987: 49). The British government was pressured even by establishment scientists to change its policy on acid rain after the collection of comprehensive evidence (Yearley 1991: 108, 113). "Greenpeace bases its endeavors on detailed technical and scientific advice and claims it has the 'most sophisticated mobile laboratory in Europe'" (Brown and May 1989: 150). A growing importance of scientific expertise also underlie the actions of Friends of the Earth, the Royal Society for the Protection of Birds, and the Society for the Promotion of Nature Reserves (Yearley 1991: 75-6). "Expert dissent seems to have been a necessary precondition for the emergence of serious protest in the nuclear case" (Rudig 1986: 371). Sensitivity to ecological hazards cannot be equated with hostility to science. "It is not the uneducated or advocates of a new Stone Age culture who are warning of the dangers, but more and more these activists are people who are themselves scientists -- nuclear engineers, physicians, geneticists or computer scientists" (Beck 1992a: 203). Although science has been a source of environmental problems, it has already begun to contribute to solutions through the work of ecologically aware scientists.

Science has led to the development of technologies that have transformed the relationship between social action and the processes of nature from traditional symbiosis to modern parasitism, but science also has the potential to be an important part of the transformation to a new symbiotic relationship. Science in this regard is a manifestation of the two sides of reason (Raynaud 1987). Through science and technology, reason has developed an ideology of mastering nature; yet through science, reason can and has already begun to develop an ecological understanding of nature that promotes a growing recognition of the need to adapt to it.

Rejection of the pursuit of mastering nature does not imply rejection of science. Thus Beck (1992a: 181) concludes that the "proof of the irrationality of the prevailing practice of science no more means the end of science than the refutation of Newtonian mechanics meant the end of physics." Science consists of the anti-dogmatic approach of learning from mistakes. Its most significant mistakes presently involve its perverse ecological consequences. These paradoxically constitute, through learning to deal with them, the opportunity for a renewed expansion of science and applied science. "Here the self-contradiction that scientific development has got into in its reflexive phase becomes tangible: *the publicly transmitted criticism of the previous development becomes the motor of expansion*" (Beck 1992a: 161).

Science and applied science can have either environmentally efficient or wasteful consequences, depending upon whether the development of partial scientific and technological knowledge is steered in a direction that is partial to a natural environment capable of sustaining living species. Science and its applications can be oriented to the pursuit of the mastery of nature under the presumption of its plasticity or to the pursuit of harmony between social action and the dynamic ecosystem of a powerful natural world. Science and applied science can be developed as enemies of nature attempting to wrestle it to submission or as friends of nature.

Bookchin (1987: 52-3) argues that the "all-encompassing image of an intractable nature that must be tamed by a rational humanity has given us a domineering form of reason, science, and technology." Although Bookchin is dead wrong in blaming this on an image of an "intractable nature" -- in fact the dominant image of nature is better characterized as unduly tractable and plastic, which is why the global ecological crisis and high technology accidents have come as such a shock especially to technocrats -- he is right in asserting that reason, science, and technology have been steered in specific directions by particular images. The type of science that developed has been influenced by the type of society that developed it, a society pursuing the mastery of nature based on the image that nature is plastic.

Redirecting science and its applications involves not a technical fix, but rather redirecting society. It involves an initiative not just of scientists, but of society as a whole. When the Nobel Prize winner Polanyi (1992: 130) was asked: "'Should we not, as scientists, see to it that science develops in a way that is beneficent, along directions most likely to have humane and advantageous consequences?' ... I have to tell them that I do not know of any way of doing that, and I think it is grossly misleading to pretend otherwise." If nuclear physicists terminated nuclear research in order to prevent the further development of nuclear weapons, then societies intent on military power would turn to biological or chemical weapons or directed-energy rays. Polanyi argues that the problem is not science but society because society can and does use any branch of science to kill.

One of the key expressions in the above quotation from Polanyi is "as scientists." Scientists can play an important role in turning science and applied science in a beneficent direction, but Polanyi (1992: 130) is correct to argue that it is misleading to pretend that scientists can "see to it that science develops in a way that is beneficent." It is not just scientists who determine whether science develops "along directions most likely to have humane and advantageous consequences" (Polanyi 1992: 130), but groups in positions of greater power in society that finance science. Furthermore, "one section of society cannot assume the right to dictate to the rest on the assumption that it has a monopoly on wisdom" (Polanyi 1992: 131). The consequences of science are too important to be left to scientists alone, if only because scientists have difficulty overcoming their short-term vested interest in equating science with the present partial form of science promoted by commercial and military interests.

If Polanyi is, however, implying that there is no way of reorienting science and applied science, then he is wrong. Science and applied science are not impartial forms of knowledge. Their development has already been oriented by broader forces in society, for example, they are presently hitched to military and commercial objectives. Although applied science is more application sensitive, even pure science has typically been funded according to its potential applications in terms of these two sets of objectives. The question of whether humans use the power of science "ill or well" is not, as Polanyi (1992: 129) claims, separate from the question of the character of the science that has been developed. Science and applied science are dialectically related, each affecting the other. Science and its applications could be harnessed to ecological goals, rather than only commercial and military ones, if society so willed.

Polanyi can not have it both ways. The responsibility of the scientist "to read out loud warning signs that say 'caution'" (Polanyi 1992: 130) contradicts, especially in ecological terms, the freedom of the scientist to go full speed ahead "wherever it leads" (Polanyi 1992: 128). The uncertainty of where science may lead combined with the ecological requirement of caution leaves as choices (1) slowing science down, (2) channelling it in an ecological direction, or (3) both. The question is not whether to halt science or to charge blindly ahead "wherever it leads," but *how* to reorient the development of science and applied science in a beneficent direction, including ecological beneficence. There is no easy answer to that question, only struggle to bring that goal onto center stage. If scientists resist the ecological reorientation of science and applied science, it will only increase the demand by the population to slow down or even to halt science as technology generates further environmental degradation.

The conclusion of Perrow about the inevitability of high-technology "normal accidents," and the prophecy of Weber of a "shell of bondage" interpreted ecologically, refer to science and its applications as they exist at the present time. They have to do with continuing the development of the present form of partial science and partial applied science. If less dangerous materials were chosen, complexity reduced, and sufficient buffers used to reduce tight coupling, then accidents would not be inevitable nor normal. Ecological recklessness would be replaced by ecological prudence as a guiding principle. Information about probable consequences could be used to choose ecologically appropriate technologies and directions for scientific development. Such information would be based on rational principles of accounting and accountability for pollution. This negative feedback, as Dryzek (1987) refers to it, might well lead, in the case of a specific technology, to the conclusion that materials are too dangerous, complexity too great, or adequate buffers unavailable, and therefore result in the ecologically rational decision to abandon that technology as too dangerous. Perrow (1984) suggests nuclear energy as a prime candidate for abandonment. In this reorientation of applied science and even science, military and commercial goals would yield to ecological goals in the determination of the partiality of science and applied science. "By changing its self-conception and political arrangement, we must, as it were, install *brakes and a steering wheel* into the 'non-steering' of the racing techno-scientific development that is setting explosive powers free" (Beck 1992a: 180).

The environmentally destructive form of science and technology known to date has resulted from particular sets of social relations that have rendered science and its applications partial against the environment. The social relations that result in the monopolization of information and knowledge, in cover ups, and especially in the monopolization of power, have prevented people from acting upon or even perceiving environmental problems until they are so serious they are beyond camouflage. Dominant classes have not been held accountable for their actions because of deficiencies in the institutionalized means of accountability.

Conversely, unblocking the channels of communication, obtaining the means to perceive harmful environmental consequences (especially to foresee such consequences before projects are undertaken), and empowering people to take action on the environment and to control the polluters would provide the institutional basis and social pressure in favor of the development of science and applied science partial to the environment instead of against it. "The recourse to scientific results for the socially binding definition of truth is becoming *more and more necessary*, but at the same time *less and less sufficient*" (Beck 1992a: 167). The "questioning mind" of the scientist would still have "the freedom to pursue the truth wherever it leads" (Polanyi 1992: 128-9), but it would be guided by the ecological values of society generally, and of scientists in particular, instead of by the military and commercial goals that presently promote the development of science. Since military and commercial goals are more extraneous to science than ecological ones, the problem of compromising "success by adding extraneous criteria of choice derived from seat-of-the-pants judgements about the ultimate utility and beneficence of understanding that is yet to be achieved" (Polanyi 1992: 128-9) would be diminished.

> This is the developmental logic in which modernization risks are constituted through a tense interplay of science, scientific practice and the public sphere, and then played back into science, precipitating 'identity crises', new forms of work and organization, new bases for theories, new methodological developments and so on. ... Nevertheless, one should not be deceived here; through all the contradictions, a path of scientific *expansion* has been taken. (Beck 1992a: 161)

This brings us to the issue of examining whether there is hope for such a transformation of science, applied science, and society generally so that, instead of being implicated in a parasitic relationship with nature, they will enter into a symbiotic one.

Notes

1. This conception of science is sometimes attributed to Merton, especially by constructivist sociologists of science who want to use him as a target, but his view is a much more balanced one of taking into consideration the influence of values and interests on the development of science without losing sight of the difference between science and pseudoscience (see Merton 1968: esp 585-91 and Merton 1977: esp. 108-12).
2. A more extensive critique of contemporary sociology of science for having obscured the importance of the processes of nature by focusing solely on the social construction of reality can be found in Murphy (forthcoming).

3. The concept of 'partial knowledge' has also been used to refer to what counts as knowledge in school (Young and Whitty 1977: 123) and to describe, from a feminist perspective, sociological knowledge constructed by men and by dominant ethnic groups (see Juteau 1981).

4. Beck is, however, wrong in his explanation of why contemporary society has become a different type of society. A risk society with Trojan horses that disgorge dangers as well as afflicted parties incompetent concerning their own affliction (Beck 1992a: 54) were precisely the characteristics of societies overwhelmed by the bubonic plague. The peculiarity of today's society comes rather from the presence of scientists who offer some hope of finding answers, from the fact that they unleashed the dangers in the first place, and from the planetary scope of the risk that threatens all life on Earth.

5. Bringing into focus the important resources of science and applied science need not imply a return to a technical-functionalism that ignores conflict and domination. On the contrary, science and applied science are best perceived as means of empowerment in social conflict leading to domination and privilege.

6. Collins uses the facility premise to buttress a sociology that claims that reality is socially constructed: "The social construction of reality is a key to all of sociology" (Collins 1975: 470). An analysis that attempts to weed out weaknesses such as this facility premise from the otherwise major contribution of Collins is under preparation by the present author.

7. As was argued in the discussion of partial knowledge and of empowerment by means of science and applied science, this does not mean objective intelligence in the sense of being unaffected by struggles for power. Objectified intelligence consists rather of intelligence and mind that has taken the form of an object: the machine or the bureaucratic organization.

10

Parasitism:
A "Light Cloak" or an "Iron Cage"?

Humans have transitory specific goals, whether they be consumption of specific commodities, travel, military conquest of particular nations, military defense against other nations, etc., which are replaced when attained. The instruments and physical means used to attain these goals constitute the material embodiment of means -- ends rationality. The instruments and means are discarded when they are used, become obsolete, or when the goals change, but they remain in the natural environment as waste to accumulate. In this process, nature is partially appropriated, social action is objectified, and the objects (effluent, emissions, left-overs from production, commodities, instruments) return to threaten their human producers in the form of waste accumulation. And the accumulation of waste consists not just of an aggregate of independent objects, but rather of a growing system of dangerous, complex, tightly coupled interactions with the ecosystem. This opposition between human activity oriented to specific subjective goals and the largely unintended, threatening consequences of that activity through the medium of the natural environment constitutes the contemporary ecological form of the classical process of alienation, as conceived of not only by Marx (1963, 1964), but also by Weber.[1] Instead of being congruent with their long-term needs, the perverse effects of human activity come back to oppress the initiators of that activity.

Weber expressed as follows the great difficulty of changing this instrumentally rational economic order.

> This order is now bound to the technical and economic conditions of machine production which to-day determine the lives of all the individuals

who are born into this mechanism, not only those directly concerned with economic acquisition, with irresistible force. Perhaps it will so determine them until the last ton of fossilized coal is burnt. In Baxter's view the care for external goods should only lie on the shoulders of the 'saint like a light cloak, which can be thrown aside at any moment.' But fate decreed that the cloak should become an iron cage. (Weber 1930: 181)

As stated previously, Mommsen (1987: 41) argues that statements such as these by Weber are best interpreted not as a fatalistic prediction but rather as a "self-denying prophecy" advanced "to mobilize counter-forces in order to arrest those trends." Can the present dangerous trends dedicated to the consumption and appropriation of nature, including the use of the natural environment as a waste sink, be thrown aside like "a light cloak" or have they become "an iron cage"?

Humanity as Nature's Master, Slave, or Friend?

A 'historic dualism' has hitherto characterized the relationship between social action and the processes of nature: the domination of humanity by nature versus "a domineering humanity whose goal is to subjugate the natural world, including human nature itself" (Bookchin 1987: 52). The pursuit of the mastery of nature -- of replacing self-regulating natural systems by systems planned by humans -- has up to now led to a parasitic relationship of humans to nature characterized by environmental degradation. The failure to correct the harmful ecological consequences of human actions, or even to perceive those consequences, has resulted in cultural, social, and economic systems being out of touch with their effects on ecosystems (Bernstein 1981).

The two poles of this dualism are not the only possibilities. "The point is surely that man need not be either nature's master -- 'transcendence' -- or nature's slave -- 'immanence'" (Dryzek 1987: 46). By placing human interventions in nature within the bounds of adapting to nature and by recognizing human embeddedness in nature, humans can become nature's friend -- compatibility -- rather than either its master or its slave. This is the message contained in the names the environmental movement gives to its own organizations: "Friends of the Earth," "Earth First," etc. Human interventions in the natural environment guided by an emphasis on adapting to the self-regulating dynamic of nature and benefiting from that dynamic, rather than an emphasis on replacing it with human planning, would constitute the basis of a symbiotic relationship between social action and the processes of nature.

The issue at the end of this century is no longer the same as that at the beginning. Then it was the mastery of nature. Now it is the mastery of social constructions so that they will become compatible with nature, in other words, human self-mastery. Whereas earlier the significant question was how to promote rationalization, now it is how to foster the ecological rationalization of the process of rationalization itself.

Dryzek (1987: 46) argues that "an ecologically rational man -- nature system is one in which human and natural components stand in a symbiotic relationship." The same conclusion has been expressed in terms of "harmony." "The Promethean quest of using technology to 'dominate nature' is replaced by the ecological ethic of using technology to harmonize humanity's relationship with nature" (Bookchin 1980: 109). Whereas Darwin's theory of natural evolution, Social Darwinism, and Human Ecology stressed competition and survival of the fittest, the ecology movement puts its "emphasis on symbiosis as the most important factor in natural evolution. ... The compensatory manner by which animals and plants foster each other's survival, fecundity, and well-being surpasses the emphasis conventional evolutionary theory places on their 'competition' with each other -- a word that, together with 'fitness', is riddled with ambiguities" (Bookchin 1987: 25). Deep ecologists too argue in favor of "actions that tend to promote symbiosis" (Fox 1990: 268). The philosopher Arne Naess (1986: 28), who coined the term "deep ecology," states: "if I had to give up the term [Self-realization] fearing its inevitable misunderstanding, I would use the term 'symbiosis'." Thus deep ecologists call for: "'treading lightly' upon the earth (i.e., lifestyles of voluntary simplicity)" (Fox 1990: 268) and practices that are "simple in means, rich in ends" (Devall 1988).

A symbiotic relationship could in principle be attained, as deep ecologists suggest, by turning back the clock and living at the population levels and in the way of life of primal peoples, that is, through derationalization. The transition back to such a time and place would, however, as social ecologists point out, most likely involve an immense amount of human suffering.[2] Dryzek argues that the idea of human non-intervention in the natural environment is untenable, that it would return us to the time when humans were nature's slave, and that a compromise must be reached between naturalness and productive artificiality. "Production for human use demands artificial suppression of ecological succession -- think, for example, of the artificiality (and extreme instability) of a cornfield" (Dryzek 1987: 45).

The ecological issue is not one of the presence or absence of human intervention in nature, but rather of the character and consequences of that intervention. All species intervene in their environment. The key question is whether humans will enter into a parasitic relationship with their natural environment in which they threaten to unleash powerful forces of nature that will destroy the capacity of their host to support them (Odum 1983: 401) and other living species, or whether the relationship will be symbiotic.

Before humans developed the means that degrade the natural environment, the relationship between social action and the processes of nature was symbiotic by necessity. It has not been so much the primacy of nature in the human hierarchy of values that prevented its degradation in the past, but rather the lack of means to exploit nature. Now that humans have developed those means, the relationship can be symbiotic only by choice. Humans have, by their accumulation of knowledge about nature and their social constructions, forced the choice between a parasitic and a symbiotic relationship with nature upon themselves, and with it struggle over that choice: "our metabolism with nature will either be mutually interdependent such that our vision of ourselves will place us firmly *within* the natural world -- not 'above it' -- or we will become its most destructive parasites" (Bookchin 1987: 96).

Reorienting the Relationship
Between Social Action and the Processes of Nature

There is no shortage of theories claiming that society is moving to a new ecological paradigm (Dunlap and Van Liere 1978, 1983; Cotgrove 1982; Milbrath 1984, 1989), or post-modern ecological awareness (Ophuls 1977; Beck 1992a, 1992b). There is even some survey evidence that attitudes have changed in an ecological direction (Council on Environmental Quality et al. 1980; Dunlap 1989; Olsen et al. 1992). What is lacking is evidence that these attitudinal changes have affected behavior, life styles, and institutions in a way that leads to a symbiotic relationship between humans and their environment. After all, pollution continues to accumulate in the atmosphere, rivers, lakes, and oceans, and proof of a decelerating rate of such contaminant accumulation has yet to be presented. Furthermore, as the costs of environmental restoration become more clear there has been an increase in organized opposition to environmentalism on the part of polluting companies and their workers. "But despite considerable opposition and attempts at denigrating environmentalism as an elitist and irresponsible social value, monopoly-capital interests and organized labor have failed to make ecology 'the last fad'" (Schnaiberg 1980: 372). Ecologically aware social action is not fading, but it is not advancing very quickly either.

Bookchin (1991: 34) has a particularly ambitious goal for humans. "Our species, gifted by the creativity of natural evolution itself, could play the role of nature rendered self-conscious." But why will humans act as the self-consciousness of nature rather than in their own immediate self-interest of exploiting nature? Dryzek (1987) has examined the possibilities and limitations of "social choice mechanisms" -- markets, administered systems, polyarchy (electoral democracy), law, moral persuasion, etc. -- for a symbiotic relationship with nature. But even if it could be proven that one of these social choice mechanisms is better suited than the others for a symbiotic relationship, how could that relationship be made to predominate? Are we not stuck with the present social choice mechanisms and the present relationship with the natural environment? How can the market, bureaucratic organization, the legal system, etc., as well as the culture underlying them, be ecologically reoriented? To express the issue in its starkest form,

> how does any highly developed society, like the US in 1980s with 235 million people, living because of the global imports and exports of transnational corporate capitalism in and out of huge metroplexes, reinhabit its bio-regions such that 'the human population lives harmoniously and dynamically by employing a sophisticated and unobtrusive technology in a world environment which is left natural'? (Luke 1988: 91)

Luke criticizes deep ecology in this way for lacking a "theory of transition," but his critique applies to all theories of a new relationship between social action and the processes of nature.

Albrow (1990: 289) is certainly correct to conclude that "in returning the focus always to the responsible agent, the sociologist can allow human beings glimpses of their own image and possibilities to control their own fate before it slips from their grasp." His conclusion receives a particularly powerful expression if interpreted in terms of the environmental crisis. The issue is, none the less, the practical one of how the agent can become responsible for a symbiotic relationship, rather than merely participating in a parasitic one. The development of a symbiotic relationship between humans and their natural environment in terms of any of the green options implies material and institutional change, and a cultural transformation to an adaptive orientation toward nature in order to implement material and institutional change. How can a symbiotic relationship between social action and the processes of nature be realized? Four main theories of transition from our present parasitic relationship between the social and the natural to a more symbiotic relationship have been proposed, theories based on (1) force, (2) practical reason, (3) ecological ethics, and (4) ecological consciousness. A fifth, based on ecological experience and ecological knowledge, is, I will argue, more complete and more convincing than the others.

Force

The assumption of the necessity of a forced transition is usually, but not only, based on Marxian theory.

> The knot of the ecological crisis cannot be cut with a paper-knife. The crisis is inseparable from the conditions of existence systematically determined by the mode of production. ... To ask the individual wage-earner to differentiate between 'real' and 'artificial' needs is to mistake the real situation. Both are so closely connected that they constitute a relationship which is subjectively and objectively indivisible. Hunger for commodities, in all its blindness, is a product of the production of commodities, which could only be suppressed by force. (Enzensburger 1976: 193-4)

Many neo-Malthusians (Hardin 1968; Weinberg 1972; Harman 1976; Ophuls 1977; Heilbroner 1980; Odum 1983) have also suggested force and coercion as solutions to urgent ecological problems, solutions that avoid the delays of electoral democracy.[3]

The hazard of environmental degradation "harbors a tendency to a *legitimate totalitarianism of hazard prevention,* which takes the right to prevent the worst and, in an all too familiar manner, creates something even worse" (Beck 1992a: 80). Force and coercion constitute threats to democratic politics. As solutions they entail their own contradictions. The group that appropriates the power to use force to implement the transition to symbiosis would then be in a position to use force for its own ends, including both the maintenance of its privileged position of power and the dissimulation of ecological problems it produces. Thus the use of force to attain ecological goals would in all probability have, as a perverse, unintended consequence, a decrease in ecological accountability to the general population and hence an increased likelihood of ecological irresponsibility. One need only examine the history of societies that forcibly overthrew capitalism to be aware of these contradictions in social change by means of force. Furthermore, proposing force as a solution begs the question of how groups promoting a symbiotic relationship with nature will gain the power to force their powerful opponents to conform. For example, even the imposition of taxes, which constitutes Schnaiberg's (1980: 431-2) socio-environmental program, sounds easy but often faces stiff resistance. In Ontario, Canada, the imposition of a tire tax engendered such opposition that it had to be repealed. Beck (1992a: 231) argues that attempts at recentralization run up against the barrier *"that modern society has no control center."*

Practical Reason

At the opposite pole to force is Habermas's (1970a; 1970b; 1973a; 1973b; 1984) theory of "practical reason." Dryzek (1987: 200-15) attempts to apply that theory as the means of enhancing the ecological rationality of collective choices. Habermas argued that reason cannot be reduced to its instrumental and technological component; the latter is but one of a plurality of different types of rational activity (see also Raynaud 1987: 189-90). Another component -- "practical reason" -- "involves a collective cultivation of virtuous behavior, rather than the administration or manipulation of people and things" (Dryzek 1987: 200). Practical choices in this sense, and not only technical means, can be rationalized (Raynaud 1987: 184). Under practical reason, action is determined by the best reasons, where good reasons are not only instrumental ones but also and especially those referring "to the moral rightness or wrongness of an act, or of the goals toward which that act seems to be directed, or of the kind of society which that act would help constitute" (Dryzek 1987: 201). The normative grounds underlying actions are rationally questioned by examining their consistency with shared value systems. This Habermas (1984) refers to as "communicative rationalization" and ideal speech.

Ideal speech is reflective and cooperative (Barber 1984), not aggressive and adversarial as in legal argumentation. Ideal speech differs from moral persuasion in that, rather than being imposed from above, norms and principles for action gain the free consent of actors and hence their compliance.

Habermas (1973a) also distinguishes between selfish particular interests and generalizable interests common to all individuals, and argues that the latter prevail under communicative rationality and ideal speech because agreement cannot be reached on the former. Although different conceptions of generalizable interests persist, he claims that consensus can be reached at least concerning general norms. Dryzek (1987: 204) then argues that "the human life-support capacity of natural systems is *the* generalizable interest *par excellence,* standing as it does in logical antecedence to competing normative principles such as utility maximization or right protection." Thus Dryzek's (1987: 7) rational ecology contends that whereas "axiomatic social choice theory is confined to interpreting society's welfare in terms of some aggregation of individual preferences, my broader treatment allows for collective interests beyond these preferences (for example, an interest in ecological integrity)."

At this point, when dealing with the relationship between social action and the processes of nature, Dryzek breaks with the work of Habermas.

> Habermas sees technical or instrumental knowledge -- natural science -- and manipulative forms of practice as thoroughly appropriate to human dealings with the natural world. Practical reason, manifested most strongly in what Habermas refers to as 'emancipatory' knowledge, is reserved for the social sciences and social practice. Thus Habermas sees a discontinuity between the systems of the human world (potential subjects) and those of the natural world (inevitable objects). From the viewpoint of ecological rationality, this discontinuity is a misplaced decomposition of a non-reducible system. (Dryzek 1987: 206)

Dryzek seeks to use practical reason to guide human dealings with nature. He implies that the dominant ideology, which shows itself even in Habermas's work, reduces nature to a static object to be manipulated and mastered. He (Dryzek 1987: 207) argues on the contrary in favor of treating ecosystems as if they were subjects, allowing for and reacting to their spontaneous actions. He suggests that official spokespersons be formally appointed for ecosystems in terms of legal status within the system of law. The environmental movement has already begun acting as unofficial, informal spokespersons for ecosystems.

Common interests substituted for selfish particular interests, reflective and cooperative speech replacing aggressive and adversarial argumentation, free consent, the collective cultivation of virtuous behavior, and action determined by the best reasons are changes worthy of promotion. Ideal speech, communicative rationalization, and practical reason are valuable as standards for judging real-life discourse and as ways to attempt to push action toward those standards.

"Practical reason" is not, however, a social choice mechanism in the sense of the other social choice mechanisms (markets, administered systems, electoral systems, law, moral persuasion) discussed by Dryzek (1987). Ecologically rational practical reason refers to the choice of a symbiotic relationship with the natural environment, whereas the others deal with a mechanism for choosing. In his discussion of practical reason, Dryzek is confusing social choice mechanisms with social choice (the choice of being virtuous, in particular, ecologically virtuous).

Practical reason reaffirms virtue, but does not explain why virtue, rather than deviance from virtue, occurs or will occur. Like all moral standards, practical reason as well as the ten commandments has the potential of eliciting deviance as well as conformity to standards. Dryzek fails to examine the relationship between, on the one hand, practical reason, communicative rationality, and ideal speech, and on the other, the unintended, and at times perverse, consequences in practice of attempts to implement them.

For example, the practical reason, communicative rationality, and ideal speech of the early Christians consisted of their preaching the "collective cultivation of virtuous behavior." They reflected upon, argued, debated, and refined their conception of virtue. Christianity has at times had a tense relationship with instrumental reason, as manifested in anti-usury laws and in the theology of liberation. Yet Christianity developed into the hierarchical social institution of the Roman Catholic Church. Why would the practical reason of Habermas and Dryzek, like virtuous Christianity before it, not also lead to the development of an elite of expert specialists who specialize in debating and defining virtue: the theologians of practical reason? Dryzek admits that this also occurred in the case of Marxist-Leninist theory and is occurring for ecological theory. "In the same way that the 'vanguard' in Marxist-Leninist theory is the guardian of the laws of history, this kind of elite [those who claim knowledge of ecology] could be the guardian of the laws of ecology. The rest of us would presumably defer to that superior knowledge" (Dryzek 1987: 94). Yet Dryzek gives no convincing argument for believing that the hierarchization that occurred in the cases of the other forms of reason and virtue would not occur for practical reason. What is it about "practical reason" that would immunize it against the hierarchization, and deviation from virtue, suffered by Christianity, Marxism, and ecology? It would seem that practical reason can only be so immunized by definition, with Dryzek's and Habermas's ideal speech about practical reason degenerating into tautological reasoning.

To take another example, "practical reason" bears a resemblance to electoral democracy in its ideal form:

> the key aspect of polyarchical mechanisms [electoral democracy] is that collective choices are the outcomes of interactions between relatively large numbers of actors, none of which is capable of exercising anything remotely approaching authoritative control over the system. Interaction should proceed in the context of relatively free exchange of argument, information, and influence, such that choices are arrived at through 'mutual adjustment' between partisans of different interests. (Dryzek 1987: 110-1)

Yet electoral democracy as it exists in practice is admittedly quite different: "outcomes consist of compromises whose content reflects the relative weight of the political resources -- votes, campaign contributions, number of activists, moral acceptability, expertise, commitment, bribes, arguments, legal powers, and the like -- which organized interests and governmental actors (such as agencies) bring to bear" (Dryzek 1987: 119). It consists of systematically distorted communication based on ideology and dogmatism and on the use of language to deceive and manipulate. Under these conditions, consensus reflects merely the particular interests of political powers, or at best, a compromise between competing particular interests of powerful groups, rather than ideal speech and practical reason in Habermas's and Dryzek's sense.

The sociologically significant phenomenon consists not in the proposal of an ideal world, which can be done easily, but in the maintenance or deformation of ideals when the attempt is made to put them into practice. The issue involves how "practical reason" would fare in practice, if it ever were to descend from the lofty level of an ideal proposal. Since the only resource is to be argument and since action is to result from the better argument, practical reason requires that all actors possess a similar degree of "communicative competence" (Habermas 1970b) in order to lead to participation rather than to domination. Furthermore, "unconstrained communication is only possible once exploitative material conditions have been abolished" (Dryzek 1987: 211). By presupposing discussion among equals and the abolition of exploitative material conditions, the theory of practical reason proposes an idealist philosophical solution that assumes away the sociological problem of class and power inequalities. It presupposes as unproblematic precisely that which is problematic, thereby ignoring rather than analyzing social hierarchy and its ecological consequences. It merely presumes an imaginary world in which communicative action is unaffected by differences in power, rather than examining why and how such an imaginary world will come into being this time. A sociology that sets up a standard of humans as cherubim is not by that fact more profound, insightful, or revolutionary than the rest of sociology.

There is little that is practical in the theory of practical reason. "Habermas is veiled by a formalism so abstract and a jargon so equivocal and dense that he is almost beyond the reach of pointed criticism" (Bookchin 1980: 222). His theory of practical reason can easily dissolve into sterile generalizations and facile platitudes: "practical reasoning is less cumbersome than bargaining, for only norms and broad principles are 'negotiated,' not the detailed contents of actions" (Dryzek 1987: 205). Consensus concerning a broad principle favoring the natural environment is easy but superficial. It is the detailed specific actions of humans that affect the environment, however "cumbersome" bargaining over them may be. During the last two millennia Christians have been in agreement concerning the broad commandment to love one's neighbor, but that has not prevented them from taking action to kill each other in numerous wars. Why will the broad norm to love nature suffer a different fate? If broad norms are not translated into detailed specific actions, they become irrelevant.

Dryzek (1987: 211) argues that "practical reason promises substantial advance on the 'coordination' aspect of ecological rationality" because the experimental literature shows that group discussion prior to individual choice increases cooperation. Yet here he merely equates practical reason and group discussion. The omnipresent group discussion in bureaucratic committees, public or private, has not led to ecological rationality.

Dryzek is silent concerning how the paradise of ideal speech, communicative rationality, and virtuous practical reason are to be arrived at and maintained. His (Dryzek 1987: 211) criticism of critical theory applies *grosso modo* to his own endeavor: "its proponents have said little about institutions which would promote 'discursive will-formation' in any set of concrete circumstances. If one cannot deduce any implications for institutional structure, however modest, from the idea of communicative rationalization, then one might as well reject it."

Dryzek (1987: 213) does suggest one mechanism for promoting practical reason, namely, environmental mediation. But he fails to show why mediation as it presently exists, which he himself criticizes as "a mere compromise between competing particular interests" (Dryzek 1987: 213) often detrimental to general environmental interests, will be replaced by his hyper-idealized mediation in which manipulation and propaganda are discarded and virtuous reason holds sway. He merely assumes an ideal state of affairs, rather than demonstrating how or why it will come into being.

Moreover, why should practical reason, communicative rationality, and ideal speech lead to ecological rationality rather than to some other conception of rationality and virtue, perhaps even a conception based on environmental mastery and plasticity? Since there are many different conceptions of virtue, it is not self-evident that virtuous reason will lead to a symbiotic relationship between social action and the processes of nature. Dryzek, and Habermas before him, fail to perceive the depth of difficulty confronting reason in arriving at consensus because they underestimate irreducible value diversity: "the various value spheres of the world stand in irreconcilable conflict with each other ... here too, different gods struggle with one another, now and for all times to come" (Weber 1958: 147-8). It is the content of reason, rationality, and speech that counts, and that will be determined by struggle, not by gods but by humans, to give priority to values that result in a symbiotic relationship between social action and the processes of nature.

Discourse about practical reason fails to advance our understanding of why humans will change from a parasitic to a symbiotic relationship with nature, that is, it fails to advance a theory of transition. The key question is: what will promote ecological rationality in its struggle with other conceptions of value rationality during reasoned debate, communicative discussion, and speech? The unavoidable answer to this question is the necessity to maintain a human-supporting natural infrastructure, that is, an ecological form of instrumental rationality to satisfy human material interests. If practical reason leads to ecological rationality, it is because of the requirements of the natural environment for satisfying long-term human needs. It is this that makes ecology reasonable to humans and stimulates the appeal of the intrinsic value of nature.

Hence the issue of developing a symbiotic relationship between social action and the processes of nature is not one of practical reason, communicative rationality and ideal speech (value rationalization in Weber's terms) versus instrumental rationality, but rather one of constructing ecological forms of both value rationality and instrumental rationality. Humans, like all other animals, have and will necessarily always have an instrumental relationship with nature, in the sense of using the natural environment as the means to survive and flourish. The problem of parasitism has been introduced in the case of humans by the scale and intensity of their instrumental relationship with nature, which threatens to destroy in the long run the capacity of the natural environment to support humans and other species. Thus ecological instrumental rationality calls for the reorientation of the human-nature relationship from parasitism (excessive and destructive instrumentalization) back to symbiosis. Ecological value rationality calls for a greater appreciation of nature and of its other species as a value in itself, deep ecologists being in the forefront of such a movement promoting the intrinsic value of nature. These two forms of ecological rationality are complementary and mutually reinforcing.

The opposition Dryzek, following Habermas, constructs between particular interests and generalizable, common interests is, although seductive at first glance, not as valuable as it seems. For example, the particular interests of native groups in maintaining traditional, small-scale hunting and fishing requiring a large, waste-free land mass is convergent with the long-run generalizable interests of all humans in unpolluted water and air and in a symbiotic relationship with the natural environment. These particular interests of natives clash, however, with the particular interests -- the pursuit of profit and jobs -- of logging companies and loggers, pulp and paper companies and their workers, mining companies and miners, oil companies and oil workers, etc. Symbiotic particular interests converge with symbiotic generalizable interests, and are in opposition to parasitic particular interests. Similarly, parasitic generalizable interests of humans are in opposition to symbiotic generalizable interests. For example, the development of a high material standard of living for all humans would appear to be a generalizable, common interest, yet it has the potential to play havoc with the environment, destroy other living species and their habitats, and thereby harm future generations of humans. The ecological opposition is not between particular and generalizable interests *per se*. Rather it is between parasitic and symbiotic interests, whether they be particular or generalizable.

Ecological Ethics

Weber examined the tensions that had developed in his time between the different spheres of value, such as religion, economics, politics, aesthetic values, and intellectual values. "The very tensions between those spheres for Weber generated a derived need, the metaphysical need to resolve those conflicts and to find a common meaning to them all and to life" (Albrow 1990: 239). The ecological sphere is extraordinary in that, although it generates one more area of tension and conflict, it is the holistic sphere *par excellence*. By the very fact that it emphasizes relationships within a global system, not only between humans but also between the human species and other living species as well as their physical environment, it forms a particularly propitious basis for holistic values created to satisfy the need for a common meaning to all the various spheres and to life. Hence one line of argument claims that a symbiotic relationship between social action and the processes of nature can best be advanced through ethical appeals founded on holistic ecological values.

The anarchist version of social ecology is one current of thought that advocates change in terms of holistic ecological ethics:

> this book is primarily intended to give voice to a revolutionary idea of social change ... authentic politics stood opposed to evil and called for its complete negation by the good ... we have dissociated politics from ethics. ... This shift is utterly subversive of any significant reconstruction of the body politic as an agent for achieving the historic goal of the good life, not merely as a practical ideal but as an ethical and spiritual one. ... To reverse this denormatization of politics by a leprous series of 'trade-offs,' to provide an ethical holism rooted in the objective values that emerge from ecology and anarchism, is fundamental to this book. ... It is on this classical ethics that all else rests in the pages that follow. (Bookchin 1980: 30-1)

The anarchist interpretation of ecology as symbiotic rather than competitive enables it to become the basis of an ethics of cooperation rather than a system of domination. Ecology is "a *participatory* realm of interactive life-forms whose most outstanding attributes are fecundity, creativity, and directiveness, marked by complementarity that renders the natural world the grounding for an ethics of freedom rather than domination" (Bookchin 1987: 55).

Anarchist social ecology has founded its proposed reconstruction of the relationship between social action and the processes of nature on an appeal to humanity's sense of justice for humans and has proposed a new ethical ideal: a social order based on the elimination of all forms of hierarchy among humans. It has not followed neo-Malthusians, advocates of sustainable development, and many scientific ecologists who have made their appeal for social change on the basis of the long-term material interests of humans. Anarchist ecologists reason as follows. "If we rely on self-interest and economic motives to evoke the popular response that will deal with these overarching [ecological and social] problems, we will be relying on the very constellation of psychological factors that have so decisively contributed to their emergence" (Bookchin 1987: 32). Hence the "entire panoply of so-called appropriate technologies ... should be seen more in terms of their ethical function than their operational efficiency. ... Fundamental to that sense of interdependence is a re-visioning of nature as a moral basis for a new ecological ethics" (Bookchin 1987: 96).

Anarchists such as Bookchin (1980: 241-2) argue that "*desire*, not merely need, *possibility*, not merely necessity, enter into her or his [the individual's] self-formation and self-activity" and they attempt to re-establish the appeal of ethics to creative subjects rather than perceiving humans as objects governed by forces that work behind their backs (Bookchin 1980: 198, 200). They argue that history is forged by intentions rather than forces. "Not to form visions that break radically with the present is to deny a future that can be qualitatively different from the present" (Bookchin 1980: 284).

Deep ecology has also appealed to humanity's sense of justice, in its case justice toward non-human species of life, and has proposed an ideal as well: an ecotopia based on biospherical equality (Devall and Sessions 1985; Sale 1988). Deep ecology too contains a proposal for change in terms of a transformation of values: away from an instrumental orientation to nature toward an appreciation of nature for its inherent value. The proposed re-enchantment of nature would give it new intrinsic meaning. Nature would be valued instead of consumed or seen as a mere instrument to consumption. This would become the basis of a code of ecological ethics that would determine how people, individually and collectively, ought to act toward the environment.

> We have a moral obligation to preserve wilderness and biodiversity, to develop a respectful and symbiotic relationship with that portion of the biosphere that we do inhabit, and to cause no unnecessary harm to non-human life. ... For social ethics to be ecologically grounded they must become consistent with this larger ecological moral imperative. That is why I am for Earth first. (Foreman 1991: 116)

The theory of transition more or less explicit in this reorientation is that of an ethical transformation and value conversion, from nature viewed as a means and instrument to nature valued intrinsically.

Ethical arguments and the attempt to emphasize the intrinsic value of nature have a significant role to play in promoting a symbiotic relationship between social action and the processes of nature. Like all proposed conversion attempts, however, the conversion to ecological ethics and/or an appreciation of nature's intrinsic appeal as a predominant ethical principle and cultural value runs into difficulties in practice. The weaknesses of practical reason specified in the previous section are just as true of theories of transition to a symbiotic relationship with nature based on ethical appeals and value conversion. Beck (1992b: 106) succinctly expresses some of the inadequacies: "An ethical renewal of the sciences, even if it were not to become entangled in the thicket of ethical viewpoints, would be like a bicycle brake on an intercontinental jet, considering the autonomization of technological development and its interconnections with economic interests." Such theories do not explain why conformity to those ethics and values will occur, rather than deviance from them. In dismissing self-interest as a catalyst to change, Bookchin fails to take advantage of a fundamental shift in the perception of self-interest fostered by environmental problems: from short-term economic self-interest to long-term ecological self-interest.

Paradoxically, Bookchin himself has forcefully expressed the limitations of ethical arguments to change the capitalist exploitation of humans and of nature.

> It is not the perversity of the bourgeois that creates production for the sake of production, but the very market nexus over which he presides and to which he succumbs. ... It requires a grotesque self-deception, or worse, an act of ideological social deception, to foster the belief that this society can undo its very law of life in response to ethical arguments or intellectual persuasion. (Bookchin 1980: 66)

Yet "ethical arguments" and "intellectual persuasion" are precisely what Bookchin emphasizes in order to promote anarchist ecology. Bookchin is of course referring to the difficulty of *reforming* capitalism to render it harmonious with nature, but his argument applies *a fortiori* to the difficulty of *replacing* capitalism with a revolutionary non-hierarchical society by means of ethical argumentation.

Bookchin also blinds himself to questions of fact and knowledge by formulating questions as purely moral issues. "Entering deeply into the factors that have produced the dilemma is a moral issue: the conviction that every benefit must be 'purchased' by a risk -- in short, that for every 'advance' humanity must pay a penalty" (Bookchin 1987: 5). Although there are moral aspects to it, benefits-versus-risks analysis is also a question of historical fact, and knowledge or lack of it. The benefits of air travel have unwittingly come at the risk of polluting the upper atmosphere. The benefits of refrigeration and air conditioning have come at the price of depleting the ozone layer. There was no conspiracy to deplete the ozone layer, rather the environmental impact of those 'advances' was unintended and indirect. The problem is not that benefits-versus-risks analysis is immoral, as Bookchin implies, but rather that benefits-versus-risks analysis in terms of environmental impact assessment has not been done. Theorists such as Bookchin can talk with facility in abstract terms about "appropriate technology" for a "post-scarcity" utopia, but in practice the determination of the ecological appropriateness of technology is problematic and requires knowledge. Such knowledge is typically incomplete from a global ecological point of view. Hence benefits often entail risks. This is particularly true for technology that is new, even technology that recycles or disposes of waste. The alternatives to a benefits-versus-risks assessment as a prelude to action are, on the one hand, brinkmanship benefits based on ignorance of risk, or on the other, stagnation in the midst of an environmental mess.

Olsen et al. (1992: 169) concluded from their survey research that an environmental ethic in the form of an ecological social paradigm is replacing the technological social paradigm in the United States and perhaps other industrial societies. However, they do not document how deeply this environmental ethic is held. For example, it is easy to say to an interviewer that something should be done to save the environment. But is this value held deeply enough to prevent the respondent from purchasing an automobile and compelling him or her to use public transportation? There is little sign of a shift to environmental ethics in the usage rates of the polluting private car as opposed to environmentally more benign public transportation. Environmental ethics only make an ecological difference if they affect human use of their environment. If not, they are mere verbal rituals. Olsen et al. (1992: 169) themselves admit that such an environmental ethic is not sufficient to deal with environmental problems.

Recently, the theory of transition based on an appeal to ethics and values has also been criticized from within deep ecology. Many deep ecologists (see Fox 1990) are now concerned that the development of ecological ethics will be ineffective in motivating an anthropocentric human species to make the transition from a parasitic to a symbiotic relationship with nature. They worry that humans are more motivated by their own material interests than by ideals or by ethical pronouncements. Thus deep ecologists now bluntly express their concern over the fecklessness of ethical appeals: 'sermons seldom hinder us from pursuing our self-interest" (Macy 1987: 20). They therefore increasingly seek a more effective way to transform the relationship between social action and the processes of nature. They are now beginning to invert Bookchin's claim by advancing the argument that need, not merely desire, necessity, not merely possibility, can shape social action.

Ecological Consciousness

The previous quotation from deep ecology continues as follows.

> Sermons seldom hinder us from pursuing our self-interest, so we need to be a little more enlightened about what our self-interest is. It would not occur to me, for example, to exhort you to refrain from cutting off your leg. That wouldn't occur to me or to you, because your leg is part of you. Well, so are the trees in the Amazon Basin; they are our external lungs. We are just beginning to wake up to that. We are gradually discovering that we *are* our world. (Macy 1987: 20)

Thus the offshoot of deep ecology -- transpersonal ecology -- argues that the transition to a symbiotic relationship with nature can be better achieved by shifting away from a focus on the intrinsic value of other species and ecosystems *per se* (biocentricity), and from ethical arguments, towards an extended view of what human self interest, and the 'self,' involves (Fox 1990).

Transpersonal ecology argues in favor of an enlarged, non-anthropocentric view of the self that goes beyond the person and encompasses other species and all of nature. The human individual is seen as but one element of its holistic ecosystem, entering into ecological relations with other elements. Human material interests and indeed the 'self' are redefined in terms of the ecosystem to which humans belong in order to promote identification with that ecosystem. Any world-view that perceives the universe as a holistic ecological process, whether it be mythological, religious, speculative philosophical, or scientific, can bring about an empathic "deep-seated realization of the fact that we and all other entities are aspects of a single unfolding reality" (Fox 1990: 252). Transpersonal ecologists postulate that "if one has a deep understanding of the way things *are* (i.e., if one empathically incorporates the fact that we and all other entities are aspects of a single unfolding reality) then one *will* (as opposed to should) naturally be inclined to care for the unfolding of the world in all its aspects" (Fox 1990: 247).

Ecological consciousness thus replaces ecological ethics as a more realistic proposal for making the transition from a parasitic relationship with nature to a symbiotic relationship.

> As the implications of evolution and ecology are internalized and replace the outmoded anthropocentric structures in your mind, there is an identification with all life. ... It is only by identification with the whole process that correct values will emerge. Otherwise we see it as self-sacrifice or effort. In shallow ecology arguments we're always trying to balance jobs and environment. If we identify with the immense process ... we see immediately our correct self-interest whereas the self-interest of the narrow ego in modern societies is mistaken self-interest. (John Seed, quoted in Fox 1990: 239-40)

However, this theory of identification with a wider ecological 'self,' as proposed by transpersonal ecologists, conflates two distinct constituents. One refers to a truly expanded self, which includes all of nature, such that protecting another species would be seen as protecting oneself, even if there were no evidence that decreased numbers of that species would be harmful to humans. In this sense, humans would identify as part of their 'expanded self' not only parts of nature useful to them, such as the Amazon forests as their external lungs, but also parts dangerous to them, like the smallpox virus, and those that are a nuisance, for example, the cockroaches in the kitchens of some old houses rented by university students. Exploiting an oil field or a mineral deposit would be seen as exploiting one's self. This constituent begs the question of the transition to a symbiotic relationship with nature. If there is no demonstrable material interest for the individual, why will humans identify with the rest of nature to the extent of conceiving of it as part of their 'selves'? Why will humans not pick and choose particular parts of nature to identify with according to their individual, and/or species, self-interest? The answer is that they will identify with those parts of nature that do not demonstrably serve their interests only to the extent that they regard nature as a whole as intrinsically valuable. This constituent brings us full circle back to the intrinsic value approach of early deep ecology -- to sermons, moral 'oughts,' ethical exhortations, sacrifice, etc. -- with all its limitations as a theory of transition to a symbiotic relationship with nature, limitations that transpersonal ecologists have themselves specified.

Rather than solving the problem of the transition to a symbiotic relationship with the natural environment, this constituent -- purportedly eschewing sacrifice -- leaves a host of unanswered questions. Why will people see forests and oilfields as part of their 'selves' to be defended, rather than as resources to be exploited? Why will they not perceive the reduction in their level of material consumption as sacrifice? Why will they not perceive deep, transpersonal ecology as ecological puritanism? In short, why will a worldview based on an all-encompassing sense of self have any appeal? Fox (1990: 251) responds weakly: "I can only reiterate that these remarks cannot and should not be analyzed through a logical lens." They belong, he claims, to the realm of the mystical, of experientially based spirituality.

The second constituent refers to the dependence of humans on their human-supporting natural environment, and appeals to a common human self-interest in its maintenance. Material self-interest at a time of ecological crisis promotes an appreciation of the long-term dependency of human selves, however narrowly defined, on the natural environment and promotes an awareness of the necessity of attaining a symbiotic relationship with nature, thereby transcending short-term material gain. It is on this basis that there is hope that humans will change, within the near future, their values, practices, and institutions to render them symbiotic with nature, because it is in their material interests, and especially those of their children and grandchildren, to do so. And it is in this sense that change is a question not just of ecological sermons, ethics, and 'moral oughts,' but of ecological self-interest. This constituent consists, not of a vague expanded conception of the self that includes all of nature, but rather the classical conception of the self as human individual who is socially and biologically related to his or her offspring. Social change can flow from the present conception of the self in instrumentally rational society rather than requiring as a necessary launching pad an all-inclusive, improbable conception of self foreign to that society.

Ecological Experience and Ecological Knowledge

In Weber's view the development of rationality, one important aspect of which aimed for the mastery of nature, paradoxically did not lead to control by individuals and in fact led to their alienation. "The vast resources this intellectualisation provided the human race in the form of accumulated knowledge and technique created for Weber a disenchanted world ... which they [individuals] knew in principle to be wholly explicable, but over which they had no control. But the development of this alienating rationality appeared to him to be inherent in any prospects for the future which he could discern" (Albrow 1990: 122).

This alienating rationality involves a process by which nature comes to appear foreign to humans and remote from their needs.

> Weber uses the term *Entfremdung*, 'alienation', to designate the position of those urban groups to mean precisely the separation of daily life from a unity with nature ... the briefest way in which one might characterise Weber's theory is that it is a developmental theory of human need in which the needs of a person are met, conditioned, created by specific social and cultural circumstances. Needs and interests (not identical, but often used almost interchangeably by Weber) are compelling forces in society which have to be satisfied one way or another. (Albrow 1990: 73-4)

The problem of alienation consists of socially and culturally developed needs that have become separate from, and indeed out of touch with, nature. This problem is closely associated with urbanization, including the more recent phenomenon of global urbanization.

Despite Weber's expression of pessimism, his analysis provides the basis for a solution to this problem. Consumption practices based on a socially and culturally conditioned sense of needs and interests can be confronted with more compelling long-term needs and interests of humans and their offspring: the need for an ozone layer, for uncontaminated water and pure air, for a chain of living species upon which the human species depends, for human contact with nature, etc. The alienation of humans from nature, and the exploitation of alien nature, can be countered by the rediscovery of the interests of humans in a natural environment capable of meeting more fundamental human needs over the long term. A better understanding of the long-term ecological needs of humans has the potential to redirect the perception of human needs and their development in a more ecological direction, thereby stimulating material ecological interests to become also ideal interests. Such understanding is promoted by the ecological experience of environmental degradation in the daily lives of people: increased frequency of skin cancer due to the depletion of the ozone layer, reduced fish stocks in rivers and oceans, polluted air in cities, accumulation of toxic and radioactive waste, inability to find dump sites, etc. The latent side effects of rationalization are losing their latency and becoming manifest.

Showing that it is in the best interests of humans to enter into a symbiotic relationship with the ecosystem as a whole, and not just specific parts of it, can be done by demonstrating that nature is a powerful force that unleashes perverse consequences when initiated by human attempts to manipulate it in a parasitic way. Nature itself provides the demonstration through ecological experience, but it can also be done with less suffering through ecological knowledge.

Dunlap and Catton have spent a lifetime studying the relationship between social action and nature, and have come to the following conclusions (Dunlap 1993, Dunlap and Catton 1993). Whereas environmental problems were seen until recently as an aesthetic concern or as an irritant, they are increasingly perceived as a direct threat to human well-being because of the changing character of those problems. (1) They have become more frequent, creating a sense of pervasiveness. (2) They have increased in scale, becoming global and potentially affecting many more people. (3) The consequences for present humans, future generations, and other species are more serious. (4) They are poorly understood, difficult to detect and predict, and the consequences may be irreversible. Hence the changing character of ecological problems is an important impetus leading them to appear riskier and more urgent.

Although some environmental classes are likely to be victimized more than others, the global disruption of the equilibrium nature has constructed puts everyone at risk. The health and wealth of even the rich and powerful are threatened, and their future and that of their offspring is uncertain as well: "the pauperization of the Third World through hazards is contagious for the wealthy. The multiplication of risks causes world society to contract into a community of danger. The boomerang effect strikes precisely those wealthy countries which had hoped to get rid of hazards by transferring them overseas, but then had to import cheaper foodstuffs" (Beck 1992a: 44). The merely partial knowledge of the forces of nature unleashed by humans results in uncertainty for everyone. This universalization of human-provoked, ecological risk is unique to advanced rationalization. Such risks threaten the health of humans and other species, and for those who remain unconcerned by these matters, they also threaten the political, social, economic, and cultural constructions of humans. Bank accounts and livelihoods may deteriorate before health. The hazards of rationalization undermine the advantages of hitherto existing forms of rationalization.

> Catastrophes that touch the vital nerves of society in a context of highly developed bureaucratic safety and welfare arouse the sensationalist greed of the mass media, threaten markets, make sales prospects unpredictable, devalue capital and set streams of voters in motion. Thus the evening news ultimately exceeds even the fantasies of countercultural dissent; daily newspaper reading becomes an exercise in technology critique. (Beck 1992b: 116)

The commonality of anxiety does not, however, take the place of the commonality of need, as Beck (1992a: 49) assumes. Rather the commonality of anxiety results precisely from the commonality of need for fresh air, clean water, healthy food, and a secure natural environment necessary for social, economic, and cultural prosperity.

The global character of ecological problems creates an accumulating dynamic of vulnerability in which nations must either negotiate international cooperation or face ecological ruin. Moreover, the need to stop environmental degradation and begin its restoration does not affect all businesses negatively. In the transition to a symbiotic relationship with nature, there will be profits made, market share increased, and jobs created. Companies do not speak with a unified voice in opposition to changes required to bring about a symbiotic relationship with nature.

The missing answer to the question of why practical reason would choose ecological rationality over a non-ecological value rationality, and why there is hope for greater ecological consciousness, becomes evident. It is because of ecological experience and ecological knowledge, with ecological knowledge being the early warning sensor of ecological experience. The finite limits of the planet, the partiality of human knowledge of the workings of nature and hence the necessity of expecting the unintended unleashing of new forces of nature when humans manipulate the natural environment, as well as the lack of certitude that human reason could artificially match the balances nature has created, stimulate an interest in prudence when purposive interventions in nature are undertaken. For example, environmental problems are already beginning to prompt the development of "social impact assessment" and "environmental risk analysis" (Short 1984; Freudenburg 1986, 1988; Dietz 1987; Dietz et al. 1989), however partial they may be at the present time. Despite his tendency to reduce ecology to its social component, Bookchin redeems himself, albeit all-too-rarely, by perceiving nature too as a causal dynamic. "All of this must be done if we are to resolve the ecological crisis that threatens the very existence of the biosphere in the decades that lie ahead. It is not a visionary 'blueprint' or 'scenario' that mandates these far-reaching alterations in our social structures and relations, but the dictates of nature itself" (Bookchin 1980: 285).

Ecological experience and ecological knowledge are socially constructed in that perceptions are influenced by contingencies, interests, and values. This is particularly evident when such knowledge is propagated by the mass media. Ecological knowledge is not, however, free-floating. The assumption that such knowledge is nothing but a socially constructed fiction is refuted by experience. There is a sensory, experiential basis underlying ecological knowledge precisely because humans are not pure spirits, rather they are themselves part of nature embedded in natural processes. People see the smog, the dead trees, the foam in rivers, and the eroded buildings and monuments. They smell the pollution in the air near heavy industry, taste the insipid water, see the dead fish wash up on beaches, die of skin cancer, etc. Even with radar, fishermen find fewer fish to catch. The deadly experience of the people of Hiroshima and Nagisaki demonstrated to all the catastrophic force of nuclear energy. Although the outcome is not straightforward, nor automatic, nor predetermined, the experience of ecological problems lends credence to constructed messages describing their development, and has the potential to put the lie to constructed messages denying their existence.[4] Thus Beck (1992a: 72) is in error when he argues that "ultimately *no one* can know about risks, so long as to know means to have consciously experienced." Just ask the people of Bhopal, or Chernobyl, or those in fishing villages or tourist areas who see an oil slick wash up on their beaches and find the lifeless fish and oil-coated birds. Science enables humans to foresee in time, and the media to communicate in distant space, what other humans will or are consciously experiencing. Human embeddedness in nature is confirmed by a process more basic than words, namely, by every breath humans take.

Take a related example. Some smokers followed the constructed message of cigarette companies and denied the equally constructed message of the connection between cigarettes and lung cancer (as well as cardio-vascular problems). Their deaths then informed other smokers concerning the credibility of the opposing messages. Death itself is a process of nature that tends to be particularly persuasive. Many have stopped smoking, and taught their children not to start, because deaths of relatives and friends or their own health problems have made medical statistics believable and those of cigarette companies untrustworthy. The executives of cigarette companies themselves have the difficult task of swallowing their own propaganda when they decide whether to encourage their offspring to smoke.

Beck (1992a: 55) is correct when he contends that the "*latency phase of risk threats is coming to an end. The invisible hazards are becoming visible.* Damage to and destruction of nature no longer occur outside our personal experience in the sphere of chemical, physical or biological chains of effects; instead they strike more and more clearly our eyes, ears and noses." Failure to satisfy the ecological requirements of the chain of life, and not just of human life, is becoming a perceptible global threat to people's health, and also to their economic and social life. The assumption that society, culture, politics, and the economy can be understood as autonomous of nature -- the presumed dualism between humans and nature that was taken for granted in the early phase of instrumental rationalization -- is being undermined as waste accumulates and environmental problems intensify.

Ecological experience and ecological knowledge are resulting in a wider identification with nature, not in terms of seeing all of nature as one's self but rather by perceiving one's self as part of nature dependent upon its broader, long-term dynamics, thereby stimulating a more adaptive orientation toward nature. Ecological experience, especially the experience of the consequences of the degradation of the natural environment, paradoxically lays the basis for the development of a new, more respectful image of the relationship between social action and the processes of nature than the images of plasticity and mastery. Hence it has the potential to predispose humans to develop science, and the technology it leads to, in a way that would be partial to a symbiotic relationship with nature instead of the present parasitic relationship. Such a symbiotic relationship can rise from the accumulated waste of the parasitic relationship that now exists.

An ecological perspective is already developing in society and in science as a result of the interaction of environmental problems, environmental science, and environmental activism (Oates 1989, Caldwell 1990, Stern et al. 1990). In science, growing evidence of mounting ecological deterioration has given credibility to a broad ecological approach -- focussing on the interaction between human societies and the ecosystems they inhabit -- in its struggle against the specialized, reductionist, and technologically optimistic perspectives that have hitherto dominated the scientific establishment (Dunlap and Catton 1993b). A U.S. National Academy of Sciences report recently argued as follows. "So potent is the human impact on the earth system that knowledge of physical processes ruling terrestrial or atmospheric change will be incomplete until scientists better understand the human dimensions of that change" (quoted in Silver and DeFries 1990: 46-7).

By demonstrating the unsuspected global impact of waste accumulation, scientific ecology can present humans with a better and more precise view of what their long-term material interests are. This is precisely what happened with the discovery of the depletion of the ozone layer. This deeper conception of material interests then has the potential to promote ecological consciousness and symbiotic practices. Scientific knowledge of ecological problems is not, however, unproblematic (Yearley 1991). It is itself partial in both senses of being incomplete and oriented to particular interests. Its provisional character can be misused to justify, for lack of scientific certainty, the continuation of environmental degradation. Despite its limitations, science is none the less the means that enables us to see most clearly, which does not mean perfectly, what the ecological problems and possibilities are.

Although Yearley (1991: 144) is correct to conclude that in "a narrow sense, science does not seem to compel people to conserve particular bits of their environment nor tell them what the conservation priorities are," it must be remembered that nothing else has compelled people to do that either. Ecological knowledge as the early warning sensor of ecological experience can, if not compel, at least influence people to take the ecological high ground. Pollutants "induce systematic and often *irreversible* harm, generally remain *invisible*, are based on *causal interpretations*, and thus initially only exist in terms of the (scientific or anti-scientific) *knowledge* about them. ... Knowledge gains a new political significance" (Beck 1992a: 22-3).

Even transpersonal ecology has now begun to suggest that scientific knowledge, as well as the experience of the effects of ecological problems, promote a wider ecological identification and ecological values.

> The other side of science is its importance for understanding our place in the larger scheme of things (and it is scarcely necessary to add that this aspect has had profoundly *non*anthropocentric implications). ... modern science is providing an increasingly detailed account of the physical and biological evolution of the universe that compels us to view reality as a single unfolding process. (Fox 1990: 253)

Allowing the character of the social-natural relationship to inform our consciousness, values, and social organization, either through experience or knowledge, has the potential to challenge reason in all its forms to proceed in the direction of a symbiotic relationship with nature. Ecological experience and/or ecological knowledge underlie decisions made through practical reason, ecological ethics, and ecological consciousness.

Reflexive and Reflective Rationalization

Beck (1992a, 1992b) argues that we are entering a new type of modernity, "reflexive modernity," and the "risk society." Science, engineering, and business are generating a revolution in which they produce threats that are knowable only through science, engineering, and the media. The archetype of such threats, radiation, is imperceptible even to its victims. "The structuring of the future is taking place indirectly and unrecognizably in research laboratories and executive suites, not in the parliament or in political parties" (Beck 1992a: 223). Attempts to deny or downplay such threats, or to interpret them as inevitable side-effects, or to propose end-of-pipe remedies rather than attack causes, constitute sub-politics that seek to legitimate present activities. There is also another side of sub-politics. "Through the influence of various centers of sub-politics -- media publicity, citizens' initiatives, new social movements, critical engineers and judges -- operational decisions and production methods can be publicly denounced instantaneously, and forced with the cudgel of lost market shares to give a *non*-economic, *discursive* justification of their measures" (Beck 1992a: 223). Primary rationalization is being replaced by the reflexive rationalization of the premises of previously taken-for-granted processes of change (Beck 1992a: 216-7).

> In this *second-degree* rationalization the principles of centralization and bureaucratization, along with the associated rigidity of social structures, come into conflict with the principles of *flexibility*. The latter gain increasing priority in the situations of risk and uncertainty that are coming into being, but also presuppose new, as yet unforeseeable, forms of *externally monitored self-coordination* of subsystems and decentralized units of action. (Beck 1992a: 231-2)

Beck's work is particularly stimulating, but there are some problems. His concept of "risk society" is of dubious value as the distinguishing feature of contemporary society because many previous societies have also been risk societies. Societies heading into war constituted risk societies, such as the Confederate American states in 1861 and the Austro-Hungarian Empire in 1914. If risk is to have anything to do with possible outcomes, the USSR was a risk society by the 1980s. Even if they remained more or less intact, European societies were risk societies during the two world wars. Economic competition has also resulted in risk societies for some time, as the case of Argentina shows. Risk can have many and varied sources. How could Ireland at the time of the repeated famines in the nineteenth century not be referred to as a risk society? If risk society is to refer to one where members are in a state of anxiety about their future, then it corresponds to Weber's characterization of salvation anxiety among Puritans. And medieval Catholic societies constituted risk societies too, for what could be more anxiety provoking to believers than the risk of the hellfires of damnation. Secular rationalization has reduced risk at least in the sense that death only comes once, whereas hell is for eternity.

It is not so much "risk society" that distinguishes contemporary societies, rather it is the peculiar character of the risk. Whereas in the past the risks involved social constructions with little effect on nature, or only local effects, today's human constructions imperil life on the planet. They have potentially global effects on ecosystems. Unlike the past, contemporary human constructions have unleashed forces of nature that threaten to return and destroy the very humans who let them loose. Modern societies are distinctive in the character of their manipulation of nature. But since nature is not plastic nor static, this involves not just social action but interaction with nature's processes, which returns to affect social action. Hence modern, rational society is reflexive in the sense that its social action turns back on the subject precisely because modern society ruins the equilibrium constructed by the dynamics of nature. The major weakness of Beck's (1992a, 1992b) work is that he does not pay sufficient and explicit attention to nature's processes and their interaction with social constructions. There has not been, as Beck (1992a: 49) claims, a transition from class society to risk society. Risk society existed in the past and class society continues to exist. Rather a new character of risk -- global, ecological risk -- has emerged from the formal rationalization processes of class society.

Moreover, unlike previous threats, those of today result from the development of science yet need science to be understood or even accurately perceived. If it were not for the development of science, there might not be a hole in the ozone layer, and we certainly would not know if a hole were present. Radiation is imperceptible until it provokes a fatal sickness, and even then science is required to attach effects to cause. Contemporary risks have the distinguishing features of being global, produced by humans, and not readily perceptible without science. They amount to science undermining itself by its very success, yet science being necessary to comprehend the problems and find solutions.

Current risks consist of the possibility that rationalization (the core feature of modernity) may lead to the ultimate irrationality of self-destruction. The chance that these consequences will occur challenges science, rationalization, and society to be more reflective, in the sense of thoughtful, about the rationalization process. The reflexive quality of rational constructions manipulating nature such that nature recoils against the constructors throws down the challenge of reflectiveness and a further intensification of rationalization in terms of a fundamental rethinking of its goals. This has the potential to make the economy less self-referential, that is, less dependent on the self-propelled stimulation of short-term desires for luxuries and gadgets that has hitherto characterized it and more dependent on the satisfaction of basic, long-term human needs.[5]

Not all threats are caused by humans. Science increases awareness of risk concerning threats that originate in nature's processes as well. The implication of the big bang theory of the universe is that the destiny of human society is oblivion. The fading of stars implies the fading of our sun, hence of life on earth. Dinosaurs are known only through science, and the causes of their extinction are only suspected. The implication of their demise is that if such powerful creatures became extinct as a result of natural forces, so could humans. Although such threats are exceedingly remote, awareness of them through science challenges the anthropocentric bias of human culture and stimulates reflection about the place of humans in the larger cosmos.

Science and rationalization involve decisions at each step of the way, and it is the results of these decisions that upset nature's equilibrium. This in turn forces us to decide new issues. Phenomena that appeared self-evident, or those where no decision was possible, now require decisions. The development of the means of fetal surgery demands decisions concerning the question of when human life begins, and life-extending technology such as artificial lungs compels decisions about when it ends. Knowledge of the effect of CFCs on the ozone layer challenges humans to decide between air-conditioning, an ozone layer, new technology that may have other deleterious properties and prove costly, etc. Knowledge of atmospheric pollution by the automobile imposes a decision between the private car, public transportation, and solar-powered vehicles that may be slower and more expensive. Even denial of problems or refusal to decide are themselves decisions. So too are the opposite extremes of holding everyone responsible for ecological problems, and therefore no one, or scapegoating a few so that others can avoid responsibility. Each of these decisions has consequences for the organizations producing air-conditioners, automobiles, and the like, for life styles, and for consumption patterns. Because of their public character, the state and civil society are increasingly involved in these decisions, which itself is a dramatic change from the past when enterprises could do as they please. Society confronts its own prior decisions because of the interaction of the effects of those decisions with the dynamic processes of nature. Reflexive rationalization is forcing reflective rationalization upon human society.

Parasitism:
From an Iron Cage to a Cloak to Be Thrown Off

However great humans believed their mastery of nature and however plastic they felt their relationship with nature, nature has succeeded in reminding them of its power by overwhelming their projects. The struggle to master nature has proved to be the pursuit of a mirage: the closer humans think they get to controlling nature, the more they learn the increasingly global environmental consequences of their actions, and mastery recedes and eludes them once more. The assumption of a plastic relationship between humans and their natural environment -- the hitherto prevailing premise of both capitalism and state socialism -- has been exposed by environmental problems and by recent detailed investigations, such as those of Perrow (1984) and Dryzek (1987), to be misleading.

Their work, as well as that of Dunlap and Catton, have established that the natural environment is not just a stage upon which human actors play out their social action. Nor is it merely "the interior furnishings of the civilizational world" (Beck 1992a: 80). Human choice and human activity take place, not in a passive context being molded by humans, but within a dynamic ecosystem of which human activity is but one part. Nature is a powerful process rather than a quiescent limiting condition. As Perrow has shown, nature reacts to human manipulations based on partial knowledge by exploding, corroding, contaminating, earthquaking, greenhousing, etc. Social action enters into a dialectical relationship with the rest of nature's dynamic processes.

Those studies have confirmed the basic Weberian intuition: "Nothing could be further from the truth than to see Weber's account of the rationalisation process as the inevitable unfolding of the power of rationality. The material world was always recalcitrant, always placed limits on what could be done" (Albrow 1990: 186). The embeddedness of social action in nature and yet the dialectical relationship between social action and the dynamic processes of nature, with society acting on nature and nature acting on society, have produced both a new social order and a new natural environment, unfortunately one characterized mainly by its degradation.

The spontaneity, complexity, and tight coupling of nature have resulted in human uncertainty about the effects of social action on the natural environment (Dryzek 1987) and through it on humanity itself. This, plus the effects of the accumulation of waste that has gone hand in hand with the accumulation of capital, and the fact that everyone is affected by the degradation of the natural environment, are conditions that challenge the human race to develop a new awareness of its long-term material interests and a greater appreciation of the natural environment that sustains it. They produce an elective affinity with an ecological consciousness and with political struggle toward reorienting social action in the direction of a more symbiotic relationship with nature. If society, by acting on nature, has generated a parasitic relationship with nature, then society, by modifying the way it acts on nature, can transform the character of that relationship. Environmental degradation only becomes inevitable when humans let it be so. If parasitism has become an iron cage, it is because humans have failed to treat it as a cloak, although not a light one, to be thrown off. The experience of the ecological consequences of human action, as well as knowledge of probable future consequences before experiencing them, have the potential to stimulate a transformation of social action, and with it social institutions and culture, towards a symbiotic relationship with the dynamic processes of nature. "If predictions of biospheric disorganization are accurate, the joint movement *may* be spurred" (Schnaiberg 1980: 440). One study (Dunlap et al. 1993) has found that environmental conditions are now recognized as problematic in almost all nations.

A new recognition is beginning to emerge of nature as an active, imperfectly understood, process rather than as a plastic thing to shape and master. This conception draws attention to what humans still don't know about nature, rather than the habitual focus on how much we have learned. It underscores the partiality of scientific and technological knowledge, and hence the fact that nature remains largely mysterious to humans. The acknowledgement of human ignorance, hence uncertainty and need to adjust to nature, lays the basis for a redefinition of the relationship between the social and the natural in terms of respect rather than plasticity, adaptation instead of exploitation, symbiosis in place of mastery, and involves new perceptions of long-term material and ideal human interests.

Whether this potential will be actualized and lead to ecological practices is problematic, not pre-determined. Short-term benefits may be chosen over long-term advantages, dangers denied, anxiety repressed, risk documenters scapegoated (Beck 1992a: 75). Disinformation may mask ecological problems and prevail over information. Environmental degradation may be left unattended, the economy and agriculture left to deteriorate, then future generations would destroy the environment out of desperation as presently happens in the Third World, and so the circle would become ever more vicious. Weber's work helps us keep in mind that objective situations do not necessarily bring about consciousness and organized, effective action. There is no predestined symbiotic relationship lying on the horizon, just struggle to attain it. The cumulative curve of waste and environmental degradation, the experience of its consequences, and knowledge of probable future consequences, are but three factors, however important, among many influencing whether the relationship between social action and the processes of nature will be directed in terms of the intensification of rationality under plasticity or greenness, rerationalization or derationalization. Global environmental change will be determined by the human response to environmental degradation and to the competing rationality claims of mastery of nature or human self-mastery, hence by the interaction of the forces of nature with the distinctively human quality of reason.

Notes

1. See Raynaud (1987: 187-9) for an insightful discussion of the idea of alienation, if not the word, in the work of Weber.

2. Although the goal of a symbiotic relationship between social action and the processes of nature is in principle shared by the proponents of (1) the intensification of rationalization under greenness, (2) rerationalization, and (3) derationalization, they differ not only in their suggested paths to it but also in their conception of what it entails.

3. See also the critique of neo-Malthusian studies in Chapter 3 for other limitations of force and coercion as solutions to environmental problems.

4. Similarly, the collapse of state socialism in eastern Europe has shown that even total media manipulation can be ineffective when it runs counter to experience.

5. Beck (1992a: 56), following Luhmann, is totally wrong on this point when he asserts the contrary.

Bibliography

Adams, Bill. 1990. *Green Development: Environment and Sustainability in the Third World*. London: Routledge.

Ahier, John. 1977. "Philosophers, Sociologists and Knowledge in Education." Pp. 59-72 in Michael F.D. Young and Geoff Whitty (eds.) *Society, State, and Schooling: Readings on the Possibilities for Radical Education*. Ringmer, England: Falmer Press.

Aitken Roshi, Robert. 1985. "Gandhi, Dogen and Deep Ecology." Appendix C in Devall, Bill and Sessions, George. *Deep Ecology*. Salt Lake City: Peregrine Smith.

Albrow, Martin. 1987. "The Application of the Weberian Concept of Rationalization to Contemporary Conditions." Pp. 164-82 in S. Whimster and S. Lash (editors) *Max Weber, Rationality and Modernity*. London: Allen and Unwin.

_____. 1990. *Max Weber's Construction of Social Theory*. London: Macmillan.

Albrow, Martin and Elizabeth King (editors). 1990. *Globalization, Knowledge and Society: Readings from International Sociology*. Newbury Park, California: Sage.

Alexander, Jeffrey C. 1988. "The New Theoretical Movement." Pp. 77-101 in Smelser, Neil J. (editor), *Handbook of Sociology*. Newbury Park, California: Sage.

Alsopp, B. 1972. *Ecological Morality*. London: Muller.

Alston, Dana (editor). 1991. *We Speak For Ourselves: Social Justice, Race and Environment*. Washington: Panos Institute.

Althusser, Louis. 1970. "Idéologie et Appareils Idéologiques d'Etat." *La Pense* 151.

_____. 1971. *Lenin and Philosophy and Other Essays*. London: New Left Books.

_____. 1977 (1965). *For Marx*. London: NLB.

_____. 1979 (1968). "The Object of Capital." Pp. 71-198 in Althusser, Louis, and Balibar, Etienne. *Reading Capital*. London: Verso.

Andreski, Stanislav. 1984. *Max Weber's Insights and Errors*. London: Routledge & Kegan Paul.

Antonio, Robert J. and Ronald M. Glassman (eds.). 1985. *A Weber-Marx Dialogue*. Lawrence, Kansas: University Press of Kansas.

Aronowitz, Stanley. 1988. *Science as Power: Discourse and Ideology in Modern Society.* Minneapolis: University of Minnesota Press.

Ashmore, Malcolm. 1988. *Knowledge and Reflexivity: New Frontiers in the Sociology of Knowledge.* London: Sage.

_____. 1989. *The Reflexive Thesis: Wrighting the Sociology of Scientific Knowledge.* Chicago: University of Chicago Press.

Baber, Zaheer. 1992. "Sociology of Scientific Knowledge: Lost in the Reflexive Funhouse?" *Theory and Society* 21: 105-19.

Baldus, Bernd. 1990. "In defense of theory: A reply to Cheal and Prus." *Canadian Journal of Sociology* 15: 470-5.

Barnes, B. 1974. *Scientific Knowledge and Sociological Theory.* London: Routledge & Kegan Paul.

_____. 1977. *Interests and the Growth of Knowledge.* London: Routledge & Kegan Paul.

_____. 1985. *About Science.* Oxford: Blackwell.

Barnes, D. and Edge, D. (eds.). 1982. *Science in Context.* London: Open University Press.

Barry, B. and Hardin, R. 1982. *Rational Man and Irrational Society.* Berkeley: Sage.

Baumol, William J. and Oates, Wallace E. 1975. *The Theory of Environmental Policy.* Englewood Cliffs, N.J.: Prentice-Hall.

Beck, Ulrich. 1992a. *Risk Society: Towards a New Modernity.* London: Sage.

_____. 1992b. 'From Industrial Society to Risk Society: Questions of Survival, Social Structure and Ecological Enlightenment'. *Theory, Culture & Society* 9: 97-123.

Becker, Garry. 1964. *Human Capital.* New York: National Bureau of Economic Research.

Beckerman, Wilfred. 1974. *In Defence of Economic Growth.* London: Jonathan Cape.

Bell, Daniel. 1960. *The End of Ideology.* New York: Free Press.

_____. 1973. *The Coming of Post-Industrial Society: A Venture in Social Forecasting.* New York: Basic Books.

_____. 1976. *The Cultural Contradictions of Capital.* New York: Basic Books.

_____. 1977. "Are There 'Social Limits' to Growth?" Pp. 13-26 in K.D. Wilson (ed.), *Prospects for Growth: Changing Expectations for the Future.* New York: Praeger.

Bendix, R. 1962. *Max Weber: An Intellectual Portrait.* New York: Doubleday.

Benton, Ted. 1989. "Marxism and Natural Limits: An Ecological Critique and Reconstruction." *New Left Review* 178: 51-86.

_____. 1991. "Biology and Social Science." *Sociology* 25: 1-29.

_____. 1992. "Ecology, Socialism and the Mastery of Nature: A Reply to Reiner Grundmann." *New Left Review* 194: 55-75.

Berger, Peter and Luckmann, Thomas. 1967 (1966). *The Social Construction of Reality.* Garden City, New York: Anchor.

Bernstein, Brock B. 1981. "Ecology and Economics: Complex Systems in Changing Environments." *Annual Review of Ecology and Systematics* 12: 309-30.

Bertell, Rosalie. 1985. *No Immediate Danger: Prognosis for a Radioactive Earth.* Summertown, Tennessee: The Book Publishing Company.

Bettelheim, Charles. 1974. *Les Luttes de classes en URSS*. Paris: Maspero - Seuil.

Bhaskar, Roy. 1978. *A Realist Theory of Science*. Atlantic Highlands: Humanities Press.

_____. 1989. *Reclaiming Reality: A Critical Introduction to Contemporary Philosophy*. London: Verso.

Biehl, Janet. 1988. "Ecofeminism and Deep Ecology: Unresolvable Conflict?" *Our Generation* 19: 19-31.

_____. 1991. *Rethinking Ecofeminist Politics*. Boston: South End Press.

Birke, Lynda. 1986. *Women, Feminism and Biology: The Feminist Challenge*. Brighton: Wheatsheaf.

Blauner, Robert. 1967. *Alienation and Freedom*. Chicago: University of Chicago Press.

Blea, Chim. 1986. "Animal Rights and Deep Ecology Movements." *Synthesis* 23: 13-4.

Bloor, D. 1976. *Knowledge and Social Imagery*. London: Routledge and Kegan Paul.

Blowers, A. 1984. "The triumph of material interests -- geography, pollution, and the environment." *Political Geography Quarterly* 3: 49-68.

Bolin, B. et al. (eds.). 1986. *The Greenhouse Effect: Climate Change, and Ecosystems*. Chichester UK: John Wiley & Sons.

Bookchin, Murray. 1971. *Post-Scarcity Anarchism*. Montreal: Black Rose

Bookchin, Murray. 1974. *Our Synthetic Environment*. New York: Colophon.

_____. 1977. *The Spanish Anarchists: The Heroic Years, 1868 - 1936*. New York: Harper Colophon.

_____. 1979. "Marxism as Bourgeois Sociology." *Our Generation* 13: 21-8.

_____. 1980a. *The Limits of the City*. Montreal: Black Rose Books.

_____. 1980b. *Toward an Ecological Society*. Montreal: Black Rose.

_____. 1982. *The Ecology of Freedom: The Emergence and Dissolution of Hierarchy*. Palo Alto, Cal.: Cheshire.

_____. 1984. *Toward an Ecological Society*. Montreal: Black Rose Books.

_____. 1987a. *The Rise of Urbanization and the Decline of Citizenship*. San Francisco: Sierra Club Books.

_____. 1987b. *The Modern Crisis*. Second revised edition. Montreal: Black Rose.

_____. 1988. "Social Ecology Versus Deep Ecology." *Socialist Review* 88 (3): 9-29.

_____. 1990a. "Recovering Evolution: A Reply to Eckersley and Fox." *Environmental Ethics* 12: 253-74.

_____. 1990b. *Remaking Society: Pathways to a Green Future*. Boston: South End Press.

_____. 1991. *Defending the Earth: Debate between Murray Bookchin and Dave Foreman*. Montreal: Black Rose Books.

Borgstrom, Georg. 1965. *The Hungry Planet*. London: Collier-Macmillan.

_____. 1969. *Too Many*. London: Collier-Macmillan.

Botkin, James et al. 1979. *No Limits to Learning*. New York: Pergamon.

Boudon, Raymond. 1977. *Effets pervers et ordre social*. Paris: PUF.

Boulding, Kenneth. 1973. "The Economics of the Coming Spaceship Earth," in Daly, Herman (ed.), *Toward a Steady-State Economy*. San Francisco: W.H. Freeman & Co.

Bourdieu, Pierre. 1966. "L'École conservatrice: Les inégalités devant l'école et devant la culture." *Revue française de sociologie.* 7: 325-47.

_____. 1977. *Reproduction in Education, Society and Culture.* Beverly Hills: Sage.

Bourdieu, Pierre and Passeron, Jean-Claude. 1970. *La Reproduction.* Paris: Minuit.

Braithwaite, R.B. 1953. *Scientific Explanation.* Cambridge: Cambridge University Press.

Braverman, Harry. 1974. *Labor and Monopoly Capital.* New York: Monthly Review Press.

Broadbent, Jeffrey. 1989. "Envirnmental Politics in Japan: An Integrated Structural Analysis." *Sociological Forum* 4: 179-202.

Brown, James Robert (ed.). 1984. *Scientific Rationality: The Sociological Turn.* Dordrecht: D. Reidel.

Brown, Lester R. 1972. *World Without Borders.* New York: Random House.

_____. 1981. *Toward a Sustainable Society.* New York: W.W. Norton.

Brown, Lester R. et al. 1988. *The State of the World 1988.* New York: W.W. Norton.

_____. 1993. *The State of the World 1993.* New York: W.W. Norton.

Brown, Michael. 1979. *Laying Waste.* New York: Pantheon.

Brown, M. and May, J. 1989. *The Greenpeace Story.* London: Dorling Kindersley.

Brown, Phil. 1992. "Popular Epidemiology and Toxic Waste Contamination: Lay and Professional Ways of Knowing." *Journal of Health and Social Behavior* 33: 267-81.

Brown, Phil and Mikkelsen, Edwin. 1990. *No Safe Place: Toxic Waste, Leukemia, and Community Action.* Berkeley: University of California Press.

Brubaker, Rogers. 1984. *The Limits of Rationality: An Essay on the Social and Moral Thought of Max Weber.* London: George Allen & Unwin.

Bullard, Robert. 1983. "Solid Waste Sites and the Black Houston Community." *Sociological Inquiry* 53: 273-88.

_____. 1990. *Dumping in Dixie: Race, Class and Environmental Quality.* Boulder: Westview Press.

Burger, T. 1976. *Max Weber's Theory of Concept Formation: History, Laws and Ideal Types.* Durham, N.C. Duke University Press.

Burgess, Ernest W. 1925. "The growth of the city." In Park, R., Burgess, E., and McKenzie, R. (eds.). *The City.* Chicago: University of Chicago Press.

Burgess, R. 1978. "The concept of nature in geography and Marxism." *Antipode* 10: 1-11.

Buttel, Frederick. 1976. "Social Science and the Environment: Competing Theories." *Social Science Quarterly* 57: 307-23.

_____. 1978. "Environmental Sociology: A New Paradigm?" *The American Sociologist* 13: 252-6.

_____. 1987. "New Directions in Environmental Sociology." *Annual Review of Sociology* 13: 465-88.

Buttel, Frederick, Hawkins, Ann, and Power, Alison. 1990. "From Limits to Growth to Global Change." *Global Environmental Change* 1: 57-66.

Buttel, Frederick and Taylor, Peter. 1992. "Environmental Sociology and Global Environmental Change": A Critical Assessment." *Society and Natural Resources* 5: 211-30.

Caldecott, Leonie and Leland, Stephanie (eds.). 1983. *Reclaim the Earth: Women Speak Out for Life on Earth*. London: The Women's Press.

Caldicott, Helen. 1992. *If You Love This Planet: A Plan to Heal the Earth*. New York: W.W. Norton.

Caldwell, Lynton Keith. 1990. *Between Two Worlds: Science, the Environmental Movement and Policy Choice*. Cambridge: Cambridge University Press.

Callicott, J.B. 1983. "Traditional American Indian and Traditional Western European Attitudes towards Nature: An Overview." Pp. 231-59 in R. Elliot and A. Gare, *Environmental Philosophy*. Milton Keynes: Open University Press.

Capra, Fritjof and Spretnak, Charlene. 1985. *Green Politics*. New York: Dutton.

Carnot, Nicolas Léonard Sadi. 1953 (1824). *Reflexions sur la Puissance Motrice du Feu*. Paris: A. Blanchard, Librairie Scientifique et Technique.

Carson, Rachel. 1962. *Silent Spring*. Boston: Houghton Mifflin.

Castells, M. 1978. *City, Class and Power*. London: Macmillan.

Castoriadis, Cornelius. 1977. "From Bolshevism to the Bureaucracy." *Our Generation* 12: 43-54.

Catton, William, Jr. 1980. *Overshoot: The Ecological Basis of Revolutionary Change*. Urbana: University of Illinois Press.

Catton, William, Jr. and Dunlap, Riley. 1978. "Environmental Sociology: A New Paradigm." *American Sociologist* 13: 41-9.

_____. 1980. "A New Ecological Paradigm for Post-Exuberant Sociology." *American Behavioral Scientist* 24: 15-48.

Chalmers, A.F. 1982. *What is this Thing Called Science?* London: Open University Press.

_____. 1990. *Science and its Fabrication*. London: Open University Press.

Charney, J.I. (ed.). 1982. *New Nationalism and the Use of Common Spaces*. Totowa, NJ: Allenheld.

Chase, Steve. 1991. "Whither the Radical Ecology Movement?" Pp. 7-24 in Bookchin, Murray and Foreman, Dave, *Defending the Earth*. Montreal: Black Rose Books.

Cheal, David. 1990. "Authority and incredulity: sociology between modernism and post-modernism." *Canadian Journal of Sociology* 15: 129-47.

Cheney, Jim. 1987. "Ecofeminism and Deep Ecology." *Environmental Ethics* 9: 115-45.

Chevalier, J.M. 1969. *La Structure financire de l'industrie amricaine*. Paris: Cujas.

Christian, James. 1981. *Philosophy*. Third edition. New York: Holt, Rinehart & Winston.

Chubin, D.E. 1981. "Constructing and Reconstructing Scientific Reality: A Meta-analysis." *International Society for the Sociology of Knowledge Newsletter* 7: 22-8.

Cicourel, Aaron V. 1964. *Method and Measurement in Sociology*. New York: The Free Press.

Cicourel, Aaron V. et al. 1974. *Language Use and School Performance*. New York: Academic Press.

Clark, Burton R. 1962. *Educating the Expert Society*. San Francisco: Chandler.

Clark, Colin. 1970. *Starvation or Plenty?* New York: Taplinger Publishing.

_____. 1975. *Population Growth: The Advantages.* Santa Anna, Calif.: R.L. Sassone.

Clark, Colin W. 1974. "The Economics of Overexploitation." *Science* 181: 630-4.

Clark, John. 1984. *The Anarchist Moment: Reflections on Culture, Nature, and Power.* Montreal: Black Rose Books.

_____ (editor). 1990. *Renewing the Earth: The Promise of Social Ecology.* London: Green Print.

Clement, Wallace. 1975. *The Canadian Corporate Elite: An Analysis of Economic Power.* Toronto: McClelland & Stewart.

_____. 1977. *Continental Corporate Power: Economic Elite Linkages Between Canada and the United States.* Toronto: McClelland & Stewart.

Clingan, C. 1981. "Safety at Sea." *Interdisciplinary Science Reviews* 6: 42.

Cole, Stephen. 1992. *Making Science.* Cambridge: Harvard.

Collins, H.M. 1975. "The Seven Sexes: A Study in the Sociology of a Phenomenon, or the Replication of Experiments in Physics." *Sociology* 9: 205-24.

_____. 1981a. "Son of the Seven Sexes: The Social Destruction of a Physical Phenomenon." *Social Studies of Science* 11: 215-24.

_____. 1981b. "Stages in the Empirical Programme of Relativism." *Social Studies of Science* 11: 3-10.

_____ (ed.). 1981c. "Knowledge and controversy: Studies of Modern Natural Science." *Social Studies of Science* 11(1).

_____. 1982. "Special Relativism - The Natural Attitude." *Social Studies of Science* 12: 136-9.

_____. 1983. "An Empirical Relativist Programme in the Sociology of Scientific Knowledge." Pp. 85-113 in Knorr-Cetina, Karin D. and Michael Mulkay (editors), *Science Observed: Perspectives on the Social study of Science.* London: Sage.

_____. 1985. *Changing Order.* London: Sage.

Collins, H.M. and Cox, G. 1976. "Recovering Relativity: Did Prophecy Fail?." *Social Studies of Science* 6: 423-44.

Collins, H.M. and Cox, G. 1977. "Relativity Revisited: Mrs. Keech - A Suitable Case for Special Treatment?" *Social Studies of Science* 7: 372-81.

Collins, H.M. and Pinch, T.J. 1979. "The Construction of the Paranormal: Nothing Unscientific is Happening." Pp. 237-70 in R. Wallis (ed.), *On the Margins of Science: The Social Construction of RejectedKnowledge.* University of Keele: Sociological Review Monograph, No. 27.

_____. 1982. *Frames of Meaning: The Social Construction of Extraordinary Science.* London: Routledge and Kegan Paul.

Collins, Patricia Hill. 1989. "Black Feminist Thought." *Signs* 14: 765-70.

Collins, Randall. 1968. "A Comparative Approach to Political Sociology." Pp. 42-67 in Reinhard Bendix (ed.), *State and Society.* Boston: Little, Brown, & Co.

_____. 1971. "Functional and Conflict Theories of Educational Stratification." *American Sociological Review* 36: 1002-1019.

_____. 1975. *Conflict Sociology: Toward an Explanatory Science.* New York: Academic Press.

_____. 1976. Review of "Schooling in Capitalist America" by Samuel Bowles and Herbert Gintis. *Harvard Educational Review 7* 46: 246-51.

_____. 1979. *The Credential Society.* New York: Academic.

_____. 1980. "Weber's Last Theory of Capitalism: A Systematization." *Amearican Sociological Review* 45: 925 -942.

_____. 1981. *Sociology Since Midcentury: Essays in Theory Cumulation.* New York: Academic.

_____ (editor). 1985. *Three Sociological Traditions.* New York: Oxford University Press.

_____. 1986. *Weberian Sociological Theory.* Cambridge: Cambridge University Press.

_____. 1988. *Theoretical Sociology.* San Diego: Harcourt Brace Jovanovich.

_____. 1989. "Sociology: Proscience or Antiscience?." *American Sociological Review* 54: 124-39.

_____. 1990. "Market Dynamics as the Engine of Historical change." *Sociological Theory* 8: 111-35.

Commoner, Barry. 1971. *The Closing Circle: Nature, Man, and Technology.* New York: Alfred A. Knopf.

_____. 1976. *The Poverty of Power: Energy and the Economic Crisis.* New York: Alfred A. Knopf.

_____. 1990. *Making Peace with the Planet.* New York: Pantheon.

Cooley. 1976. "Contradictions of Science and Technology in the Production Process." In Hillary Rose and Steve Rose (eds.) *The Political Economy of Science.* Cambridge, Mass.: Schenkman.

Cotgrove, Stephen. 1982. *Catastrophe or Cornucopia: The Environment, Politics and the Future.* New York: Wiley.

Couch, Stephen and Kroll-Smith, Stephen. 1985. "The Chronic Technical Disaster: Toward a Social Scientific Perspective." *Social Science Quarterly* 66: 564-75.

Council on Environmental Quality, Department of Agriculture, Department of Energy, and Environmental Protection Agency. 1980. *Public Opinion on Environmental Issues: Results of a National Opinion Study.* Washington: U.S. Government Printing Office.

Covello, V.T., Lave, L.B., Moghissi, A., and Uppuluri, V.R. (eds.). 1984. *Uncertainty in Risk Assessment, Risk Management, and Decision Making.* New York: Plenum.

Cramer, J. 1987. *Mission-Orientation in Ecology: the Case of Dutch Fresh-Water Ecology.* Amsterdam: Rodopi.

Crozier, Michel. 1964. *The Bureaucratic Phenomenon.* Chicago: University of Chicago Press.

_____. 1970. La Société Bloquée. Paris: Seuil.

Cuomo, Christine. 1992. "Unravelling the Problems in Ecofeminism." *Environmental Ethics* 14: 351-63.

Dahl, Robert A. 1971. *Polyarchy.* New Haven, Conn.: Yale University Press.

Dahrendorf, Ralf. 1977. "Observations on science and technology in a changing socio-economic climate." Pp. 73-82 in Ralf Dahrendorf et al. (eds.), *Scientific-Technological Revolution.* London: Sage.

Daly, Herman E. 1973. "The Steady-State Economy: Toward a Political Economy of Biophysical Equilibrium and Moral Growth." Pp. 149-74 in Daly, Herman (ed.) *Toward a Steady-State Economy*. San Francisco: W.H. Freeman & Co.

Daugherty, Howard, Jeanneret-Grosjean, Charles, and Fletcher, H.F. 1979. *Ecodevelopment and International Cooperation*. Joint Project on Environment and development 6. Ottawa: Environment Canada, Cida.

Davidoff, Linda. 1991. "Radical Visions and Strategies." Pp. 63-5 in Bookchin, Murray, and Foreman, Dave, *Defending the Earth*. Montreal: Black Rose Books.

Davis, K. and Moore, W.E. 1945. "Some Principles of Stratification." *American Sociological Review* 10: 242-9.

Dawe, Alan. 1978. "Theories of Social Action." Pp. 362-417 in Bottomore, Tom, and Nisbet, Robert (editors). *A History of Sociological Analysis*. New York: Basic Books.

d'Eaubonne, Françoise. 1974. *Le Féminisme ou la Mort*. Paris: Pierre Horay.

Debeir, J.C., Deléage, J.P., and Hémery, D. 1986. *Les servitudes de la puissance, une histoire de l'energie*. Paris: Flammarion.

De Montbrial, Thierry, et al. 1979. *Energy: The Countdown*. New York: Pergamon.

Derber, Charles. 1982. *Professionals as Workers: Mental Labor in Advanced Capitalism*. Boston: G.K. Hall and Co.

Devall, Bill. 1979. "Ecological Consciousness and Ecological Resisting: Guidelines for Comprehension and Research." *Humboldt Journal of Social Relations* 9: 177-96.

_____. 1988. *Simple in Means, Rich in Ends: Practicing Deep Ecology*. Salt Lake City: Peregrine Smith Books.

Devall, Bill and Sessions, George. 1985. *Deep Ecology: Living As If Nature Mattered*. Salt Lake City: Peregrine Smith.

_____. 1988. *Simple in Means, Rich in Ends. Practicing Deep Ecology*. Salt Lake City: Peregrine Smith.

Dials, G.E. and Moore, E.C. 1974. "The Cost of Coal," *Environment* 16.

Diamond, Irene and Feman Orenstein, Gloria (editors). 1990. *Reweaving the World: The Emergence of Ecofeminism*. San Francisco: Sierra Club Books.

Dickens, Peter. 1992. *Science and Nature: Towards a Green Social Theory*. Philadelphia: Temple University Press.

Dietz, Thomas. 1987. "Theory and Method in Social Impact Assessment." *Sociological Inquiry* 57: 54-69.

Dietz, Thomas and Kalof, Linda. 1992. "Environmentalism Among Nation States." *Social Indicators Research* 26: 353-66.

Dietz, Thomas, Stern, Paul and Rycroft, Robert. 1989. "Definitions of Conflict and Legitimation of Resources: The Case of Environmental Risk." *Sociological Forum* 4: 47-70.

Dobson, Andrew. 1990. *Green Political Thought*. London: Unwin Hyman.

Dolman, Antony (ed.). 1977. *RIO, Reshaping the International Order*. New York: The New American Library Inc.

Domhoff, G. William. 1967. *Who Rules America?* New York: Prentice-Hall.

_____. 1970. *The Higher Circles*. New York: Random House.

_____. 1972. *Fat Cats and Democrats*. Englewood Cliffs, N.J.: Prentice-Hall.

_____. 1979. *The Powers That Be*. New York: Random House.

Douglas, Mary. 1985. *Risk Acceptability According to the Social Social Sciences*. New York: Sage.

_____. 1992. *Risk and Blame: Essays in Cultural Theory*. London: Routledge.

Douglas, M. and Wildavsky, A. 1982. *Risk and Culture: An Essay on the Selection of Technical and Environmental Dangers*. Berkeley: University of California Press.

Dryzek, John S. 1983. "Present Choices, Future Consequences: A Case for Thinking Strategically." *World Futures* 19: 1-19.

_____. 1987. *Rational Ecology: Environment and Political Economy*. Oxford: Basil Blackwell.

Dubos, Rene. 1968. *So Human an Animal*. New York: Scribners.

_____. 1980. *The Wooing of the Earth*. New York: Scribners.

Dunlap, Riley. 1980. "Paradigmatic Change in Social Science: From Human Exceptionalism to an Ecological Paradigm." *American Behavioral Scientist* 24: 5-14.

_____. 1983. "Ecologist Versus Exemptionalist: The Ehrlich-Simon Debate." *Social Science Quarterly* 64: 200-3.

_____. 1989. "Public Opinion and Environmental Policy." In Lester, James (ed.), *Environmental Politics and Policy*. Durham, N.C.: Duke University Press.

_____. 1993. "From Environmental to Ecological Problems." In C. Calhoun and G. Ritzer (eds.), *Social Problems*. New York: McGraw-Hill.

Dunlap, Riley and Catton, William, Jr. 1979. "Environmental Sociology." *Annual Review of Sociology* 5: 243-73.

_____. 1993a. "Toward an Ecological Sociology." *Annals of the International Institute of Sociology* 3: 263-84.

_____. 1993b. "Struggling With Human Exemptionalism: The Rise, Decline and Revitalization of Environmental Sociology." Paper presented to the Annual Meeting of the American Sociological Association, Miami Beach.

Dunlap, Riley, Gallup, George Jr., and Gallup Alec. 1993. *Health of the Planet*. Princeton: George Gallup International Institute.

Dunlap, Riley and Mertig, Angela (eds.). 1992. *American Environmentalism: The U.S. Environmental Movement, 1970-1990*. Washington: Taylor and Francis.

Dunlap, Riley and Scarce, Rik. 1991. "The Polls-Poll Trends: Environmental Problems and Protection." *Public Opinion Quarterly* 55: 651-72.

Dunlap, Riley and Van Liere, Kent. 1984. "Commitment to the Dominant Social Paradigm and Concern for Environmental Quality." *Social Science Quarterly* 65: 1013-1028.

Durham, W.H. 1979. *Scarcity and Survival in Central America: Ecological Origins of the Soccer War*. Stanford, Calif.: Stanford University Press.

Eckersley, Robyn. 1989. "Divining Evolution: The Ecological Ethics of Murray Bookchin." *Environmental Ethics* 11: 99-116.

Edelstein, Michael R. 1988. *Contaminated Communities: The Social and Psychological Impacts of Residential Toxic Exposure*. Boulder, Col.: Westview.

Edwards, A.W.F. 1986. "How many reactor accidents?." *Nature* No. 324: 417-18.

Edwards, Richard. 1979. *Contested Terrain*. New York: Basic Books.

Egginton, Joyce. 1980. *The Poisoning of Michigan*. New York: W.W. Norton.

Ehrenfeld, David. 1976. "The Conservation of Non-Resources." *American Scientist* 64: 648-56.

_____. 1978. *The Arrogance of Humanism.* New York: Oxford University Press.

Ehrlich, Paul. 1968. *The Population Bomb.* New York: Ballantine.

Ehrlich, Paul and Ehrlich, Anne. 1972. *Population, Resources, Environment: Issues in Human Ecology.* San Francisco: W.H. Freeman & Co.

_____. 1983. *Extinction: The Causes and Consequences of the Disappearance of Species.* New York: Random House.

Ehrlich, Paul and Pirages, Dennis. 1974. *Ark II: Social Response to Environmental Imperatives.* San Francisco: W.H. Freeman & Co.

El-Hinnawi, E. 1985. *Environmental Refugees.* Nairobi: United Nations Environment Programme.

Elliott, D.K. (ed.). 1986. *Dynamics of Extinction.* Chicester, UK: John Wiley & Sons.

Endo, Shusaku. 1992. "In Pursuit of an Elusive Happiness'. *The Ottawa Citizen*: September 8, A13 (first published in *The Guardian*).

Enzensberger, Hans Magnus. 1976. "A Critique of Political Ecology." Pp. 161-95 in Rose, Hilary and Rose Steven (eds.) *The Political Economy of Science: Ideology of/in the Natural Sciences.* London: Macmillan.

Erickson, Brad (editor). 1990. *Call to Action: A Handbook for Ecology, Peace and Justice.* San Francisco: Sierra Club Books.

Escobar, Arturo. 1989. "Sustainable Development or Sustainable Profits." *Capitalism, Nature, Socialism: A Journal of Socialist Ecology* (fall).

Estes, Caroline. 1989. "Consensus and Community." In Judith Plant (ed.), *Healing the Wounds.* Philadelphia: New Society Publishers.

Evernden, Neil. 1993. *The Social Creation of Nature.* New Haven: Yale University Press.

Eysenck, J. 1971. *The I.Q. Argument.* New York: Library Press.

Faber, Daniel, and O'Connor, James. 1989. "The Struggle for Nature: The Environmental Crisis and the Crisis of Environmentalism." *Capitalism, Nature, Socialism: A Journal of Socialist Ecology* (summer).

Ferguson, Marilyn. 1980. *The Aquarian Conspiracy: Personal and Social Transformation in the 1980s.* Los Angeles: J.P. Tarcher.

Fernandes, W. and Kulkarni, S. (eds.). 1983. *Towards a New Forest Policy: People's Rights and Environmental Needs.* New Delhi, India: Indian Social Institute.

Ferrarotti, Franco. 1982. *Max Weber and the Destiny of Reason.* New York: M.E. Sharpe, Inc..

Ferry, Luc. 1992. *Le nouvel ordre écologique.* Paris: Grasset.

Firestone, Shulamith. 1970. *The Dialectic of Sex.* New York: Bantam.

Fischhoff, B., Lichtenstein, S., Slovic, P., Derby, S.L., and Keeney, R.L. 1981. *Acceptable Risk.* New York: Cambridge University Press.

Flader, Susan. 1974. *Thinking Like a Mountain: Aldo Leopold and the Evolution of an Ecological Attitude Toward Deer, Wolves, and Forests.* Columbia: University of Missouri Press.

Fleck, Ludwik. 1979. *Genesis and Development of a Scientific Fact.* Chicago: University of Chicago Press.

Foreman, David, editor. 1985. *Ecodefense: A Field Guide to Monkey Wrenching*. Tucson: Earth First! Books.

_____. 1987. "Whither Earth First!" *Earth First*. November 1.

_____. 1991a. *Confessions of an Eco-Warrior*. New York: Harmony Books.

_____. 1991b. *Defending the Earth: Debate between Murray Bookchin and Dave Foreman*. Montreal: Black Rose Books.

Fox, Nick. 1991. "Green Sociology." *Network* (Newslettr of the British Sociological Association). No. 50: 23-4.

Fox, R. 1971. "The XYY offender: a modern myth?." *Journal of Criminal Law, Criminology and Police Science* 62: 59-73.

Fox, Warwick. 1989. "The Deep Ecology - Ecofeminism Debate and its Parallels." *Environmental Ethics* 11: 5-25.

_____. 1990. *Toward A Transpersonal Ecology: Developing New Foundations For Environmentalism*. Boston: Shambhala.

Frankel, O.H. and Soule, M.E. 1981. *Conservation and Evolution*. Cambridge: Cambridge University Press.

Freudenburg, William. 1986. "Social Impact Assessment." *Annual Review of Sociology* 12: 451-78.

_____. 1988. "Perceived Risk, Real Risk: Social Science and the Art of Probabilistic Risk Assessment." *Science* 242: 44-9.

Freudenburg, William and Gramling, Robert. 1989. "The Emergence of Environmental Sociology." *Sociological Inquiry* 59: 439-52.

_____. 1993. "Coastal Crude and the Dualism of Society - Environment Relationships: Understanding Opposition and Support for Offshore Oil Development." *Sociological Forum* 8 (forthcoming).

Freund, Julien. 1966. *Sociologie de Max Weber*. Paris: PUF le sociologue.

_____. 1969. *Max Weber*. Paris: PUF.

_____. 1983. *Sociologie du conflit*. Paris: PUF.

Fullenbach, Josef. 1981. *European Environmental Policy: East and West*. London: Butterworths.

Fuller, R. Buckminster. 1971. *An Operating Manual for Spaceship Earth*. New York: Dutton.

Galbraith, John Kenneth. 1967. *The New Industrial State*. Boston: Houghton Mifflin.

Garfinkel, H. 1952. *The Perception of the Other: A Study in Social Order*. Unpublished Ph.D. dissertation, Harvard University.

_____. 1967. *Studies in Ethnomethodology*. Englewood Cliffs, N.J.: Prentice-Hall.

_____. 1982. *Ethnomethodological Studies of Work in the Discovering Sciences*. London: Routledge and Kegan Paul.

Garfinkel, Harold, Lynch, Michael, and Livingston, Eric. 1981. "The Work of a Discovering Science Construed with Materials from the Optically Discovered Pulsar." *Philosophy of the Social Sciences* 11(2): 131-58.

Gerth, H.H. and Mills, C. Wright. (1946) 1958. "Introduction: The Man And His Work." Pp. 1-74 in H.H. Gerth and C. Wright Mills (eds.), *From Max Weber: Essays in Sociology*. New York: Galaxy (Oxford University Press).

Giarini, Orio. 1980. *Dialogue on Wealth and Warfare*. New York: Pergamon.

Gibbons, K.G. 1979. "Orbital Saturation: The Necessity for International Regulation of Geosynchronous Orbits." *California Western International Law Journal*, Winter.

Giddens, Anthony. 1980. "Classes, Capitalism, and the State." *Theory and Society* 9: 877-90.

_____. 1990. *The Consequences of Modernity*. Stanford: Stanford University Press.

_____. 1991. *Modernity and Self-Identity in the Late Modern Age*. Stanford: Standord University Press.

Giere, Ronald N. 1988. *Explaining Science: A Cognitive Approach*. Cambridge: Cambridge University Press.

Gieryn, T.F. 1982. "Relativist/Constructivist Programmes in the Sociology of Science: Redundance and Retreat." *Social Studies of Science* 12: 279-97.

Glaeser, B. (ed.). 1984. *Ecodevelopment*. London: Pergammon.

Glueck, Sheldon, and Glueck, E. 1966. *Physique and Delinquency*. New York: Harper and Row.

Godelier, Maurice. 1984. *L'idel et le matriel*. Paris: Fayard.

Goldman, Marshall I. 1972. *The Spoils of Progress: Environmental Pollution in the Soviet Union*. Cambridge: Cambridge University Press.

Goodfield, N. 1981. *An Imagined World*. New York: Harper & Row.

Goodin, Robert E. 1982. *Political Theory and Public Policy*. Chicago: University of Chicago Press.

Goodman, N. 1978. *Ways of World-Making*. Indianapolis: Hackett.

Gore, Al. 1992. *Earth in the Balance: Ecology and the Human Spirit*. Boston: Houghton Mifflin.

Gorz, Andre. 1964. *Strategy for Labor*. Boston: Beacon Press.

_____. 1980. *Ecology as Politics*. Montreal: Black Rose Press.

_____. 1982. *Farewell to the Working Class: An Essay on Post Industrial Socialism*. London: Pluto Press.

_____. 1985. *Paths to Paradise: On the Liberation from Work*. Boston: South End Press.

Gould, L.G., Gardner, .T., DeLuca, D.R., Tiemann, A.R., Doob, L.W., and Stolwijk, J.A. 1988. *Perceptions of Technological Risks and Benefits*. New York: Russell Sage Foundation.

Gouldner, Alvin. 1970. *The Coming Crisis of Western Sociology*. New York: Basic Books.

_____. 1978. "The New Class Project, Parts I and II." *Theory and Society 6(2) and 6(3)*.

_____. 1979. *The Rise of Intellectuals and the Rise of the New Class*. New York: Seabury.

Graham, Frank. 1970. *Since Silent Spring*. Boston: Houghton Mifflin.

Gray, Elizabeth Dodson. 1979. *Green Paradise Lost*. Massachusetts: Roundtable Press.

Grove, J.W. 1989. *In Defence of Science: Science, Technology, and Politics in Modern Society*. Toronto: University of Toronto Press.

Grundmann, Reiner. 1991. "The Ecological Challenge to Marxism." *New Left Review* 187.

Guha, Ramachandra. 1990. *The Unquiet Woods: Ecological Change and Peasant Resistance in the Himalaya.* Delhi: Oxford University Press.

Guillaumin, Colette. 1978. "Pratique du pouvoir et idée de Nature." *Questions fministes*, Paris, Tierce, numéro 2 et 3.

Guimaraes, R.P. 1991. *The Ecopolitics of Development in the Third World: Politics and Environment in Brazil.* Boulder: Lynne Reinner.

Gusfield, J.R. 1981. *The Culture of Public Problems.* Chicago: Chicago University Press.

Habermas, Jurgen. 1970a. "On Systematically Distorted Communication." *Inquiry* 13: 205-18.

_____. 1970b. "Toward a Theory of Communicative Competence." *Inquiry* 13: 360-75.

_____. 1973a. *Legitimation Crisis.* Boston: Beacon Press.

_____. 1973b. *Theory and Practice.* Boston: Beacon Press.

_____. 1979. *Communication and the Evolution of Society.* Boston: Beacon Press.

_____. 1984. *The Theory of Communicative Action I: Reason and the Rationalization of Society.* Boston: Beacon Press.

Hagen, E.W. 1980. "Common-Mode/Common Cause Failure: A Review." *Nuclear Safety* 21: 184-92.

Hagman, G. et al. 1984. *Prevention Better Than Cure: Report on Human and Environmental Disasters in the Third World.* Stockholm: Swedish Red Cross.

Hall, Anthony L. 1989. *Developing Amazonia: Deforestation and Social Conflict in Brazil's Carajas Programme.* Manchester: Manchester University Press.

Hamilton, David. 1973. *Technology, Man and the Environment.* London: Faber and Faber.

Hardin, Garrett. 1968. "The Tragedy of the Commons." *Science* 162.

_____. 1969. *Population, Evolution and Birth Control: A Collage of Controversial Ideas.* San Francisco: W.H. Freeman & Co.

Hardin, Garrett and Baden, John (eds.). 1977. *Managing the Commons.* San Francisco: W.H. Freeman.

Hare, Kenneth. 1989. *The Ottawa Citizen.* October.

Hare, Nathan. 1981. "Black Ecology." Pp. 229-36 in Shrader-Frechette, K.S. (ed.) *Environmental Ethics*, Pacific Grove, Calif.: Boxwood Press.

Haritos, Rosa. 1993. "Scientists at Work: Contexts of Scientific Discovery." Paper presented at the 88th Annual ASA Meetings, Miami Beach.

Harman, Willis W. 1976. *An Incomplete Guide to the Future.* New York: W.W. Norton.

Hartwell, M.A. and Hutchinson, T.C. 1985. *Environmental Consequences of Nuclear War, Volume II: Ecological and Agricultural Effects.* Chichester, UK: John Wiley & Sons.

Hazard, John N. 1964. *The Soviet System of Government.* Third edition. Chicago: University of Chicago Press.

Heilbroner, Robert L. 1980. *An Inquiry Into the Human Prospect: Updated and Reconsidered forthe 1980s.* New York: W.W. Norton.

Heims, Steve J. 1991. *The Cybernetics Group.* Cambridge: MIT Press.

Hess, Karl. 1979. *Community Technology.* New York: Harper and Row.

Hill, Stephen. 1990. *The "Tragedy" of Technology.* London: Pluto.

Holden, Constance. 1984. "A 'profile' Population Delegation?" *Science* 224: 1321-2.

Holton, Robert J. 1991. *Max Weber on Economy and Society.* London: Routledge.

Horkheimer, Max and Adorno, Theodor. 1972 (1944). *Dialectic of Enlightenment.* New York: Seabury.

Horowitz, Irving Louis. 1972. "The Environmental Cleavage: Social Ecology Versus Political Economy." *Social Theory and Practice* 2: 125-34.

Howard, Frank. 1989. "Ecologists take heed: The End is not near." *The Ottawa Citizen* 18 November: B3.

Humphrey, Craig R. and Butell, Frederick R. 1983. *Environment, Energy and Society.* Belmont, Ca.: Wadsworth.

Huggett, Richard. 1989. *Cataclysms and Earth History.* Oxford: Oxford University Press (Clarendon).

Ignatieff, Michael. 1992. "Misunderstanding Human Ecology: The Green Movement is Moralizing Instead of Connecting with Daily Life." *London Observer.*

Illich, I. 1973. *Tools for Conviviality.* New York: Harper and Row.

Islam, S. and K. Lindgren. 1986. "How many reactor accidents will there be?." *Nature* No. 322: 691-2.

Israel, Joachim. 1972. "Max Weber et la rationalité." Pages 161-197 dans Joachim Israel, L"aliénation de Marx à ls sociologie contemporaine. Paris, Editions Anthropos.

James, Roger. 1980. *Return to Reason: Popper's Thought in Public Life.* Shepton Mallet, Somerset, UK: Open Books.

Johnson, B.B. and Covello, V.T. 1987. *The Social and Cultural Construction of Risk.* Boston: D. Reidel.

Jones, Alwyn. 1990. "Social Symbiosis: A Gaian Critique of Contemporary Social theory." *The Ecologist* 20: 108-13.

Jones, R.A. 1986. "Durkheim, Frazer and Smith: the role of analogies and exemplars in the development of Durkheim's sociology of religion." *American Journal of Sociology* 92: 596-627.

Juster, Thomas (ed.). 1975. *Education, Income and Human Behavior.* New York: McGraw-Hill.

Juteau, Danielle. 1981. "Visions partielles, visions partiales: visions (des) minoritaires en sociologie." *Sociologie et Sociétés* XIII: 33-47.

Kahn, Herman and Wiener, Anthony. 1967. *The Year 2000.* London, Canada: Collier-Macmillan.

Kahn, Herman. 1979. *World Economic Development: 1979 and Beyond.* Boulder: Westview.

Kalberg, Stephen. 1979. "The Search for Thematic Orientations in a Fragmented Oeuvre: The Discussion of Max Weber in Recent German Sociological Literature", *Sociology* 13: 127-39.

_____. 1980. "Max Weber's Types of Rationality." *American Journal of Sociology,* vol. 85, pp. 1145-1179.

_____. 1983. "Max Weber's Universal-Historical Architectonic of Economically-Oriented Action: A Preliminary Reconstruction", *Current Perspectives in Social Theory* 4: 253-88.

Kapp, K. William. 1971. *The Social Costs of Private Enterprise.* New York: Shocken.

Kelley, Donald R. 1976. "Environmental Policy Making in the USSR." *Soviet Studies* 28: 570-89.

Kelley, Donald R., Stunkel, Kenneth R., and Wescott, Richard R. 1976. *The Economic Superpowers and the Environment.* San Francisco: W.H. Freeman.

Kelly, Colin. 1990. "Methods of reading and the discipline of sociology: The case of Durkheim studies." *The Canadian Journal of Sociology* 15: 301-24.

Kerr, Clark, Dunlop, John R., Harbison, Frederick, and Myers, Charles. 1960. *Industrialism and Industrial Man.* Cambridge: Harvard University Press.

King, Ynestra. 1989. "The Ecology of Feminism and the Feminism of Ecology." Pp. 18-28 in Judith Plant (ed.), *Healing the Wounds: The Promise of Ecofeminism.* Toronto: Between the Lines.

Knorr, K.D. 1977. "Producing and Reproducing Knowledge: Descriptive or Constructive? Toward a Model of Research Production." *Social Science Information* 16: 669-96.

Knorr-Cetina, K.D. 1981. *The Manufacture of Knowledge: An Essay on the Constructivist and Contextual Nature of Science.* Oxford: Pergamon Press.

_____. 1982. "The Constructivist Programme in Sociology of Science: Retreats or Advances?" *Social Studies of Science* 12: 320-4.

_____. 1983. "The Ethnographic Study of Scientific Work: Towards a Constructivist Interpretation of Science." Pp. 115-140 in Knorr-Cetina, Karin D. and Michael Mulkay (editors), *Science Observed: Perspectives on the Social Study of Science.* London: Sage.

Knorr-Cetina, Karin and Cicourel, Aaron (eds.). 1981. *Advances in Social Theory and Methodology: Towards an Integration of Micro and Macro Sociology.* London: Routledge & Kegan Paul.

Knorr, K.D. and Knorr, D.W. 1982. "From Scenes to Scripts: On the Relationship between Laboratory Research and Published Papers in Science." *Social Studies of Science* 12(4).

Knorr-Cetina, Karin D. and Michael Mulkay (editors). 1983. *Science Observed: Perspectives on the Social Study of Science.* London: Sage.

Kolinsky, Eva. 1988. *The Greens in West Germany: Organization and Policy Making.* Birmingham: Berg Publishers.

Kolko, G. 1962. *Wealth and Power in America.* New York: Praeger.

Kornhauser, William. 1963. *Scientists in Industry.* Berkeley: University of California Press.

Krieger, Martin H. 1973. "What's Wrong With Plastic Trees?" *Science* 179.

_____. 1992. *Doing Physics: How Physicists Take Hold of the World.* Bloomington: Indiana University Press.

Krimsky, S. and Plough, A. 1988. *Environmental Hazards: Communicating Risk as a Social Process.* Dover, Mass.: Auburn House.

Kroll-Smith, Stephen and Couch, Stephen. 1991. "What is a Disaster? An Ecological-Symbolic Approach to Resolving the Definitional Debate." *International Journal of Mass Emergencies and Disasters* 9: 355-66.

Kuhn, Thomas. 1962. *The Structure of Scientific Revolutions.* Chicago: University of Chicago Press.

Kuklick, H. and Jones, R.A. 1984. "Preface." Pp. ix-xii in H. Kuklick and Jones, R.A. (eds.), *Knowledge and Society: Studies in the Sociology of Culture Past and Present*, Vol. 4. Grenwich, Conn.: JAI Press.

Lagadec, Patrick. 1982. *Major Technological Risk*. New York: Pergamon.

Lambert, B. 1990. *How Safe is Safe? Radiation Controversies Explained*. London: Unwin.

Lane, David. 1976. *The Socialist Industrial State: Towards a Political Sociology of State Socialism*. London: George Allen & Unwin.

Larson, Magali Sarfatti. 1977. *The Rise of Professionalism: A Sociological Analysis*. Berkeley: University of California Press.

Lasch, Christopher. 1978a. *Haven in a Heartless World*. New York: Basic Books.

_____. 1978b. *The Culture of Narcissism: American Life in an Age of Diminishing Expectations*. New York: Norton.

_____. 1984. *The Minimal Self*. New York: Norton.

_____. 1990. *The True and Only Heaven: Progress and its Critics*. New York: Norton.

Lash, Scott, and Whimster, Sam (eds.), *Max Weber, Rationality and Modernity*. London: Allen & Unwin.

Latour, Bruno. 1981. "Insiders and Outsiders in the Sociology of Science: Or, How Can We Foster Agnosticism." *Knowledge and Society* 3: 199-216.

_____. 1983. "Give Me a Laboratory and I Will Raise the World." Pp. 141-70 in Knorr-Cetina, K. and Mulkay, M. (eds.) *Science Observed*. London: Sage.

_____. 1987. *Science in Action. How to Follow Scientists and Engineers through Society*. Cambridge, Massachusetts: Harvard University Press.

_____. 1990. "Postmodern? No, Simply Amodern! Steps Towards an Anthropology of Science." *Studies in History and Philosophy of Science* 21: 145-71.

Latour, B. and Woolgar, S. 1979. *Laboratory Life: The Social Construction of Scientific Facts*. London: Sage.

Laudan, L. 1982. "A Note on Collins's Blend of Relativism and Empiricism." *Social Studies of Science* 12: 131-2.

Law, J. 1977. "Prophecy Failed (for the Actors)!: A Note on 'Recovering Relativity.'" *Social Studies of Science* 7: 367-72.

Lazlo, Ervin, et al. 1977. *Goals for Mankind*. New York: E.P. Dutton.

Leiss, William. 1974. *The Domination of Nature*. Boston: Beacon Press.

_____. 1976. *The Limits to Satisfaction*. Toronto: University of Toronto Press.

_____ (ed.). 1979. *Ecology Versus Politics in Canada*. Toronto: University of Toronto Press.

Leonard, H.J. (ed.). 1985. *Divesting Nature's Capital: The Political Economy of Envirnmental Abuse in the Third World*. New York: Holmes and Meier.

_____. 1986. "Hazardous Wastes: The Crisis Spreads." *National Development*, April.

Leopold, Aldo. 1949. *Sand County Almanac*. London: Oxford University Press.

Levi, I. 1980. *The Enterprise of Knowledge*. Cambridge, Mass.: MIT.

Levine, Adeline Gordon. 1982. *Love Canal: Science, Politics, and People*. Lexington, MA: Lexington Books.

Levine, Donald N. "Rationality and Freedom: Weber and Beyond." *Sociological Inquiry*, 51 (1): 5-25.

Lindblom, Charles E. 1977. *Politics and Markets: The World's Political-Economic Systems*. New York: Basic Books.

Lipset, Seymour Martin. 1979. "Predicting the Future of Post-Industrial Society: Can We Do It?" Pp. 1-35 in S. M. Lipset (ed.), *The Third Century: America as a Post-Industrial Society*. Stanford: Hoover Institution Press.

List, Peter (ed.). 1993. *Radical Environmentalism*. Belmont: Wadsworth.

Loewith, Karl. (1932) 1970. "Weber's Interpretation of the Bourgeois-Capitalistic world in terms of the guiding principle of 'Rationalization'." In Wrong, Dennis (ed.), *Max Weber*. Englewood Cliffs: Prentice-Hall.

_____. 1982. *Max Weber and Karl Marx*. London: Allen & Unwin.

Lombroso, C. 1911. *Crime: Its Causes and Remedies*. Boston: Little, Brown.

Lovelock, J.E. 1979. *Gaia: A New Look at Life on Earth*. Oxford: Oxford University Press.

_____. 1989. *The Ages of Gaia: A Biography of Our Living Earth*. Oxford: Oxford University Press.

Lowe, Philip and Goyder, Jane. 1983. *Environmental Groups in Politics*. London: George Allen.

Lowe, Philip and Rudig, Wolfgang. 1986. "Political Ecology and the Social Sciences: The State of the Art." *British Journal of Political Science* 16: 513-50.

Luke, Timothy. 1983. "Notes for a Deconstructionist Ecology." *New Political Science* 11.

_____. 1988. "The Dreams of Deep Ecology." *Telos* 76: 65-92.

Luke, Timothy and White, Stephen. 1985. "Critical Theory, the Informational Revolution, and an Ecological Modernity." In John Forester (ed.), *Critical Theory and Public Life*. Cambridge, Mass.: MIT Press.

Lynch, Michael. 1982a. *Art and Artefacts in Laboratory Science*. London: Routledge and Kegan Paul.

_____. 1982b. "Technical Work and Critical Inquiry: Investigations in a Scientific Laboratory." *Social Studies of Science* 12(4): 499-534.

Lynch, Michael, Livingston, and Garfinkel, Harold. 1983. "Temporal Order in Laboratory Work." Pp. 205-38 in Knorr-Cetina, Karin D. and Michael Mulkay (editors) *Science Observed: Perspectives on the Social Study of Science*. London: Sage.

MacKenzie, D. and Wajcman, J. 1985. *The Social Shaping of Technology*. London: Open University Press.

Macy, Joanna. 1987. "Faith and Ecology." *Resurgence*. July/August: 18-21.

Maddox, John. 1972. *The Doomsday Syndrome*. London: Macmillan.

Malthus, Thomas. 1965 (1798). *An Essay on the Principle of Population, as it Affects the Future Improvement of Society, with Remarks on the Speculations of Mr. Godwin, M. Condorcet, and other Writers*. 1798 edition. New York: Reprints of Economic Classics.

_____. 1963 (1801). *An Essay on the Principle of Population or a View of its Past and Present Effects on Human Happiness with an Inquiry into our Prospects Respecting the Future Removal or Mitigation of the Evil which it Occasions*. 1801 edition. Homewood, Illinois: Richard D. Irwin.

Manes, Christopher. 1990. *Green Rage: Radical Environmentalism and the Unmaking of Civilization*. Boston: Little, Brown & Company.

Marglin, Stephen. 1974. "What the bosses do: The Origins and functions of hierarchy in capitalist production." *Review of Radical Political Economics* 6: 60-112.

Marples, D.R. 1988. *The Social Impact of the Chernobyl Disaster*. New York: St. Martin's.

Marshall, Thomas H. 1939. "The recent history of professionalism in relation to social structure and social policy." *Canadian Journal of Economics and Political Science* V: 325-40.

_____. 1965 (1939). *Class, Citizenship and Social Development*. Garden City, N. Y.: Doubleday - Anchor.

Marx, Karl. 1959 (1887). *Capital*. Vol. 1. Moscow: Foreign Languages Publishing House.

_____. 1963. "Alienated Labour." In T.B. Bottomore (ed.), *Karl Marx: Early Writings*. New York: McGraw-Hill.

_____. 1964 (1932). *Economic and Philosophic Manuscripts of 1844*. Dirk J. Struik (ed.). New York: International Publishers.

_____. 1966 (1894). *Capital*. Vol. 3. Moscow: Progress Publishers.

Marx, Karl and Engels, Frederick. 1956. *The Holy Family*. Progress Publishers.

Mason, E.S. 1958. "The Apologetics of Managerialism." *Journal of Business* 31: 1-11.

Matthews, Mervyn. 1978. *Privilege in the Soviet Union: A Study of Elite Life-Styles under Communism*. London: George Allen & Unwin.

May, John. 1989. *The Greenpeace Book of the Nuclear Age*. Markham, Canada: McClelland & Stewart.

Mazur, Alan. 1987. "Does Public Perception of Risk Explain the Social Response to Potential Hazard?" *Quarterly Journal of Ideology* 11: 41-5.

McGibben, Bill. 1989. *The End of Nature*. New York: Random House.

McInnes, Simon, McGrath, William, and Potichnyj, Peter J. 1978. *The Soviet Union and East Europe into the 1980s: Multidisciplinary Perspectives*. Oakville, Ontario: Mosaic Press.

McKenzie, Roderick D. 1933. *The Metropolitan Community*. New York: McGraw-Hill.

McLuhan, Marshall. 1965. *Understanding Media: The Extensions of Man*. New York: McGraw-Hill.

Meadows, Donella et al. 1972. *The Limits to Growth*. New York: New American Library.

Meadows, Donella H., Meadows, Dennis L., and Randers, Jorgen. 1992. *Beyond the Limits*. Toronto: McClelland and Stewart.

Mellor, Mary. 1992. "Èco-Feminism and Eco-Socialism: Dilemmas of Essentialism and Materialism." *Capitalism, Nature, Socialism* 3: 1-20.

Mellos, Koula. 1988. *Perspectives on Ecology: A Critical Essay*. London: Macmillan.

Merchant, Carolyn. 1980. *The Death of Nature: Women, Ecology and the Scientific Revolution*. San Francisco: Harper Collins.

_____. 1989. *Ecological Revolutions: Nature, Gender and Science in New England*. Chapel Hill: University of North Carolina Press.

_____. 1992. *Radical Ecology: The Search for a Livable World*. New York: Routledge.

Merton, Robert. 1968 (1949). *Social Theory and Social Structure*. New York: Free Press.

_____. 1970 (1938). *Science, Technology & Society in Seventeenth Century England*. New York: Harper & Row.

_____. 1977. "The Sociology of Science: An Episodic Memoir." P. 3-141 in Merton, Robert and Gaston, Jerry (eds.), *The Sociology of Science in Europe*. Carbondale: Southern Illinois University Press.

Mesarovic, Mihajlo and Pestel, Eduard. 1974. *Mankind at the Turning Point*. New York: New American Library.

Michelson, William. 1970. *Man and His Urban Environment*. Reading, Mass.: Addison-Wesley.

Milbrath, Lester. 1984. *Environmentalists: Vanguard for a New Society*. Albany: State University of New York Press.

_____. 1989. *Envisioning a Sustainable Society: Learning Our Way Out*. Albany: State University of New York Press.

Milisavljevic, Ratko. 1978. *Environnement, idologie et science*. Paris: Editions Anthropos.

Mitchell, Robert Cameron. 1990. "Public Opinion and the Green Lobby: Poised for the 1990s?" Pp. 81-99 in N.J. Vig and M.E. Kraft (eds.), *Environmental Policy in the 1990s: Toward A New Agenda*. Washington: CQ Press.

Mitzman, Arthur. 1971. *The Iron Cage*. New York: Grosset & Dunlap.

Mommsen, Wolfgang J. 1974. *The Age of Bureaucracy: Perspectives on the Political Sociology of Max Weber*. Oxford: Basil Blackwell.

_____. 1987. "Personal conduct and Societal change." Pp. 35-51 in Lash, Scott, and Whimster, Sam (eds.), *Max Weber, Rationality and Modernity*. London: Allen & Unwin.

Monroe, Joseph G., and Woodhouse, Edward J. 1989. *The Demise of Nuclear Energy? Lessons for Democratic Control of Technology*. New Haven: Yale University Press.

Moore, N.W. 1987. *The Bird of Time: The Science and Politics of Nature Conservation*. Cambridge: Cambridge University Press.

Moore Lappe, Frances and Collins, Joseph. 1977. *Food First: Beyond the Myth of Scarity*. Boston: Houghton-Mifflin.

Morgan, M.G. and Henrion, M. 1990. *Uncertainty: A Guide to Dealing with Uncertainty in Quantitative Risk and Policy Analysis*. New York: Cambridge University Press.

Morrison, Denton. 1976. "Growth, Environment, Equity, and Scarcity." *Social Science Quarterly* 57: 292-306.

Mukerju, Chandra. 1989. *A Fragile Power: Scientists and the State*. Princeton: Princeton University Press.

Mulkay, Michael. 1979a. *Science and the Sociology of Knowledge*. London: Allen & Unwin.

_____. 1979b. "Knowledge and Utility: Implications for the Sociology of Knowledge." *Social Studies of Science* 9: 63-80.

_____. 1980. "Sociology of Science in the West." *Current Sociology* 28: 1-116.

_____. 1985. *The Word and the World: Explorations in the Form of Sociological Analysis.* London: Allen and Unwin.

_____. 1990. *Sociology of Science: A Social Pilgrimage.* London: Open University Press.

Mulkay, M. and Gilbert, G.N. 1982. "Accounting for Error: How Scientists construct their social world when they account for correct and incorrect belief." *Sociology* 16: 165-83.

Mulkay, M. and Gilbert, S.N. 1984. *Opening Pandora's Box: A Sociological Analysis of Scientists' Discourse.* Cambridge: Cambridge University Press.

Murphy, Raymond. 1979. *Sociological Theories of Education.* Toronto: McGraw-Hill Ryerson.

_____. 1981. "Teachers and the Evolving Structural Context Economic and Political Attitudes in Quebec Society." *The Canadian Review of Sociology and Anthropology,* Vol. 18: 157-182.

_____. 1982a. "Power and Autonomy in the Sociology of Education." *Theory and Society,* Vol. 11: 179-203.

_____. 1982b. Review of "Colonial Immigrants in a British City: A Class Analysis" by John Rex and Sally Tomlinson. *Canadian Journal of Sociology* 7: 87-90.

_____. 1983. "The Struggle for Scholarly Recognition: The Development of the Closure Problematic in Sociology." *Theory and Society,* Vol. 12: 631-658.

_____. 1984. "The Structure of Closure: A Critique and Development of the Theories of Weber, Collins, and Parkin." *British Journal of Sociology* 35: 547-67.

_____. 1985. "Exploitation or Exclusion?." *Sociology: The Journal of the British Sociological Association,* Vol. 19: 225-243.

_____. 1986a. "Weberian Closure Theory: A Contribution to the Ongoing Assessment." *British Journal of Sociology,* Vol. 37: 21-41.

_____. 1986b. "The Concept of Class in Closure Theory: Learning From Rather Than Falling Into the Problems Encountered by Neo-Marxism." *Sociology: The Journal of the British Sociological Association,* Vol. 20: 247-264.

_____. 1987. "The Basis of Class, Status Group, and Party: The Power to Monopolize and the Monopolization of Power." Paper prepared for Unesco.

_____. 1988. *Social Closure: The Theory of Monopolization and Exclusion.* Oxford, England: Oxford University Press (Clarendon).

_____. 1990. "Proletarianization or Bureaucratization: The Fall of the Professional?" Chapter 5 in Rolf Torstendahl and Michael Burrage (editors), *The Formation of Professions: Knowledge, State and Strategy.* London: Sage.

_____. Forthcoming. "The Sociological Construction of Science Without Nature." *Sociology: The Journal of the British Sociological Association.*

Myers, Norman. 1979. *The Sinking Ark.* Oxford: Pergamon Press.

_____ (editor). 1984. *Gaia: An Atlas of Planet Management.* New York: Anchor.

_____. 1986. "The Environmental Dimension to Security Issues." *The Environmentalist,* Winter.

Naess, Arne. 1973. "The shallow and Deep, Long-Range Ecology Movement: A Summary." *Inquiry* 16: 95-100.

_____. 1986. "The Deep Ecological Movement: Some Philosophical Aspects." *Philosophical Inquiry* 8: 10-31.

_____. 1988. *Ecology, Community and Lifestyle: An Outline of Ecosophy.* Cambridge: Cambridge University Press.

Nash, Roderick. 1982. *Wilderness and the American Mind.* New Haven: Yale University Press.

_____. 1989. *The Rights of Nature: A History of Environmental Ethics.* Madison: University of Wisconsin Press.

National Research Council. 1985. *The Effects on the Atmosphere of a Major Nuclear Exchange.* Washington: National Academy Press.

Newby, Howard. 1991. "One World, Two Cultures: Sociology and the Environment." *Network* 50: 1-8.

Newton-Smith, W.H. 1981. *The Rationality of Science.* London: Routledge and Kegan Paul.

Nicholson, M. 1987. *The New Environmental Age.* Cambridge: Cambridge University Press.

Nisbet, Robert. 1979. "The Rape of Progress." *Public Opinion* 2: 2-6, 55.

Norton, Bryan G. 1984. "Environmental Ethics and Weak Anthropocentrism." *Environmental Ethics* 6.

Nowotny, H. 1973. "On the Feasibility of a Cognitive Approach to the Study of Science." *Zeitschrift fur Soziologie* 2: 282-96.

Oates, David. 1989. *Earth Rising: Ecological Belief in an Age of Science.* Corvallis: Oregon State University.

O'Connor, James. 1988. "Capitalism, Nature, Socialism: A Theoretical Introduction." *Capitalism, Nature, Socialism* 1: 11-38.

_____. 1989. "Ecological Crisis." *Capitalism, Nature, Socialism: A Journal of Socialist Ecology* (fall).

_____. 1991. "The Second Contradiction of Capitalism. Causes and Consequences." *Capitalism, Nature, Socialism,* Pamphlet 1.

Odum, Eugene P. 1983. *Basic Ecology.* Philadelphia: Saunders.

Olsen, Marvin, Lodwick, Dora, and Dunlap, Riley. 1992. *Viewing the World Ecologically.* Boulder: Westview.

Ophuls, William. 1977. *Ecology and the Politics of Scarcity: Prologue to a Political Theory of the Steady State.* San Francisco: W.H. Freeman & Co.

Orr, David. 1992. *Ecological Literacy: Education and the Transition to a Postmodern World.* Albany: State University of New York Press.

Paehlke, Robert C. 1990. *Environmentalism and the Future of Progressive Politics.* Yale University Press.

Page, Talbot. 1977. *Conservation and Economic Efficiency.* Baltimore: Johns Hopkins University Press for resources for the Future.

Park, Robert E. 1952. *Human Communities.* New York: Free Press.

Park, R., Burgess, E., and McKenzie, R. (eds.). 1925. *The City.* Chicago: University of Chicago Press.

Parkin, Frank. (1971) 1972. *Class Inequality and Political Order.* Frogmore: Paladin.

_____. 1974. "Strategies of Social Closure in Class Formation." In Frank Parkin (ed.), *The Social Analysis of Class Structure.* London: Tavistock.

_____. 1979. *Marxism and Class Theory: A Bourgeois Critique.* London: Tavistock.

_____. 1980. "Reply to Giddens." *Theory and Society* 9: 891-4.

_____. 1982. *Max Weber*. London: Tavistock.

Parsons, Talcott. 1968 (1937). *The Structure of Social Action*. New York: Free Press.

_____. 1964 (1951). *The Social System*. New York: Free Press.

_____. 1966. *Societies: Evolutionary and Comparative Perspectives*. Englewood Cliffs, N. J.: Prentice-Hall.

_____. 1971. *The System of Modern Societies*. Englewood Clifs, N. J.: Prentice-Hall.

Pearce, F. 1989. *Turning up the Heat*. London: Paladin.

Peccei, Aurelio. 1981. *One Hundred Pages for the Future, Reflection of the President of the Club of Rome*. New York: Pergamon.

Peck, Dennis L. (ed.). 1989. *"Psychological Effects of Hazardous Toxic Waste Disposal on Communities."* Springfield, Ill.: Charles C. Thomas.

Pepper, David. 1984. *The Roots of Modern Environmentalism*. London: Croom Helm.

Perlo, V. 1958. "People's Capitalism and Stock Ownership." *American Economic Review* 48: 333-47.

Perrow, Charles. 1984. *Normal Accidents: Living with High-Risk Technologies*. New York: Basic Books.

Peters, R.L. and Darling, J.D.S. 1984. "The Greenhouse Effect of Nature Reserves." *Bioscience* 35: 707-17.

Pfohl, S.J. 1977. "The 'Discovery' of Child Abuse." *Social Problems* 23: 310-24.

Pickering, A. 1980. "The Role of Interests in High Energy Physics: The Choice Between Charm and Colour." In K. Knorr, R. Krohn and R. Whitley (eds.), *The Social Process of Scientific Investigation, Sociology of the Sciences Yearbook*, vol. 4. Boston/Dordrecht: D. Reidel.

Pinchot, Gifford. 1947. *Breaking New Ground*. New York: Harcourt, Brace and Co.

Pirages, Dennis C. 1977. *The Sustainable Society: Implications for Limited Growth*. New York: Praeger.

Pittock, A.B. et al. 1986. *Environmental Consequences of Nuclear War, Volume I: Physical and Atmospheric Effects*. Chichester, UK: John Wiley & Sons.

Plant, Christopher and Plant, Judith (eds.). 1991. *Green Business: Hope or Hoax?* Philadelphia: New Society Publishers.

Plant, Judith (ed.). 1989. *Healing the Wounds: The Promise of Ecofeminism*. Toronto: Between the Lines.

Plumwood, Val. 1986. "Ecofeminism: An Overview and Discussion of Positions and Arguments." *Australasian Journal of Philosophy* 64: 120-38.

_____. 1990. "Women, Humanity and Nature." In Sean Sayers and Peter Osborne (eds.), *Feminism and Philosophy: A Radical Philosophy Reader*. London: Routledge.

_____. 1992. "Feminism and Ecofeminism: Beyond the Dualistic Assumptions of Women, Men and Nature." *The Ecologist* 22: 8-13.

Polanyi, John C. 1992. "The Scientist as Citizen: Freedom and Responsibility in Science." *Queen's Quarterly* 99: 125-33.

Polanyi, Karl. 1957. *The Great Transformation*. Boston: Beacon Press.

Pollner, M. 1974. "Sociological and Common-Sense Models of the Labelling Process." Pp. 27-40 in Turner, R. (ed.), *Ethnomethodology* Harmondsworth: Penguin.

Popper, Karl. 1960. *The Logic of Scientific Discovery.* London: Hutchinson and Co.
_____. 1963. *Conjectures and Refutations: The Growth of Scientific Knowledge.* New York: Basic.
Porritt, Jonathon. 1985. *Seeing Green: The Politics of Ecology Explained.* New York: Basil Blackwell.
Porter, John. 1965. *The Vertical Mosaic.* Toronto: University of Toronto Press.
Poulantzas, Nicos. 1976. "The Capitalist State: A Reply to Miliband and Laclau." *New Left Review* 95: a63-83.
_____. 1977. "The New Petty Bourgeoisie." Pp. 113-124 in A. Hunt (ed.) *Class and Class Structure.* London: Lawrence & Wishart.
_____. 1978. *Classes in Contemporary Capitalism.* London: Verso.
Prentice, Susan. 1988. "Taking Sides: What's Wrong with Eco-   Feminism?" *Women and Envirnments* 10.
Prus, Robert. 1990. "The interpretive challenge: The impending crisis in sociology." *The Canadian Journal of sociology* 15: 355-63.
Pryde, Philip R. 1972. "The Quest for Environmental Quality in the USSR." *American Scientist* 60: 739-45.
Ravetz, Jerome R. 1987. "Usable knowledge, usable ignorance." *Knowledge* 9: 87-116.
Raynaud, Philippe. 1987. *Max Weber et les dilemmes de la raison moderne.* Paris: PUF.
Redclift, M. 1984. *Development and the Environmental Crisis.* London: Methuen.
_____. 1987. *Sustainable Development.* London: Metheun.
Regis, Ed. 1990. *Great Mambo Chicken and the Transhuman Experiment.* Addison-Wesley.
Rifkin, Jeremy. 1981. *Entropy: A New World View.* New York: Bantam Books.
Rodda, Annabel. 1991. *Women and the Environment.* London: Zed.
Roemer, John. 1982. "New Directions in the Marxian Theory of Exploitation and Class." *Politics and Society* 11: 253-87.
Rose, Hillary, and Rose, Steve. 1976. *The Political Economy of Science.* Cambridge, Mass.: Schenkman.
Roszak, Theodore. 1975. *Unfinished Animal: The Aquarian Frontier and the Evolution of Consciousness.* New York: Harper & Row.
Roth, Guenther and Schluchter, Wolfgang. 1981. *Max Weber's Vision of History.* Berkeley: University of California Press.
Rothman, Harry. 1972. *Murderous Providence: A Study of Pollution in Industrial Societies.* London: Rupert Hart-Davis.
Rudig, W. 1986. "Nuclear power: an international comparison of public protest in the USA, Great Britain, France and West Germany." Pp. 364-417 in R. Williams and S. Mills (eds), *Public Acceptance of New Technologies: An International Review.* London: Croom Helm.
Sachs, Ignacy. 1980. *Stratgies de l'codveloppement.* Paris: Editions ouvrières.
Sachs, Ignacy et al. 1981. *Initiation l'codveloppement.* Toulouse: Privat.
Sale, Kirkpatrick. 1980. *Human Scale.* New York: G.P. Putnam's Sons.
_____. 1985. *Dwellers in the Land: The Bioregional Vision.* San Francisco: Sierra Club Books.
_____. 1988. "Deep Ecology And Its Critics." *The Nation* May 14: 670-5.

_____. 1991. *Dwellers in the Land: The Bioregional Vision*. Philadelphia: New Society Publishers.

Salleh, Ariel. 1984. "Deeper Than Deep Ecology": The Ecofeminist Connection." *Environmental Ethics* 6: 339-45.

Sandbach, F. 1978. "Ecology and the 'Limits to Growth' debate." *Antipode* 10: 22-32.

Sandman, P.M., Sachsman, M.R., Greenberg, M.R., and Gochfield, M. 1987. *Environmental Risk and the Press*. Oxford: Transaction.

Sayer, Derek. 1990. *Capitalism and Modernity: An Excursus on Marx and Weber*. London: Routledge.

Scaff, Lawrence A. 1981. "Max Weber and Robert Michels." *American Journal of Sociology*.

_____. 1984. "Weber before Weberian Sociology." *British Journal of Sociology*.

Scarce, Rik. 1990. *Eco-Warriors: Understanding the Radical Environmental Movement*. Chicago: Noble Press.

Schluchter, Wolfgang. 1979. "The Paradox of Rationalization" in *Max Weber's Vision of History*, Guenther Roth and Wolfgang Schluchter, editors. Berkeley: University of California Press .

_____. 1981. *The Rise of Western Rationalism: Max Weber's Developmental History*. Berkeley: University of California Press.

Schmidt, Alfred. 1971. *The Concept of Nature in Marx*. London: New Left Books.

Schnaiberg, Allan. 1975. "Social Syntheses of the Societal - Environmental Dialectic: The Role of Distributional Impacts." *Social Science Quarterly* 56: 5-20.

_____. 1980. *The Environment: From Surplus to Scarcity*. New York: Oxford.

Schnaiberg, Allan, Watts, Nicholas, and Zimmerman, Klaus (eds.). 1986. *Distributional Conflicts in Environmental-Resource Policy*. New York: St. Martin's.

Schonewald-Cox, C.M. et al. (eds.). 1983. *Genetics and Conservation*. Menlo Park, Calif.: Benjamin/Cummings.

Schrader-Frechette, K.S. 1985. *Risk Analysis and Scientific Method*. Boston: D. Reidel.

Schroeter, Gerd. 1985. "The Marx-Weber Nexus." *Canadian Journal of Sociology*.

Scope. 1985. *Environmental Consequences of Nuclear War*. Chichester, UK: John Wiley & Sons.

Sessons, George. 1981. "Shallow and Deep Ecology: A Review of the Philosophical Literature." *Ecological Consciousness: Essays From the Earthday X Colloquium*. Washington, D.C.: University Press of America.

_____. 1985. "A Postscript." Appendix H in Devall, Bill and Sessions, George, *Deep Ecology*. Salt Lake City: Peregrine Smith.

_____. 1991. "Deep Ecology versus Ecofeminism: Healthy Differences or Incompatible Philosophies?." *Hypatia* 6: 90-107.

_____. 1987. "The Deep Ecology Movement." *Environmental Review* VII: 105-26.

Shabad, T. 1979. "Communist environmentalism." *Problems of Communism* May-June: 64-7.

Shapin, S. 1982. "History of Science and its Sociological Reconstructions." *History of Science* 20: 157-211.

Sheldon, William. 1949. *Varieties of Delinquent Youth: An Introduction to Constitutional Psychiatry*. New York: Harper and Row.

Shepard, Paul. 1978. *Thinking Animals: Animals and the Development of Human Intelligence*. New York: Viking.

_____. 1982. *Nature and Madness*. San Francisco: Sierra Club Books.

Sherman, Howard. 1972. *Radical Political Economy: Capitalism and Socialism from a Marxist-Humanist Perspective*. New York: Basic.

Shiva, Vandana. 1988. *Staying Alive: Women, Ecology and Survival in India*. London: Zed Books.

Short, James Jr. 1984. "The Social Fabric at Risk: Toward the Social Transformation of Risk Analysis." *American Sociological Review* 49: 711-25.

Sibley, Mulford Q. 1977. *Nature and Civilization: Some Implications for Politics*. Ithaca, NY: F.E. Peacock.

Sills, David, Wolf, C. P., and Shelanski, Vivien (eds.). 1982. *Accident at Three Mile Island: The Human Dimensions*. Boulder: Westview.

Silver, Cheryl Simon with DeFries, Ruth. 1990. *One Earth / One Future: Our Changing Global Environment*. Washington: National Academy Press.

Silverton, J. and Sarre, P. 1990. *Environment and Society*. London: Hodder and Stoughton.

Simon, Julian. 1977. *The Economics of Population Growth*. Princeton: Princeton University Press.

_____. 1981. *The Ultimate Resource*. Princeton: Princeton University Press.

Simon, Julian and Kahn, Herman (eds.). 1984. *The Resourceful Earth*. Oxford: Basil Blackwell.

Singleton, Fred (ed.). 1976. *Environmental Misuse in the Soviet Union*. New York: Praeger.

Sjoberg, L. (ed.). 1987. *Risk and Society*. Boston: Allen & Unwin.

Skolimowski, H. 1984. "The Dogma of Anti-Anthropocentrism and Ecophilosophy." *Environmental Ethics* 6: 283-8.

Smelser, Neil J. 1959. *Social Change in the Industrial Revolution*. Chicago: University of Chicago Press.

Smil, Vaclav 1984. *The Bad Earth: Environmental Degradation in China*. New York: M.E. Sharpe.

Smith, Adam. 1776 (1977). *The Wealth of Nations*. Chicago: The University of Chicago Press.

Smith, Murray E.G. 1991. "Understanding Marx's theory of value: an assessment of a controversy." *The Canadian Review of Sociology and Anthropology* 28 (3): 357-376.

Smith, V. Kerry (ed.). 1979. *Scarcity and Growth Reconsidered*. Baltimore: Johns Hopkins University Press for Resources for the Future.

Son, Sambra. 1970. *Systeme et Environnement*. Editions Anthropos.

_____. 1972. *Socialism and Environment*. London: Spokisman Books.

Soule, M.E. (ed.). 1986. *Conservation Biology: Science of Scarcity and Diversity*. Sunderland, Mass.: Sinauer Associates.

Southam Newspapers. 1989. *Our Fragile Future*. October 7. Ottawa.

Spector, M. and Kitsuse, J.I. 1977. *Constructing Social Problems*. Menlo Park, California: Cummings.

Spencer, Herbert. 1898-9. *Principles of Sociology.* New York: Appleton.

Spretnak, Charlene. 1989. "Towards an Ecofeminist Spirituality." Pp. 127-32 in Judith Plant (ed.), *Healing the Wounds: The Promise of Ecofeminism.* Toronto: Between the Lines.

_____. 1990. "Ecofeminism: Our Roots and Flowering." Pp. 3-14 in Irene Diamond and Gloria Feman Orenstein (ed.), *Reweaving the World.* San Francisco: Sierra Club.

Sprout, Margaret and Sprout, Harold. 1971. *Toward a Politics of the Planet Earth.* New York: Van Nostrand Reinhold.

Stack, Carol. 1986. "The Culture of Gender: Women and Men of Color." *Signs* 11: 321-4.

Stehr, Nico. 1991. "The Power of Scientific Knowledge - and its Limits." *Canadian Review of Sociology and Anthropology* 28: 460-82.

Stern, Paul, Young, Oran, and Druckman, Daniel (eds.). 1990. *Global Environmetal Change: Understanding the Human Dimensions.* Washington: National Academy Press.

Stretton, Hugh. 1976. *Capitalism, Socialism, and the Environment.* Cambridge, England: Cambridge University Press.

Suzuki, David. 1990a. "The Ecocrisis: The direct result of the values and beliefs of our institutions." *The Ottawa Citizen.* February 11: E6.

_____. 1990b. "Broader Implications of Work to Decode Human DNA Need Contemplation." *The Ottawa Citizen,* December 9.

Sweezy, Paul. (1942) 1967. *The Theory of Capitalist Development.* New York: Dobson.

Sweezy, Paul and Baran, P. 1966. *Monopoly Capital.* New York: Monthly Review.

Taylor, Michael. 1976. *Anarchy and Cooperation.* London: John Wiley.

_____. 1982. *Community, Anarchy, and Liberty.* Cambridge: Cambridge University Press.

Taylor, Paul. 1986. *Respect for Nature: A Theory of Environmental Ethics.* Princeton: Princeton University Press.

Taylor, Peter and Buttel, Frederick. 1992. "How Do We Know We Have Global Environmental Problems?" *Geoforum* 23: 405-16.

Teilhard de Chardin, Pierre. 1965. *The Phenomenon of Man.* London: Fontana.

Tenbruck, F.H. 1980. "The problem of thematic unity in the works of Max Weber." *British Journal of Sociology* 31: 316-351.

Tetlock, Philip E., Husbands, Jo. L., Jervis, Robert, Stern, Paul C., and Tilly, Charles. 1989. *Behavior, Society, and Nuclear War.* Volume 1. New York: Oxford University Press.

Thayer, Frederick C. 1981. *An End to Hierarchy and Competition.* New York: New Viewpoints.

Therborn, G. 1980. *The Ideology of Power and the Power of Ideology.* London: Verso.

Thomas, J.J.R. 1985. "Rationalization and the Status of Gender Divisions." *British Journal of Sociology* 19: 409-420.

Thompson, P.B. 1986. "Uncertainty Arguments in Environmental Issues." *Environmental Ethics* 8: 59-76.

Thurow, Lester C. 1980. *The Zero-Sum Society: distribution and the Possibilities for Economic Change.* New York: Basic Books.

Timpanaro, S. 1975. *On Materialism.* London: NLB.

Timberlake, L. 1987. *Only One Earth: Living for the Future.* London: BBC/Earthscan.

Tobias, Michael, ed. 1985. *Deep Ecology.* San Diego: Avant Books.

Toffler, Alvin. 1984. *The Third Wave.* New York: Bantam.

Tolba, Mostafa. 1987. *Sustainable Development: Constraints and Opportunities.* London: Butterworth.

_____. 1992. *Saving Our Planet: Challenges and Hopes.* London: Chapman & Hall.

Tolba, Mostafa and El-Khaly, Osama (eds.) 1992. *The World Environment 1972-1992: Two Decades of Challenge.* London: Chapman & Hall.

Touraine, Alain. 1973. *Production de la société.* Paris: Seuil.

Travis, G.D.L. 1981. "Replicating Replication? Aspects of the Social Construction of Learning in Planarian Worms." *Social Studies of Science* 11: 11-32.

Trigger, Bruce G. 1989. "Hyperrelativism, responsibility, and the social sciences." *The Canadian Review of Sociology and Anthropology* 26 (5): 776-797.

Trow, Martin. 1961. "The Second Transformation of American Secondary Education." *International Journal of Comparative Sociology* 2: 144-66.

Turner, Bryan S. 1981. *For Weber: Essays on the Sociology of Fate.* London: Routledge & Kegan Paul.

_____. 1987. "Marx, Weber, and the Coherence of Capitalism: The Problem of Ideology." Pp. 169-204 in Norbert Wiley, ed., *The Marx - Weber Debate.* Newbury Park, Calif.: Sage.

_____. 1992. *Max Weber: From History to Modernity.* London: Unwin Hyman Academic.

United Nations Environment Programme. 1986. *The State of the Environment: Environment and Health.* Nairobi.

Unseld, Charles, Morrison, Denton, Sills, David, and Wolf, C. P. (eds.). 1979. *Sociopolitical Effects of Energy Use and Policy.* Washington: National Academy of Sciences.

Van den Berghe, Pierre L. 1980. "Race, Ethnicity, and Class in Britain: A Dialectical Duel with the Ghosts of Marx and Weber." *Contemporary Sociology* 9: 662-5.

Vander Tak, Jean, Hamb, Carl, and Murphy, Elaine. 1979. *Our Population Predicament: A New Look.* Population Bulletin, vol. 34, no. 5. Washington: Population Reference Bureau, Inc.

Vayk, J. Peter. 1978. *Doomsday Has Been Cancelled.* Menlo Park, Ca.: Peace Publishers.

Veblen, Thorstein. (1899) 1953. *The Theory of the Leisure Class.* New York: Mentor.

Vernadsky, V.I. 1945. "The Biosphere and the Noosphere." *American Scientist* 33: 1-12.

Viscusi, W.K. 1992. *Fatal Tradeoffs: Public and Private Responsibilities for Risk.* New York: Oxford.

Von Furstenberg, G.M. 1990. *Acting Under Uncertainty.* Boston: Kluwer Academic Publishers.

Voros, M. and Honti, Gy. 1974. "Explosion of a Liquid CO_2 Storage Vessel in a Carbon Dioxide Plant." Pp. 337-46 in C.H. Buschmann (editor) *Loss Prevention and Safety Promotion in the Process Industries*. New York: Elsevier Scientific Publishing Co.

Wajcman, Judy. 1991. *Feminism Confronts Technology*. Cambridge: Polity Press.

Walker, Charles A., Gould, Leroy C., and Woodhouse, Edward J. 1983. *Too Hot to Handle? Social and Policy Issues in the Management of Radioactive Wastes*. New Haven, Conn.: Yale University Press.

Wallerstein, Immanuel. 1979. *The Capitalist World Economy*. London: Cambridge University Press.

_____. 1983. *Historical Capitalism*. London: Verso.

_____. 1984. *The Politics of the World-Economy*. London: Cambridge University Press.

Wallis, R. (ed.). 1979. "On the Margins of Science: The Social Construction of Rejected Knowledge." *Sociological Review Monograph* 27.

Walsh, Mary Williams. 1991. "Artic villagers have world's highest levels of PCBs in their blood." *The Ottawa Citizen* June 30: E3.

Warren, Karen. 1987. "Feminism and Ecology: Making Connections." *Environmental Ethics* 9: 3-20.

_____. 1990. "The Power and the Promise of Ecological Feminism." *Environmental Ethics* 12: 125-46.

Watson, James D. 1968. *The Double Helix: A Personal Account of the Structure of DNA*. New York: Signet.

Watson, Richard A. 1983. "A Critique of Anti-Anthropocentric Biocentrism." *Environmental Ethics* 5.

_____. 1985. "Ecoethics: Challenging the Underlying Dogmas of Environmentalism." *Whole Earth Review* March: 5-13.

Wattenberg, Ben. 1984. *The Good News is the Bad News is Wrong*. New York: Simon and Schuster.

Weber, Max. (1904-5) 1930. *The Protestant Ethic and the Spirit of Capitalism*. Translated by Talcott Parsons. London: Unwin.

_____. (1946) 1958. *From Max Weber: Essays in Sociology*, H.H. Gerth and C. Wright Mills (eds.). New York: Oxford University Press.

_____. (1922) 1978. *Economy and Society: An Outline of Interpretive Sociology*, Guenther Roth and Claus Wittich (eds.). Berkeley: University of California.

Weinberg, Alvin M. 1972. "Social Institutions and Nuclear Energy." *Science* 177: 27-34.

Weiss, Johannes. 1985. "On the Marxist Reception and Critique of Max Weber in Eastern Europe." Pp. 117-31 in Antonio, Robert and Glassman, Ronald (editors), *A Weber-Marx Dialogue*. Lawrence, Kansas: University of Kansas Press.

Wenger, Morton G. 1987. "Class Closure and the Historical/Structural Limits of the Marx-Weber Convergence." Pp. 43-64 in Norbert Wiley, ed., *The Marx - Weber Debate*. Newbury Park, Calif.: Sage.

Westing, A.H. (ed.). 1986. *Global Resources and International Conflict*. Oxford: Oxford University Press.

Westoby, Jack. 1989. *The Purpose of Forests*. London: Basil Blackwell.

Whipple, C. 1987. *De Minimis Risk*. New York: Plenum.

White, Lynn Jr. 1967. "The Historical Roots of Our Ecological Crisis." *Science* 155: 1203-7.

Whitty, Geoff. 1977. "Sociology and the Problem of Radical Educational Change: Notes towards a reconceptualization of the 'new' sociology of education." In Young and Whitty (1977).

Whitty, Geoff and Young, M.F.D. (eds.). 1976. *Explorations in the Politics of School Knowledge*. Nefferton, England: Nefferton Books.

Wijkman, A. and Timberlake, L. 1984. *Natural Disasters: Acts of God and Acts of Man?* London: Earthscan for the International Institute for Environment and Development and the Swedish Red Cross.

Wilber, Ken. 1981. *Up from Eden: A Transpersonal View of Human Evolution*. New York: Doubleday.

_____. 1983. *Eye to Eye: The Quest for the New Paradigm*. Garden City, N.Y.: Anchor Books.

Wiley, Norbert. 1987. "Introduction." Pp. 7-27 in Norbert Wiley, ed., *The Marx - Weber Debate*. Newbury Park, Calif.: Sage.

Williams, R. and Law, J. 1980. "Beyond the Bounds of Credibility." *Fundamenta Scientiae* 1: 295-315.

Williams, Trevor. 1977. "Education and Biosocial Processes." Pp. 248-80 in Carlton, R., Colley, L., and MacKinnon, N. (eds.), *Education, Change, and Society*. Toronto: Gage.

Winner, Langdon. 1975. "Complexity and the Limits of Human Understanding." Pp. 40-76 in Todd R. LaPorte (ed.), *Organized Social Complexity: Challenges to Politics and Policy*. Princeton: Princeton University Press.

Wolff, Kurt. 1978. Pp. in Tom Bottomore and Robert Nisbet, editors, *A History of Sociological Analysis*. New York: Basic Books.

Woodcock, George. 1977. *The Anarchist Reader*. London: Fontana.

Woolgar, S. 1981. "Interests and Explanation in the Social Study of Science." *Social Studies of Science* 11: 365-94.

_____. 1983. "Irony in the Social Study of Science." Pp. 239-66 in Karin D. Knorr-Cetina and Michael Mulkay (eds.), *Science Observed: Perspectives on the Social Study of Science*. London: Sage.

_____. 1988a. *Science: the Very Idea*. London: Tavistock.

_____. (editor). 1988b. *Knowledge and Reflexivity: New Frontiers in the Sociology of Knowledge*. London: Sage.

Woolgar, S. and Pawluch, D. 1985a. "Ontological gerrymandering: The anatomy of social problems explanations." *Social Problems* 32: 214-27.

_____. 1985b. "How shall we move beyond constructivism?" *Social Problems* 33: 159-62.

World Commission on Environment and Development. 1987. *Our Common Future*. Oxford, England: Oxford University Press.

Worster, Donald. 1977. *Nature's Economy: A History of Ecological Ideas*. Cambridge: Cambridge University Press.

Wright, Erik Olin. 1976. "Class Boundaries in Advanced Capitalist Societies." *New Left Review* 98: 3-41.

_____. 1977. "Alternative Perspectives in Marxist Theory of Accumulation and Crisis." Pp. 195-231 in Jesse Schwartz, ed., *The Subtle Anatomy of Capitalism.* Santa Monica, Calif.: Goodyear Publishing.

Wrong, D. 1961. "The Oversocialized Conception of Man in Modern Sociology." *American sociological Review* 26: 183-93.

Yankelovich, Daniel. 1974. "Corporate Ownership and Control: The Large Corporation and the Capitalist Class." *American Journal of Sociology* 79: 1073-1119.

Yearley, Steven. 1988. *Science, Technology and Social Change.* London: Unwin Hyman.

_____. 1991. *The Green Case.* London: Harper Collins Academic.

_____. 1992. "Green Ambivalence about Science: Legal-rational Authority and the Scientific Legitimation of a social Movement." *British Journal of Sociology* 43: 511-32.

Young, Michael F.D. (ed.). 1971. *Knowledge and Control: New Directions for the Sociology of Education.* London: Collier-MacMillan.

_____. 1976. "Curriculum Change: Limits and Possibilities." Pp. 185-91 in Roger Dale, Geoff Esland, and Madeleine MacDonald (eds.), *Schooling and Capitalism: A Sociological Reader.* London: Routledge & Kegan Paul.

Young, Michael F.D. and Whitty, Geoff (eds.). 1977. *Society, State, and Schooling: Readings on the Possibilities for Radical Education.* Ringmer, England: Falmer Press.

Zile, Zigurds L. 1982. "Glimpses of the Scientific Revolution in Soviet Environmental Law." Pp. 187-216 in Peter B. Maggs, Gordon B. Smith, and George Ginsburg (eds.), *Law and Economic Development in the Soviet Union.* Boulder, Col.: Westview Press.

Index

About the Book and Author

Divergent beliefs about humanity's relationship to nature collide as the second millenium ends. One belief emphasizes that a distinctive characteristic of humans—reason—enables them to reshape and master nature. Another insists that nature is not so plastic, hence humans must adapt to nature and render development sustainable, or even limit growth.

"Social ecology" asserts that environmental problems result from institutional hierarchies and suggests decentralized institutions and egalitarian ethics. According to "deep ecology" such problems originate in cultures assuming only humans are worthwhile, thus it stresses the intrinsic value of nature. Feminists are torn between values based on the equality of men and women and ecofeminist values postulating that women are inherently closer to nature than men. *Rationality and Nature* critically assesses these conflicting cultural tendencies.

Waste has been the forgotten element of political economy. Western society has sophisticated methods of financial accounting but does little to account for the losses—financial and human—of waste. Raymond Murphy proposes in this book a theory of environmental debt as a source of capital accumulation. He develops a model of "environmental classes" that helps us to understand the political and economic basis of conflict over the environment.

Environmental degradation did not occur on a vast scale until science and applied science were developed. Are they responsible for it and can they be reoriented toward a more symbiotic relationship with nature? Other ways of bringing about a symbiotic relationship are also explored in this book: compulsion, ecological values, ecological experience, and ecological knowledge.

Raymond Murphy, professor of sociology at the University of Ottawa, Canada, is author of *Social Closure: The Theory of Monopolization and Exclusion* (1988) and other books.